Human-AI Leadership for Transforming Schools

Asma Khaleel Abdallah
https://orcid.org/0000-0003-1028-7618
Sharjah Education Academy, UAE

Ahmed Khaleel Akaabi
https://orcid.org/0000-0001-7220-8087
United Arab Emirates University, UAE

Markus Talvio
https://orcid.org/0000-0003-0177-5118
University of Helsinki, Finland

IGI Global
Scientific Publishing
Publishing Tomorrow's Research Today

Vice President of Editorial Melissa Wagner
Director of Acquisitions Mikaela Felty
Director of Book Development Jocelynn Hessler
Production Manager Mike Brehm
Cover Design Jose Rosado

Published in the United States of America by
IGI Global Scientific Publishing
701 East Chocolate Avenue
Hershey, PA, 17033, USA
Tel: 717-533-8845 | Fax: 717-533-7115
Website: https://www.igi-global.com E-mail: cust@igi-global.com

Library of Congress Cataloging-in-Publication Data

LCCN: (CIP Data Pending)
ISBN13: 9798260003886
Isbn13Softcover: 9798260003893
EISBN13: 9798260003909
British Cataloguing in Publication Data
A Cataloguing in Publication record for this book is available from the British Library.

Table of Contents

Detailed Table of Contents

The chapter is considered as the exploration of the transformational opportunities of artificial intelligence (AI) and the application of information analytics in creating a culture supportive of educational leadership reiterates the need to establish inclusive and fair systems of decision making. The chapter outlines principles for data-driven leadership that can overcome a key shortcoming of AI tools: their frequent inability to identify underlying systemic biases that traditional methods also miss. It involves a step-by-step analysis of the questions related to the use of algorithms, ethical aspects of the manipulation of information, and confidentiality and thus emphasizes the importance of providing balancing between automation and human control in the field of educational administration. This current study presents practical recommendations on the ethical implementation of AI, the improvement of professional abilities, and transparent data behavior through the synthesis of the internationally recognized paradigms with practical case studies.

School leaders face rapid change. They manage the spread of artificial intelligence and digital technologies, climate-related disruption, and shifting enrolment linked to migration. At the same time, persistent gaps in access, participation, and outcomes remain. Many leadership approaches address innovation, technology, and equity as separate priorities, which fragments action. This chapter presents ITEQ Leadership—Innovation, Technology, and Equity—as a single, integrated playbook for school leaders. The chapter brings together equity-focused leadership, responsible technology use, and disciplined innovation so principals and leadership teams act with clarity. It is written for principals, deputy heads, and researchers working in diverse contexts, including low-resource, multilingual, and crisis-affected settings. The chapter translates research into leader competencies, an 18-month implementation roadmap, practical tools, and global vignettes. The aim is to support innovation that advances equity in ways that are measurable, sustainable, and grounded in community voice.

Preface

LEADING THE FUTURE: HUMAN WISDOM IN THE AGE OF INTELLIGENT SCHOOLS

Education systems across the globe are standing at a defining crossroads. Rapid technological acceleration, widening equity gaps, post-pandemic disruptions, geopolitical instability, and growing demands for wellbeing and inclusion have fundamentally reshaped what it means to lead schools. Artificial intelligence (AI), advanced analytics, smart technologies, and digital infrastructures are no longer peripheral tools that support educational administration; they are becoming deeply embedded in teaching, assessment, governance, and strategic planning. Yet technology alone does not transform schools—leadership does.

Human–AI Leadership for Transforming Schools emerges at this pivotal historical moment. As indicated in the official project documentation, this book brings together international scholars and practitioners to explore how school leaders can responsibly integrate AI and human judgment to advance equity, wellbeing, and systemic transformation. The contributors collectively argue that the future of schooling depends not on replacing human leadership with algorithms, but on designing synergistic models in which human values, ethical commitments, and contextual intelligence guide technological implementation.

The subject matter of this book lies at the intersection of three powerful and interdependent forces shaping contemporary education: artificial intelligence and digital innovation, leadership theory and practice, and the pursuit of equity and inclusion. The central premise is that leadership must evolve in response to technological transformation. AI systems can analyze large datasets, predict patterns, personalize learning experiences, and optimize organizational processes. However, they cannot independently define ethical priorities, interpret cultural nuance, or safeguard social justice. These responsibilities remain firmly within the domain of human leadership.

Across its chapters, this book explores how leaders can govern AI ethically and transparently, use data-informed systems to identify and address inequities, design inclusive learning environments, foster wellbeing amidst rapid digital change, and build resilience during times of crisis. It positions "Human–AI Leadership" as an emerging paradigm—one that integrates technological sophistication with moral responsibility, relational intelligence, and a deep commitment to educational equity. Rather than viewing AI as a technical add-on, the book conceptualizes it as a leadership challenge that requires new frameworks, competencies, and dispositions.

The relevance of this topic in today's world cannot be overstated. Governments are embedding AI within national development strategies, industries are restructuring around automation and data analytics, and educational systems are under pressure to prepare students for rapidly changing labor markets. At the same time, concerns about algorithmic bias, data privacy, digital surveillance, and unequal access to technology have intensified. School leaders are increasingly required to make decisions about technologies that influence instructional design, student assessment, resource allocation, and institutional accountability. Yet many leadership preparation programs have not fully addressed AI governance, digital ethics, or data literacy at the depth required by contemporary realities.

This book therefore responds to a pressing global need. It situates school leadership within the broader context of the Fourth Industrial Revolution while maintaining a clear focus on educational values. It recognizes that AI implementation without equity-centered leadership risks amplifying existing disparities. Conversely, when guided by thoughtful and ethical leadership, AI has the potential to illuminate hidden inequities, personalize support for diverse learners, and strengthen strategic decision-making.

The intended audience for this book is diverse yet unified by a shared commitment to improving educational systems. School principals and system leaders will find frameworks and practical insights for navigating AI integration within their institutions. Policymakers and regulatory bodies will encounter discussions on governance, accountability, and inclusive policy design. Scholars and doctoral students in educational leadership, policy, and technology will engage with emerging theoretical paradigms that redefine leadership in digitally mediated contexts. Educational technology designers and professional development providers will gain perspectives on aligning innovation with ethical and equity-driven objectives. The book is equally suitable for advanced coursework in leadership programs and for practitioners seeking guidance on responsible digital transformation.

CHAPTER OVERVIEW

Each chapter makes a distinctive contribution to the book's overarching narrative. The opening chapter examines leadership styles within multicultural for-profit schools, focusing on transformational leadership as a model for navigating diversity and performance demands. By situating leadership within complex sociocultural environments, it establishes a foundational understanding of how leadership identity shapes institutional direction and organizational climate. This theoretical grounding sets the stage for later discussions of how leadership must further adapt in technologically enriched contexts.

The second chapter provides a comprehensive analysis of artificial intelligence in schools, addressing both its opportunities and its risks. It examines governance mechanisms necessary to ensure inclusive learning and ethical oversight. By carefully balancing innovation with caution, this chapter establishes the ethical parameters that inform the rest of the book. It underscores that technological advancement must be accompanied by transparent policies, stakeholder engagement, and safeguards against unintended harm.

The third chapter introduces the concept of engineering Human–AI leadership for school equity. It proposes integrative frameworks that combine algorithmic tools with human judgment to address disparities in educational outcomes. By bridging systems design and leadership theory, the chapter offers a structured approach to ensuring that data-driven practices remain aligned with equity goals.

The fourth chapter explores AI-enhanced learning environments through the lens of school leadership perceptions. It investigates how leaders interpret and enact AI-supported pedagogical and assessment practices, and how these practices can either reinforce or reduce inequities. By grounding theoretical discussions in lived leadership experiences, the chapter adds empirical depth and highlights the importance of leader sense-making in technological adoption.

The fifth chapter moves from perception to action by examining AI and data-informed leadership for inclusive decision-making. It demonstrates how analytics can be leveraged to identify achievement gaps, allocate resources strategically, and monitor institutional progress toward inclusion targets. This chapter provides actionable models that enable leaders to transform data into meaningful interventions.

The sixth chapter reframes school leadership for innovation, technology, and inclusion. It challenges traditional leadership paradigms and calls for adaptive, forward-thinking approaches capable of aligning digital transformation with inclusive values. In doing so, it broadens the conceptual boundaries of educational leadership in the digital era.

The seventh chapter centers on wellbeing and equity, reminding readers that digital transformation must not eclipse the relational core of schooling. It argues that

AI adoption should enhance—not undermine—psychological safety, professional collaboration, and a sense of belonging for students and staff. This chapter reinforces the idea that technological efficiency must remain subordinate to human flourishing.

The eighth chapter addresses resilience, safety, and continuity in times of crisis. Drawing from contemporary disruptions, it examines how digital infrastructures and AI systems can support learning continuity while maintaining equity. The chapter highlights adaptive leadership, preparedness, and strategic foresight as essential competencies for navigating uncertainty.

The ninth chapter offers a policy-oriented case study of AI-enabled reform within the context of India's National Education Policy 2020. By analyzing large-scale implementation efforts, it demonstrates how Human–AI leadership principles can be embedded within national transformation agendas. This chapter situates the book within a global reform landscape and illustrates the scalability of its central concepts.

Collectively, these chapters contribute to the advancement of the field in several important ways. The book articulates Human–AI Leadership as a distinct and emerging paradigm that integrates ethics, equity, governance, and technological innovation. It aligns leadership scholarship with contemporary digital transformation agendas while maintaining a steadfast commitment to social justice. It offers practical frameworks that can be adapted across diverse educational systems and cultural contexts. Most importantly, it affirms that the purpose of technological integration in schools is not efficiency alone, but the advancement of inclusive, equitable, and humane educational environments.

CONCLUSION

As schools evolve into increasingly intelligent and interconnected ecosystems, the defining question is not whether artificial intelligence will influence leadership, but how leaders will shape its use. This book invites readers to move beyond reactive adaptation and toward intentional design. It calls upon educational leaders to become architects of ethical digital futures—professionals who harness AI thoughtfully, critically, and compassionately in service of students, communities, and society at large.

Asma Khaleel Abdallah
Sharjah Education Academy, United Arab Emirates

Ahmed Khaleel Akaabi
United Arab Emirates University, United Arab Emirates

Markus Talvio
Helsinki University, Finland

Acknowledgment

The completion of this book has been a collaborative journey shaped by the intellectual generosity, commitment, and shared vision of many individuals and institutions. We are deeply grateful to all those who contributed to bringing this work to fruition.

First and foremost, we extend our sincere appreciation to all contributing authors from different countries. Their scholarship, diverse perspectives, and dedication to advancing equitable and responsible educational leadership have enriched this book in profound ways. Each chapter reflects not only rigorous academic inquiry but also a shared commitment to shaping a more inclusive and ethically grounded future for schools worldwide.

We would like to recognize the invaluable partnership of the editors and their institutions. Our gratitude goes to Sharjah Education Academy, United Arab Emirates University, and the University of Helsinki for their continued support of scholarly collaboration and international engagement. The institutional environments that foster research, dialogue, and innovation made this book possible.

We are especially thankful to the reviewers who generously dedicated their time and expertise to evaluating the submitted chapters. Their constructive feedback, careful reading, and professional integrity significantly enhanced the quality, clarity, and rigor of this book. Peer review remains a cornerstone of academic excellence, and we deeply value the important role reviewers played in strengthening the final manuscript.

Our sincere appreciation is also extended to the team at IGI Global. Their professional guidance, editorial support, and commitment to high publishing standards have been instrumental in transforming this project from concept to publication. We are grateful for their responsiveness, organization, and dedication to ensuring that this book reaches a global audience.

Finally, we acknowledge the broader educational leadership community whose ongoing work in schools, universities, and policy environments continues to inspire research and innovation. This book stands as a collective effort grounded in collaboration, mutual respect, and a shared aspiration to advance equitable, ethical, and forward-looking educational leadership.

To all who contributed directly or indirectly to this book, we offer our heartfelt thanks.

Chapter 1
Leadership Styles of Multicultural For-Profit Schools:
A Transformation Leadership Style

Ziad Younes Shatat
http://orcid.org/0009-0007-3304-3794
Sharjah Private Education Authority, UAE

ABSTRACT

This chapter examines key leadership models—instructional, participative, directive, shared, transactional, and transformational—and their influence on teaching quality, professional relationships, and school culture. Instructional and participative approaches enhance collaboration, motivation, and shared decision-making, while directive and transactional models provide structure, accountability, and performance consistency. Building on these foundations, transformational and transformative leadership emerge as effective models for managing change, promoting inclusivity, and supporting diverse, multicultural school environments. Such leaders foster alignment between individual and organizational goals, encourage creativity, and strengthen professional growth. The chapter highlights strategic communication, continuous development, and active stakeholder engagement as essential tools for navigating complex educational contexts.

INTRODUCTION

Historically, leadership has played a central role as a determining factor when it comes to shaping up societies as well as cultural set-ups. According to antiquity and

DOI: 10.4018/979-8-2600-0388-6.ch001

the modern era, rulers have acted as agents of change, guiding societies through the time of transition, growth, and creative steps. The role of leadership has escalated in the modern globalized environment, where there is cultural heterogeneity. Most of the modern organizations and schools are becoming more and more functions in multicultural milieus, making cross cultural leadership a prerequisite to success rather than just an admirable quality. The modern day leaders are thus tasked with navigating the intricacies of different belief systems, value systems, and normative networks, and at the same time making their teams and institutions become cohesive and have a feeling of direction. As an analysis of leadership in its cultural context shows, it is an event that goes far beyond the limits of administrative or managerial roles and is a highly cultural one. Leadership reflects as well as shapes the values, beliefs and attitudes that define societies thus shaping the trends of cooperation and interaction in organisational settings. Leaders who focus on change and development of the society therein therefore have an inspirational effect on the moral and ethical foundations of their societies. This interdependence of culture and leadership is an important aspect to note that intelligent leaders do not just perform management functions but rather implement and promote the cultural scripts that individuals use to connect with one another. It is based on this assumption that there has been a consistent movement by scholars to focus scholarly interest on the intra-personally oriented aspects of leadership with the recognition that cultural acuity needs to be accompanied by personal authenticity and emotional intelligence (Ibrahim, 2020). Credibility in leadership that encompasses both ethical behaviors and character, spirituality and self awareness have been cited as a pillar of effective leadership.As opposed to the traditional understanding of leadership as a strictly behavioral or strictly technical phenomenon, the modern school of thought states that leadership is a holistic integration of cognitive, physiological, affective, and spiritual aspects. In this integrative paradigm, leadership is viewed both as a process of inner growth and movement and as an outer process of directing social success(El Zaatari& Ibrahim, 2021). The growing awareness of the internal milieu of leaders is as such contributing to the broader discourse of globalization and cultural pluralism. The nexus between leadership modalities and culture mediated expectations is made more and more complex as firms and pedagogical institutions multiply across national boundaries. An explication of this interrelation has the requisite knowledge of strategies by which leaders can effectively engage, motivate, and guide people who are attracted by diverse cultural backgrounds (Sarfraz et al., 2024; Chkheidze, 2024; Paulienė, 2012b).

Leadership and culture merge in the dynamic relationship of interdependence in the globalized society. Cultural values define what good leadership is and leadership practices in turn define cultural development in the organizational setting. This two-way impact requires the leaders to develop cultural intelligence as well as adaptive strategies in order to be sure that their decisions are heard in various social and organizational environments (Ibrahim,2012). By exploring the meaning of leadership in a diverse cultural context, researchers bring insights into how the beliefs, traditions, and social norms shape the attitudes to power, teamwork, and creativity (Aldous & Ismail, 2025). Additionally, those cultural views have direct consequences related to the leadership development in multinational settings. As organizations expand their business activities to international boundaries, the leaders have to identify the nature of skills and competencies that attract the highest valuation across cultures. This consciousness eases the inclusion promotion, cultural conflict management, and productive international teamwork. Traditionally, the leadership theories were mostly based on Western or North American paradigms, which often ignored the values and practices of the non-Western societies. There has been a strong need to review these theories to determine their relevance to non-Western contexts. This critical re-evaluation does not only broaden the area of the leadership theory but also increases its applicability in the context of the ever-growing interconnected and multi-cultural world. The growing change of thinking in leadership globally provides the smooth way to exploring transformational leadership as the model that is especially applicable to the complex, culturally blended, and quickly changing environments (Sarfraz et al., 2024; Chkheidze, 2024;Paulienė, 2012b).

Transformation leadership has developed in the environment of growing globalization and technological advancement and is now considered to be one of the most effective forms of organizational leadership in the era of changes. Unlike transactional or directive leadership approaches, which focus on legal matters and stability, transformational leadership aims at inspiring, motivating, and uplifting followers as they relate personal goals and desires with those of the organization. Transformational leaders also promote creativity and commitment through vision-based communication and emotional connection nurturing and suborinates empowerment, which leads to innovation and resilience (Abdallah & Musah, 2023). This type of leadership is especially useful at the time when there is a social and institutional crisis, the flexibility and innovativeness are the most important qualities. Transformational leaders help create a feeling of purpose whereby the teams cross cultural and organizational boundaries. Their focus on empowerment and team building is aimed at developing trust so that the members of different backgrounds feel appreciated and involved (Ibrahim, 2013). In its turn, transformational leadership is particularly relevant in the multicultural settings, where inclusivity and empathy represent the essential factors of organizational success. The logical approach to this idea can be seen in the sphere of education, which is directly connected with the social change and cultural progress. With educational systems across the globe going through the process of reform and modernization, transformational leadership provides the necessary model that is required to skillfully guide these complex undertakings (Sarfraz et al., 2024; Chkheidze, 2024;Paulienė, 2012b)..

Education leaders are in an environment that requires a certain level of intellectual discipline as well as moral accountability. Unlike the competitive and profit-seeking business arena, institutions of higher-learning will have to balance various missions, such as teaching, enhancing inclusiveness, and equipping students with skills that enable them to be global citizens. Transformational leaders in the school and university setting are empirically linked to increased teacher motivation, strengthened professional teamwork and student performance. They develop cultures that are based on trust and creativity and thus not only can enhance the performance of the institutions, but also help in improving the satisfaction of the teachers and their retention. These leaders recommend reflective practice, lifelong learning, and malleability - virtues that cannot be ignored in the face of the fast-changing technologies and transforming educational models. The concept of change management in the context of education, however, presents a unique challenge, as it is essential that the leaders are paying attention to the organisational structures, as well as cultural and emotional aspects of the educational communities. Transformational leadership is empathetic, empowering, and shares the vision, which provides an all-inclusive solution to this dilemma (Aldous & Ismail, 2025). Transformational leaders are crucial in making learning institutions sustainable and relevant as they become diverse, technologically integrated, and responsive to changes in the world in terms of knowledge and learning (Ibrahim,2018). As a result, the interdependence between culture, leadership and education is a holistic concept where leadership acts as a cultural socializing agent and a means of change; it indicates the values of the times and it also determines the direction of institutions and societies towards inclusiveness, novelty and justice (Sarfraz et al., 2024; Chkheidze, 2024;Paulienė, 2012b).

BACKGROUND: THE LEADERSHIP EFFECT ON THE CHANGE TO THE CULTURE OF INNOVATION AND SCHOOL REFORM

Understand Leadership

The leadership is a critical issue in organizations, and it can be easily described as the act of influencing people or groups in order to accomplish the set goals, which can be the development of innovation. By setting up shared goals and defining the capacity of innovation, leaders can foster organization innovation, performance, and strategy by means of values and behaviors. The importance of leadership has been increased with developing of the global business environment as competitive. There is no single definition of leadership, on the contrary, a variety of styles are born, such as autocratic, transactional, democratic, and transformational, depending on the behavior of the leaders. The role of leadership has been identified as one of the key sources of innovation despite its different forms. The human capital which involves individual and collective knowledge of the employees is critical to the development of organizational innovation. It is also made of tacit knowledge, competencies and personal attributes. Employee performance depends on leadership and management support in the process of implementing innovation strategies. Innovation performance may be significantly different depending on the leadership styles that organizations adopt. Still, it is untenable to claim that one of the styles is better than another because innovation depends on various contextual and organizational factors. The contributions made by each leadership style are different and various firms might need different approaches. The available literature recognizes at least 21 other styles of leadership; the other styles are not specifically connected with the innovation strategies in organizations. Two main paths of connection, which are direct and indirect impacts, are identified. The four main types of leadership emphasized below vary in the level of staff involvement they offer and the reason behind why they are critical in the realization of innovation strategies, which underlines their importance to nurturing an innovative attitude (Costa et al., 2023).

Autocratic Leadership

The concept of autocratic leadership was initially developed by Lewin in 1935 and can be utilized in terms of an inclusive approach, with a focus on human capital, team balance, and a separatist approach to quantitative results. Furthermore, this style may be especially effective in situations when the leader is characterized by a high level of emotional intelligence, especially in those moments when the person is stressed or when he or she has to make a decision fast. Regardless of whether the organization is in a high-technology industry or in a more traditional modality, autocracy is considered necessary in ensuring the deadlines and accountability. Therefore, innovation processes can be supported by such leadership. Moreover, autocratic leaders are very critical in situations of high stress. Organization One aspect of the organizational culture observed in autocratic leaders is the presence of a traditionally masculine culture, hierarchical organization, high power distance, and collectivist orientation. In line with this, this type of leadership has been pegged on an externally oriented environment and is common in small companies in their initial maturity stages. In autocratic leadership, the leader gathers all the power and control by pressing the subordinates into following the established rules (Ibrahim, 2010). On the other hand, these leaders make procedural steps clear and give clear instructions. But the autocratic leaders usually do not allow the subordinates to adopt their own styles, which shows a widespread lack of trust in the abilities of the followers. One of the main distinguishing features of this style is extreme control and rejection of subordinate opinions as well as assertive communication of job instructions. With regards to creativity and innovation, such leaders are characterized by low creative ability and mostly restricted to communicative roles and this negatively affects employee satisfaction and triggers low motivation trends. As a result, these types of leadership relationship can lead to the development of high levels of absenteeism and employee turnover. On the contrary, autocratic leaders take a position where, though seen as apparently beneficial, it ends up trapping highly talented employees, and inhibiting creativity in the long term. In organizations that use this paradigm of leadership, the strict hierarchical structure is dominant. However, the autocratic approach can be justified in certain situations. Autocratic leadership will be necessary in organizations where perfection of execution is mandatory such as in manufacturing sectors. This leadership is highly prevalent in military, political and sports coaches as well as some chief executives in industries(Alkaabi *et al.*, 2025). The authoritarian type is especially applicable in situations where employees have to be trained quickly, as it is the case with fast-food businesses. This leadership is also apparent in the music industry, specifically in the large orchestras, thus highlighting its prevalence in various industries as well as its ability to maintain high standards of operational efficiency in the results provided. Nevertheless, this style might not be motivating subordinates and the rates of attrition and focus on innovation processes might increase (Costa et al., 2023).

Transactional Leadership

Weber (1947) was the first scholar who defined transactional leadership in the process of studying transformational leadership. The construct is determined by how the leaders make gain out of employees, depending on how well the followers conform to the demands of their leaders in a scheme of reciprocal performance. Such a leadership arrangement arises when one of them takes the initiative of initiating contacts with the rest of the people in the effort to achieve mutually valuable results. The values that underlie the process of the exchange such as integrity, responsibility, and reciprocity cannot be disregarded and are tightly connected with the needs of the followers and their job performance. Two orthogonal dimensions, which characterize rewards and managerial practices, include active or passive exception handling and, therefore, three modalities of leaders, namely, contingent reward, exception management, and laissez-faire. The transactional leader will therefore focus on gains, awards, prizes, and self-interest between the leader and the follower, and failure to meet the goals will result in punishment. Transactional leadership may be a hindrance to innovation and provide minimal input to organizational learning. Additionally, it is a contextual style, which frequently takes the form of micromanagement or traditional management, in the event that leaders have risk aversion towards new directions. These leaders would also wish to maintain control to reduce risks in projects or routine activities, thus creating a feeling of obligation in subordinates who are forced to respond to high quality results and effort to meet deliberative behaviors of the leader. In relation to human capital, transactional leaders have been known to develop specialized skills through prioritizing individual roles in lieu of teamwork; they are also known to be more likely to invest in the current talent as opposed to outsourcing since they believe it is more beneficial to utilize an in-house talent. Therefore, transactional leadership is linked to decreased performance in innovation, whereby creativity is limited by a set of objectives. However, it can have a benefit to organizations that seek to achieve short-term goals within a short time especially in the large institutional contexts (Costa et al., 2023).

Democratic Leadership

Democratic leadership or participative leadership became highly visible in the second half of the twentieth century, and its empirical roots can be traced to the Hawthorne experiments. This leadership structure is based on a distributive model of making decisions whereby everyone among the subordinate members shares power. The peculiarity of this style is that it allows active participation, which is also quite similar to the ethos of functioning of democratic governmental systems. Typically, the democratic leaders are seen in organization where there is low power distance, high dimensionality of femininity and individualism, and low uncertainty avoidance. This leadership paradigm is based on participation as the central aspect, which makes it especially different compared to other styles. Based on empirical data, it is believed that democratic leadership is especially fitting in the framework of a startup setting and technology based firms, and in companies or initiatives where heterogeneous teams have to work collaboratively to coordinate and co-produce. Democratic leaders possess motivation as a salient trait, which helps in improving the organizational performance. Practically, democratic leaders create a sense of trust and support of the initiatives of followers by approving and spreading their intellectual input. They show developments of behaviors and pass leadership of methodologies of work to the followers. Democratic leadership is generally considered to be a normative form of organizational practice. In this context, notions receive the value of their own regardless of their origin, which is observed in educational establishments. However, there can also be drawbacks of the democratic leaders, such as the slow decision making, a decreased capacity to scale in very large organizations as well as a possible rigidity of strategic deliberations (Costa et al., 2023).

Transformational Leadership

Transformational leadership was initially defined by Burns & Ward (1978) and then furthered work of Bass and Bass (1985) who utilized Multifactor Leadership Questionnaire to identify the psychological processes that made the difference between transformational and transactional leadership. The ability of transformational leadership to create and promote creativity and organizational innovation has led to a growing scholarly interest in it. It is the most thoroughly examined style of leadership in the area of innovation. Moreover, the given construct can be operationalized in four sub-dimensions, including individualized influence, inspirational motivation, intellectual stimulation, and individualized consideration. The combination of these sub-dimensions explains the way transformational leaders influence innovation processes; as an example, they show followers the importance of particular goals and create intrinsic motivation to work on the achievement of these goals, which positively impacts performance. The transformational leaders are often located in the companies where there are flexible working conditions and the environment where the work is innovational, and which encourage the unity by underlining the shared interests and goals. Compared to transactional, transformational leaders are more oriented towards innovation since they engage the employees in the mission of the organization and allow them to experiment with new approaches to solving problems. Therefore, transformational leaders are often described as being champions of innovation. Transformational leaders who promote learning are effective in generating learning cultures which support innovation outcomes in situations where employees have strong learning abilities. This leadership style plays a great role in promoting the innovation by setting simple common goals, mobilizing the employees with vision, and creating trust and confidence. By such practices, leaders give followers the power and enable them to provide good climates where innovation can take place and produce high results and competitive advantages. Transformational leaders encourage the staff to look beyond the normal limits, and the energy that they convey often creates enormous passion towards work among the followers. One of the acute areas of transformational leaders is the promotion of the ownership of employees through searching the variety of opinions that can be applied to solving a problem. Team dynamics are also directly related to their communication skills as well as risk tolerance, which leads to the creation of ideas, new products, services, or technologies. Transformational leadership depends on the quality of mentoring and coaching as the high quality lead to intellectual stimulation and charismatic leadership that makes the followers efficient without imposing a judgmental attitude. Transformational leadership has been more effective where the mentors are skilled and experienced. However, leaders should facilitate followers by providing specialized training and the supply of resources that will facilitate innovation. Transformational leaders provoke systematic feedback and track motivation through systematically soliciting employee feedback. This leadership paradigm is beyond motivation or compliance, and it is based on the beliefs, needs, and values of subordinates. The interpersonal basis of this style is based on relationships that are long lasting, positive and well founded on trust. Transformational leadership possesses both incremental and radical innovation which facilitate the development of follower innovation capacities as well as affect organizational learning that intensifies innovation. This effect of style on the success of the project takes place both directly and indirectly (Costa et al., 2023).

Profit School: Profitability, Policy and Student Achievement

The growth of for-profit higher education occurred exponentially in the 1990s and the first years of the 2000s, after which it reversed itself in the 2010s. Changes in the for-profit postsecondary sector are closely connected to the federal funding and regulation, or an absence of it. Deregulation in the 1970s and 1980s led to the appearance of for-profit colleges that responded to massive inflations of Title4 grants and subsidized student loans in the 1990s. The constant increase in tuition has resulted in millions of students complementing their federally-subsidized grants and loans with unsubsidized and personal loans. The question of whether or not the for-profit colleges hold effective human capital to the disadvantaged students who cannot afford postsecondary education provided in the public and nonprofit sphere, or whether the for-profit colleges are taking advantage of the disadvantaged students and the federal funds to make money without the quality education remains a contentious issue. Further, the amount of student loan debt of degree-seeking students in for-profit colleges is significantly higher (over 20000 and 13000 at 2-year and 4-year colleges respectively) than that of students in the same groups at public colleges. These findings, together with those of other scholars, indicate that the for-profit colleges are neither educationally nor economically comparable to the publicly and privately owned non-profit colleges, to which they should be subjected in order to obtain Title IV federal funding, as per the Education Amendments of 1972 (Tucker, 2021).

Unregulated and Growth of For-Profit Colleges

According to the Higher Education Act of 1965, Title IV of which provides the federal government with the power to support college students by granting them and providing them with subsidized loans, the Commissioner is authorized to grant money to the institutions of higher education and other agencies, organizations, and institutions but, with one exception, not a nonprofit organization. The Education

Amendments of 1972, which became infamous due to Title IX, which, barring discrimination based on sex, allowed federal aid to be given to for-profit colleges on the condition that they would offer substantially equivalent education, training, or services more easily or more cheaply, or by avoiding unnecessary duplication of costly physical plant and equipment, or by offering needed education or training... otherwise, it would not be available. For-profit institutions did not have an instant influx of enrollments with the access to federal funding, although further deregulation of student loans in 1986 facilitated the jumpstarting of the for-profit sector, which expanded, in terms of higher education enrollments, by 1.5 3/4 percent of the total in 1990 to 9 percent by 2009. The students who join the for-profit colleges are overrepresented more likely to be drawn in the traditionally marginalized group and have characteristics that are generally linked with low college attendance rates. Survey data on the sample of beginning postsecondary students of 2004-2009 have revealed that the for-profit students are disproportionately Black and Latino, have low-income, are single parents, and hold GEDs. More likely, such students are not financially dependent on their parents and receive federal financial support. Three-quarters of federal government financial aid to students at for-profits is through federal grants, which is compared to only 90 percent in non-profit colleges. The rise in for-profit enrollments can be, in part, explained by the overcrowded community colleges that have difficulties in enrolling students in the necessary courses and this is mostly explained by the fact that the budgets of the public schools are short. State tax higher education appropriations doubled or tripled in 2000-2010, whereas Pell Grants and Stafford Loans tripled and doubled respectively. This is one of the features of a wider neoliberal trend in which higher education is privatized and financialized. The state is less involved in the provision and more involved in financing, thus providing an opportunity to influential private entities to externalize liabilities through covering them with loan default (Tucker, 2021).

Student Loans and Earnings After College

The results of large and multiple student loans and poor post-college incomes by the students explain the high rates of default by students of the for-profit colleges. Student loans in for-profit colleges account for more than 90 percent of all students compared to about 13 percent in 2-year publics. The probability of students in non-profit making private colleges to borrow student loans is about 50 percent less. The median student debt to graduates with bachelors degrees in for-profit institutions is about four times bigger than the debt to graduates of four-year public colleges, and almost two times bigger than the debt to graduates in non-profits. Average tuition at the for-profit colleges is so exorbitant that over 40 percent of those students to the college complete federally subsidized Stafford Loans with other unsubsidized loans. It is discovered that post-college earnings of students receiving associate degrees or certificates conferred by the for-profit colleges do not differ significantly with those who do not receive an associate degree or a certificate. The application of the IRS data shows that certificate-seeking students in the for-profits receive lower incomes and are less likely to get employment compared with students in public schools. The data on two state community colleges systems in 2001-2006 indicates that community college students who move to for-profit, four-year programs earn much less than students who move to four-year programs of non-profit and public colleges (Tucker, 2021).

School Culture: The Focal Stick of Education Quality

School culture refers to the institutional image of an actual school and includes internalized rules and standards that determine attitudes, behaviors and expectations of the stakeholders. In case schools desire to maximize their ability to promote learning, and cultural development among students, they ought to focus on building collaborative cultures. It is crucial to make a collaborative culture where everyone in an organization subscribes to beliefs, rules, policies, mission, and goals to enhance the schools. There are four main practices that can be used in organising school learning culture: (a) shared leadership, (b) collaborative culture, (c) collective learning, and (d) shared values and vision, which are often evaluated with the help of the Brown Learning Culture Assessment. Culture in school cuts across every aspect of school life. The cultural patterns have to be related to the requirements of the institution; the quality of leadership practice is related to the development of a favorable school culture. School culture change is a challenging task, but it is at the core of successful school improvement. The processes of school improvement are linked with the attempts to influence learning conditions and to change the elements of the institution culture so that to meet the organizational goals. Principals play a pivotal role in shaping the school culture and take center stage in school improvement agenda; but this is not an easy task as they are expected to not only bring about change but also create a sense of belongingness among teachers and students thus creating benefits in the school organizational culture by aligning organizational and individual values. Principals are able to achieve a positive culture by instilling confidence in teachers and students. Successful leaders learn to adjust and work in the existing climate and culture of their school and community which in turn facilitates a school that initiates constant improvement. Separating climate and culture: climate is the emotional sense of the school climate and culture is the wider system of everything environmental and the beliefs and values of the members. The two have an effect upon group member behaviors. Culture refers to a product of past relations in a school whereas climate is a process of present-day perceptions of the past relations. Every school has a unique culture, and it can fall within a spectrum between a conducive and a toxic culture in relation to the effect on the learning outcomes in the school fraternity. It involves norms, values, beliefs, traditions, rituals which build up through time as the stakeholders work together, solve problems and come up with outcomes which inform expectations that influence cognition, affect, and behavior. The school culture has a very strong influence on the attitudes and performance of the students. A holistic model suggests that every single member of the extended school community is involved in the development of a motivational school culture (Heenan et al., 2023).

FOCUS OF CHAPTER: THE TRANSFORMATIONAL LEADERSHIP IN SCHOOL DEVELOPMENT

Leadership and School

The decisions made by the principals in the leadership of schools will greatly affect the standards of instruction, teaching and learning in the school. Still, it is crucial to note that the leadership styles of principals must be dependent on a range of factors, such as the environment, the challenges, and a certain problem that the school faces at the moment. According to a literature review, various types of school leadership can significantly improve classroom learning and instruction, and at the same time reduce institutional issues (Agyeman and Aphane, 2024).

Institutional Leadership of School

Instructional leadership is critical in improving schools, considering that it is basically involved with teaching and learning. This form of leadership gives equal significance to school, teachers, parents as well as students towards teaching and learning. It does this by creating a favorable school climate, helping teachers and students to live up to curriculum requirements as well as enhancing the teaching and learning culture of the school (Ramadan & Ismail, 2023). A research in South Africa was focused on high performing schools in low-resource settings, where primary schools were sampled. The research found that instructional leaders are important in influencing the performance of learners in a positive manner. Indicatively, the research contended that educational administrators would lead changes in underachieving schools that are functioning under resource restraint. The adoption of the concept of instructional leadership is especially beneficial in cases when the teachers need guidance in coordinating the curriculum as well as the process of teaching and learning. The roles of instructional leaders, therefore, are to improve the instructional abilities of teachers and create an atmosphere that helps in learning. The role and the ability of the instructional leader to mobilise various actors and stakeholders enhances teaching and learning. Instructional leadership plays a vital role in the development of a school, therefore, it creates the right environment that leads to improved performance and achievement (Agyeman and Aphane, 2024).

Participation School Leadership

Participative leadership is a management model where employees are given the ability to make decisions together with their managers. The ability to organize is also one of the major attributes of participative leadership in education. Principals use different forms of coordination which include giving out authority, empowering employees, encouraging collaboration with stakeholders as well as enhancing interaction and communication with teachers and learners. It has been established that the utilization of participative leadership by school principals is extremely significant in school administration and management since it helps in the facilitation of the routine instructional performance. In this regard, these leaders lead the pack in engaging the employees in decision-making. Participative leadership is an undertaking in which the principals and teachers make joint decisions. This approach to school decision-making has been found to encourage teachers to work harder, have better performance, and increase their school commitment thereby proving the past arguments. Such leadership also focuses on the teacher as a crucial human and intellectual capital, which is core in the institution. A participative leader will always have the element of involving teachers in decision-making, which will guarantee social cohesion and team building (Agyeman & Aphane, 2024).

Directive School Leadership

Directive leadership gives the subordinates a model to follow and make decisions that help them correspond to the goals of the leader. The leader is expected to spell out what the followers should achieve, the strategy as well as the quality levels that are required. As a result, a school principal who practices such kind of leadership has the ultimate control and authority in all the decision-making within the school. Direct instructions define what is expected, which process to follow, and the schedule, which is normally told by leaders who adopt a directive style (Agyeman & Aphane, 2024).

Shared School Leadership

Shared leadership refers to a collaborative exercise whereby group members lead each other towards a common goal. This type of leadership exhibits group and team attributes regarding dynamic aspects of shared influence amongst particular group members in pursuit of shared goals. Shared leadership as explained entails a large number of the teachers who, although not necessarily holding an official or senior post in the school, are considered to be the leaders in the school. This is essential as it will enable leaders to devolve authority and power to team members who will participate in decision making that will be abilitate them to undertake roles of decision making as well as be rewarded to do so. This kind of leadership brings out the hidden talents in the employees and allows the followers to overcome relevant to their constraints. By contrast, shared leadership emphasizes the achievement of goals within schools rather than the personal self-interests of the followers, (Agyeman and Aphane, 2024).

Educational Leadership: Transactional Leadership

Transactional leadership is based on the association between the leader and the team and focuses on the advantages of a contractual agreement, where the leader will reward loyal and committed employees with their efforts. The main objective of transactional leadership is to force the subordinates to pull themselves to get a good reward. Transactional leaders, therefore, enhance the motivation of employees by rewarding them. Towards this end, leaders have clear goals and explaining how the actions of the followers concerning the goals. The leadership style was the most widely used in schools and was called transactional leadership orienting towards organisational effectiveness and supervisory control. However, the transactional school leaders are expected to engage followers in following a scheduled goal prior to committing to it, thus restricting the leader to evaluate its results and make changes as needed (Agyeman and Aphane, 2024).

Transformational School Leadership

The transformational leadership defines leaders who motivate the followers to reach their potential capacity and to deliver effectively in line with the demands of the school. A transformational leader plays an essential role in a school because he or she focuses on the vision and mission of the institution. In addition, the influence of a transformational leader is considered by the majority of scholars to be deep, as they are oriented to the creation of the needed changes in the school setting. Transformational leadership promotes sustainable dedication of both learners and teachers in support. However, the impact of transformational leadership is mitigated in case a school requires an urgent change (Agyeman and Aphane, 2024).

School Culture and Transformation

Multicultural education offers the teachers and senior management teams (SMTs) to join forces with different school populations and establish justice in the societies characterized by ethnic, language, religion, gender and socioeconomic inequality. Programmes targeting the need to accommodate diversity should be actively incorporated by teachers and SMTs in an attempt to help learners achieve higher academic performance and holistic human growth. Transformative leadership can be used as an avenue to remodel the learning outcomes of multicultural school students. It involves something to be done in order to rectify inequalities and to ensure that learners receive equal chances to achieve their full potential, are treated with dignity and acquire competences. Inequities negatively impact the performance of learners and require inclusive practices that would promote historically marginalised learners. Inclusive education took center stage in the 1994 Salamanca Statement, which was adopted at the World Conference on Special Needs Education: Access and Quality held in Spain under the auspices of the UNESCO. Inclusive education was recognized in the conference as the most prolific way of making sure that all people have equal education. Transformative leaders should be social just and should therefore take the initiative of challenging the political and social challenges that continue to propagate inequities in schools. The perspectives and behaviors that multicultural schools represent are the ones that value and appreciate the existence of various groups within the society, appreciate and acknowledge the existence of socio-cultural diversity, and promote a continuous involvement in an inclusive cultural environment. Transformative leadership is seen to be optimal when it comes to the practices of teachers and the roles of principals in leading schools in multicultural settings. It challenges people to assume responsibility in envisioning what kind of world they want to build to their interactions, opinions and beliefs which is associated with the ideal school environment. It means that transformative leadership can be considered the source that must encourage people to be more creative, interdependent, and interpersonal-valued, which reflect their ideals and help them provide results that could represent their ethics, expectations, and concerns. Transformative leadership therefore focuses the leadership in the multicultural contexts and this may help teachers and principals make positive contributions to school development. This is because as transformative leaders, the senior management in schools ought to foster teacher autonomy and provide inclusive teaching and learning environments as a way of leading in multicultural school settings. By so doing, SMTs ought to promote the emergence of autonomous, socially responsible and critically aware individuals in the perspective of providing education as (inter)personal empowerment and social change. In-service teachers should be given teacher autonomy to critically and independently contemplate the existing cultural benefits and power dynamics, their own space in schools, and to critically examine the dimensions of multiculturalism with the aim of creating equal and inclusive learning environments by the way they practice their teaching profession. The development of inclusive learning spaces is one direction where many opportunities of engagement may be created, e.g., providing flexible and versatile platforms of specific learning, teamwork, and collaboration. An inclusive, learning friendly classroom (ILFC) welcomes, fosters and educates all learners regardless of language, intellectual, gender, emotional and social attributes. An ILFC is, thus, a place where educators acknowledge the importance of diversity and organize their work to treat all students equally (Kgothule et al., 2021).

INSPIRATIONAL LEADERSHIP THAT BRINGS ABOUT CHANGE IN PROFIT DRIVEN SCHOOLS

Transformational leadership has become a crucial strategy of dealing with change in education and promoting institutional growth. Transformational leaders help schools, colleges, and universities overcome tough change processes, and in the process, these institutions will overcome challenges and achieve a long-term success. This ability to motivate, inspire and align the stakeholders on a common vision makes them invaluable agents of positive change in the education sector. Transformational leadership is one of the pillars of strong educational change management. Transformational leaders also support innovation and inclusiveness by working through complicated reforms in institutions, as well as stimulating change, with vision, inspiration, and individualized attention. Their skill in balancing regulation needs and organisational culture makes sure that change not just happens, but is sustained hence developing not only educators and students, but the educational community in general (Chkheidze, 2024; Alainati et al., 2023).

Transformational Leadership and Change Management at School

Transformational leaders play a crucial role in facilitating change in the learning institutions. They describe the powerful vision, which is rather consistent with the goals of reform efforts and provides an effective guidance to all parties. This vision serves as a road map through which the educators, staff, and students are brought together because of the similar goals and the benefits and purpose of the change are also clarified. These leaders manage to create a sense of commitment by encouraging a vision of the reasoning behind change and reduce opposition (Fang et al., 2024). Transformational leaders also make sure the institutional missions keep up with changing educational needs like inclusion, the use of innovative pedagogies, or technology. Transformational leaders identify the sense of purpose and encourage it among their subordinates through inspirational motivation that help its team and foster enthusiasm. By maintaining interest in the difficult shifts and using emotional bonds as a means of increasing trust and decreasing anxiety in the course of reforms, they support each other. Credibility and respect are built on their idealistic influence, which is by example. Transformational leaders encourage teachers and employees to embrace new practices and be flexible and accountable by modeling the values and attitudes that they promote as part of the educational development (Chkheidze, 2024; Alainati et al., 2023).

Promoting Innovation and the Intellect

Promotion of creativity and problem solving is another major element of transformational leadership. Transformational leaders provoke the development of the intellect through the ability of stakeholders to think and come up with creative solutions. In instruction, this can be very frequently realized through encouraging the use of experimental teaching techniques, digital technology, and methods of instruction. These leaders facilitate teamwork in solving problems, which helps them to provide an environment where the educators are confident to develop new ways of doing things without the fear of failure. Such an innovation culture will allow schools to be more responsive to change and will help them maintain prolonged improvement (Chkheidze, 2024; Alainati et al., 2023).

Customized Attention and Support of the Stakeholders

Transformational leaders also extend individualized attention to the needs, concerns, and aspirations of teachers, staff and students based on their personal needs. Through empathy, guidance and professional support, they will make sure that every individual in the school community feels appreciated throughout the transformations. This concern decreases change resistance and boosts morale. The individualized strategy will help educational leaders build inclusive settings where all stakeholders feel valued and assisted, thus, providing an easier way to transition and greater institutional cohesiveness (Chkheidze, 2024; Alainati et al., 2023).

Influence on Personnel and Student Growth

The trait of transformational leadership is that it aims at building the potential and the desires of followers. Transformational leadership focuses on empowerment, motivation, and moral purpose unlike transactional leadership which focuses on achieving set goals. Transformational leaders increase commitment, creativity, and self-efficacy by motivating teachers and students to pursue their potential in the future. When teachers work under transformational leadership, they have more chances to perform to the best of their abilities driven by group objectives and ethical intent. This correlation can be backed up by the results of research on Leadership for Organisational Learning and Student Outcomes (LOLSOs), which showed that the role of transformational leaders in enhancing student engagement and performance is indirect, mediated by the effect they have on teacher motivation, teamwork, and professional development (Chkheidze, 2024; Alainati et al., 2023).

Control by Regulation and Centralization of Curriculum

Regulatory control, especially in systems where curricula have a centralized nature, is one of the external threats that transformational leaders have to grapple with. Centralization is the situation whereby educational leaders require certain curriculum to be followed depending on national or economic agendas. Though this control may lead to consistency, it tends to limit innovativeness and local flexibility. Transformational leaders can prevent these effects by applying policies in a flexible way and adjusting centralized needs to suit the specifics of their school. Where leaders have to choose between compliance and creativity to retain holistic skill development in situations where national priorities dominate like STEM education. The problem of potential disadvantages inherent in strict centralization can be minimized in the context of distributed and transformational leadership styles, which make teachers more autonomous and participatory in decision-making (Chkheidze, 2024; Alainati et al., 2023).

Organizational Factors Within an Organization That Affect Leadership

There are numerous internal forces affecting educational organizations amongst them being shared values, organizational culture, structures and policies. These factors influence leadership practices enactment and maintenance in schools. Individual qualities like integrity, vision, and empathy of a leader are very essential but not enough without facilitating organizational structures. Such internal factors as administrative support, teamwork, and positive learning climate are relevant influencing factors on leadership effectiveness and the improvement of schools overall (Chkheidze, 2024; Alainati et al., 2023).

Organizational Culture and Leadership, and Its Role

Organizational culture is a set of common values, beliefs and norms that dictate the work of an educational institution. Culture in schools arises through its constant interaction between the teachers, students and administrators. It influences the attitude to teaching, learning and innovation. Good, well cultivated cultures help in teamwork, credibility and responsibility which is in tandem with transformational concepts. On the other hand, negative or rigid cultures have the potential to slow development. School culture has a significant impact on the quality of leadership; it defines the ability to implement and maintain educational reforms. Transformational leaders are highly involved in constructing culture through openness, inclusiveness, and shared vision of success; that organisational values strengthened change instead of opposing it (Chkheidze, 2024; Alainati et al., 2023).

CASE STUDY, PROBLEMS, STRATEGY AND FUTURE DIRECTION

Case Studies

Transformational leadership has positioned itself as one of the key models to promote good school culture, teacher motivation and better student performance in multicultural learning institutions across the globe. The cultural diversity of schools in the United Arab Emirates (U.A.E.) is striking in terms of the availability of teachers and students of diverse background, providing potential opportunities and challenges to the school leaders. Empirical evidence shows that the principals who use transformational practices, which include stating a common vision, professional growth, and participative decision-making, can help to improve the climate of schools and staff collaboration to a significant extent. However, in many cases, the perception of the effectiveness of transformational leadership by principals and teachers is often different, mainly because of the differences in the cultural expectations, the types of communication, and the standards of leadership among nationalities. More studies indicate that culturally intelligent school leaders can more readily adjust transformational strategies to support this diversity, and hence the need to train leaders with cultural proficiency.

Transformational leadership in the United States has a close connection with teacher job satisfaction and commitment especially in urban schools with diverse populations. When principals integrate transformational behaviors with culturally responsive leadership by being equity-based in their visioning and involving communities demonstrate the greater levels of teacher trust and school performance. Likewise, in the United Kingdom, the transformational leadership can be seen through school improvement with a vision and the development of staff collaboratively, but there is often a tension between visionary leadership and the national accountability standards (Heenan et al., 2023). Transformational leadership of principals has also been reported to improve the mastery goals and self-efficacy of teachers in Singapore, where multiculturalism is a central aspect of the society, as long as it is accompanied by the systematic professional learning systems. At the same time, in Indonesia, transformational leadership outcomes positively affect multicultural education, but only when the school culture is not obstructive; otherwise, the transformational work of the leader is often ineffective (Research on School Culture and Multicultural Education in Indonesia, 2025).

In all settings, one thing comes out strongly and that is transformational leadership works in the multicultural schools most effectively when combined with cultural intelligence, distributed leadership and contextual adaptation. The leaders of the school strongly understanding and valuing cultural subtleties have a better chance of vision, motivation, and teacher empowerment attainments with different groups of staff (Bass & Avolio, 1995; Heenan et al., 2023). As it has been proved in all these countries, the effectiveness of transformational leadership in multicultural schools relies not only on the ability to inspire the vision but also to introduce inclusivity and ongoing professional learning as the part of the daily school routine. In turn, leadership development programs with the focus on cultural proficiency, reflective practice, and evidence-based collaboration are being promoted by policy initiatives in such nations as the U.A.E., the U.S., and Singapore as key tools to maintain successful multicultural school climate.

Global Leadership

The process of global leadership requires the development of interpersonal skills that would enable the growth of companies in international markets. However, the leadership functions do not follow the national boundaries; it holds a unique place of global location. Cross-cultural leadership goes beyond the geographical considerations, hence realising the vision of an organization at large. Leaders are also essential in the management of cultural diversity in order to remain central in the global system. Strategic leaders in culture hence create change in structures of the organization. Leaders who work in the environment of various business settings develop strong interpersonal relations with the representatives of the heterogeneous groups. Leaders have a great impact on teams to conform to deeply rooted cultural values and beliefs at the workplace in a cross-cultural situation. Leaders inspire different team and handle change effectively, to overcome cultural difference in such a way that business can realize its goals. Therefore, although the leadership functions in cultural management are prominent, how the leaders are able to contribute to cross-cultural practices is not well comprehended. Due to this reason, the substantive influence of leadership in the cultural context should be discussed at international scales. In the contemporary world, leadership has not been universal to many businesses. Therefore, this special investigation is essential to clarify the method, issues and plans of this changing paradigm, which now seems to be practicable in various situations. There is no doubt that in recent years the interest in global leadership has become very high. As a result, the character of work of the leaders has been subjected to a fundamental change(Ismail & Aldous, 2025). Globalization, competition, and innovation have brought about the phenomenon, which has increased the complexity in the global workplace. The growing uncertainties of various cultures have increased personal standards in terms of leadership. Lack of cultural knowledge may present challenges to the leaders including cultural differences, conflict and insensitivity. Such obstacles may hinder the flexibility of leaders to figure out divergent norms and values, which may result in firms making mistakes in the global market. The changing diversity can not be considered in everyone. Thus, cultural challenges and cultural diversity acceptance can help organizations to reach new levels of success. There are emerging tools and strategies that enable organizations to be more effective using cross-cultural leadership that is salient. Globalization has certainly brought a lot of intricacies in decision making and strategic planning. Based on this, embracing new approaches that accommodate different views will allow leaders to deal with international operational issues. In such a fast changing business world, a more thorough perception of cross-cultural leadership can be used to direct companies to the foreign diversification. Cultural competency, training, cross cultural team building and frequent communication promote knowledge and correspondence of different sets of cultures. In fact, successful cross-cultural leadership necessitates cultural awareness, versatility, communication, and a vision to settle the ever-increasing challenges of globalization and thus reap the benefits of leadership to achieve business success (Sarfraz et al., 2024).

Difficulties in Change Management

Although change management in education is a necessity towards innovation and growth, it presents several challenges which transformational leaders should overcome successfully. Lack of resistance to change is also a significant challenge as educators and employees are often reluctant to use new methods due to their uncertainty, the fear of failure, or the need to remain loyal to the proven methods. This resistance can stop or interrupt initiatives especially when the stakeholders feel that they are being sidelined in making the decisions. Another challenge is resource constraints since new programs and technologies are usually challenging to implement due to lack of infrastructure and funding. With a low level of funding, schools may lack the finances, skills and time to effectively execute and sustain transformation initiatives (Ismail & Ismail, 2024). Also, the existing expectations of various stakeholders create cultural barriers whose existence complicates the process of reaching an agreement. The conflict and lack of growth may be caused by different priorities of parents, teachers, administrators, and children. Transformational leaders can work around these barriers through encouraging change through open communication, ensuring that all the parties are informed about the aims and benefits of the change (Abdallah, 2024). Although continuous professional growth provides an educator with the skills and confidence to change to new approaches, participatory decision-making reduces resistance through the establishment of trust and ownership. By addressing these problems strategically, educational leaders can make a major, lasting change that can be beneficial to all stakeholders (Chkheidze, 2024).

Practice: Strategic Plans of Transformational Leaders

Transformational leaders are important in achieving good change within the learning setting through the use of strategies that enable the stakeholders and realign them with the goals of the organization. One of the strategies that should be encouraged is inclusiveness and ensuring that every voice will be heard and respected: teaching, students, parents, and staff. Inclusive decision-making creates a feeling of ownership to the change process, reduces resistance, and builds trust. Another important strategy is the use of technology to enhance teaching programs and also to facilitate administrative work. Digital solutions, such as learning management systems and artificial intelligence-based platforms, may improve collaboration, efficiency, and engagement and help a teacher to address the requirements of the modern learning process. Leaders should also help teachers to develop professionally by offering them opportunities to learn and develop and share best practices. Professional development also encourages the spirit of continuous improvement besides equipping teachers with new skills. Finally, the maintenance of motivation and morale needs to be done by recognition and praise of achievement. It reinforces devotion and enthusiasm when the endeavors receive recognition and reward, in the form of prizes, recognition and small tokens. Through these strategies, transformational leaders create an environment where everyone subscribing to the strategy will be inspired, motivated, and dedicated to achieving firm goals to ensure sustainable improvements in education (Chkheidze, 2024).

Future Directions

The significance of transformational leadership in change management will continue to increase as institutions of education bargain an ever-evolving world. Besides the new problems, leaders have to promote creativity and justice within their organizations.The primary issue is that they have to integrate digital learning materials and artificial intelligence (AI) in the classroom. The tools might enhance the effectiveness of the administration, individualize the teaching, and prepare kids to go into a technologically-driven future. To guarantee proper training and dispel the concerns on the impact that technology will have on the traditional education, transformational leaders will be required to guide the stakeholders on the transition. Another emerging area of concern is the use of education to solve global problems such as climatic change. To create awareness and empower the students to actively participate in addressing the issues facing the environment, teachers need to include sustainability in their curriculum. This would require collaboration with communities and educators in order to develop novel programs. It is also important to ensure the inclusion and access by marginalized groups. Transformational leaders should strive to bridge gaps in education systems, opportunity, and resources in order to make sure that every student irrespective of his or her background can succeed. By adopting these future directions, the transformational leaders will shape the education to meet the requirements of a global, just, and sustainable society besides managing the change. Their adaptability and vision will be necessary in ensuring the development of substantial progress (Chkheidze, 2024).

CONCLUSION

Transformational leadership is a major element of effective change management within learning institutions. Transformational leadership is increasingly being a significant job requirement in the face of unprecedented challenges in schools, colleges, and institutions with little-to-no previous experience of what they can, cannot, and cannot do in the context of rapid technical change, emerging social demand and complex global calamities. These leaders establish the foundations of long-term development and innovation in education through promoting change outlook, driving the stakeholders, and empowering individuals to achieve group goals. One of the most significant contributions to transformational leadership is the need to address the human side of change. Education reform often involves curriculum, pedagogy, or policy change, which has a direct impact on administrators, teachers and students. It is a normal human nature to resist change, either due to fear, doubt, or a feeling of dedication to the status quo. Transformational leaders reduce this resistance through open communication, inclusive decision making and customized support so that the parties involved all feel appreciated and understood. Openness and flexibility of these leaders is created through trust and bonding of having a common purpose and makes change not as threatening and cooperative. Moreover, transformative leaders have the sense of innovation in the classroom. Being the ones who challenge the system of doing things and foster an attitude towards considering new ideas, they provoke the minds of the employees. In the classroom, as one example, technology application which is commonly viewed with suspicion is an opportunity to grow under transformational leadership. Leaders enhance both the learning and teaching experience by providing educators with the tools to exploit digital tools as well as professional development. Such a flexibility ensures that learning institutions remain relevant and able to meet the demands of a fast changing world. Equity and diversity are another fundamental aspect that transformational leadership is committed to. The requirements and perspectives of every stakeholder in educational institutions are diverse and thus divergent communities. Transformational leaders are highly concerned with inclusivity by ensuring that no voices are left out and fostering a setting of respect and collaboration. It is important particularly in addressing systematic injustices, such as closing the digital divide in underserved communities or providing resources to marginalized communities. These leaders, through promoting equality, create a more inclusive and fair learning atmosphere besides enhancing educational accessibility. Transformational leadership is also very effective in terms of sustaining change. Reforming education does not only entail bringing about changes in a temporary manner but also incorporating new processes into the institutions ethos. Transformational leaders achieve this by recognizing efforts, recognizing success, and maintaining a long-term view of the destination when they are rewarding positive behavior. They are able to inspire and motivate even when the odds are against them ensuring that the change is sustained. Transformational leadership will continue to be more significant as learning institutions prepare to face the future. New issues such as the adoption of the artificial intelligence, addressing such existential issues as climate change, and ensuring that all people receive high-quality education require visionary and flexible leaders. Such leaders must balance between creativity and compassion to ensure that nothing goes wrong with change. To conclude, transformational leadership is an evolutionary phenomenon that shapes the course of education instead of being an instrument of change management. Transformational leaders create environments in which individuals and businesses thrive through promoting inclusion, promoting innovation, and fostering trust. Their ability to manage the issues of change will ensure that learning institutions remain strong, adaptable, and able to prepare students to live in a continuously evolving world. The role of transformational leadership cannot possibly be overestimated with the process of guiding the change as education keeps evolving.

REFERENCES

Abdallah, A. K. (2024). The impact of gender, psychology, and cultural dimensions on leadership development in distance education. *Scientific Reports*, *14*(1), 68495. Advance online publication. DOI: 10.1038/s41598-024-68495-4 PMID: 39112564

Abdallah, A. K., & Musah, M. B. (2023). Principal and teacher licensing as a tool to school improvement. In *Restructuring leadership for school improvement and reform*. IGI Global., DOI: 10.4018/978-1-6684-7818-9.ch014

Agyeman, N. Y., & Aphane, V. (2024). Exploring school leadership styles used to improve instruction and learning in schools. *Journal of Research Initiatives*, *8*(1). https://digitalcommons.uncfsu.edu/jri/vol8/iss3/1

Alainati, N. D. S. J., Almonawer, N. D. N. S., & Al-Hammad, N. D. F. A. (2023). Transformational Leadership in Education: Review of literature. *International Journal of Business and Management*. Advance online publication. DOI: 10.24940/theijbm/2023/v11/i2/bm2302-016

Aldous, S. M., & Ismail, G. A. (2025). AI for sustainable emergency preparedness and response in schools. In *Convergence of AI, education, and business for sustainability*. IGI Global., DOI: 10.4018/979-8-3373-1917-9.ch003

Alkaabi, A. M., Abdallah, A. K., Abdallah, R., Al Hasan, M., & Mohamed, A. (2025). Principal engagement in the teacher evaluation process in remote schools: A narrative inquiry of language teachers. *Forum for Linguistic Studies*, *7*(3), 209–230. DOI: 10.30564/fls.v7i3.8502

Bass, B. M., & Avolio, B. J. (1995). Theory of transformational leadership redux. *The Leadership Quarterly*.

Bass, B. M., & Bass Bernard, M. (1985). *No. 3* (Vol. 25). Leadership and performance beyond expectations. Free press.

Burns, E. M., & Ward, W. D. (1978). Categorical perception—phenomenon or epiphenomenon: Evidence from experiments in the perception of melodic musical intervals. *The Journal of the Acoustical Society of America*, *63*(2), 456–468. PMID: 670543

Chkheidze, S. (2024). Transformational leadership in change management in educational organizations. *International Journal of Teaching and Learning Sciences*, *2*(1). Advance online publication. DOI: 10.71010/IJTLS.2025.e110

Costa, J., Pádua, M., & Moreira, A. C. (2023). Leadership styles and innovation management: What is the role of human capital? *Administrative Sciences, 13*(2), 47. DOI: 10.3390/admsci13020047

El Zaatari, W., & Ibrahim, A. (2021). What promotes adolescent students' school belonging? Students' and teachers' convergent/divergent views. *Cogent Education, 8*(1), 1–20. DOI: 10.1080/2331186X.2021.1984628

Fang, M., Abdallah, A. K., & Vorfolomeyeva, O. (2024). Collaborative AI-enhanced digital mind-mapping as a tool for stimulating creative thinking in inclusive education for students with neurodevelopmental disorders. *BMC Psychology, 12*(1), 1975. Advance online publication. DOI: 10.1186/s40359-024-01975-4 PMID: 39289718

Heenan, I. W., De Paor, D., Lafferty, N., & McNamara, P. M. (2023). The Impact of Transformational School Leadership on School Staff and School Culture in Primary Schools—A Systematic Review of International literature. *Societies (Basel, Switzerland), 13*(6), 133. DOI: 10.3390/soc13060133

Ibrahim, A. (2010). *Education in the UAE: A socio-cultural analysis.* In Y. Zhao et al., *Handbook of Asian Education: A Cultural Perspective* (pp. 327-344). Routledge. https://doi.org/DOI: 10.4324/9780203816318

Ibrahim, A. (2018). *Directive, collaborative, or non-directive? Supervision perceptions of UAE thesis/dissertation approaches.* Issues in Educational Research, 28(3), 679–700. https://www.iier.org.au/iier28/ibrahim.pdf

Ibrahim, A. (2020). *What hurts or helps teacher collaboration? Evidence from UAE schools.* Prospects: Comparative Journal of Curriculum, Learning, and Assessment. https://doi.org/.DOI: 10.1007/s11125-019-09459-9

Ibrahim, A. S. (2012). Induction and mentoring of novice teachers: A scheme for the United Arab Emirates. *Teacher Development, 16*(2), 235–253. DOI: 10.1080/13664530.2012.688676

Ibrahim, A. S. (2013). The learning needs of beginning teachers in the United Arab Emirates. *Journal of Education for Teaching: International Research and Pedagogy, 39*(5), 491–506. DOI: 10.1080/02607476.2013.739791

Ismail, G. A., & Aldous, S. M. (2025). Integrating health and safety standards in teacher licensing systems: A GCC perspective. In *Building a unified teacher licensing system: Policies, education reforms, and cultural integration.* IGI Global., DOI: 10.4018/979-8-3373-0837-1.ch015

Ismail, L. S., & Ismail, O. A. S. (2024). Adaptive strategies for success: Monitoring and evaluating blue-green infrastructure in urban development. In *Integrating blue-green infrastructure into urban development*. IGI Global., DOI: 10.4018/979-8-3693-8069-7.ch001

Kgothule, R., Palmer, J., Alexander, G., & De Klerk, E. (2021). Transformative leadership in multicultural schooling contexts: A critical reflection of in-service teachers practices and school manager roles. *Education and New Developments, 620–624*. Advance online publication. DOI: 10.36315/2021end131

Paulienė, R. (2012b). Transforming Leadership Styles and Knowledge Sharing in a Multicultural Context. *Business Management and Education, 10*(1), 91–109. DOI: 10.3846/bme.2012.08

Ramadan, R. S., & Ismail, O. A. S. (2023). Building a better future: The role of school inspection in driving educational excellence. In *Restructuring leadership for school improvement and reform*. IGI Global., DOI: 10.4018/978-1-6684-7818-9.ch011

Research on School Culture and Multicultural Education in Indonesia. (2025). *The influence of school's culture on multicultural education in Indonesia*. ResearchGate.

Sarfraz, M., Bhutta, M., & Ivascu, L. (2024). Leadership in Cross-Cultural Contexts: Strategies for Global success. *International Journal of Organizational Leadership, 13. First, 2024*(Special Issue), 1–5. DOI: 10.33844/ijol.2024.60410

Tucker, F. (2021). For-Profit colleges: Neither educationally nor economically equivalent. *Research in Higher Education, 40*. https://files.eric.ed.gov/fulltext/EJ1296449.pdf

Chapter 2
Artificial Intelligence in Schools:
Opportunities, Risks, and Governance for Inclusive Learning

Noha Zoelfakar
United Arab Emirates University, UAE

Ali Ibrahim
http://orcid.org/0000-0002-1070-6256
United Arab Emirates University, UAE

ABSTRACT

Artificial Intelligence (AI) is reshaping education systems worldwide and placing schools at a critical crossroads. While AI offers opportunities to support learning and decision-making, it also raises concerns related to bias, equity, ethics, and pedagogical integrity. This chapter examines AI's impact across three dimensions: operational, strategic, and pedagogical. Operationally, it explores how AI can support personalized learning, reduce administrative demands, and assist teachers, while addressing risks such as data privacy, algorithmic bias, and unequal access. Strategically, it considers AI governance in schools, including data-informed leadership and resource allocation, alongside ethical and regulatory gaps. Pedagogically, it focuses on inclusive learning, examining AI's role in differentiation, accessibility, and linguistic diversity, while safeguarding fairness, human interaction, and educational values. The chapter concludes by arguing that meaningful AI integration requires governance frameworks grounded in inclusion, transparency, and ethical accountability.

DOI: 10.4018/979-8-2600-0388-6.ch002

1 INTRODUCTION: THE GROWING USE OF AI IN EDUCATION

Artificial Intelligence (AI) has been increasingly incorporated into various practices across schools and education systems worldwide. Practices that were previously confined mainly to information technology or computer science classes in schools are now increasingly embedded across lesson planning, assessment, feedback, and administrative decisions. The rapid rise of AI tools, machine learning, and generative technologies has accelerated this shift, introducing schools to new work mechanisms that automate routine tasks and offer students personalized learning experiences that were previously difficult to achieve at scale (OECD, 2021).

What distinguishes the current wave of AI from earlier educational technologies is not only its widespread adoption, but the extent to which it is now involved in core educational processes. Earlier digital tools supported teaching by organizing information or facilitating communication. In contrast, contemporary AI systems, particularly generative and predictive applications, increasingly perform functions that were previously predominantly human, producing explanations, generating feedback, anticipating learner performance, and recommending instructional or administrative actions. In doing so, these systems reconfigure boundaries that have traditionally structured schooling. Whether it is between content creation and assessment, between formative feedback and summative evaluation, or between human expertise and automated support, boundaries are being redefined.

AI systems can operate at speeds and scales that may exceed direct human oversight, enabling functions such as continuous feedback, real-time profiling, and automated decision support within classrooms and education systems. As a result, AI may not simply enhance existing practices, but also introduce alternative assumptions about authorship, effort, and expertise, while raising broader questions about responsibility for knowledge production, evaluation, and pedagogical authority within schools.

This shift is also reflected in emerging international policy responses, with several global organizations issuing system-level guidance that reflects AI's move from a novel innovation to a more routine part of schooling. UNESCO's guidance on generative AI in education calls for both immediate action and longer-term policy planning to ensure that pedagogy, academic integrity, and equity remain integral in educational systems as AI use expands (UNESCO, 2023). UNICEF approaches AI in schools through a child-rights lens, emphasizing fairness, participation, privacy, transparency, and accessibility as core principles for both design and implementation (UNICEF, 2021; UNICEF, 2025). These developments signal that AI integration is no longer peripheral and has moved towards the institutionalization of AI within education systems.

At the same time, the rapid rise and integration of AI in education is neither uniform nor neutral. Research consistently demonstrates that the effects of AI in education are shaped not only by technical capacity or access, but by governance arrangements, teacher preparation, professional judgment, and institutional interpretation (Selwyn, 2024; Williamson & Eynon, 2020). Schools do not introduce AI into a vacuum. Existing policies, available resources, and professional norms influence how AI is applied in practice. As a result, AI operates across several interconnected layers, including classroom-level teaching and learning practices, governance-level leadership decisions, system management, and pedagogical considerations related to inclusion, access, and the overall learner experience.

This chapter examines three interconnected dimensions of AI in education within the context of K–12 schooling. It considers both predictive and generative forms of AI, conceptualizing these technologies as embedded capabilities within educational systems and platforms, rather than as standalone tools or products. The analysis draws, where available, on evidence from large-scale system reviews and international policy frameworks to situate school-level practices within broader structural contexts.

The chapter first addresses the operational dimension, examining how AI is integrated into everyday school practices such as teaching, assessment, feedback, and the management of teachers' administrative workload. The discussion then turns to the strategic dimension, examining how AI shapes governance, leadership decisions, resource allocation, and policy implementation. Finally, the pedagogical dimension is explored, with a focus on inclusive learning, learner diversity, and the conditions under which AI may either support equity or risk undermining it.

These dimensions are not treated as isolated domains but as interdependent aspects of how AI is being integrated into schools and how educational institutions respond to this integration. Operational applications of AI cannot be effective or equitable without sound governance structures and clear pedagogical principles. Similarly, strategic governance decisions must be informed by both operational realities and pedagogical goals. In turn, pedagogical commitments to inclusion and equity depend on both operational tools and governance frameworks that protect learner rights and ensure accountability. Bringing these perspectives together reflects a growing consensus in the literature that the educational impact of AI is best understood not through isolated tools or individual use cases, but as part of a broader sociotechnical system (UNESCO, 2023).

The significance of this discussion extends across a wide range of educational stakeholders. AI integration is increasingly reshaping roles, responsibilities, and decision-making for every group within school systems. For teachers, AI may influence instructional practice, professional judgment, and the distribution of workload. For school leaders and policymakers, AI introduces a new form of governance driven by data and automated feedback, while seeking to uphold ethical and inclusive guidelines (Gökçe, 2025). For students and families, AI can be associated with expanded access to learning opportunities and increased risks related to privacy, fairness, and inclusion.

Evidence from global monitoring initiatives suggests that when digital and AI-enabled tools are scaled up without adequate safeguards in place, risks to equity and trust are likely to emerge, particularly for learners who are already at risk of being marginalized (UNESCO, 2023). Without careful design and governance, AI may reinforce existing inequalities and constrain educational relationships. By contrast, when developed and implemented with attention to ethical, pedagogical, and systemic considerations, it holds potential to support more responsive, equitable, and sustainable education systems (Baker & Hawn, 2022; OECD, 2023).

The objective of this chapter is not to advocate for or against the use of AI in education, but to provide a balanced, evidence-informed examination of its opportunities and risks across operational, strategic, and pedagogical domains. It aims to support educators, school leaders, and decision-makers in making more informed choices about when, how, and for what purposes AI may be appropriately utilized in schools. By synthesising empirical research and policy guidance, the chapter highlights where the potential benefits are most credible, where risks are most acute, and most importantly, why professional judgment, strong governance, and inclusive design remain essential for the responsible use of AI in schools. At a time when educational norms are increasingly shaped by new norms defined by the rapid evolution of AI, this helps align everyday classroom practice with expectations regarding equity, accountability, and safeguarding learners' rights. Accordingly, the central question guiding this chapter is not whether AI can enhance educational efficiency or performance, but how schools can govern and pedagogically mediate AI systems so that these tools can strengthen, rather than displace, human-centred educational experiences.

2 THE OPERATIONAL DIMENSION: AI OPPORTUNITIES AND RISKS FOR TEACHING AND LEARNING

From an operational perspective, artificial intelligence is deployed in schools through its incorporation into everyday teaching and learning practices. This includes tools used for lesson preparation, assessment, feedback, and instructional support. Within school contexts, two broad perspectives inform how artificial intelligence is understood and used. The first perspective emphasizes the technical capabilities of AI, suggesting that advances in algorithms and data processing can drive improvements in teaching and learning outcomes (Martin et al., 2024; Semwaiko et al., 2024). The second perspective highlights the extent to which AI's impact on schools is mediated by human and institutional contexts, with teachers, leaders, and policies shaping how technologies are interpreted and used in practice (Michopoulou & Chin Gan, 2025). Building on these two perspectives, this section presents an analysis of the opportunities offered by AI for improving educational practice, while critically examining the risks and challenges that require careful attention to support equitable, responsible, and ethical implementation.

Beyond questions of efficiency or learning gains, the routine use of AI in classrooms may also reshape instructional authority in less visible but significant ways. Historically, teachers held the authority to design learning activities, deliver instruction to students, and assess their progression. AI-enabled systems can now contribute to many of these functions by recommending content, generating explanations, and anticipating learner trajectories. As such, when recommendations become embedded in everyday classroom routines, authority over instructional decisions is no longer retained solely with the teacher, but is instead reassigned and shared between human and algorithmic actors (Jose et al., 2025). This shift does not necessarily weaken the teacher's role, but it does reconfigure its nature. Authority moves from direct control toward the teacher's capacity to interpret, contextualize, and, where necessary, challenge AI-generated outputs in ways that serve learners' needs. In settings where AI provides immediate and continuous feedback, students may also begin to orient their learning behavior toward system-generated responses rather than teacher cues, subtly repositioning where evaluative authority is located.

Research on learning analytics and AI-mediated feedback suggests that, without clear teacher guidance, students may assign disproportionate weight to automated feedback, treating system outputs as authoritative even when their underlying logic is partial or opaque. This tendency may limit opportunities for critical interpretation and reduce the likelihood that students seek further clarification from teachers or peers. In other words, such developments have implications for classroom relationships and learning dynamics. AI-supported instruction can redefine patterns of interaction, sometimes increasing individualization at the expense of shared discussion and peer collaboration. While adaptive AI systems can support differentiated pacing and personalized learning, they may also fragment classrooms into parallel learning pathways, which can reduce social learning and collaborative problem-solving.

The growing presence of algorithmic feedback may also influence how students understand success and failure, especially when system-generated suggestions are perceived as objective or final. Research on learning analytics and AI-mediated feedback indicates that, without clear teacher guidance, students may place more weight on automated feedback even when the system's reasoning is incomplete or limited in scope (Lim *et al.*, 2020; Jose *et al.*, 2025). Under these conditions, operational decisions about when, how, and for whom AI feedback is introduced become pedagogical decisions as they have an impact on shaping the learner's trust, motivation, and progression. At the same time, studies show that students generally express a higher preference for human-mediated feedback than for AI-generated feedback, particularly in relation to teaching complex academic skills (Kotlyar & Krasman, 2025; Weidlich *et al.*, 2025). These findings do not diminish the instructional value of AI tools in education, but they underscore the continued importance of instructional authority, professional judgment, and human-mediated learning experiences in AI-supported classrooms.

3 AI OPPORTUNITIES IN SCHOOLS

3.1. Types of Opportunities

3.1.1 AI-Powered Tutors and Personalized Learning Pathways

AI-powered tutoring systems and adaptive learning platforms are among the most frequently cited opportunities for AI integration in schools. Intelligent tutoring systems (ITS) are designed to provide personalized, adaptive learning experiences tailored to individual student needs. These systems analyze patterns in learner performance to adjust learning content, sequence, and pace in real time. Evidence suggests that, when implemented effectively, these systems can support tailored learning experiences that address students' individual needs (Kulik & Fletcher, 2016; Ma et al., 2014; Létourneau et al., 2025; Dubey, 2025). A large-scale systematic review by Martin et al. (2024) concludes that AI applications in K–12 education, including personalized learning tools, can enhance student learning experiences and offer more flexible responses to learner diversity than traditional fixed instructional formats. Further, Kulik and Fletcher's (2016) meta-analysis review of 50 controlled studies found that students using intelligent tutoring systems outperformed those in conventional classroom settings in 46 cases (92%), with performance gains significant enough to be considered substantively meaningful.

Additionally, when implemented thoughtfully, adaptive learning systems may support students who require additional scaffolding, while simultaneously providing advanced learning opportunities for those who are ready to progress at a faster pace. Evidence from inclusive education contexts indicates that AI-driven personalization can be particularly beneficial for students with special educational needs and for learners facing language barriers, as these systems may offer alternative representations, adaptive content, formative assessment, and assistive communication tools (Irawan & Anwar, 2025). From a pedagogical perspective, the value of

AI tutors lies in their capacity to augment the teacher's ability to identify learning needs, detect gaps, and adjust instructional support accordingly. This support can both save instructional time and reduce the risk that some learners may experience delayed or limited support. In this sense, AI systems function as diagnostic tools and decision-support resources that inform professional judgment rather than substitute it (Durães et al., 2024; Kim, 2025). However, the effectiveness of AI-powered tutors depends on the quality of the data on which they rely and the extent to which teachers interpret, contextualise, and integrate system recommendations into their instructional practice.

3.1.2 Real-Time Feedback and Formative Assessment

AI-enabled feedback and assessment tools represent another significant operational opportunity for the use of AI in school settings. Automated systems can provide immediate responses to quizzes, assessments, and class activities. This can enable students to address misconceptions while learning is still in progress, rather than after summative evaluation has occurred (Lim et al., 2020; Zheldibayeva et al., 2025). The literature links timely feedback with improved learning outcomes, particularly in skill-based domains such as writing, mathematics, and language learning, where iterative feedback can support sustained engagement and incremental skill development (Martin et al., 2024; Semwaiko et al., 2024).

In addition, automated grading and scoring systems may reduce the time teachers spend on grading assignments, thereby allowing more time for instructional focus on feedback dialogue, differentiation, and teacher–student interactions. Learning analytics and pattern recognition tools can also help identify misconceptions, disengagement, or uneven progress across groups of students (Durães et al., 2024; Aileni, 2025). However, evidence suggests that these tools are pedagogically effective only when embedded within appropriate instructional design supported by adequate infrastructure, teacher preparation, and strong ethical and human oversight (Melo-López et al., 2025; Semwaiko et al., 2024).

Beyond system design and teacher capacity, another operational consideration is students' ability to interpret and act on AI-generated feedback. Research on learning analytics shows that the effectiveness of feedback depends not only on its timeliness or accuracy, but on learners' feedback literacy, including their capacity to critically interpret suggestions and integrate feedback into their own learning strategies (Lim et al., 2020). Without explicit scaffolding, students may treat system-generated feedback as definitive judgments rather than provisional inputs, which can limit reflection and deeper engagement. This risk is heightened in AI-supported assessment environments where automated feedback may appear authoritative or opaque, particularly when learners lack understanding of how such systems generate recommendations (Swiecki et al., 2022). Supporting feedback literacy, therefore, becomes an essential operational task, and evidence shows that students' ability to benefit from AI- and analytics-based feedback depends on teachers' active mediation of how feedback is interpreted, contextualized, and acted upon within broader learning goals (Weidlich et al., 2025).

3.1.3 Enhancing Teacher Capabilities and Reducing Administrative Load

Teachers often report more positive perceptions of AI when its use contributes to time savings and workload reduction. AI technologies are increasingly used to support teachers by automating routine administrative tasks and assisting with instructional planning. Applications that support automated grading, attendance tracking, and lesson planning have been shown to reduce the time teachers spend on repetitive tasks and alleviate workload pressures, which are frequently linked to teacher burnout and attrition (Woodruff et al., 2023; Raza et al., 2025). When used strategically, such tools can significantly enhance teacher effectiveness and allow educators to reallocate time toward high-impact pedagogical activities, student interaction, and reflective practice.

Beyond efficiency gains, AI systems may also inform professional decision-making, though this potential warrants careful consideration. Predictive analytics, for example, can help teachers identify students who may require additional support or early intervention (Durães et al., 2024). Crucially, these outputs must be treated as advisory rather than prescriptive. If interpreted uncritically, predictive systems may constrain professional agency and contribute to the deskilling of educators by narrowing the scope of pedagogical judgment (Michopoulou & Chin Gan, 2025).

3.2 AI Risks and Challenges in Schools

It is also important to recognize that not all operational uses of AI in schools are visible to teachers or learners. Beyond explicit instructional tools, AI increasingly operates through background systems that shape scheduling, prioritization of support, behavioral flagging, and resource allocation, often without direct human awareness. Critical research on educational technology highlights that such forms of invisible automation can influence educational decisions while remaining largely unquestioned, particularly once they become normalized within institutional routines (Williamson & Eynon, 2020). When AI functions are embedded into everyday systems rather than presented as discrete tools, accountability and oversight become more challenging to sustain, increasing the risk that automated decisions are accepted as neutral or inevitable. This normalization of AI within educational infrastructure reinforces the need for professional awareness, transparency, and institutional monitoring, especially in contexts where automation reshapes decision-making power and responsibility (Selwyn, 2024; UNESCO, 2023).

3.2.1 Algorithmic Bias and Fairness Concerns

AI systems are trained on data that reflect historical patterns, so they may reproduce and sometimes amplify existing disparities. As a result, algorithmic bias represents one of the most serious operational risks associated with AI use in schools. Educational data frequently reflect existing inequalities related to socioeconomic status, language background, and disability (Utterberg Modén et al., 2023). When such patterns are embedded within algorithmic systems, there is a risk that inequities are reproduced and legitimized, particularly when outputs are presented as objective or neutral. In other words, biased algorithms may influence learner profiling and instructional recommendations in ways that can disadvantage marginalized groups (Baker & Hawn, 2022; Utterberg Modén et al., 2023; Faisal, 2025). Moreover, the logic behind how AI generates these decisions or recommendations is often only partially transparent or insufficiently specified. While some AI tools offer limited explanations of their recommendations, others operate as black boxes, constraining meaningful oversight and contestation. As a result, mitigating algorithmic bias cannot rely solely on technical design features but also depends on educators' capacity to interpret and critically engage with, and sometimes override, AI-generated outputs and recommendations (Michopoulou & Chin Gan, 2025).

In practice, algorithmic bias rarely manifests as explicit or intentional discrimination. Instead, it is more likely to enter classrooms through routine instructional decisions shaped by AI-generated signals. Recommendation systems may suggest differentiated pathways, flag students as “at risk,” or prioritise specific learners for intervention based on historical patterns embedded in training data. Although these outputs are usually framed as neutral, they may subtly lower expectations for students, especially those from disadvantaged socioeconomic backgrounds, linguistic minorities, or students with disabilities. When teachers are presented with predictive labels, these classifications can influence grouping decisions, pacing, and the additional focus and support they offer to students. Over time, early indicators may shift from early signals or recommendations to reinforced trajectories, in which learners keep receiving feedback that reflects past performance rather than developing capabilities.

It is important to acknowledge that these dynamics do not suggest that bias is inevitable. Rather, they highlight the central role of professional judgment in mediating AI use in everyday school practice. Research on equity and AI in compulsory education shows that algorithmic effects often become normalized through routine use unless they are made visible and open to challenge (Utterberg Modén et al., 2023). Bias becomes most consequential when AI outputs are accepted without questioning, particularly in high-pressure contexts where teachers face time constraints and heavy workloads. Research suggests that when educators lack training in data literacy or algorithmic reasoning, there is a greater risk that AI-generated insights are treated as authoritative judgments rather than provisional indicators (Sperling et al., 2024). In such contexts, operational bias is less a technical failure than a governance and professional capacity issue (Michopoulou & Chin Gan, 2025). Mitigating these risks requires making bias visible in everyday use, equipping teachers to interrogate system recommendations, and ensuring that AI-supported decisions remain open to contestation, revision, and contextual override. Accordingly, algorithmic bias in schools cannot be addressed solely through technical fixes, but must be viewed as an operational challenge shaped by daily instructional practices and professional judgment.

3.2.2 Data Privacy, Security, and Ethical Issues

The large-scale deployment of digital and AI-enabled tools in schools, particularly in the absence of robust safeguards, raises significant concerns related to learner privacy and institutional data security. Global reporting has documented widespread harvesting of student data and weak statutory protections, particularly during the COVID-19 pandemic and remote schooling (UNESCO, 2023). These developments raise substantial concerns regarding privacy, data security, consent, and long-term data use. Akgün and Greenhow (2022) highlight the ethical challenges of AI in K-12 education, identifying privacy concerns as one of the biggest ethical issues surrounding AI use in schools. Children occupy a particularly vulnerable position within these systems, as they have limited capacity to provide informed consent and restricted control over how their data may be stored, shared, or reused in the future.

Empirical and policy-oriented studies highlight that many schools lack sufficient governance capacity to fully evaluate vendor data practices or enforce strict data protection standards (Irawan & Anwar, 2025). Southgate et al. (2025) found that parents express significant concerns about privacy in AI systems, including questions about how student data are collected, used, and protected. These findings underscore the importance of ethical implementation practices that prioritise data minimisation, transparency with students and families, and clearly defined boundaries around acceptable data use.

From an operational standpoint, privacy and data protection should not be understood solely as matters of regulatory compliance, but as foundational conditions for trust in AI-enabled schooling. Without clear governance frameworks, transparent practices, and ongoing oversight, the legitimacy of AI-supported educational practices may be undermined, particularly in relation to equity, accountability, and learner rights (Michopoulou & Chin Gan, 2025; UNESCO, 2023).

3.2.3 Digital Divide and Equity of Access

The potential benefits associated with AI use in education are not evenly distributed and may exacerbate existing disparities between more and less resourced communities. Unequal access to digital devices, reliable connectivity, and language support can limit the extent to which schools and learners are able to engage meaningfully with AI-enabled educational tools. Research shows that schools with robust digital infrastructure, reliable connectivity, and access to high-quality tools are better positioned to adopt and benefit from AI applications (Woodruff et al., 2023). In contrast, under-resourced schools often face material and organizational barriers that limit AI adoption (Raza & Farooq, 2025), thereby reinforcing existing educational inequalities.

Equity concerns related to AI extend beyond access to devices and applications. Variations in teacher training, professional development opportunities, and student digital literacy influence who is able to benefit from AI-enhanced learning environments and who may be excluded (Semwaiko et al., 2024; OECD, 2023; Florentino et al., 2025). In this context, AI-enabled education risks contributing to the emergence of stratified learning experiences, where technological advantage aligns closely with socioeconomic privilege.

Addressing these challenges requires deliberate policy interventions and targeted investment, rather than assuming that technology alone will deliver equitable outcomes (Khan et al., 2025; Aileni, 2025). Such disparities are not accidental, but reflect broader policy choices, funding priorities, and governance arrangements that determine which schools are selected to benefit from AI-enabled educational innovations. From an operational perspective, efforts to mitigate the digital divide must therefore be understood as integral to responsible AI integration, rather than as a secondary consideration.

3.2.4 Impact on Student Engagement, Critical Thinking, and Academic Integrity

Another operational concern relates to the influence of AI on student engagement, learning dispositions, and academic integrity. While AI can increase the frequency and immediacy of feedback, it can also encourage over-reliance when students substitute system-generated answers for their own reasoning. Such practices may reduce opportunities for productive struggle, critical thinking, and creative engagement, which are central to meaningful learning (Barr et al., 2015; Risko & Gilbert,

2016; Gerlich, 2025). Generative AI tools also challenge traditional understandings of authorship and independent work, raising questions about academic integrity in educational contexts (Peterson, 2025; Dwivedi et al., 2023). In response, schools are encouraged to redesign assessment practices that foreground process, reflection, and applied understanding, which are more aligned with meaningful learning goals.

At the operational level, the central issue is not whether students use AI, but how they use it in an ethical, transparent, and pedagogically sound way. Generative AI tools can produce fluent explanations and complete assignments that closely resemble students' work. This has introduced a central challenge in the use of AI tools, as the boundary between independent student work and system-generated outputs has become increasingly difficult to delineate, complicating the attribution of authorship (Dwivedi *et al.*, 2023).

Research on cognitive offloading helps explain why this matters. When learners consistently delegate problem-solving, synthesis, or explanation tasks to automated systems, there is a risk that deeper cognitive engagement and critical thinking are diminished (Risko & Gilbert, 2016; Barr *et al.*, 2015). While generative AI feedback and explanations can support learning, evidence suggests that uncritical reliance may weaken students' capacity for sustained reasoning and self-directed learning, with implications for long-term learning outcomes (Pitts *et al.*, 2025).

Addressing these challenges does not require increased surveillance or blanket restrictions. Literature points to pedagogical redesign as a more effective safeguard for academic integrity. Assessment practices that emphasise process, reflection, oral explanation, and applied reasoning can help reduce AI-generated shortcuts while preserving legitimate learning support (Swiecki *et al.*, 2022; Eaton, 2023). From an operational perspective, the key question is therefore not whether students will engage with AI tools, but whether schools are prepared to design and sustain learning environments that promote cognitive depth, fairness, and integrity in contexts where generative AI is increasingly present.

4 THE STRATEGIC PERSPECTIVE: OPPORTUNITIES AND RISKS FOR SCHOOL GOVERNANCE

Beyond the operational aspects of classroom practices, AI increasingly operates at the strategic level of school governance. It influences leadership decision-making, system planning, accountability, and policy implementation. System-level research indicates that AI and learning analytics are increasingly used not only to support instruction, but also to inform organizational management, planning, and governance across education systems (OECD, 2023).

From this perspective, AI functions not solely as a pedagogical resource but rather as a managerial and governance instrument that shapes how schools allocate resources, monitor performance, develop staff capacity, and demonstrate compliance with regulatory expectations. This section explores both how AI can support more effective strategic school leadership and the associated risks related to ethics, accountability, and leadership capacity that arise when algorithmic decision-making is implemented with limited transparency or insufficient professional judgment.

4.1 Opportunities

4.1.1 Data-Driven Decision-Making and Policy Formulation

One strategic opportunity associated with AI use in school governance is its potential to support more informed, evidence-based decision-making through the analysis of large volumes of administrative, academic, and operational data. Predictive analytics and data dashboards can be used to identify trends in student achievement, attendance, attrition, and resource allocation. Such tools may assist leaders in turning data into well-informed decisions and eliminating background noise, which helps them to anticipate challenges and design targeted interventions (Durães et al., 2024). From a policy perspective, these data insights can also inform evidence-based planning and support responsive governance approaches.

International policy analyses suggest that AI can strengthen system-level decision-making when its use is aligned with clear educational goals and accompanied by safeguards for equity, transparency, and accountability (OECD, 2023; UNESCO, 2023). However, the quality of data-driven governance remains contingent on the quality of available data and the interpretive capacity of educational leaders. AI-generated insights do not carry inherent meaning; they require contextual understanding and professional judgment to avoid misleading conclusions (Semwaiko et al., 2024). In practice, the value of these tools depends not only on data quality but also on local context and leaders' capacity to interpret AI outputs critically, rather than treat them as self-evident truths (OECD, 2023).

AI tools are commonly viewed as neutral decision-support tools. Yet, their influence extends beyond offering recommendations, as their growing role in school governance subtly reshapes administrative decisions. Beyond generating recommendations, such systems have started to shape which issues are framed as important, which learners need additional support, and which outcomes are considered indicators of success. This carries the risk of redirecting the attention of leadership away from contextual and relational aspects of schooling, which are usually not reflected in algorithmic representation. Furthermore, these systems typically generate results aggregated across classrooms, assessments, and overall learning performance, relying on underlying models and assumptions that are not always transparent.

For these reasons, AI-generated outputs intended to inform policy development or resource allocation require careful professional scrutiny before being acted upon. Strategic decision-making must remain anchored in human judgment, professional experience, and ethical consideration, with AI functioning as a prompt for deliberation rather than a substitute for leadership responsibility. Without such mediation, the boundary between professional judgment and algorithmic recommendation risks becoming blurred, with implications for accountability, governance capacity, and institutional trust.

4.1.2 Optimizing Resource Allocation and Operational Efficiency

AI-driven analytics may support more strategic allocation of financial, human, and infrastructural resources within school systems. By identifying patterns related to student needs, staffing demands, and organizational inefficiencies, such tools can assist leaders in making informed decisions about resources and staffing, while remaining anchored in professional judgment rather than automated prescription (OECD, 2023; Williamson & Eynon, 2020). In addition, AI-supported budget forecasting and financial planning can draw on historical expenditure data and projected trends to inform future resource needs. When implemented effectively, these efficiencies may release capacity that can be redirected toward instructional support and student services.

From an equity perspective, AI-driven approaches to resource optimization have the potential to contribute to more balanced provision across regions, including differences between urban and rural contexts and between schools with varying levels of resourcing (Chen et al., 2025). By identifying resource disparities and recommending more equitable allocation patterns, AI can support school leaders in directing additional resources to high-need schools and students. However, the literature cautions that such strategic use of AI should be guided by explicit commitments to equity and educational quality. Without such commitments, resource optimisation processes risk reinforcing existing disadvantages rather than addressing them (Khan et al., 2025; Utterberg Modén et al., 2023).

4.1.3 Teacher Professional Development

At the strategic level, AI also offers opportunities to enhance teacher professional development through more data-informed planning and targeted capacity building. This responds to long-standing concerns that uniform, one-size-fits-all professional development is often ineffective. Rather than requiring all teachers to attend the same professional development sessions, AI can recommend personalized learning pathways tailored to each teacher's professional development needs, experience level, and career goals (Woodruff et al., 2023). In addition, AI-supported platforms may assist school leaders in monitoring the impact of professional development initiatives, supporting more adaptive and responsive program design.

Recognizing the growing importance of AI literacy for educators, major organizations have invested in professional development. The International Society for Technology in Education (ISTE) and the Association for Supervision and Curriculum Development (ASCD) have partnered to provide large-scale, coordinated professional development initiatives focused on AI for educators, reflecting growing institutional investment in teacher AI literacy (International Society for Technology in Education & Association for Supervision and Curriculum Development, 2025). Such initiatives emphasise not only technical familiarity, but also ethical awareness, pedagogical integration, and professional judgment. Policy-oriented research further emphasizes that effective AI integration depends on continuous investment in teacher development, including data literacy, ethical awareness, and the capacity to exercise informed professional judgment when engaging with AI-supported systems (OECD, 2023; UNESCO, 2023).

4.1.4 Streamlined Compliance and Reporting

School leaders and district administrators devote considerable time and resources to compliance monitoring to meet federal, state, and system-level accountability requirements. These obligations often involve the collection, organization, and reporting of large volumes of administrative and performance data across multiple domains. Digital data systems, including AI-supported tools, may assist in organizing evidence, supporting monitoring, flagging reporting gaps, and reporting processes (OECD, 2023). When implemented carefully, such systems can improve consistency in reporting practices and reduce the administrative burden associated with compliance-related tasks.

From a strategic perspective, AI-enabled compliance and reporting tools may also enhance transparency and comparability across schools and districts by standardising data structures and reporting formats. This can support clearer communication with oversight bodies and stakeholders, while also enabling leadership teams to track progress against regulatory benchmarks more efficiently. However, the use of AI in this domain does not eliminate the need for human oversight. Professional judgment remains essential in interpreting compliance indicators, contextualising reported data, and ensuring that accountability measures are applied in ways that are educationally meaningful rather than procedurally reductive.

Importantly, the potential efficiency gains associated with AI-supported compliance systems should be understood as a means rather than an end. When routine reporting and monitoring tasks are partially automated, leadership capacity may be redirected toward instructional leadership, staff development, and school improvement initiatives. At the same time, strategic use of AI in compliance contexts requires careful governance to avoid the risk of narrowing educational priorities to what is most easily measured. Ensuring that AI-supported reporting serves broader educational goals, rather than driving them, should remain a central leadership responsibility within AI-enabled governance structures.

4.2 Risks

4.2.1 Ethical Implications in Administrative Decision-Making

One of the most serious risks in AI-enabled school governance is over-reliance on AI recommendations without sufficient critical human judgment. Such reliance may contribute to the reinforcement of existing biases embedded within educational data systems (Utterberg Modén et al., 2023). When algorithms are used to inform high-stakes decisions, such as predicting student performance or dropout risk, there is a risk that administrators may privilege automated outputs over their own professional judgment and ethical reasoning. Studies further suggest that predictive models often yield less reliable results when applied to student groups different from those on which they were trained, increasing the likelihood that contextual differences are overlooked and that marginalised groups are disadvantaged (Baker & Hawn, 2022).

Research suggests that AI systems introduce new forms of digital governance in education, where commercial infrastructures and opaque decision-making processes shape educational practices with limited transparency (Williamson & Eynon, 2020). Because many of these systems are typically developed and managed by private companies with limited transparency, opportunities for students, families, educators, and communities to scrutinize and contest them are constrained. These risks are amplified when algorithmic bias intersects with high-stakes administrative decision-making. Together, these concerns highlight the responsibility of school leaders to maintain human judgment, promote transparency, and treat AI as a supportive tool rather than a decision-maker.

4.2.2 Need for Robust AI Governance and Policy Frameworks

The strategic deployment of AI in school governance requires clear, coherent, and enforceable governance frameworks. Fragmented or underdeveloped policies create operational and ethical risks, particularly when AI systems are introduced across multiple administrative and decision-making functions. International frameworks increasingly emphasize risk-based governance approaches for AI systems used in educational administration. For example, regulatory developments such as the European Union Artificial Intelligence Act classify AI systems used in educational contexts as high-risk applications, requiring human oversight, transparency, and documentation of decision-making processes (European Union, 2024).

Complementary frameworks such as the National Institute of Standards and Technology (NIST) AI Risk Management Framework provide practical guidance for identifying, assessing, and mitigating AI-related risks across organizations (Autio et al., 2024). Similarly, ISO/IEC 42001:2023 establishes a structured, auditable international standard for AI management systems, integrating governance elements such as risk management, policy frameworks, and ongoing improvement throughout the AI lifecycle (ISO, 2023). Taken together, these frameworks emphasise that AI use must be embedded within formal governance structures rather than treated as a purely technical or operational matter.

Without explicit policies addressing data use, transparency, accountability, and oversight, the adoption of AI in schools may outpace institutional capacity to manage its broader implications (UNESCO, 2023; OECD, 2023). From a strategic perspective, school systems and education authorities therefore face the challenge of adapting international governance frameworks to local legal, institutional, and cultural contexts, ensuring that AI implementation aligns with educational values, regulatory obligations, and public trust.

4.2.3 Fostering Sustainable Leadership and Managing Change

Finally, AI introduces complex challenges for school leadership in change management. These challenges are not limited to technical adoption but extend to shifts in organizational culture, professional roles, and established decision-making routines. Effective implementation requires building organizational capacity for change and sustaining leadership commitment over time. This includes developing a shared vision, aligning AI initiatives with school improvement goals, and ensuring coherence across different levels of the system. Research shows that successful technology adoption depends on leadership capacity, stakeholder engagement, and teacher readiness rather than technical readiness alone (Dexter & Richardson, 2020). In this sense, leadership involves not only initiating innovation but also supporting sense-making and trust among staff.

A sustainable approach implements a clear communication plan and allocates time for teacher collaboration and professional development. Such approaches recognise that meaningful change requires time, dialogue, and opportunities for collective learning, rather than rapid implementation driven by external pressures. It is equally important to recognise the need for ongoing monitoring and evaluation of the AI initiatives to learn from early missteps before scaling. This iterative process allows leaders to identify unintended consequences, adjust implementation strategies, and maintain alignment with ethical, pedagogical, and organizational priorities.

Taken together, these strategic opportunities and risks illustrate that AI governance in schools cannot be treated as a purely technical or administrative concern. Strategic decisions about data use, accountability, and oversight directly shape the pedagogical conditions under which AI is enacted in classrooms. This consequently influences how inclusion, professional judgment, and learner agency are realized in practice.

5 THE PEDAGOGICAL PERSPECTIVE: OPPORTUNITIES AND RISKS FOR INCLUSIVE LEARNING

5.1 Opportunities

5.1.1 Differentiated Instruction: AI Tutors and Adaptive Learning Platforms

Intelligent Tutoring Systems (ITS) and adaptive practice tools can adjust the sequence of learning activities, the type of hints offered, and the ways in which student understanding is assessed, thereby helping students work toward grade-level expectations while recognizing their different levels of readiness. Recent reviews of K-12 education report positive effects on achievement when ITS are designed to rely on personalization, adjust content and difficulty in real time, and offer immediate feedback, particularly when systems are curriculum-aligned and used in conjunction with teacher mediation (Létourneau et al., 2025). At the same time, while ITS may help students learn more effectively than other common instructional formats, they do not replace or surpass the instructional value of close human guidance (Ma et al., 2014).

Generative AI tools can further support adaptive learning systems by generating explanations, presentations, and leveled examples that assist teachers in scaffolding instruction. However, the effectiveness of these supports depends on how they are pedagogically integrated. Learning gains are most reliable when tutoring is aligned with the taught curriculum and when teachers actively use the system-generated signals to adjust instruction, rather than allowing the tools to operate unattended.

AI-enabled adaptive systems in education have been applauded for their ability to support inclusive learning. Adaptive systems can offer timely support, adaptive pacing, alternative representations, and scaffolding that may help learners engage more effectively with curriculum content. However, excessive automated scaffolding can foster dependency, where learners may become reliant on system prompts, feedback, or generated explanations rather than developing independent problem-solving strategies. Evidence from literature suggests that learners with prior knowledge of AI-supported environments, who are self-motivated and have higher levels of self-regulation, respond better to AI tools and automated feedback (Ma et al., 2014; Kotlyar & Krasman, 2025). On the other hand, learners who face barriers related to language, disability, or prior attainment may experience reduced opportunities for developing independence if AI supports are not carefully mediated. In such cases, tools designed to support inclusion may inadvertently widen learning gaps if they are not embedded within pedagogical structures.

These patterns reinforce the central role of teachers in inclusive AI use. Drawing on their experience and professional judgment, teachers know when to intervene, withdraw support, and challenge learners. Teacher-mediated use helps scaffolding remain purposeful, adaptive, and temporary rather than permanent. In this sense, AI functions most effectively as a pedagogical amplifier rather than a substitute for teaching. Its value lies in extending teachers' capacity to respond to learner diversity, rather than automating instructional decisions. Inclusive AI use in schools, therefore, depends less on the presence of adaptive features and more on the professional judgment that governs how, when, and for whom those features are deployed.

5.1.2 AI-Driven Assistive Technologies for Students with Disabilities

AI-enabled assistive technologies such as text-to-speech, speech-to-text, word prediction, and computer vision–based supports can improve participation and communication for many learners with disabilities. These tools can support how learners interact with curriculum content, classroom tasks, and assessment formats, allowing students to demonstrate understanding in ways that align with their functional needs and learning profiles.

Recent systematic reviews in K-12 contexts indicate that assistive technologies and digital devices have a positive impact on both learning experiences and academic outcomes of Special Educational Needs and Disabilities (SEND) students (Mukhtarkyzy et al., 2025). These findings suggest that, when appropriately integrated, AI-driven assistive tools can contribute to more accessible and flexible learning environments.

At the same time, international policy guidance emphasises that the benefits of AI-enabled assistive technologies depend on the conditions under which they are deployed. UNESCO (2023) highlights the importance of ensuring that such tools are accessible to students, protective of their privacy, and transparent to students and families. It also stresses the need for precise mechanisms to address exclusion, system failures, and unintended consequences (UNESCO, 2023). From this perspective, inclusive use of AI-driven assistive technologies relies not only on technological capability but also on thoughtful pedagogical integration, ethical design, and robust governance frameworks.

5.1.3 Overcoming Language Barriers in Multilingual Classrooms

AI-enabled translation and language support tools can help reduce barriers for multilingual learners by making instructional materials and key vocabulary more comprehensible while students continue to develop academic language proficiency. Reviews of machine translation-assisted language in education generally report positive learner attitudes and potential learning benefits, particularly when teachers explicitly teach how to use these tools and integrate them into pedagogical practice.

The literature further suggests that such tools have been particularly effective in foreign language learning, with notable benefits for writing development through guided routines such as task-based application and reflection (Lee, 2023). Reviews indicate that neutral machine translation can support foreign language teaching and learning in receptive and productive language skills, especially for more advanced second-language learners.

However, these tools best support inclusion when they are teacher-mediated. These tools appear most effective when teachers provide guidance on appropriate use and support learners in moving progressively toward greater linguistic independence. Without such mediation, AI-based language supports may inadvertently widen disparities between students who are able to use these tools effectively and those who are not, reinforcing existing differences in language proficiency and digital literacy (Klimova et al., 2023).

5.1.4 Enhanced Teacher Capacity for Inclusion

AI has the potential to expand teachers' capacity for inclusive practice by supporting differentiation without increasing administrative and instructional workload. By redistributing effort away from routine tasks and toward learner-centred practice, AI-enabled tools can support inclusive, inquiry-based teaching by helping educators adapt learning styles, materials, and feedback to the diverse needs of students, including students with disabilities and multilingual learners (Moundridou et al., 2024).

Empirical studies examining AI use in instructional and administrative contexts indicate that teachers can save time and improve targeted support, particularly in areas such as lesson planning, feedback preparation, and monitoring learner progress (Woodruff et al., 2023; Raza et al., 2025). When such efficiencies are realised, they may enable teachers to allocate greater attention to responsive instruction and individualized support within everyday classroom constraints. In this manner, AI enhances teacher capacity for inclusion not by replacing professional expertise, but by strengthening educators' ability to respond thoughtfully and equitably to learner diversity.

It is important to emphasize that AI tools should always remain under human supervision and be applied through educators' professional experience. AI-generated outputs must be carefully interpreted, validated, and refined rather than accepted as authoritative judgments (UNESCO, 2023).

5.2 Risks

5.2.1 Risk of Unequal Access and Widening Educational Inequities

While AI tools are often presented as scalable solutions, their benefits are not distributed evenly across educational contexts. Unequal access to devices, reliable connectivity, language support, and assistive features means that opportunities to benefit from AI-enabled learning vary considerably across schools and communities. Students' ability to access and meaningfully use AI-supported learning continues to be shaped by socioeconomic conditions, geographic location, and language and literacy backgrounds.

Research shows that uneven access to AI tools and digital devices limits the potential benefits, particularly for learners in low-income and remote areas (OECD, 2023). Language and literacy challenges add an additional layer of constraint, as many of these AI tools assume a certain level of language literacy and digital knowledge, which is not always the case. Without deliberate attention to accessibility, localization, and teacher mediation, AI tools risk reinforcing existing patterns of inequality and continuing to benefit the already advantaged and well-resourced students while offering fewer supports to those who need additional scaffolding (UNESCO, 2023; Williamson & Eynon, 2020).

5.2.2 Risk of Reinforcing Algorithmic Bias and Structural Inequality

AI systems are trained on historical data, which may encode existing biases. As such, these systems do not operate independently of the social contexts in which they are developed and deployed. When trained on biased or incomplete datasets, educational AI systems can reproduce and, in some cases, amplify existing inequalities. Empirical studies show that algorithmic systems may reflect historical patterns of exclusion, resulting in biased feedback, predictions, or evaluations that disadvantage marginalised learners (Baker & Hawn, 2022).

Within educational settings, such dynamics may translate into lowered expectations, limited learning pathways, or inaccurate representations of student ability (Ray, 2023). These risks are particularly pronounced when AI-generated outputs are treated as neutral or objective assessments, rather than as tools that require interpretation and professional judgment. Without active professional mediation and contextual oversight, reliance on algorithmic systems may inadvertently legitimise biased assumptions and obscure structural factors shaping student performance.

5.2.3 Risk of Over-Automation and Eroding Human Interaction

Concerns about AI use in education are not limited to data access and governance but extend to how technology reshapes relationships and learning experiences. Over-reliance on automated systems can weaken human interaction and connection, teacher-student relationships, and reduce opportunities for peer interaction, potentially contributing to increased learner isolation (Selwyn, 2024). Consequently, when efficiency and automation are prioritized over human connection, AI risks narrowing the social and relational dimensions of learning, which may also constrain learner agency by encouraging dependence on automated guidance rather than reflective, self-directed engagement (Darvishi et al., 2023).

Research on teacher practice consistently suggests that the educational value of AI emerges most clearly when educators understand its limitations, apply professional judgment, and use these tools as supplementary support rather than a substitute for human interaction (Tan et al., 2025). From this perspective, teacher training and human-centred pedagogical design are not optional additions, but essential conditions for sustaining healthy learning environments and supporting inclusive educational practices.

6 RECOMMENDATIONS AND IMPLEMENTATION STRATEGIES

6.1 Synthesizing Key Opportunities and Risks

The evidence reviewed in this chapter suggests that the central question facing schools is no longer whether artificial intelligence can be used to support teaching and learning, but rather under what conditions such use is educationally appropriate and ethically responsible. Across the operational, strategic, and pedagogical dimensions, a consistent pattern emerges. AI appears most valuable when it supports everyday teaching and learning while preserving human relationships and professional judgment, thereby sustaining equitable and trustworthy schooling experiences for all learners. By contrast, AI poses risks when it is treated as an authoritative substitute for human decision-making or when it displaces the relational work of teaching.

These tensions cannot be resolved at the level of individual tools or isolated classroom practices. Instead, they require deliberate alignment between pedagogy, governance, and institutional values. Evidence from studies on intelligent tutoring systems suggests that learning gains are possible, particularly when these systems are mediated by teachers through structured feedback and targeted practice, rather than left to operate as unattended automation (Létourneau et al., 2025; Ma et al., 2014).

At the same time, significant risks persist. Bias can be reproduced when historical inequities are embedded in training data or when outputs are treated as neutral truths without critical review or questioning (Baker & Hawn, 2022; Williamson & Eynon, 2020). Concerns related to privacy, transparency, and child protection have also been consistently documented, particularly as AI tools that rely on student data for training and decision-making are scaled across education systems in the absence of coherent and enforceable governance frameworks (UNESCO, 2023; UNICEF, 2021). This shifts the practical question from whether AI "works" to whether it works in ways that protect learners' rights and strengthen professional judgment rather than displacing it. From this perspective, the appropriate governance response should focus on establishing clear management systems and proportionate risk controls that prioritise children's safety and security and ensure inclusivity (ISO, 2023; Autio et al., 2024; European Union, 2024; U.S. Department of Education, 2023).

6.2 Core Principles for an AI-Ready School System

An AI-ready school system is defined not by how many tools it adopts, but by the quality of the decisions it makes about their use, the safeguards it puts in place, and the learning experiences it designs. Across the evidence and policy guidance discussed in this chapter, a small set of principles emerges that consistently shape whether AI supports schooling in meaningful and responsible ways.

First, a human-centred learning experience must remain non-negotiable. AI is most effective when it functions as a supportive tool rather than an authority that controls decision-making. Guidance on generative AI repeatedly emphasises the importance of human agency and capacity building, so that pedagogy, academic integrity, and professional responsibility remain central rather than being implicitly delegated to automated systems (UNESCO, 2023). In practice, this means that teachers and leaders should retain the right and responsibility to question outputs, interpret recommendations within the local context, and make final decisions informed by professional experience and concern for student wellbeing (U.S. Department of Education, 2023). Such mediation reduces the risk of delegating control to AI tools and systems, whose decisions are driven by pre-designed algorithms that are neither tailored to all contexts nor always transparent in their underlying logic.

Second, equity and accessibility must be built in from the start, not patched later on. UNICEF's child rights guidance frames inclusion, non-discrimination, privacy, and transparency as baseline requirements whenever AI systems affect children (UNICEF, 2021; UNICEF, 2025). OECD system-level analyses similarly highlight that countries' readiness is uneven, and that governance and capacity gaps can leave systems unable to guide responsible AI use (OECD, 2023). For schools, equity is not abstract. It is visible in whether AI tools work across languages, abilities, and access conditions, and in whether learners with the greatest needs are prioritised rather than further marginalised.

Third, data governance and privacy should be treated as learning conditions, not administrative paperwork. UNESCO's global monitoring work shows that technology can scale faster than safeguards required to govern it are developed, which, in turn, threatens privacy, trust, and equity when oversight is weak (UNESCO, 2023). At the school level, this translates into practical choices such as minimising data collection, setting clear boundaries on use, communicating transparently with families, and documenting who has access to data, for what purpose, and under what conditions.

Fourth, assessment practices and academic integrity must evolve in parallel with the use of AI. As generative tools become more widespread, they are already reshaping long-standing practices around homework, assignments, and examinations (OECD, 2023). This does not require turning classrooms into surveillance zones. Instead, it points to the need for a stronger assessment design that values reasoning and applied understanding, alongside clear expectations about acceptable AI use. Supporting students in developing ethical and reflective engagement with AI is more sustainable than assuming these tools can be excluded from learning contexts (UNESCO, 2023; OECD, 2023; Gökçe, 2025).

Fifth, implementation must be evidence-led, continuously monitored, and designed to improve over time. Risk-based approaches offer a practical structure, emphasising that responsible AI use depends on ongoing oversight rather than one-time approval. The NIST AI Risk Management Framework outlines a lifecycle approach to governing, mapping, measuring, and managing AI-related risks, with its Generative AI Profile extending this approach to address the specific risks associated with generative systems (Autio et al., 2024). ISO/IEC 42001 similarly adopts a management-systems perspective, highlighting the importance of continuous monitoring and improvement (ISO, 2023). For schools, this implies clarity of purpose, explicit success criteria, and regular review of outcomes across learner groups, alongside the capacity to adapt, pause, or discontinue AI use when unintended consequences or inequities emerge.

6.3 Recommendations for Educators, Policymakers, Developers, and Researchers

For educators, the central task is to ensure AI is embedded within pedagogy rather than positioned alongside it as an optional or parallel activity. Teachers can use AI to support planning, differentiation, and feedback, but the most reliable benefits appear when teachers retain control over learning goals, success criteria, and interpretation of student progress (UNESCO, 2023). It is also important for students to get clear guidance from teachers on how and why AI tools are used, rather than leaving them to experiment informally. A large systematic review of research on AI in teaching and teacher professional development highlights the uneven and fragmented support teachers receive and reinforces the need for coherent support so teachers can integrate AI proactively and thoughtfully rather than defensively (Tan et al., 2025). Evidence on teachers' engagement with generative AI indicates that teachers are motivated to use AI when resources are available and when they are confident about their knowledge and ability to use it, suggesting that schools need to create supportive conditions rather than merely issuing expectations (Collie et al., 2024).

For policymakers and school leaders, the priority lies in creating enabling conditions that support responsible innovation while protecting learners' rights. This includes clear guidance on acceptable use, investing in teacher AI literacy, and establishing accountability structures that enable contestability. Cross-country analysis shows that governance readiness often lags behind technological adoption, increasing the risk of fragmented practice and uneven protection across schools (OECD, 2023). Child-centred policy guidance similarly emphasises that effective AI governance cannot rely on individual schools to improvise safeguards, but requires system-level oversight, privacy protection, inclusion, and clear lines of responsibility (UNICEF, 2025).

For developers and vendors, the recommendation is straightforward and equally clear. Educational AI systems need to be designed with real classroom contexts in mind and with explicit attention to educational values. This includes transparent communication about system limitations, appropriate safeguards for child users and their data privacy, and clarity regarding the rationale underlying algorithmic recommendations, enabling educators to make informed decisions before using them. UNICEF's guidance explicitly places particular emphasis on inclusion, non-discrimination, privacy, transparency, and accountability, making clear that responsibility for ethical design rests with developers as well as institutions (UNICEF, 2021; UNICEF, 2025). UNESCO similarly stresses the importance of human-centred design and ethical validation for educational use, rather than assuming general-purpose tools are automatically suitable for learning environments (UNESCO, 2023).

For researchers, the current evidence base still leaves important gaps. Reviews of intelligent tutoring systems in K–12 settings report generally positive trends, but also note considerable variation in study quality, design, and implementation conditions, which limits comparability and generalisation (Létourneau et al., 2025). Hence, future research should move beyond the question of whether AI works to examine for whom it works, under what conditions, and with what trade-offs. This includes closer attention to subgroup effects related to disability, language background, and socioeconomic context, as well as the roles of teacher mediation and educational leaders in shaping and reinforcing implementation and governance.

6.4 Future Directions for Research and Practice

Looking ahead, three priorities stand out for advancing both research and practice in AI in education. The first is the need for stronger causal evidence generated in authentic school settings. This includes longer-term studies that follow learning outcomes alongside indicators of wellbeing, engagement, and equity, rather than focusing narrowly on short-term performance gains. Such work is essential for understanding not only whether AI appears effective, but how its effects unfold over time and across different groups of learners.

The second priority is the systematic evaluation of governance and implementation models, rather than a narrow focus on individual tools. There is a clear need for comparative research on which forms of professional development and classroom routines are most effective in reducing bias, protecting privacy, and supporting academic integrity. Without this level of insight, schools and systems are left to navigate adoption through trial and error.

The third priority lies in design-focused research that foregrounds inclusive learning. This involves testing AI systems with, rather than merely on, diverse learners, including multilingual students and learners with disabilities. It also means treating accessibility and usability as outcomes that must be examined, rather than assumptions built into the technology. International policy guidance has highlighted the importance of this shift, particularly in relation to children's rights and equitable access to educational technologies (UNESCO, 2023; UNICEF, 2025).

Across all three areas, there is clear evidence that the most promising direction is not in greater automation but stronger human stewardship, meaning careful attention to how AI is researched, designed, and governed within educational contexts. This means shaping AI tools around clearly defined educational purposes, keeping human expertise and professional judgment at the centre of decision-making, and ensuring that educational processes remain grounded in human interaction rather than shifting toward a predominantly human-machine-facing process.

7 CONCLUSION

Artificial intelligence is no longer a peripheral innovation in education. It is rapidly being woven into the fabric of schooling. Whether it is in lesson planning, feedback, assessment, student monitoring, or system-level decision-making, AI-enabled tools are now present in many aspects of educational practice. The analysis presented in this chapter indicates that the most significant opportunities emerge when AI is used to extend human capacity and support it rather than replace it. At the operational level, evidence suggests that tools such as intelligent tutoring systems can support learning gains, especially when used within structured, teacher-mediated routines (Létourneau et al., 2025; Ma et al., 2014). At the same time, the chapter highlights that these benefits are not automatic. They depend on implementation conditions, teacher expertise, and the school capacity to interpret AI outputs through contextual understanding and professional judgment, rather than treating them as authoritative decision-makers (UNESCO, 2023; Selwyn, 2024).

Across the operational, strategic, and pedagogical perspectives examined in this chapter, the risks are equally tangible. Algorithmic bias and data-driven profiling can reproduce historical inequities and subtly legitimise them when systems are treated as neutral or objective (Baker & Hawn, 2022; Williamson & Eynon, 2020). Privacy risks and governance gaps become more pronounced as AI tools scale, particularly when children's data are collected, processed, or reused without robust safeguards and transparent communication with families (UNESCO, 2023; UNICEF, 2021; UNICEF, 2025). Equity concerns also remain central. Uneven access, differences in digital literacy, and variability in institutional capacity can create a two-tier pattern of benefits, where the learners and schools with the strongest resources are best positioned to benefit from AI-supported learning (OECD, 2023). In this sense, the central challenge is not simply adoption, but the ability of education systems to ensure that AI use strengthens inclusion rather than widening gaps.

The synthesis offered in Section 5 reinforces a practical conclusion. AI-ready schooling is not defined by how many tools are used, but by the quality of the governance and pedagogy shaping their use. Human-centred teaching and learning remain the anchor, and teacher professional judgment must remain central to goals, criteria, and interpretation (U.S. Department of Education, 2023; UNESCO, 2023). Equity and accessibility must be designed in from the start, with clear accountability for transparency, privacy protections, and meaningful ways to respond when tools fail or exclude learners (UNICEF, 2021; UNICEF, 2025). Risk-based governance frameworks provide a usable structure for schools and systems to map use cases, define controls, monitor impacts across learner groups, and refine practice over time rather than relying on one-time approvals or informal norms (Autio et al., 2024;

ISO, 2023). These frameworks should not be understood as additional administrative burdens, but as enabling conditions for responsible implementation.

Looking ahead, this chapter argues for a deliberate and careful recalibration of educational practice. The most promising direction lies not in greater automation, but in strengthened human stewardship of AI within classrooms and across systems. This includes stronger evidence generated in authentic school settings, deeper evaluation of implementation and governance models, and inclusive design that treats accessibility, transparency, and equity outcomes as core success criteria rather than secondary considerations (UNESCO, 2023; OECD, 2023). Ultimately, AI should be treated neither as a threat to be avoided nor as a panacea for all educational issues without critique. It should be treated as a powerful sociotechnical force that must be shaped by educational purpose, human responsibility, and a rights-by-design approach that protects learners while enabling meaningful innovation.

REFERENCES

Aileni, A. R. (2025). AI-Driven Educational Equity: A Data Architecture for Addressing Achievement Gaps in Public Education Systems. *Journal of Computer Science and Technology Studies*, *7*(4), 535–540. DOI: 10.32996/jcsts.2025.7.4.63

Akgün, S., & Greenhow, C. (2022). Artificial intelligence in education: Addressing ethical challenges in K-12 settings. *AI and Ethics*, *2*(3), 431–440. DOI: 10.1007/s43681-021-00096-7 PMID: 34790956

Autio, C., Schwartz, R., Dunietz, J., Jain, S., Stanley, M., Tabassi, E., Hall, P., & Roberts, K. (2024). *Artificial intelligence risk management framework: Generative artificial intelligence profile* (NIST AI 600-1). National Institute of Standards and Technology. https://doi.org/DOI: 10.6028/NIST.AI.600-1

Baker, R. S., & Hawn, A. (2022). Algorithmic bias in education. *International Journal of Artificial Intelligence in Education*, *32*, 1052–1092. DOI: 10.1007/s40593-021-00285-9

Barr, N., Pennycook, G., Stolz, J. A., & Fugelsang, J. A. (2015). The brain in your pocket: Evidence that Smartphones are used to supplant thinking. *Computers in Human Behavior*, *48*, 473–480. DOI: 10.1016/j.chb.2015.02.029

Chen, R., Wu, Y., Chen, Z., & Zhou, P. (2025). Advancing educational equity in rural China: The impact of AI devices on teaching quality and learning outcomes for sustainable development. *Frontiers in Psychology*, *16*, 1588047. Advance online publication. DOI: 10.3389/fpsyg.2025.1588047 PMID: 41267767

Collie, R. J., Martin, A. J., & Gasevic, D. (2024). Teachers' generative AI self-efficacy, valuing, and integration at work: Examining job resources and demands. *Computers and Education: Artificial Intelligence*, *7*, 100333. DOI: 10.1016/j.caeai.2024.100333

Darvishi, A., Khosravi, H., Sadiq, S., Gašević, D., & Siemens, G. (2023). *Impact of AI assistance on student agency*. Computers & Education. *Article*, *104967*. Advance online publication. DOI: 10.1016/j.compedu.2023.104967

Dexter, S., & Richardson, J. W. (2020). What does technology integration research tell us about the leadership of technology? *Journal of Research on Technology in Education*, *52*(1), 17–36. DOI: 10.1080/15391523.2019.1668316

Dubey, P. K. (2025). Personalized Learning and Pedagogy: Harnessing AI for Tailored Education. In Wang, V. (Ed.), *Integrating AI Into Pedagogical Education* (pp. 81–102). IGI Global Scientific Publishing., DOI: 10.4018/979-8-3693-6130-6.ch004

Durães, D., Bezerra, R. M. A., & Novais, P. (2024). AI-driven educational transformation in secondary schools: Leveraging data insights for inclusive learning environments. In *Proceedings of the IEEE Global Engineering Education Conference (EDUCON)*. https://doi.org/DOI: 10.1109/EDUCON60312.2024.10578910

Dwivedi, Y. K., Kshetri, N., Hughes, L., Slade, E. L., Jeyaraj, A., Kumar Kar, A., Baabdullah, A. M., Koohang, A., Raghavan, V., Ahuja, M., Albanna, H., Albashrawi, M. A., Al-Busaidi, A. S., & Balakrishnan, J. (2023). "So what if ChatGPT wrote it?": Multidisciplinary perspectives on opportunities, challenges and implications of generative conversational AI for research, practice and policy. *International Journal of Information Management*, *71*, 102642. Advance online publication. DOI: 10.1016/j.ijinfomgt.2023.102642

Eaton, S. E. (2023). Postplagiarism: Transdisciplinary ethics and integrity in the age of artificial intelligence and neurotechnology. *International Journal for Educational Integrity*, *19*, 23. Advance online publication. DOI: 10.1007/s40979-023-00144-1

European Union. (2024). *Regulation (EU) 2024/1689 of the European Parliament and of the Council of 13 June 2024 laying down harmonised rules on artificial intelligence (Artificial Intelligence Act)*. https://data.europa.eu/eli/reg/2024/1689/oj

Faisal, R. (2025). Ethical AI Integration in Education: Policies, Challenges, and Strategies for Bridging Digital Divides in Emerging Economies. *Crossroads of Social Inquiry*, *1*(2), 1–18. DOI: 10.64851/csi.v1i2.28

Florentino, B., Sestito, C., Cruz, W., de Carvalho, A., & Bonidia, R. (2025). *Artificial intelligence for all? Brazilian teachers on ethics, equity, and the everyday challenges of AI in education* (Preprint). https://doi.org//arXiv.2512.23834DOI: 10.48550

Gerlich, M. (2025). AI tools in society: Impacts on cognitive offloading and the future of critical thinking. *Societies (Basel, Switzerland)*, *15*(1), 6. Advance online publication. DOI: 10.3390/soc15010006

Gökçe, A. (2025). Revolutionizing education with AI: Ethical considerations in K–12 settings. In *IntechOpen*. https://doi.org/DOI: 10.5772/intechopen.1012230

International Society for Technology in Education & Association for Supervision and Curriculum Development. (2025). *AI in education: Professional learning and support for educators*. ISTE+ASCD. https://iste.org/ai

Irawan, M. A., & Anwar, Z. (2025). Harnessing artificial intelligence for inclusive education management: Strategies for supporting students with special needs. [JEMIN]. *Journal of Educational Management and Instruction*, *5*(2), 350–370. DOI: 10.22515/jemin.v5i2.11650

ISO. (2023). *ISO/IEC 42001:2023 Artificial intelligence management system.* https://www.iso.org/standard/81230.html

Jose, B., Cleetus, A., Joseph, B., Joseph, L., Jose, B., & John, A. K. (2025, August). Epistemic authority and generative AI in learning spaces: rethinking knowledge in the algorithmic age. In *Frontiers in Education* (Vol. 10, p. 1647687). Frontiers Media SA. https://doi.org/DOI: 10.3389/feduc.2025.1647687

Khan, M., Thongnun, W., Zamani, M., Siripap, P., Channuwong, S., & Lertatthakornkit, T. (2025). Strategies for reducing educational inequality in primary schools using adaptive learning technologies. *International Journal of Environmental Sciences, 11*(7), 416–424. DOI: 10.64252/13f8wm17

Kim, J. (2025). Perspectives on AI integration in K-12 schools: Opportunities, challenges, and strategic approaches. *Midwest Journal of Education, 2*(1). Advance online publication. DOI: 10.69670/mje.2.1.4

Klimova, B., Pikhart, M., Benites, A. D., Lehr, C., & Sanchez-Stockhammer, C. (2023). Neural machine translation in foreign language teaching and learning: A systematic review. *Education and Information Technologies, 28*(1), 663–682. DOI: 10.1007/s10639-022-11194-2

Kotlyar, I., & Krasman, J. (2025). Student reactions to AI versus human feedback in teamwork skills assessment. *International Journal of Educational Technology in Higher Education, 22*, 57. Advance online publication. DOI: 10.1186/s41239-025-00555-9

Kulik, J. A., & Fletcher, J. D. (2016). Effectiveness of Intelligent Tutoring Systems: A Meta-Analytic Review. *Review of Educational Research, 86*(1), 42–78. https://www.jstor.org/stable/resrep22695

Lee, S. M. (2023). The effectiveness of machine translation in foreign language education: A systematic review and meta-analysis. *Computer Assisted Language Learning, 36*(1–2), 103–125. DOI: 10.1080/09588221.2021.1901745

Létourneau, A., Deslandes Martineau, M., Charland, P., Karran, J. A., Boasen, J., & Léger, P. M. (2025). *A systematic review of AI-driven intelligent tutoring systems (ITS) in K-12 education.* npj Science of Learning, 10, Article 29. https://doi.org/DOI: 10.1038/s41539-025-00320-7

Lim, L.-A., Dawson, S., Gašević, D., Joksimović, S., Fudge, A., Pardo, A., & Gentili, S. (2020). Students' sense-making of personalised feedback based on learning analytics. *Australasian Journal of Educational Technology, 36*(6), 15–33. DOI: 10.14742/ajet.6370

Ma, W., Adesope, O. O., Nesbit, J. C., & Liu, Q. (2014). Intelligent tutoring systems and learning outcomes: A meta-analysis. *Journal of Educational Psychology*, *106*(4), 901. DOI: 10.1037/a0037123

Martin, F., Zhuang, M., & Schaefer, D. (2024). Systematic review of research on artificial intelligence in K–12 education (2017–2022). *Computers and Education: Artificial Intelligence*, *6*, 100195. DOI: 10.1016/j.caeai.2023.100195

Melo-López, V.-A., Basantes-Andrade, A., Gudiño-Mejía, C.-B., & Hernández-Martínez, E. (2025). The impact of artificial intelligence on inclusive education: A systematic review. *Education Sciences*, *15*(5), 539. DOI: 10.3390/educsci15050539

Michopoulou, K., & Chin Gan, J. K. (2025). Ethical leadership in AI-enabled schools: Navigating human rights, equity, and justice in education. *European Journal of Education and Pedagogy*, *6*(5), 988. Advance online publication. DOI: 10.24018/ejedu.2025.6.5.988

Moundridou, M., Matzakos, N., & Doukakis, S. (2024). Generative AI tools as educators' assistants: Designing and implementing inquiry-based lesson plans. *Computers and Education: Artificial Intelligence*, *7*, 100277. Advance online publication. DOI: 10.1016/j.caeai.2024.100277

Mukhtarkyzy, K., Smagulova, L., Tokzhigitova, A., Serikbayeva, N., Sayakov, O., Turkmenbayev, A., & Assilbayeva, R. (2025). A systematic review of the utility of assistive technologies for SEND students in schools. *Frontiers in Education*, *10*, 1523797. Advance online publication. DOI: 10.3389/feduc.2025.1523797

OECD. (2021). *OECD digital education outlook 2021: Pushing the frontiers with artificial intelligence, blockchain and robots*. OECD Publishing. https://www.oecd.org/content/dam/oecd/en/publications/reports/2021/06/oecd-digital-education-outlook-2021_0f1487d9/589b283f-en.pdf

OECD. (2023). *Digital education outlook 2023: Towards an effective digital education ecosystem*. OECD Publishing., DOI: 10.1787/c74f03de-

Peterson, S. (2025). Addressing student use of generative AI in schools and higher education: Academic integrity and assessment design challenges. *Frontiers in Education*, *10*, 1610836. DOI: 10.3389/feduc.2025.1610836

Pitts, G., Rani, N., Mildort, W., & Cook, E.-M. (2025). *Students' reliance on AI in higher education: Identifying contributing factors* (Preprint). arXiv. https://doi.org//arXiv.2506.13845DOI: 10.48550

Ray, P. P. (2023). ChatGPT: A comprehensive review on background, applications, key challenges, bias, ethics, limitations and future scope. *Internet of Things and Cyber-Physical Systems*, *3*, 121–154. DOI: 10.1016/j.iotcps.2023.04.003

Raza, S. H., & Farooq, A. (2025). AI in Pakistani schools: Adoption, usage, and perceived impact among educators. *arXiv*. https://doi.org//arXiv.2509.25293DOI: 10.48550

Risko, E. F., & Gilbert, S. J. (2016). Cognitive offloading: How the mind extends itself. *Trends in Cognitive Sciences*, *20*(9), 676–688. DOI: 10.1016/j.tics.2016.07.002 PMID: 27542527

Selwyn, N. (2024). On the limits of artificial intelligence (AI) in education. *Nordisk Tidsskrift for Pedagogikk og Kritikk*, *10*(1), 3–14. DOI: 10.23865/ntpk.v10.6062

Semwaiko, G. S., Chao, W.-H., & Yang, C.-Y. (2024). Transforming K–12 education: A systematic review of AI integration. *International Journal of Educational Technology and Learning*, *17*(2), 43–63. DOI: 10.55217/101.v17i2.847

Southgate, E., Naghizade, E., Corman, A., & Atherton, M. (2025). Towards a governance roadmap for educational technology in Australian schools. *Journal of Educational Technology & Society*, *28*(4). Advance online publication. DOI: 10.1007/s13384-025-00916-3

Sperling, K., Stenberg, C. J., McGrath, C., Åkerfeldt, A., Heintz, F., & Stenliden, L. (2024). In search of artificial intelligence (AI) literacy in teacher education: A scoping review. *Computers and Education Open*, *6*, 100169. Advance online publication. DOI: 10.1016/j.caeo.2024.100169

Swiecki, Z., Khosravi, H., Chen, G., Martinez-Maldonado, R., Lodge, J. M., Milligan, S., & Gašević, D. (2022). Assessment in the age of artificial intelligence. *Computers and Education: Artificial Intelligence*, *3*, 100075. DOI: 10.1016/j.caeai.2022.100075

Tan, X., Cheng, G., & Ling, M. H. (2025). Artificial intelligence in teaching and teacher professional development: A systematic review. *Computers and Education: Artificial Intelligence*, *8*, 100355. DOI: 10.1016/j.caeai.2024.100355

UNESCO. (2023). *Global Education Monitoring Report 2023: Technology in education — A tool on whose terms?* United Nations Educational, Scientific and Cultural Organization. https://unesdoc.unesco.org/ark:/48223/pf0000385723

UNICEF. (2021). *Policy guidance on AI for children 2.0: Recommendations for governments and businesses to support child-centred AI systems that uphold children's rights*. UNICEF Innocenti. https://www.unicef.org/innocenti/media/1341/file/UNICEF-Global-Insight-policy-guidance-AI-children-2.0-2021.pdf

UNICEF. (2025). *Guidance on AI and children 3.0: Updated guidance for governments and businesses to create AI policies and systems that uphold children's rights.* UNICEF Innocenti. https://www.unicef.org/innocenti/media/11991/file/UNICEF-Innocenti-Guidance-on-AI-and-Children-3-2025.pdf

U.S. Department of Education, Office of Educational Technology. (2023). *Artificial intelligence and the future of teaching and learning: Insights and recommendations.* https://eric.ed.gov/?id=ED631201

Utterberg Modén, M., Ponti, M., Lundin, J., & Tallvid, M. (2023). *When fairness is an abstraction: Equity and AI in Swedish compulsory education* (arXiv:2311.01838) [Preprint]. arXiv. https://doi.org//arXiv.2311.01838DOI: 10.48550

Weidlich, J., Gotsch, F., Schudel, K., Marusic-Würscher, C., Mazzarella, J., Bolten, H., & Merki, K. M. (2025). Teacher, peer, or AI? Comparing effects of feedback sources in higher education. *Computers and Education Open, 100300.* Advance online publication. DOI: 10.1016/j.caeo.2025.100300

Williamson, B., & Eynon, R. (2020). Historical threads, missing links, and future directions in AI in education. *Learning, Media and Technology, 45*(3), 223–235. DOI: 10.1080/17439884.2020.1798995

Woodruff, K., Hutson, J., & Arnone, K. (2023). *Perceptions and barriers to adopting artificial intelligence in K–12 education: A survey of educators in fifty states. Artificial intelligence in education.* IntechOpen., DOI: 10.5772/intechopen.1002741

Zheldibayeva, R., Nascimento, A. K. de O., Castro, V., Kalantzis, M., & Cope, B. (2025). The impact of AI-driven tools on student writing development: A case study from the CGScholar AI Helper Project. https://doi.org//arXiv.2501.08473DOI: 10.48550

Chapter 3
Engineering Human-AI Leadership for School Equity

Mohammad Ahmad Ismail
http://orcid.org/0009-0004-3104-445X
Abu Dhabi University, UAE

ABSTRACT

This chapter examines human–artificial intelligence (AI) collaboration in school leadership as a means of advancing educational equity, grounded in credibility, transparency, and ethical governance, with reference to the Finnish education system. As AI-based tools increasingly influence decision-making in areas such as student assessment, learning analytics, and resource allocation, school leaders face both new opportunities and ethical challenges. Drawing on Finland's long-standing commitment to equity, professional trust, and decentralized leadership, the chapter emphasizes positioning AI as a decision-support tool rather than a substitute for human judgment. Key concerns—including algorithmic bias, data governance, transparency, and accountability—are critically examined. In response, the chapter outlines leadership approaches centered on ethical oversight, human responsibility, and stakeholder trust. It proposes an equity-driven human–AI collaborative leadership framework that balances technological innovation with democratic values and social justice in higher education.

INTRODUCTION

The sphere of education in the world is passing through a significant shift with the integration of the aspect of Artificial Intelligence (AI) into institutional decision-

DOI: 10.4018/979-8-2600-0388-6.ch003

making. What started as an exploratory application of data analytics and adaptive learning systems has developed into medium-scale systems that can forecast student results, resource distribution, learning hazards, and administrator priorities. Human judgment, professional experience, and relational authority are no longer the sole form of school leadership, which is being mediated in more and more instances through algorithmic systems that promise efficiency and objectivity as well as data-driven insight. The change comes with unprecedented opportunities as well as some serious ethical issues, especially as far as equity in education is concerned (METWALLI, 2024).

In Finland, where education policy has been traditionally based on equality, trust, and professional autonomy, the establishment of AI in school leadership reminds us of vital concerns regarding governance, responsibility, and equity. The Finnish education system has been known to be internationally committed to reducing differences among schools, eliminating high-stakes accountability regimes, and empowering teachers and principals as reflective professionals. Such characteristics render Finland an especially informative case in the study on how AI can be incorporated in leadership without compromising democracies and enhancing inequality (Papa & Jackson, 2021).

It is already happening; artificial intelligence technologies are affecting leadership decisions in subtle yet essential ways. Learning analytics systems can identify students who are likely to perform poorly; predictive control can be used to determine early interventions; automated systems can use timetabling, staffing, and resource allocation. Such tools can contribute to the improvement of equity when they are used responsibly, supporting it earlier, distributing resources more accurately, and making the leadership evidence-based. Nevertheless, unless well monitored, AI systems may equally involve bias, blur responsibility, and undermine trust, especially when the decision-making mechanisms lose touch with the surrounding reality or are located elsewhere (Mariyono et al., 2025).

The equity concern of AI-driven leadership is particularly great. Historical data is fed into algorithm systems and usually represents the social disparities that are already present concerning socioeconomic status, language background, disability, or migration history. Unquestioned, AI tools will only enforce these tendencies in the name of neutrality. In a system of education that values and upholds fairness, like that of Finland, this would become a dilemma in itself: how can leaders embrace the strength of AI and, at the same time, take care of the fact that technology is not used to destroy the same principle of equity that the system is intended to defend(Kundu & Bej, 2025).

The key to this question is trust. The education governance in Finland is subject to high institutional trust: institutional trust in the professional judgment of teachers, institutional trust between the schools and the municipalities, and institutional trust between the families and the schools. These relations are complicated by the introduction of AI (Ibrahim, 2010). Trust is likely to be undermined when algorithms that are not perfectly understood by educators, parents, or students shape decisions. Transparency is thus not just one of the technical issues, but it is also a leadership requirement. The school leaders should be able to clarify the nature of the AI-informed decisions, the data that is used, and how the human judgment is retained in the process (Wittka, 2020).

Even ethical leadership in the era of AI needs more than adherence to data protection laws. It requires an active process of responsibility, explainability, and moral agency questions. Who would be held responsible in cases when an AI decision-making fails to favor a student? What is the protection of the rights of students when predictive analytics defines the path of education? What do leaders need to do to make sure that AI helps them to be more inclusive than to be observed or excluded? The questions are quite urgent, especially in Nordic welfare-state systems, where education is considered a state good instead of a commodity on the market (Guardiola, 2025).

These issues can be solved by considering human-AI collaborative leadership as a conceptual perspective. Instead of making AI look like a free agent in making decisions, this strategy presents AI as a supportive resource that enhances- but does not supplant- human leadership. Under this model, AI offers analytical value, pattern recognition, and scenario modeling, whereas the human leader still has accountability to interpret, exercise any form of ethical judgment, and make a decision in context (Ibrahim, 2012). This partnership is very much in line with the Finnish leadership values that focus on deliberation, shared responsibility, and professional discretion (Dobrescu et al., 2024).

The chapter claims that the integration of AI into school leadership is successful only when three principles are interdependent and include trustworthiness, transparency, and ethics. Trustworthiness demands that the AI systems should be trustworthy, just, and correspond to the educational values. The transparency feature requires the processes of AI to be transparent and subject to inspection by the stakeholders. Ethical leadership is the one that ensures that human rights, equity, and democratic accountability are maintained in use. Collectively, these principles bring about the basis of AI-improved leadership that empowers, as opposed to undermines, educational justice.

There are three objectives of the chapter. To start with, it conceptualizes the topic of human-AI collaborative leadership as a part of the general literature on educational equity, ethical governance, and digital transformation. Second, it critically analyzes issues and controversies linked to the application of AI in school leadership with particular focus on algorithmic bias, data governance, and trust. Third, it suggests evidence-based leadership approaches to the development of AI-enhanced school systems that support the values of equity-based education, which are prevalent in Finland (Joshi, 2025b).

The chapter is divided into the following way. The background section places human-AI collaborative leadership in the framework of current studies on AI in education, ethical leadership, and equity-oriented governance based on international frameworks and Finnish policy traditions. The principal analytical part is an analysis of the issues and tensions that the introduction of AI to the school leadership is likely to create, such as bias, transparency, and accountability. The solutions and recommendations area describes the ethical AI implementation leadership strategies, stakeholder engagement, and capacity-building(Ibrahim, 2013) . At the end of the chapter, the author thinks about the future of fair school leadership in Finland and other countries, influenced by AI.

BACKGROUND

The implementation of artificial intelligence in the educational leadership process should be perceived in the framework of a larger theoretical, ethical, and governance-focused perspective. Human-AI collaborative leadership cannot appear in a vacuum; it is developed under the influence of extensive discussions about fairness in education, professional responsibility, the control of technologies, and the ethical obligations of educational establishments. The implementation of AI-powered systems in Finland, where the traditional education is traditionally based on social justice, trust, and decentralization principles, should be grounded in notions very carefully aligned with the traditional educational principles (LI & Tian, 2025).

Human–AI Collaborative Leadership

Human-AI collaborative leadership can be described as a combination of decision-making wherein artificial intelligence systems reinforce, inform, or supplement leadership judgment and not substitute it. This partnership might take the form of AI-assisted analytics or predictive modeling, or automated administrative operations that give leaders a better understanding of learning, resource utilization, and organizational performance patterns (Ibrahim, 2020) . Nevertheless, human responsibility and moral agency are the hallmark of collaborative leadership. AI systems are driving forces of sense-making, whereas school leaders are responsible for the interpretation, decision-making, and results (Joshi, 2025b).

This notion is close to the Finnish tradition of leadership. Finnish leaders of schools are based on the principles of professional trust, the spread of responsibility, and pedagogical knowledge, not on managerial monitoring or the authority of the top. Leadership is generally practised in collegial dialogue, evidence-based reflection, and responsiveness to local situations. In such a system, AI needs to be placed as a supportive tool, which supports the professional judgment, and not an official tool that forces action (LI & Tian, 2025).

Equity in Education and Algorithmic Risk

The Finnish policy and international literature define the concept of educational equity in a broader way than equal access to schooling, as it involves not only equal opportunities afforded to learners, but also differentiated provision and the inclusion of the outcomes of education. Equity-based systems acknowledge that students come to school with different needs based on socioeconomic status, language, disability, and immigration history, and the educational response needs to be proportional instead of universal (Joshi, 2025a).

New threats to this equity framework are presented by AI systems. The training of algorithmic tools is based on historical data, which can be full of inequalities, institutional biases, or structural exclusions. When these systems are applied to predict student performance, learn risk profiles, or guide resource allocation, they can inadvertently perpetuate disparity by reproducing patterns within historic data. As an illustration, students of lower socioeconomic status will be disproportionately identified as at risk by predictive models, which will then shape expectations and interventions in ways that perceive students as stigmatized, rather than being enabled (Joshi, 2025b).

The risks are especially pronounced in a system such as Finland one, where early tracking, labeling, and stratification is an eschewed value. The ethical issue is not only how to avoid explicit discrimination, but also it is necessary to protect against insidious manifestations of algorithmic discrimination that are hidden behind the facade of ostensibly objective analytics. Equity-oriented leadership consequently involves leaders subjecting AI outputs to critical questioning instead of accepting them as neutral or authoritative (Ali et al., 2025).

Transparency, Explainability, and Trust

Transparency is one of the major issues of AI-mediated leadership. Most AI systems become black boxes, giving recommendations or classifications without any clear explanation of the manner in which decisions are made. Such an opaque nature in the leadership of education compromises professional trust and democratic accountability. It might be hard to comprehend or contest decisions that are based on algorithms, especially when the decisions are made to have an impact on learning paths, support delivery, and assessment (Puerta-Beldarrain et al., 2025).

Transparency and mutual understanding are very important in Finnish education governance. Communication of policy decisions is usually open, and school leaders are supposed to explain their behaviours using pedagogical and ethical arguments. The implementation of opaque AI systems in this environment will likely disturb the existing trust relationships unless the explainability and openness are prioritized (Baran, 2025).

Explainable AI (XAI) has consequently become a significant educational leadership issue. On the side of leadership, transparency is a technical matter as well as a communicative and relationship matter. Leaders should be capable of describing what an AI system is, what data it works with, what constraints it has, and how human judgment relates to its output. In the absence of this clarity, AI-based leadership will undermine trust in school leadership and make stakeholder participation frail (El Zaatari & Ibrahim, 2021) .

Ethical AI and Educational Governance

Ethical AI in education is based on the ideas of fairness, accountability, privacy, and human rights. International standards such as the recommendation of AI in education by UNESCO and European ethical AI standards at large, note that AI systems must be used to enhance human well-being, dignity, and that they should fall under human control. These values are quite similar to the values of Finnish education, specifically, the focus on child welfare, inclusion, and social cohesion. A very important ethical aspect is data governance. The AI systems are based on massive data gathering, student performance, behavioral metrics, and occasionally biometric/engagement metrics. Although this type of data can be used to provide early intervention and individual support, it also poses the question of surveillance, consent, and abuse of data. The data protection norms in Finland have become fairly robust, following the European legislation and a culture of institutional responsibility. However, the growth of AI analytics increases the necessity of the apparent governance frameworks specifying data ownership, accessibility, and purpose elimination (Gao et al., 2025).

Ethical leadership where AI is mediated thus concerns defining the scopes of what and how data is collected, used, and who is supposed to make the decision. It also requires mechanisms for redress and review in cases where AI-informed decisions are challenged. In Finnish schools, where student voice and welfare are the primary focus, ethical AI leadership should ensure that technology does not limit the agency and rights of students. The other underlying problem is AI literacy among school heads and teachers. The successful collaboration between human beings and AI systems assumes that leaders will have adequate knowledge of AI mechanisms to critically interpret its outputs, understand its limitations, and detect possible bias. In the absence of this ability, leaders may be more than willing to give too much credence to algorithmic advice, undermining professional autonomy and ethical accountability (Dissanayake & Al-Sharify, 2025).

In Finland, preparation of leadership has long been focused on pedagogical leadership, curriculum development, and collaboration between staff members. With the spread of AI, the leadership development program should be broadened to encompass digital ethics, data literacy, and algorithmic accountability. It does not mean that leaders should turn into technical professionals, but instead, they should be skilled critical users of AI-informed systems. Another area in which AI literacy is needed is among teachers, students, and parents. Open and participatory leadership is about building common ground on the use of AI in schools and the reasoning. This type of involvement aids democratic governance and can help avoid mistrust or resistance that is based on misunderstanding or exclusion (Sai Rama Krishna et al., 2025).

Situating AI Leadership within the Finnish Context

The Finnish educational system offers an unusual environment to investigate the issue of human-AI collaborative leadership. Its decentralized form of governance, the high extent of professional trust, and focus on equity provide both opportunities and limitations to integrating AI. On the one hand, the lack of high-stakes accountability does not pressure the necessity to utilize AI as a surveillance or control tool. Another side of decentralization is that more responsibility is given to the local leaders to ensure ethical and fair implementation (Szmelter-Jarosz & Nozari, 2025).

This background highlights the significance of the agency of leadership. The selection, interpretation, and governance of the use of AI systems do not predetermine their results; instead, leaders define them. In Finland, where leadership is perceived as a moral and pedagogical activity, AI integration should not be directed by efficiency but by the specific ethical intent. Combined, the reviewed literature and contextual issues in this section create the background upon which the analysis of the main issues of human-AI collaborative leadership may take place. They emphasize that AI as a school leader is not a technological breakthrough but a change in governance with deep consequences in the areas of equity, trust, and ethical accountability. The following section discusses these issues in more detail, dwelling upon the controversies and risks it brings once AI systems begin to intersect with educational leadership and decision-making (Zarate-Torres et al., 2025).

MAIN FOCUS OF THE CHAPTER

Issues, Controversies, and Problems

The introduction of artificial intelligence into school leadership is a complex process that goes well beyond the implementation. Although AI systems can be used to improve efficiency, predictive ability, and decisions made with the help of data, their application to educational governance raises fundamental issues in terms of equity, predictability, accountability, and professional autonomy. These issues are especially relevant in Finland, where the historical leadership of education has been based on trust-based governance and professional ethics. These problems are not isolated technical issues but the structural tensions that occur when the algorithm systems collide with the educational systems that are democratic and equity-focused (Obed & Bright, 2025).

Algorithmic Bias and the Reproduction of Inequality

The danger of algorithmic bias is one of the most crucial issues in human-AI collaborative leadership. The AI systems are conditioned on historical data that is representative of current tendencies of success, involvement, and intervention in educational systems. These data sets are not often neutral. They tend to encode socioeconomic differences, linguistic differences, the disadvantages associated with migration, and exclusions associated with disability. When the AI tools are implemented to detect at-risk students, forecast their academic progress, or recommend the allocation of resources, the chance of repeating the trends instead of curbing them remains significant (Baker & Hawn, 2021).

Algorithms' bias is conceptually contradictory in Finland (where comprehensive schooling, delayed tracking, and individualized support have been used to achieve equity). Predictive models that sort the students by previous performance can have an unintended effectiveness of sabotaging the long-established Finnish culture of growth, support, and second chances. As an example, AI systems might unfairly flag students of immigrant background, or those in need of special educational support, and feed their perceived expectations and interventions in a subtly stigmatizing way (Idowu, 2024).

It is not only the threat of biased outputs but the normalization of bias in automation. In cases where the algorithmic recommendations are seen to be objective or scientific, they can be seen to hold greater authority than human judgment as long as they are based on incomplete or biased information. It may result in an insidious loss of equity values, whereby decisions might seem to be data-driven and, at the same time, have a systematic disadvantage for some groups. To school leaders, the problem would be to understand that bias in AI is not a coincidence but a logical consequence of systems based on data being reflected under unequal social settings (Idowu, 2024).

Opacity, Explainability, and Leadership Accountability

The second great controversy touches upon the opaqueness of AI systems and the implications it has on leadership responsibility. Most of the AI-based education tools are based on sophisticated machine-learning models that cannot be easily understood by non-experts. Consequently, school leaders might be left with having to rely on the recommendations that they are unable to clarify to teachers, students, and parents. This discredits one of the most important roles of educational leadership, the capacity to explain decisions by using transparent, pedagogical, and ethical arguments (Vibhuti & Divyansh, 2024).

Opaque AI systems in Finland have destabilized the norms of governance in Finland, where school leadership is largely connected to professional legitimacy and shared decision-making. Unless leaders are able to explain how AI-based decisions are made coherently (e.g., why some students are provided with more support or why the resources should be distributed in a specific manner), trust can be undermined. Transparency is not a procedural tool; it is a relationship practice that builds confidence in institutions (Vibhuti & Divyansh, 2024).

Accountability is also difficult due to the absence of explainability. In case an AI-driven decision has negative outcomes for a student, it can be frequently unclear to whom the responsibility is attributed, whether it is the software vendor, the algorithm itself, the data, or the human leader who consented to use this software. This spreading of responsibility is a subject of grave ethical issues. Trust-based systems, such as Finland, where accountability to leadership is personal and professional but not a punitive system, can thwart governance systems and compromise ethical regulation (Michopoulou, 2025).

Data Governance, Privacy, and Surveillance Risks

Artificial intelligence (AI) leadership is highly dependent on gathering, analyzing, and managing student information. Learning analytics, behavioral observation mechanisms, and predictive systems are increasingly based on huge volumes of data that incorporate academic achievement, attendance records, and occasionally emotional or behavioral ones. Although this kind of data could be used in early intervention and individualized learning, it is alarmingly concerning, as it implies privacy, consent, and surveillance issues (Michopoulou, 2025).

Data protection in Finnish education is within a robust regulatory framework of data protection, influenced by the European standards of data protection and the cultural focus of institutional responsibility (Abdallah & Abdallah, 2023).

. Nonetheless, the growth of AI analytics will only compound the bulk, fineness, and sensitivity of the information gathered on students. The line between support and surveillance becomes unclear when AI tools track the learning behaviors or predict the forthcoming results (Michopoulou, 2025).

One of the major issues is proportionality. Equity-oriented leadership requires that the data that is collected be based on obvious educational rewards and restricted to the required extent. Overindulgence in data collection would turn schools into surveillance spaces, which may have some implications for the autonomy and mental security of students. To the marginalized students, this surveillance can be quite invasive, making them feel controlled and not cared about. The leadership in schools, hence, has to balance the pressure of using data-driven support and also uphold student dignity and privacy (Ouedraogo-Thomas, 2025).

Erosion of Professional Autonomy and Judgment

The other major concern is associated with the effects of AI on professional autonomy. The culture of Finnish school leadership and teaching is based on the high levels of trust in professional knowledge. The judgment of teachers and principals is supposed to be guided by pedagogical knowledge, contextual understanding, as well as ethical reflection. The AI systems, in turn, offer a novel position of power that may quietly take the decision-making authority out of the specialists and give it to the algorithmic reasoning (Elabied, 2024).

The possibility of secondary human judgment ensues when AI recommendations are incorporated into daily routine, e.g., when identifying students who should be subjected to intervention or determining the effectiveness of a program. Leaders might also be under pressure to adhere to algorithmic results that indicate efficiency or conformity to regulations, whereas results that do not align with contextual knowledge or professional intuition may not be adhered to. This may deteriorate the reflective practice and lead to leadership procedural automatisms over time {Sierra Noakes, 2024 #32}.

This is especially problematic in equity-based systems. Professional judgment enables leaders to take into consideration subtlety, lived experience, and relational aspects, which cannot be comprehensively reflected in AI systems. When AI-directed decision-making reduces this ability, leadership will lose its ability to be sensitive to the nuances of the lives of students, and make the leadership less inclusive instead of more inclusive (Kim et al., 2022).

Stakeholder Trust and Democratic Legitimacy

Finnish education is characterized by trust, which is spread in the relationships between schools and families, between municipalities and the state (Abdallah & Alkaabi, 2023).. The implementation of AI in leadership processes may interfere with this trust in case the decisions are viewed as alien, technologically obscured, and unethical by the stakeholders. The use of data, whether consent is relevant, and whether AI systems mirror community values are some of the issues that may concern parents and students (Sargiotis, 2025).

One issue that can be reiterated is that stakeholders are not fully involved in AI adoption decisions. AI tools are implemented in most education systems with little consultation, either at the administrative or procurement levels (Abdallah & Alkaabi, 2023).This hierarchy method is opposite to the principles of democratic governance, and it may lead to the estrangement of communities. Marginalized groups who may already have less power in relation to institutional decisions in the equity-oriented systems also have the risk of being disproportionately influenced by the absent voices of the stakeholders (Sikander et al., 2024).

To school leaders, a democratic legitimacy cannot be destroyed without taking affirmative action, communicating effectively, and holding a dialogue. In the absence of such practices, it is likely that AI integration remains seen as another technocratic intrusion, as opposed to a supportive innovation (Topali et al., 2024).

Unequal Capacity and Digital Stratification

The ability to introduce ethical and fair AI is not consistent between schools and municipalities. There are disparities in leadership experience, digital infrastructure, and even access to professional development in an otherwise fairly equal system in Finland. To a larger extent, schools that have more resources and technical assistance can be in a better position to critically analyze AI tools, perform bias analysis, and maintain transparency (Abdallah & Musah, 2023). Less-resourced schools can implement AI systems without much scrutiny, which exposes them to potential ethical and equity risks (Holstein & Aleven, 2022).

This disproportionate ability results in the likelihood of digital stratification, in which the proceeds of AI-enhanced leadership will be unevenly distributed throughout the system. This stratification is incompatible with Finland, which is determined not to create differences between schools and make educational opportunities of students dependent on the geographical location and the impressiveness of the institutions (Chang et al., 2025).

All these show that human-AI collaborative leadership is not an apolitical or technical process. It is a very political and ethical change that alters the way of making decisions, authority, and prioritizing interests. Even in equity-based systems like the Finnish, these issues should be addressed directly instead of being treated as a secondary consideration (Abdallah et al., 2024). The next part proceeds to specific measures and leadership solutions that would help to overcome these tensions and to make sure AI integration can empower and not weaken fair, transparent, and ethical school governance (Revolusi & Febriandy, 2025).

SOLUTIONS AND RECOMMENDATIONS

The solutions to the challenges of artificial intelligence in the leadership of schools cannot be met by technical protective measures or solitary policy changes. In equity systems, like Finland, ethical leadership, institutional trust, and democratic accountability should be used as solutions. Human-AI collaborative leadership should be thus designed in a very intentional way, but AI systems should be used as an assistant tool within a human-guided system and not be viewed as independent decision-makers. In this section, I describe a proposed cluster of strategies that allow school leaders to utilize the power of AI without damaging equity, transparency, and ethical accountability (METWALLI, 2024).

Embedding Ethical AI Frameworks in Educational Leadership

One of the initial steps in ensuring fair human-AI relations is creating clear ethical AI guidelines both at the system and school levels. Informal norms cannot be considered a sufficient element of ethical governance, especially during the period when the decision-making processes are mediated even more by complex technologies (Fang et al., 2024). School leaders are expected to work with well-defined principles where fairness, accountability, transparency, and respect for human rights are the key aspects (Papa & Jackson, 2021).

Such frameworks are expected to be consistent with the current values of education in Finland, where inclusion, student wellbeing, and professional trust are the main focus. To become an ethical AI, algorithms need to be assessed on a regular basis to minimize bias, and there should be explicit rules on what is acceptable use and protection against discrimination (Alqodsi & Abdallah, 2024). Audits, such as a bias audit, may be useful in determining whether predictive models are disproportionately disadvantageous to some groups of students, including learners of immigrant backgrounds or students with special educational needs. Notably, these evaluations must not be a single affair but processes that are integrated into the leadership practice (Mariyono et al., 2025).

Responsibility is also explained with the aid of ethical frameworks. AI systems should not be seen as decision-makers; it should be human leaders who are to be held responsible. This principle supports the moral agency of school leadership and keeps the ethical judgment as a central issue in the governance of schools (Abdallah, 2023 ; Kundu & Bej, 2025).

Maintaining Human-in-the-Loop Decision-Making

The main tenet of human-AI collaborative leadership is that human control will always be present in any consequential decision. Any use of AI tools must be as a decision-support system, which will deliver insights and scenarios, not decisions (Alqodsi & Abdallah, 2024). It is especially critical in settings that touch on student placement, eligibility in interventions, or prioritization of resources, which have long-term effects on educational trajectory (Wittka, 2020).

The school leadership traditions in Finland uphold this approach highly. Leadership legitimacy is based on professional discretion, sensitivity to the situation, and understanding through relationships (Aldous & Ismail, 2024). Adopting a human-in-the-loop model will ensure that the outputs of AI are analyzed by pedagogical skills and ethics and not implemented without further thought(Abdallah, Ismail, & Alkaabi, 2024). Leaders should be motivated- institutionalized to challenge the recommendations of the algorithms, contextualize data, and overturn the outputs of AI when equity requires otherwise (Guardiola, 2025).

To be able to implement this principle, schools and municipalities are recommended to develop clear guidelines outlining the decisions that can be informed by AI and those that should be left entirely human-controlled. These limits defend against automation bias and strengthen the primacy of professional judgment (Abdallah, 2024).

Strengthening Transparency and Explainability

To maintain trust in AI-augmented leadership, transparency is mandatory. The leaders of schools should be capable of stating how AI systems work, what information they utilize, and how their results are applied in decision-making (Al-Qodsi et al., 2024). This is not restricted to technical documentation, but rather to significant communication with teachers, students, parents, and other interested parties. Practically, this would mean choosing AI systems that are more explainable and resisting opaque black box tools (Alqodsi, 2021). The leaders must make sure that employees are trained on how to interpret AI-produced insights and that the stakeholders are enlightened on how AI impacts school practices. Another element of transparent communication involves the creation of review and appeal mechanisms that allow people to challenge or dispute AI-informed decisions that impact them (Dobrescu et al., 2024).

This transparency would be consistent with the culture of democratic rule that Finland has and helps build institutional legitimacy (Al-Qodsi et al., 2024). Artificial intelligence can be used as a collaborative tool instead of a distrustful one when the stakeholders learn about the way of decision-making and develop trust in it (Joshi, 2025b).

Building AI Literacy and Leadership Capacity

Successful human-AI collaboration requires that leaders and educators can interact with AI systems critically. Artificial intelligence literacy ought to be, consequently, a part of the modern-day school leadership (Ismail & Ismail, 2024). This is not a technical specialization, but one has to be competent in the knowledge of capabilities, limitations, and ethical implications of AI. Finland's Leadership development programs need to incorporate AI-related skills with the current existing focus on pedagogical and distributed leadership (Ismail & Ismail, 2024). Among the topics to be covered by training, there should be algorithmic bias, data ethics, explainability, and responsible data use. Providing this knowledge to leaders enhances the power to make decisions, question vendors, and promote equity-driven implementations (LI & Tian, 2025).

Teachers should also be aware of AI and, where suitable, students and parents. The aspect of inclusive leadership is that it encourages collective knowledge instead of building expertise by a small group of administrative elites (Ismail, 2024). This type of capacity-building can help in terms of transparency, minimizing mistrust, and fostering collective responsibility (Joshi, 2025a).

Engaging Stakeholders and Democratic Participation

AI introduction should be done with serious stakeholder involvement. Administrative and technical spheres should not be the ones that make the decision regarding the implementation of AI tools, but the educators, families, and representatives of the community (Ismail, 2024). This form of participation echoes the Finland tradition of collaborative governance and expounds the legitimacy of technological innovation (Ismail & Aldous, 2024). Interaction has a moral and functional value. Stakeholders are able to express their concerns regarding the use of data, privacy, and unintended consequences that system designers may not be aware of (Abdallah,

Ismail, & Ismail, 2024). Considering various views, especially those of the marginalized groups, will contribute to the assurance that the AI systems will not favor the dominant norms and experiences {Joshi, 2025 #12}s.

The leaders ought to develop formal communication, feedback, and the rate of evaluation of AI efforts. These practices increasingly support the notion that AI is not a technocratic solution that is imposed on the population, but it should be subjected to democratic supervision and shared values (Ramadan & Ismail, 2023; Ali et al., 2025).

Ensuring System-Level Equity and Capacity Alignment

Equity-based human-AI collaboration needs to consider system-level differences in capacity. Even in the comparatively harmonized system in Finland, there is a disparity in digital infrastructure, leadership skills, and access to professional growth. AI integration cannot be introduced without the support, and without the coordinated support, it may favor certain schools at the expense of others and produce new kinds of stratification (Ismail & Aldous, 2025). There is a role for the national and municipal authorities, therefore, to set the direction, common standards, and technical advice to have a uniform implementation of the ethical practices in various contexts. Distribution of platforms, joint assessment of AI tools, and joint buying can be used to lessen inequalities and secure smaller or less resourceful schools against disproportionate danger (Puerta-Beldarrain et al., 2025).

A combination of all these strategies highlights the point that ethical and fair AI implementation is essentially a leadership issue, not a technological one. Human-AI collaborative leadership works effectively where the AI systems are incorporated into a governance system that values human judgment, transparency, and justice (Aldous & Ismail, 2025). When it comes to Finland, where trust and equity have traditionally been conceptualized in educational leadership, these two principles offer a substantial basis when it comes to ensuring that AI supports and does not neglect the social purpose of schooling. The final part is a reflection on these lessons and the ways these lessons apply to the future of educational leadership in an increasingly algorithmic world (Baran, 2025).

FUTURE RESEARCH DIRECTIONS

Whereas the literature on artificial intelligence in education has grown at an extremely fast rate, the scientific study of human-AI collaborative leadership (specifically through the prism of equity) is still in its initial and disjointed phases. With the increased integration of AI systems into school governance and leadership practices, systematic interdisciplinary research has an immediate urgency to guide ethically sound and context-specific application, particularly in education systems that have made social justice a core value, as Finland has (Gao et al., 2025).

The future research question is one of the most important as it is related to the long-term equity implications of AI-informed leadership decisions (Ismail & Aldous, 2025). Although the short-term advantages of AI tools, including the possibility to detect the causes of learning problems in the early stages or improve administrative effectiveness, are frequently emphasized, few empirical studies have investigated the impacts of consistent AI use on the educational paths of various student groups (Aldous & Ismail, 2025). Longitudinal research is required to investigate whether AI-based interventions cause or even increase achievement gaps based on socioeconomic status, migration background, language, or disability. Such research would be of great use in Finland, where equity is characterized by reducing inter-school and intra-school inequalities (Dissanayake & Al-Sharify, 2025).

The second priority is to develop evidence-based research on explainable and transparent AI models that apply to the field of educational leadership (Abdallah *et al.*, 2023). A lot of the current research on explainable AI (XAI) is technical in nature and fails to support the interpretive requirements of school leaders, teachers, or families in an adequate manner. Research into ways of designing AI explanations to facilitate pedagogic reasoning, moral deliberation, and communication with stakeholders should be conducted in the future. Research on the way school leaders perceive, challenge, and respond to AI-generated insights would have a significant impact on leadership theory and practice (Szmelter-Jarosz & Nozari, 2025).

It is also evident that comparative studies of governance and policy frameworks of ethical AI in education are lacking. New regulatory efforts, including the developing AI governance policies of the European Union, will have an even greater influence on the possibilities of applying AI in the educational systems of the state (Abdallah *et al.*, 2023). A study on the relationship between national policies and local leadership practices can be used to determine governance models that can offer a balance between innovation and accountability. Within the decentralized model of Finland, this piece of work would shed light on the alignment of municipal autonomy and national standards to provide the same level of ethical protection in all schools (Zarate-Torres et al., 2025).

The other valuable way is the issue of AI literacy and leadership training. Though the technical discourses of AI continue to multiply, there is scant empirical study on how school leaders are being trained to use AI ethically and critically (Abdallah & Awad, 2026). In a future study, the researcher should consider leadership development models that combine AI ethics, data governance, and equity analysis and evaluate their ability to enhance the confidence of leaders and their decision-making abilities. Future comparative research involving Nordic or European settings would help better understand how technological change is represented in professional trust-based systems through leadership training (Obed & Bright, 2025).

Lastly, interdisciplinary practice should be considered to understand the social and relationship aspects of AI implementation in schools. AI can be viewed as an instrument of technology, but there is a transformation of leader, teacher, student, and community relations with the use of AI. A qualitative study that focuses on the perceptions of the stakeholders, the dynamics of trust, and the feeling of being included or excluded can give a perspective that cannot be indicated by the quantitative analytics. This would contribute to the realization that ethical AI leadership is a social practice as much as it is a technological practice (Papa & Jackson, 2021).

These research directions, taken together, emphasize the fact that the future of AI in the field of school leadership is not limited to the level of technological development but is predetermined by the continuity of research on equity and ethics, governance, and human judgment (Alkaabi *et al.*, 2025). Further study will be necessary to make sure that AI can improve, but not undermine the core principles of publicly-provided education (Idowu, 2024).

CONCLUSION

Human-AI collaborative leadership has been the subject of discussion in this chapter as an emerging and consequential facet of educational governance, with a specific emphasis being placed on promoting equity within the professional environment of trust, transparency, and ethical practices. The analysis was conducted within the Finnish education system, which is known to be highly egalitarian, professionally trusted, and inclusive in its leadership approaches, which has proven that the implementation of artificial intelligence in school leadership is not a neutral technological phenomenon but a normative and ethical one.

The chapter has indicated that AI has a great potential to assist in the fair decision-making processes by increasing the ability of the leaders to determine the learning needs, to allocate the resources in a more efficient manner, and to react in a timely fashion to the changes in the situation. Simultaneously, it has drawn attention to severe dangers related to algorithmic bias, the lack of transparency, data control, and professional autonomy degradation. These hazards are particularly disastrous within equity-based systems, in which even minor manifestations of automated inequality can roll back years of pledges of equity and inclusion.

The chapter has furthered a model of leadership that does not squander human judgment, moral responsibility, and sensitivity to context through presenting AI as a team player and not as an authoritative decision-maker. Ethical AI systems, human-in-the-loop control, openness, interaction with stakeholders, and capacity-building of leadership were found to be the most important circumstances of making sure that AI can be used to deliver educational justice and not efficiency only. These conditions in the trust context of Finland are tightly connected with the established leadership norms, which provide a good basis for responsible innovation.

Finally, the chapter also posits that the issues of equitable AI integration are not a technical problem but a leadership one. Algorithms will have little influence on the future of AI in education because the use of AI relies not only on algorithms themselves but also on the values and decision-making frameworks that will guide their utilization. Education leaders can make certain that technological innovation reinforces, not undermines, the social mission of schooling by creating AI-enhanced, transparent, accountable, and ethically sound school systems. This way, the human-AI collaborative leadership will be a strong tool in maintaining equity, trust, and democratic legitimacy within the education systems that have an increasingly digital future.

REFERENCES

Abdallah, A. K. (2023). Teacher-led, student-focused, and unleashing the power of teacher empowerment for school improvement and success. In *Restructuring leadership for school improvement and reform*. IGI Global., DOI: 10.4018/978-1-6684-7818-9.ch001

Abdallah, A. K. (2024). The impact of gender, psychology, and cultural dimensions on leadership development in distance education. *Scientific Reports*, *14*(1), 68495. Advance online publication. DOI: 10.1038/s41598-024-68495-4

Abdallah, A. K., & Abdallah, R. K. (2023). Achieving academic excellence: The intersection of teacher development, quality education, and entrepreneurship. In *Innovations in teacher development, personalized learning, and upskilling the workforce*. IGI Global., DOI: 10.4018/978-1-6684-5518-0.ch007

Abdallah, A. K., & Abdallah, R. K. (2023). Achieving academic excellence: The intersection of teacher development, quality education, and entrepreneurship. In *Innovations in teacher development, personalized learning, and upskilling the workforce*. IGI Global., DOI: 10.4018/978-1-6684-5518-0.ch007

Abdallah, A. K., & Alkaabi, A. A. M. (2023). *Restructuring leadership for school improvement and reform*. IGI Global., DOI: 10.4018/978-1-6684-7818-9

Abdallah, A. K., Ismail, L. S., & Alkaabi, A. M. (2024). Green careers: Educating for the future of sustainability. In *Legal frameworks and educational strategies for sustainable development*. IGI Global., DOI: 10.4018/979-8-3693-2987-0.ch017

Abdallah, A. K., & Musah, M. B. (2023). Principal and teacher licensing as a tool to school improvement. In *Restructuring leadership for school improvement and reform*. IGI Global., DOI: 10.4018/978-1-6684-7818-9.ch014

Abdallah, R. K., Al Maktoum, S. B., & Al Mansoori, M. K. (2023). The road to lesson observation as a tool to school improvement: Accountability vs. perfunctory. In *Restructuring leadership for school improvement and reform* (pp. 222–252). IGI Global., DOI: 10.4018/978-1-6684-7818-9.ch012

Abdallah, R. K., & Awad, M. J. (2026). Integrating artificial intelligence and technology into UAE teacher licensing systems for global education reforms. In *Building a unified teacher licensing system: Policies, education reforms, and cultural integration* (pp. 211–250). IGI Global., DOI: 10.4018/979-8-3373-0837-1.ch008

Al-Qodsi, E. M., Jadalhaq, I. M., & El-Maknouzi, M. E. H. (2024). The place of UAE's food security in the national legislation and its role in supporting global food security. *Cogent Social Sciences, 10*(1), 2319379. Advance online publication. DOI: 10.1080/23311886.2024.2319379

Aldous, S. M., & Ismail, G. A. (2025). AI for sustainable emergency preparedness and response in schools. In *Convergence of AI, education, and business for sustainability*. IGI Global., DOI: 10.4018/979-8-3373-1917-9.ch003

Aldous, S. M., & Ismail, G. A. (2025). Crisis management and teacher preparedness: Embedding health and safety in teacher education programs. In *Building a unified teacher licensing system: Policies, education reforms, and cultural integration*. IGI Global., DOI: 10.4018/979-8-3373-0837-1.ch013

Ali, I., Nguyen, K., Ali, A. M., & Cui, T. (2025). Human–AI collaboration in knowledge ecosystems: A multidisciplinary review, integrative framework and future directions. *Journal of Knowledge Management*, •••, 1–22.

Alkaabi, A. M., Abdallah, A. K., Abdallah, R., Al Hasan, M., & Mohamed, A. (2025). Principal engagement in the teacher evaluation process in remote schools: A narrative inquiry of language teachers. *Forum for Linguistic Studies*, *7*(3), 209–230. DOI: 10.30564/fls.v7i3.8502

Alqodsi, E. M. (2021). Analyzing the implementation of usufruct rights and obligations in the UAE Civil Transactions Law. *International Journal of Criminal Justice Sciences, 16*(1), 95–109.

Alqodsi, E. M., & Abdallah, A. K. (2024). *Legal frameworks and educational strategies for sustainable development*. IGI Global., DOI: 10.4018/979-8-3693-2987-0

Alqodsi, E. M., & Abdallah, A. K. (2024). Preface. In *Legal frameworks and educational strategies for sustainable development*. IGI Global.

Baker, R. S., & Hawn, A. (2021). Algorithmic Bias in Education. *International Journal of Artificial Intelligence in Education, 32*(4), 1052–1092. DOI: 10.1007/s40593-021-00285-9

Baran, M. (2025). AI-augmented leadership: Redefining leaders' style and competencies. In *AI and Humanistic Management* (pp. 147–169). Routledge.

Chang, M. A., Tissenbaum, M., Philip, T. M., & D'Mello, S. K. (2025). Co-designing AI with youth partners: Enabling ideal classroom relationships through a novel AI relational privacy ethical framework. *Computers and Education: Artificial Intelligence, 8*. Advance online publication. DOI: 10.1016/j.caeai.2025.100364

Dissanayake, L., & Al-Sharify, A. (2025). AI and Decision Making: How does the integration of AI influence leadership decision making within technology driven companies? In Dobrescu, P., Vladu, L., & Durach, F. (2024). INNOVATION AND EDUCATION: A CHALLENGING RELATIONSHIP. INTED2024 Proceedings, Elabied, N. (2024). Collaborative Leadership With AI: New Paradigms in University Administration. *International Research Journal of Engineering & Applied Sciences, 12*(3), 01-06. https://doi.org/DOI: 10.55083/irjeas.2024.v12i03001

El Zaatari, W., & Ibrahim, A. (2021). What promotes adolescent students' school belonging? Students' and teachers' convergent/divergent views. *Cogent Education, 8*(1), 1–20. DOI: 10.1080/2331186X.2021.1984628

Fang, M., Abdallah, A. K., & Vorfolomeyeva, O. (2024). Collaborative AI-enhanced digital mind-mapping as a tool for stimulating creative thinking in inclusive education for students with neurodevelopmental disorders. *BMC Psychology, 12*(1), 1975. Advance online publication. DOI: 10.1186/s40359-024-01975-4

Gao, Q., Xu, W., Pan, H., Shen, M., & Gao, Z. (2025). Human-Centered Human-AI Collaboration (HCHAC). *arXiv preprint arXiv:2505.22477.*

Guardiola, M.-A. (2025). Educational Leadership and AI in the Post-COVID-19 Era: Ethical Challenges and Opportunities in Catalonia. *Digital Citizenship and the Future of AI Engagement, Ethics, and Privacy*, 569-602.

Holstein, K., & Aleven, V. (2022). Designing for human–AI complementarity in K-12 education. *AI Magazine, 43*(2), 239–248. DOI: 10.1002/aaai.12058

Ibrahim, A. (2010). Education in the UAE: A socio-cultural analysis. In Zhao, Y. (Ed.), *Handbook of Asian education: A cultural perspective* (pp. 327–344). Routledge., DOI: 10.4324/9780203816318

Ibrahim, A. (2020). *What hurts or helps teacher collaboration? Evidence from UAE schools. Prospects: Comparative Journal of Curriculum*. Learning, and Assessment., DOI: 10.1007/s11125-019-09459-9

Ibrahim, A. S. (2012). Induction and mentoring of novice teachers: A scheme for the United Arab Emirates. *Teacher Development, 16*(2), 235–253. DOI: 10.1080/13664530.2012.688676

Ibrahim, A. S. (2013). The learning needs of beginning teachers in the United Arab Emirates. *Journal of Education for Teaching: International Research and Pedagogy, 39*(5), 491–506. DOI: 10.1080/02607476.2013.739791

Idowu, J. A. (2024). Debiasing Education Algorithms. *International Journal of Artificial Intelligence in Education*, *34*(4), 1510–1540. DOI: 10.1007/s40593-023-00389-4

Ismail, G. A., & Aldous, S. M. (2024). Digital innovation in green learning: Ensuring safety while fostering environmental stewardship. In *Legal frameworks and educational strategies for sustainable development*. IGI Global., DOI: 10.4018/979-8-3693-2987-0.ch016

Ismail, G. A., & Aldous, S. M. (2025). AI-driven health and safety management in school facilities. In *Convergence of AI, education, and business for sustainability*. IGI Global., DOI: 10.4018/979-8-3373-1917-9.ch002

Ismail, L. S., & Ismail, O. A. S. (2024). Adaptive strategies for success: Monitoring and evaluating blue-green infrastructure in urban development. In *Integrating blue-green infrastructure into urban development*. IGI Global., DOI: 10.4018/979-8-3693-8069-7.ch001

Ismail, O. A. S. (2024). Sustainable automotive engineering: Empowering the next generation of eco-conscious engineers. In *Legal frameworks and educational strategies for sustainable development*. IGI Global., DOI: 10.4018/979-8-3693-2987-0.ch019

Joshi, S. (2025a). Comprehensive Review of Artificial Intelligence in Management, Leadership, Decision-Making and Collaboration. *Decision-Making and Collaboration (April 15, 2025).*

Joshi, S. (2025b). Review of Artificial Intelligence in Management, Leadership, Decision-Making and Collaboration.

Kim, J., Lee, H., & Cho, Y. H. (2022). Learning design to support student-AI collaboration: Perspectives of leading teachers for AI in education. *Education and Information Technologies*, *27*(5), 6069–6104. DOI: 10.1007/s10639-021-10831-6

Kundu, A., & Bej, T. (2025). AI policies in school education: A comparative study on China, Singapore, Finland, and the US. *Journal of Science and Technology Policy Management*.

LI, H., & Tian, F. (2025). Advancing decision-making through AI-human collaboration: A systematic review and conceptual framework.

Mariyono, D., Hidayatullah, A. N. A., & Kamila, A. N. A. (2025). Integrating Artificial Intelligence in Inclusive Leadership: Transforming Educational Management for a Globalized Future. *Authorea Preprints*.

METWALLI, M. M. A. S. (2024). *ARTIFICIAL INTELLIGENCE IN EDUCATIONAL LEADERSHIP: CHALLENGES AND OPPORTUNITIES* LIVERPOOL JOHN MOORES UNIVERSITY].

Michopoulou, K. (2025). The principle of equality in education: Exploring the legal aspects of the right to inclusive and equitable quality education for achieving the development of a democratic citizenship. *European Journal of Education and Pedagogy*, *6*(2), 64–69.

Obed, B., & Bright, B. (2025). Algorithmic bias in educational systems: Examining the impact of AI-driven decision making in modern education. *World Journal of Advanced Research and Reviews*, *25*(1), 2012–2017. DOI: 10.30574/wjarr.2025.25.1.0253

Ouedraogo-Thomas, R. (2025). From Tool to Digitized Co-Conspirator: A Reflective Analysis of GPT-Based Engagement with Educational Equity. *American Journal of STEM Education*. https://doi.org/DOI: 10.32674/jxz8hn16

Papa, R., & Jackson, K. M. (2021). *Artificial intelligence, human agency and the educational leader*. Springer Nature.

Puerta-Beldarrain, M., Gomez-Carmona, O., Sanchez-Corcuera, R., Casado-Mansilla, D., Lopez-de-Ipina, D., & Chen, L. (2025). A multifaceted vision of the Human-AI collaboration: A comprehensive review. *IEEE Access : Practical Innovations, Open Solutions*.

Ramadan, R. S., & Ismail, O. A. S. (2023). Building a better future: The role of school inspection in driving educational excellence. In *Restructuring leadership for school improvement and reform*. IGI Global., DOI: 10.4018/978-1-6684-7818-9.ch011

Revolusi, P., & Febriandy, R. K. (2025). Human-AI Educational Collaboration: Facing Learning Challenges in the Digital Age. *International Journal of Management, Entrepreneurship. Social Science and Humanities*, *8*(2), 289–312. DOI: 10.31098/ijmesh.v8i2.3229

Sai Rama Krishna, M., Monika Singh, T., Karuna, D., Divya, R., & Shuaib, M. (2025). Synergic Thinking: A New Era of Human-AI Decision-Making. In *The Power of Agentic AI: Redefining Human Life and Decision-Making: In Industry 6.0* (pp. 139-150). Springer.

Sargiotis, D. (2025). Fostering Ethical and Inclusive AI: A Human-Centric Paradigm for Social Impact. *International Journal of Research Publication and Reviews*, *6*(1), 3754–3779. DOI: 10.55248/gengpi.6.0125.0529

Sikander, N., Zeeshan, A., Muhammad Nouman, S., Muhammad Mudaber, J., & Ahmed, H. (2024). Ai for Inclusive Educational Governance and Digital Equity Examining the Impact of Ai Adoption and Open Data on Community Trust and Policy Effectiveness. *Contemporary Journal of Social Science Review*, *2*(04), 2557–2567. DOI: 10.63878/cjssr.v2i04.1502

Szmelter-Jarosz, A., & Nozari, H. (2025). AI-Driven Decision Intelligence and Human-AI Collaboration in Economic Systems. In *Dynamic and Safe Economy in the Age of Smart Technologies* (pp. 171–190). IGI Global Scientific Publishing.

Topali, P., Ortega-Arranz, A., Rodríguez-Triana, M. J., Er, E., Khalil, M., & Akçapınar, G. (2024). Designing human-centered learning analytics and artificial intelligence in education solutions: A systematic literature review. *Behaviour & Information Technology*, *44*(5), 1071–1098. DOI: 10.1080/0144929x.2024.2345295

Vibhuti, C., & Divyansh, C. (2024). Towards trustworthy AI: An analysis of the relationship between explainability and trust in AI systems. *International Journal of Science and Research Archive*, *11*(1), 2219–2226. DOI: 10.30574/ijsra.2024.11.1.0300

Wittka, M. (2020). Designed agency in collaborations: Exploring cross-sector collaboration in Finland's artificial intelligence programme AuroraAI.

Zarate-Torres, R., Rey-Sarmiento, C. F., Acosta-Prado, J. C., Gomez-Cruz, N. A., Rodriguez Castro, D. Y., & Camargo, J. (2025). Influence of Leadership on Human-Artificial Intelligence Collaboration. *Behavioral Sciences (Basel, Switzerland)*, *15*(7), 873. DOI: 10.3390/bs15070873

Chapter 4
AI-Enhanced Learning Environments:
School Leadership Perceptions of Bridging Equity Pedagogical and Assessment Practices

Safeya Alkatheeri
United Arab Emirates University, UAE

Eman Y. Mahmoud
http://orcid.org/0000-0003-0793-8686
United Arab Emirates University, UAE

ABSTRACT

Artificial intelligence (AI) integration became indispensable in various educational aspects. This chapter investigates school principals' perspectives on AI-enhanced learning environments and their potential in creating and maintaining equity in pedagogy and assessment in UAE schools. Equity practices are highlighted through culturally responsive pedagogy (CRP) for teaching and learning and culturally responsive evaluation (CRE) for assessment. A qualitative case study approach was implemented to explore principals' perceptions through semi-structured interviews. Two participants piloted the instrument and responded to its questions. The results show that AI is currently used by teachers and students. Both principals confirmed that the Ministry of Education provides staff with training on AI tools; however, it is not directed to enhance CRP or CRE, so teachers are not fully equipped with AI tools that enhance equity for students, and AI tools, if suitable, are still emerging. Finally, implications, challenges, recommendations, and future research directions conclude the chapter.

DOI: 10.4018/979-8-2600-0388-6.ch004

INTRODUCTION

Advanced technological tools have become essential in the modern era, part of which is technology enhanced education. As noticed recently, artificial intelligence (AI) became a trend in most educational workshops, forums, and conferences indicating the necessity of recognizing it in school contexts. Nowadays, a more particular concept has emerged in educational fields, that is AI-enhanced learning, which implies including AI in meaningful ways to enhance teaching and learning. The use of AI can facilitate pedagogy and inclusion through instruction and evaluation, so decision makers and school leaders should ensure achieving authenticity and inclusion through its applications (Umoke et al., 2025). Although AI integrations hold various benefits, "there are still concerns about their impact on educational practice and the teaching profession in the future" (Barbu & Sbughea, 2024).

Moreover, educators need to consider the difference between equity and equality to create and maintain equity-based education (Sibanda, 2023). Many educators relate equity education to essential educational practices that pertain to differentiated instruction, inclusion of all learners, and anti-racist education. However, this paper focuses on two major equity-centered aspects; that are culturally responsive pedagogy (CRP) and culturally responsive evaluation (CRE), and it investigates the potential of AI-enhanced environments to enhance them. Evaluation is tightly linked to pedagogy because the bridging of teaching, learning, and evaluation approaches is a critical educational need (Mahmoud, 2024). Multicultural classrooms require more attention in this regard; thus, all school stakeholders need to collaborate to achieve culturally responsive education. Educational policies are also advised to regulate the use of AI to ensure equity for diverse learners (Umoke et al., 2025). Within the UAE context, no similar studies were found as equity in available literature was linked to aspects other than culturally relevant pedagogy or evaluation. Therefore, this study aims to investigate school principals' perceptions of equity education in both pedagogy and evaluation as well as how AI can be meaningfully included to achieve equity.

CHAPTER OVERVIEW

This chapter discussed equity-relevant concepts in the following sections. It started with an overview of AI-enhanced learning. Then, literature was reviewed on culturally responsive pedagogy, culturally responsive evaluation, bridging pedagogy and assessment considering equity-centered education, and school principals' views and perceptions of these practices. To shed light on current issues, a qualitative case study was conducted with a semi-structured interview used as its instrument. Two school principals were interviewed to pilot and improve the instrument, and the initial findings were reported and discussed afterwards. Finally, possible implications were emphasized, challenges were highlighted, and limitations and further research recommendations were included.

LITERATURE REVIEW

AI-Enhanced Learning Environments

School learning environments have increased efficiency and quality elevated ever since the integration of AI. Hariharan (2025) explains that technology was initially viewed as a supplementary and adjunctive tool in teaching and learning; however, with technology advancement, it became pivotal in forming and delivering students' learning. In such settings, diverse students' needs, interests, aptitudes, and learning styles are catered to and tailored, so that students are ready for the requirements of the technology-driven global market (Anchal, 2025). The pedagogical aspect is not only influenced by technology, but also by educational outcomes, accessibility, engagement, and assessment. Eslit (2024) argues that the learning environment eventually becomes globally connected, inclusive, and equitable. Eslit also highlights additional benefits of AI in education in terms of students boosting their learning when they learn in a culturally supportive and simulated context and having a tailored tutoring system as well as adaptive platforms. AI is also useful when students receive instant translation and on-time constructive feedback.

Murari and Parmar (2025) include other advantages of AI in education when learning shifts to customize learning experiences for students from diverse backgrounds through including flexible contents and suggesting creative solutions to challenges those students might encounter. In addition, AI encourages personalized learning that enhances students' enthusiasm and motivation to learn (Xu, 2024). AI can simplify complex content and sophisticated knowledge for students in ways that resonate with them, such as using concept map virtual tools (Li, 2023). Through AI, teachers also get to know more about their students' emotions, interests, and feelings, and that creates mutual and effective relationships.

Alternatively, Murari and Parmar (2025) and Li (2023) bring to educators' attention an important debatable question whether artificial intelligence provides equitable access and implications for students from diverse needs and backgrounds in educational settings where gaps, divisions, and inequalities exist. Howard (2019) notes that time and money are needed to bridge such gaps and inequalities, especially when one school setting include some students who represent diversity in their backgrounds, languages, learning readiness, learning styles, needs, and interests. Students without equal access to AI can feel disadvantaged in the classroom (Hariharan, 2025). In addition, the significance of analyzing and regulating AI educational policies and implications relies in ensuring access equity of AI opportunities and challenges for students in diverse educational environments (Umoke et al., 2025).

More critically, integrating AI in classrooms can have major challenges because school leaders and teachers lack comprehensive professional development to consider effective AI tools planning and implementation (Chen et al., 2024). Such issues relate to ensuring data privacy and security, especially when personal data is required, as well as ensuring equitable accessibility to technology and AI for learners in various learning contexts and resources. Chiang et al. (2024) also emphasized how AI might negatively impact authentic interactions among peers and the teacher, which is required to enhance hands-on skills and emotional intelligence. Additionally, AI might not grant exposing learners to neutral anti-bias learning materials and resources which reduces the effectiveness of learning for diverse learners.

Since the target is providing equitable access and implications to learning from diverse backgrounds in any educational context, the difference between equity and equality should be highlighted. Espinoza (2007) and Buchholtz et al. (2021) define equity as justice and fairness when individual needs and differences are considered, which provides equal chances for students in educational settings. The term equity can be assessed quantitatively and qualitatively as it entails a fair distribution of resources and facilities to individuals. In contrast, equality is when students have the same support, opportunities, and resources, regardless of their individual differences and needs. In this sense, students' needs are considered equally and assessed quantitatively. The notion of a national curriculum represents the idea of equality when the emphasis is on equal educational attainment regardless of students' abilities, location, or diversity. Students must develop their potential and capabilities to exercise their rights in ways that emphasize social justice and seek equal results (Roche, 2013).

Burbules et al. (1982) noted that both equity and equality are not complementary to each other. If educators look for greater equity in a school, this may lead to reduced equality. For example, if resources are allocated equally to top-achieving students to enrich their performance, or low-achieving students to improve their level, this act might result in increased differences in their educational results. In this case, who should get more resources, the former or the latter, or rather, each group should receive different resources and support based on their needs and abilities. Applying equity in education is more needed than equality because students are not alike (Espinoza, 2007).

Culturally Responsive Pedagogy (CRP)

Culturally responsive pedagogy (CRP) is proposed as a framework to address gaps, divisions, and inequalities that exist among diverse students in their learning environments due to various factors (Allen et al., 2017). Ladson-Billings (2023) states that the culturally relevant pedagogy liberates teaching methods as its aim stands for equity when it comes to critical awareness, cultural ability, and academic achievement. Moreover, Cross (2005) urges teachers to be conscious, acknowledgeable, and well prepared to adequately teach students in diverse contexts. Teachers also need to be reflective of their teaching methods and curriculum to make sure it is free of bias or disorder in sociocultural concepts as that may make a group of students feel excluded. Ladson-Billings (2023) suggests incorporating CRP in teacher education programs, policies, and curriculum. As such, teachers need to be involved in continuous learning and reflection about themselves and others to map suitable teaching methods away from any personal and professional preferences. Teachers are eventually culturally responsive beings who are aware of knowledge and value being constructed without any prejudices (Ryan & Dixson, 2006).

Brown-Jeffy and Cooper (2011) and Hernandez (2022) recommend that teachers should be informed about appropriate education theories. This is because not all teachers receive proper education about teaching students in multicultural settings, in which teachers influence students' achievement and social development without any bias. At a given societal context, each class might include students representing the majority as well as minority groups. Unfortunately, minority students may be labelled or stereotyped, which affects their educational opportunities. Thus, CRP acts to ensure that students' achievement, critical awareness, and cultural competence are enhanced. This helps students improve academically and personally by incorporating culture into education. CRP not only addresses students' curriculum, but also guides teaching and management strategies, classroom atmosphere, relationships, assessment, and performance. When CRP is implemented properly, students become confident enough to come to the classroom with their prior knowledge and cultural experience without being intimidated (Harding-DeKam, 2014).

In addition, Gay (2018) highlights key considerations to be taken while implementing CRP. Teachers need to be aware of students' cultural backgrounds, knowledge, identities, and experiences. This will help teachers tailor their lessons and activities in a way that reflects students' diversity. This way, students feel more included and connected to the curriculum and enjoy learning experiences which enhance their academic, personal, and social development. In a CRP classroom, students are actively engaged in discussion and activities (Fahadah & Thomps, 2025). Students also demonstrate interest and motivation in learning that relate to their culture, which eventually improves their academic responsibility and personal interest in learning.

In practice, Aceves and Orosco (2014) propose several evidence-based CRP for culturally and linguistically diverse (CLD) learners which are: guided instruction, cooperative instruction, prompt feedback, and demonstration. Teachers can implement CRP differently to fill the academic and behavior gap in CLD classrooms (Hernandez & Burrows, 2021). For example, teachers can use teamwork, modifying tasks, introducing different topics, incorporating videos and reading, seminars, heterogenous and homogeneous groups, rating scales, writing, projects, discussion, and group work.

Equity Assessment Practices

Whenever the word 'equity' is mentioned in educational contexts, culturally relevant (or responsive) pedagogy dominates the scene, and the same applies to assessment. Hood et al. (2015) define culturally responsive evaluation (CRE) as a comprehensive framework that builds evaluation aspects on culture, in which context specific values and beliefs are considered. Concepts such as socially just assessment, culturally responsive assessment, and equity minded assessment can be interchangeably used for equity-centered assessment (Henning & Lundquist, 2022). Heiser et al. (2023) explain that equity-centered assessment "leverages the assessment process to foster equity, address issues of oppression and privilege, improve student learning, and reshape systems and structures influencing the environments in which students learn" (p. 7).

Hood et al. (2015) outline historical milestones and key characteristics of CRE from core literature organized in an extended table (see pp. 288-290). Heiser et al. (2023) also illustrate fundamental constructs that support collaborative actions and prioritize the lived experiences of marginalized students, such as the critical theory, social justice, and cultural responsiveness. To justify the need for CRE, Henning et al. (2023) explain that not all students start at the same point, so students' different abilities and backgrounds should be taken into consideration in order to get 'fair' assessment for everyone. Moreover, any assessment should ethically avoid any intentional harm, and at the same time, promote social equity and inclusion (Henning & Lundquist, 2022). Organizational policies also need to include students of various cultural backgrounds to ensure no harm in all assessment elements, and that should be a moral and practical imperative (Henning et al., 2023).

In addition, CRE can highlight implications of cultural contexts in evaluation; that is, "rather than simply serving as a lens or acknowledgment of the role of culture in evaluation, CRE comprised theoretical, conceptual, and political elements" (Henning & Lundquist, 2022, p. 186). Henning and Lundquist also move beyond theories of equity-centered assessment to practical implications to include determining outcomes, selecting methods, collecting data, analyzing data, and using and sharing results. Furthermore, there is a lack of awareness towards equity-centered assessment among teachers and educators while assessment can be used to advance equity (Henning & Lundquist, 2022). On the contrary, traditional summative tests can be barriers to equity practices because they reinforce standardized testing and report collective data (Henning et al., 2023). To overcome assessment injustice, culturally responsive assessment and equity-centered practices that encourage student agency should be adopted by practitioners (Henning et al., 2023). Examples of AI evaluation tools include assessment and quiz generators, grading and feedback assistants, and adaptive platforms. Any suggestions recommend using rubric, keeping humans in control, and checking biases because AI creates output over stereotypes and common knowledge.

In a practical study, Scott et al. (2014) investigated ways to promote fairness and equity in student assessment practices, and they found five key principles. First, educators need to anticipate the impact of evaluation practices on their students. Second, differentiation is key to accommodate all students' differences, needs, abilities, linguistic and cultural backgrounds. Third, stakeholders should not be satisfied with traditional assessment practices that passively or negatively view minorities. Fourth, the intensity and frequency of assessment should not be overwhelming to students or their families. Finally, any assessment practice should not target reward or punishment to students from any cultural background.

Like all assessment types, multicultural assessment requires validation by practitioners. Hood et al. (2015) suggests a nine-stage framework for practitioners to implement. This framework starts with educators' self-reflection on their biases and awareness of their students' backgrounds, which also calls for stakeholders' meaningful involvement. Then, it is essential to identify the purpose of the evaluation, whether it is curriculum related or meant for social justice. Designing evaluation tools requires scrutinizing assessment of bias items as well as using the right questions, and that design should favor mixed methods that contain learners' differences. This framework also advises evaluators to follow cultural protocols during data collection and eventually share data in a student-friendly way to ensure utility (Hood et al., 2015).

Bridging Pedagogical and Assessment Practices

To maintain culturally responsive education, CRP and CRE should be properly aligned. This is essential because "the proper alignment between teaching and assessment in content and methods can provide learners with confidence and autonomy because they are assessed in the same way they practiced in class" (Mahmoud, 2024, p. 176). In addition, the 'missing link' between learning and testing was investigated in an experimental study by Alderson et al. (2017), and they found that assessment 'washback' emphasizes how a test can influence instruction. Alderson et al. also urge educational leaders, policy makers, and teachers to improve their literacy of assessment to properly bond it with pedagogy.

Aligning assessment to teaching and learning, by bridging CRP and CRE, can advance learners' achievement and enhance their autonomous skills to foster quality education. Quality education has a multifaceted nature, indicating that true learning is not linked to standardized tests, but it extends to include critical thinking, problem solving, and holistic personal growth (Chand, 2024). Achieving quality education prioritizes the improvement of practical life skills, and it calls stakeholders to promote inclusive and responsive educational frameworks as well as revise policies to remove items that marginalize minorities (Chand, 2024). In addition, AI can positively contribute to education because its advanced application can significantly advance teaching and learning (Al-Tarawneh et al., 2024).

Furthermore, Wiliam (2013) describes formative assessment practices as 'the bridge between teaching and learning' and the summative assessment as an 'autopsy'. Wiliam argues that students do not necessarily learn what teachers teach, so there is only one way to measure students' learning, that is assessment. To illustrate, assessment can be an effective way to align teaching and learning because it measures learners' knowledge at a certain time or stage. To Wiliam, any assessment can be formative considering three key learning concepts, "1. Where the learner is right now, 2. Where the learner needs to be [, and] 3. How to get there" (p. 16). Hence, it is essential to reside over key formative assessment strategies, such as learning intentions, eliciting evidence, giving feedback, students learning from one another, and students owning their learning (Wiliam, 2013). If students own their learning, they "would not mind making mistakes, because mistakes are evidence that the work they are doing is hard enough to make them smarter" (Wiliam, 2013, p. 19). Wiliam concludes that teachers' adaptation of instructions upon collected data, and what students get out of that, are what really matters to increase learners' engagement and achievement.

One way of advancing equity in assessment practices is using assessments that evaluate how students meet the course outcomes by considering both the process and product. Summative tests only focus on the correct answer (product) rather than the method or reason behind it. However, alternative assessment approaches that are mainly formative evaluate students on various aspects relevant to the process and product, which matches the suggestion of using mixed methods (quantitative and qualitative) tools and questions to assess students by Hood et al. (2015). This means that more students can meet the targeted outcome, but at different production levels, and here comes the importance of selecting comprehensive evaluation criteria. For instance, task-based learning and project-based learning are effective ways to include all students in the learning environment, and thus, evaluation should similarly be task-based.

On a relevant note, Bin Rashed and Mahmoud (2023, p. 382) argue that sustaining CRP is closely linked to social-emotional learning (SEL) aspects, and that "necessitates developing teachers' knowledge and skills to create an inclusive environment where diverse racial, ethnic, social, and linguistic backgrounds." The SEL framework consists of self-awareness, social awareness, self-management, relationship management, and responsible decision-making, which caters to the diversity among learners inside and outside the classroom (Neimi, 2020 as cited in Bin Rashed & Mahmoud, 2023). Based on that, considering SEL throughout pedagogical and evaluation processes, and while constructing assessment tools, involves learners more in their learning and advances their autonomy.

School Leadership Perceptions of Equity in Pedagogy and Assessment

School leaders' perceptions of education equity are formed by several attributes that are expressed differently because the mindset of equity is also influenced by personal, professional, and school contextual variables (Nadelson et al., 2020). Harding-DeKam (2014) argues that school leaders play a major role in promoting the school climate and the culture of equity by demonstrating data-based practices, collaboration, transformation, and advocacy. Such a school culture is required by the school leaders to embrace equity and demonstrate it through their actions and support to all students to achieve optimal competency. It is recommended that any teacher education program should equip teachers with knowledge on how to implement CRP effectively in any school setting.

When attempts to implement CRP at schools fail or become superficial, this could be due to the lack of alignment needed in the curriculum and instruction as well as the lack of support in policies and dispositions (Boutte, 2012). When CRP is effectively practiced at a school, it can enhance the values and performance of involved students, and this makes them feel more equitable and included (Fahadah & Thomps, 2025). These advantages become more evident when both the majority and minority students work on activities related to their cultures and identity. As a result, the gap between students from different groups would be reduced, and the focus would be on their academic progress rather than social or cultural aspects. Students eventually feel valued and appreciated, and this creates a more positive school atmosphere.

Villegas and Lucas (2007) state that there are challenges along with the CRP implementation. One of the challenges is that teachers are not well informed or prepared about the proper CRP either due to not receiving sufficient training, lack of resources, or even the school system that is not culturally supportive. In other cases, teachers may receive insufficient training or resources that support the CRE or assessment. Another challenge is that the school culture, curriculum, and policy should support CRP and CRE because a rigid curriculum requires a lot of central testing and learning outcomes, which may hinder implementing CRP.

AI and Equity Studies in the UAE

This study aims to explore equity practices from school leadership perspectives and find AI tools that can enhance cultural responsiveness within educational processes. Although some AI tools are criticized by being culturally biased, irrelevant, ignorant, and sometimes inappropriate (Chen et al., 2024; Chiang et al., 2024), culturally responsive features can be installed within educational AI tools. Algorithm bias, which is defined as "the production of undesirable and unfair results by AI applications in a typically systemic way" is found in AI tools, mainly because they "rely on social injustices that have already been established and that they have learned about during training" (Farheen et al., 2025, p. 70). Such biases are spotted through unfair interpretation of learning outcomes due to differences in race, gender, linguistic abilities, or socioeconomic status (Farheen et al., 2025).

Linking equity to AI-enhanced learning environments in UAE schools and higher education, Khurma et al. (2023) studied ChatGPT equity and governance issues to ensure ethical use, safe access, and positive learning to maximize AI benefits. One instructor explained that "all students should have an equal chance to gain important skills and knowledge that will enable them to lead fulfilling lives and make positive contributions to society, according to the principles of equity in education" (Khurma et al., 2023, p. 194). Along with benefits, they indicated multiple risks and drawbacks, and recommended fair and ethical use of AI tools, not to hinder students' learning. In this study, equity was not linked to culturally relevant pedagogy or evaluation.

In the UAE context, some studies linked the role of school principals to being updated about current issues that emerge in the educational field. For instance, Rai and Beresford-Dey (2025) focused on the important role of school leaders in forming an effective learning environment to serve learners from different backgrounds in the era of rapid technological changes. The researchers reviewed research focusing on school leadership in the UAE and noticed that the majority of research addresses aspects that relate to school reform, leaders' roles, competency, characteristics, and professional development. There is a need to explore the cultural, reasoning, and affective aspects of leadership. School leaders should be informed about updated reforms and practices to lead school effectively, especially when the diversity of students increases. In this respect, leaders need to be culturally relevant with knowledge and affection.

Furthermore, Hassanien et al. (2025) discussed the UAE efforts to bridge the digital divide results to ethical challenges in terms of equitable accessibility and responsible use of AI. This is done by following ethical guidelines, strategic plans, regulation frameworks, and strategic management for responsible and equitable AI implementation with accountability. For long term goals, the study recommended collaboration among sectors and education to regulate AI ethics by conducting continuous assessment to AI ethics, its policies, and interdisciplinary models. The UAE made additional attempts to establish AI ethical and inclusive educational system by incorporating smart initiatives, digital learning materials and reforms, and preparing teachers and learners for AI by building their capacity to address challenges of data security, bias of algorithm, inequity of AI accessibility among learners (Oloyede, 2025).

As seen from the previous review, the current topic is not properly investigated in the UAE context, or the Gulf region. Therefore, this paper aims to explore school leadership perceptions of equity pedagogical and assessment practices in AI-enhanced learning environments in the UAE context. This study will address the following research questions:

1. What are the school principals' perceptions on AI-enhanced learning environments for equity pedagogical practices?
2. In what ways can AI applications bridge equity pedagogical and assessment practices from school leadership perceptions?

METHODOLOGY

Contextual Background

It is essential to have a look at the context of the United Arab Emirates (UAE) where the study was conducted. The UAE is described as multicultural because residents from various nationalities outnumber Emiratis. On the contrary, the population of public schools include a majority of local students (80-85%), and the rest are from other nationalities, usually from Arab countries. This description varies in other school systems, such as private and international schools. According to the Ministry of Education (MOE) the total number of enrolled students this year at public schools in the Emirate of Abu Dhabi is 1,161,169; about 1,159,849 are local UAE students distributed over Abu Dhabi city, Al Ain city, and Al Dhafra area (MOE, 2026).

Along with technology advancement, AI has become increasingly implemented by the MOE, school principals, and teachers due to its benefits in tailoring learning to the needs, abilities, learning styles, and interests of diverse learners. For instance, the MOE has recently circulated a policy on the responsible and safe use of generative artificial intelligence in classrooms to regulate teachers and students use of AI in activities, assignments, tests, etc. There are numerous training workshops and programs to empower education staff with artificial intelligence technologies. These topics include becoming certified AI trainers, nomination to form teams of AI leadership and teachers, assigning purposeful AI, AI and cybersecurity community workshop between challenges and opportunities, initiative of a million talent to empower a million teacher in AI to shape the future of learning, practical skills to use AI tools, AI for the community, AI in education, understanding AI effects on individuals and society. These workshops are part of the efforts the MOE provides for its staff and students to prepare them to meaningfully include AI, make them more AI knowledgeable, and create confident users.

Research Design and Procedure

This study implemented a qualitative case study design. The case study design suits exploring a real-life issue, and semi-structured interviews allow participants to represent their contexts (Creswell & Poth, 2018). In this research, the case study is needed to investigate pedagogical and assessment equity practices from principals' perspectives along with the emergence of AI in educational practices.

A semi-structured interview was used as an instrument for this study. The instrument was constructed, refined, and validated by two experts before piloting it. The included interview questions were inspired by the reviewed literature to illustrate the concepts investigated. These questions aim at exploring principals' knowledge regarding equity practices as well as AI opportunities in advancing them, their perceptions, practices, the support they receive from the Ministry of Education (MOE), challenges, and suggestions towards a more inclusive educational future. The nine questions were also translated to Arabic to allow principals who prefer Arabic as their first language to freely elaborate on their ideas and views. The interviewed sample in this paper is considered the pilot sample, after which the tool will be further improved and validated to be used on a wider scale and different school systems.

Participants

To have better insights on the above-mentioned issues, two school principals were interviewed. The interviews were virtually conducted in January 2026 in Al Ain city, Abu Dhabi Emirate, the capital of the UAE. Each interview lasted about 30 minutes. One researcher (and author) interviewed the first principal in English and the second one in Arabic upon their preference. The findings of these interviews helped to shed light on the current situation and issues within one context.

The first principal, Sara (pseudonym), is from the United States of America. First, she worked as a teacher in the USA for about 9 years. When she moved to the UAE, she worked initially as a classroom teacher, then as a head of faculty, a vice principal, and now she has been working as an acting principal for the last five years. Her professional background includes working in culturally and linguistically diverse school environments, particularly within bilingual contexts where Arabic is the first language for most students and English is the second language (ESL) of instruction.

The second principal, Reem (pseudonym), is from the United Arab Emirates. In the beginning of her career, she worked as an Arabic Language kindergarten teacher for about 10 years. Then, she was promoted to be a head of faculty and a vice principal afterwards. She has been working as an acting principal for the last four years. Similarly, Reem works in a bilingual context with Arabic speaking students using English as the instruction language at school.

Data Analysis

Data is planned to be analyzed thematically when collected from the larger sample. Thematic analysis will be guided by Bernard et al. (2017) and follow Creswell and Poth's (2018) stages, which include initial analysis, coding of data, and generating themes. Those themes will be constructed through observation techniques, locating repetitions, similarities and differences, selecting experts that support themes, and linking those themes to theoretical models and concepts (Bernard et al., 2017). However, the small piloting sample in this paper did not allow for a clear thematic analysis, but the initial stages were conducted. The available results gave us a glimpse of what to expect from the larger sample. Below are the responses organized by question in the results section. After that, key takeaways are briefly discussed to highlight the case of two principals' perception in Al Ain city, Abu Dhabi Emirate.

RESULTS

This section summarizes the results of each question collected from both interviewees. The Arabic responses provided by the second participant were translated to English.

The principals were first asked if they knew about culturally relevant/responsive pedagogy and culturally relevant evaluation. Both principals confirmed having knowledge about both CRP and CRE. For example, Sara learned about CRP from a course and said, "Culturally responsive pedagogy refers to teaching approaches that recognize students' cultural identities, linguistic backgrounds, and their life experiences as a central resource for their learning." Sare described culturally responsive evaluation as it "focuses on designing assessment practices that are equitable, inclusive, and sensitive to the diversity of the students they are assessing." Reem added alternative assessment and evaluation methods to CRE explaining, "giving students fair opportunities to demonstrate what they have learned in multiple ways such as projects, portfolios, oral work, or hands-on activities, rather than relying solely on traditional quizzes."

Moving to the second question, the principals were asked about describing cultural diversity within their school contexts. Sara said that "Most students are locals; most are native Arabic speakers learning in a bilingual environment where English is the primary language of instruction in several core subjects". She specified that the culture should be deeply associated with values and identities within each family rather than a general description of Emirati culture for all students. Reem described her school context as less diverse in terms of students' backgrounds and nationalities. She emphasized the linguistic diversity according to students' abilities of ESL and family communication and support.

The third question was 'How do you perceive culturally responsive teaching in relation to AI-enhanced learning environments?' Both principals showed potential in the meaningful use of AI because it can facilitate learning, adjust reading levels, and bridge linguistic gaps, in particular. However, AI implementation was conditioned by "teachers' awareness and their effective role in assisting students and promoting their learning [Reem]" and only "IF done well and with intentional planning and design [Sara]".

The fourth question was about describing the support the principal and her teachers received from the MOE to include AI in teaching students from diverse cultures. Sara said that the MOE has already provided teachers with "strategic direction and encouragement for digital transformation and the integration of AI in education. This includes policy guidance, digital platforms, and professional development initiatives aimed at enhancing teachers' technological competencies." She noted that the training her staff received lacks in-depth orientation or meaningful and subject-relevant focus. On the other hand, Reem commended the MOE efforts in training teachers and gave an example of a "specific training via Jahiz platform to learn how to effectively integrate AI into lessons and apply it with students from different backgrounds."

The fifth question was on the support the school leadership provides for teachers and students to accommodate AI instruction and make the school culturally responsive. Both principals said that they support their teachers through professional development (PD) sessions on differentiated instructions, effective and reflective AI implementation, and intentional planning. Reem encourages teachers to "share successful practices, and supports projects, activities, and events that allow students to express their learning in a creative way." Sara also "encourages action research and collaborative inquiry, so that teachers can critically examine how AI influences student learning and equity."

The sixth question moved to evaluation inquiring whether the teachers at the participant's school are prepared (with knowledge, orientation, and training) to implement equity assessment practices, or not. Sara gave a direct answer, "Honestly, no. I don't think they are prepared for this. They are very good at following instructions but want explicit steps to follow. They are less likely to recognize the need for equity aside from SEN IEPs [special educational needs; individual educational plans]." Reem, on the other hand, said that teachers use "a variety of assessment strategies, including cross-portfolio assessment like PBLA [project-based learning and assessment], formative assessments, projects, quizzes, and classroom feedback." Reem also illustrated that "all assessments are monitored and reviewed by the school leadership team to ensure consistency, fairness, and alignment with learning objectives. She finally added that "some teachers need ongoing support and examples of best practices to apply them consistently across all grades," which echoes Sara's response.

The seventh question was about issues, challenges, or barriers that principals encounter when implementing AI in both instruction and evaluation. Sara highlighted structural constraints like "curriculum demands, time limitations, miscommunication between curriculum and assessment departments" as well as ethical and technical concerns in terms of "data privacy, algorithm bias, and unequal access to digital resources." However, the main issue that Sara brought to attention is "the mindset of how to align AI use with pedagogical principles of equity and cultural responsiveness." Reem added an additional challenge that hinders the proper implementation of AI in instruction and evaluation, that is "when AI does not consider the cultural and linguistic context of learners, this require teachers to decide whenever AI should be used in the classroom."

The eight question was about if principals think using AI can help bridge educational gaps and align equity teaching and assessment practices. Sara believed that it could be possible, but certain conditions must be followed critically and intentionally. Reem also agreed that AI can bridge educational gaps and align equity in pedagogical and assessment practices if it is properly used. Reem provided examples of how students get additional support and instant feedback based on their levels as she urges teachers to be present to ensure students do not completely rely on AI.

The last question asked interviewees to give recommendations for better AI implementation to support CRP and CRE in the future. Reem suggested "hands-on training for teachers on the use of AI tools via *Jahiz* platform" among useful practices that echoed Sara's suggestions. Sara recommended policy makers to include "clear frameworks that explicitly connect AI integration with equity, cultural responsiveness and inclusive assessment practices." She added that schools should encourage "PLCs [professional learning communities] supported by action research and shared assessment frameworks" to create and maintain the intersection between CRP and CRE.

DISCUSSION

The findings of this study were used to address two research questions discussed in this section accordingly. Then, challenges and issues of implementing AI in CRP and CRE as well as solutions and recommendations are included.

The first research question (RQ1) is 'What are the school principals' perceptions on AI-enhanced learning environments for equity pedagogical practices?' In the present study, both principals generally believed that AI-enhanced learning environments have potential in promoting equity pedagogical practices. Sara and Reem assumed that culturally responsive pedagogy is linked to students' cultural identities, linguistic backgrounds, needs, and experiences as a central resource for their learning which are influenced by AI. This aligns with the study of Anchal (2025), which noted that AI plays a pivotal role in creating and tailoring learning for diverse students' needs, interests, aptitudes, and learning styles that eventually make them ready for technology-driven requirements and global market.

Sara indicated variations in school contexts as they can be very diverse or less diverse based on enrolled students. According to her, a family itself represents a unique culture at home since a culture is not only about heritage, but it is also about the values and identity of everyone in a family. In her school, most students are locals (and Arabic speakers) learning ESL. She considers herself and one Chinese teacher as exacts which makes the school context less diverse. Reem's response confirmed the less diversity of public schools; however, she considered diversity through students' English linguistic abilities, especially when students' exposure to English outside the school is limited, which could be due to the variation in family support, academic achievement, access to technology, and readiness to learn. Considering these facts adds extra pressure on the teachers to tailor lessons based on individual needs and to provide extra support to students. Similarly, Howard (2019) stated that diversity can be represented in students' backgrounds, languages, learning readiness, learning styles, needs, and interests. Murari and Parmar (2025) and Li (2023) findings support Reem's worries whether AI provides equitable access and implications for students from diverse needs and backgrounds or not.

In the same regard, both principals' responses revealed their advocacy to the meaningful use of AI. This is because of its unlimited benefits for both students and teachers. AI can support students from different academic levels, make learning enjoyable, tailor difficulty of learning contents to student's level, and bridge linguistic gaps, in particular. Many scholars described such advantages of using AI-enhanced learning environments to promote equity pedagogical practices (e.g., Li, 2023; Murari & Parmar, 2025; Xu, 2024). However, both principals raised attention to that AI systems are generally designed based on a dominant international culture, assumptions, and linguistic forms that lack neutrality and may not be suitable for the use of students in the Middle East. Thus, it is critical that teachers and administrators become aware of such issues, so they select and experiment with AI before using them with students to make sure they do not threaten equity, and that was similarly stated by Chen et al. (2024). Reem agreed that teachers should be conscious when it comes to understanding students' backgrounds and be responsible for assigning AI materials based on students' diverse needs. AI is a supplementary resource that does not replace teachers, which Reem insisted on conveying through her interview. Umoke et al. (2025) noted the importance of analyzing and regulating AI educational policies and implications to ensure equity in accessing AI opportunities and reduce challenges for students in diverse educational environments.

Fortunately, the school system supports the implementation of AI transformation and integration in the classroom in terms of policies and regulations to some extent. Sara commented that "policy guidance, digital platforms, and professional development initiatives aimed at enhancing teachers' technological competencies." Reem added that the MOE directed teachers on how to implement AI in the classroom with students from different proficiency levels of English to bridge the gap in their academic achievement and meet their needs. Reem's response supports Ladson-Billings' (2023) findings on providing equity though CRP implementation to bridge gaps in academic achievement along with cultural ability and critical awareness. However, Sara noticed that culturally responsive practices are not sufficiently linked to AI integration, saying that "It is still emerging. While there is growing emphasis on innovation and digital skills, explicit frameworks linking AI use with equity, cultural responsiveness, and inclusive assessment practices are less developed." In such settings, schools end up attempting to translate policy directions to cope with cultural and linguistic realities through contextually meaningful practices as well as avoid using AI tools that might cause harm to students' culture. Thus, Ladson-Billings (2023) suggested that CRP should be part of the education program of teachers, curriculum, and policies along with continuous professional development and reflection to be conscious about personal and professional prejudices. Eventually, teachers can become advocates of the proper CRP implementation in their classrooms as Ryan and Dixson (2006) aimed for.

The second research question (RQ2) is 'In what ways can AI applications bridge equity pedagogical and assessment practices from school leadership perceptions?'

The results show that both principals know what CRE means, but their teachers are not yet fully equipped with differentiated and culturally responsive assessment tools. Both principals showed willingness to adapt AI practices and support their teachers further than what the MOE provided to include cultural variations and ensure equity. This falls into leaders' roles in promoting the culture of equity and creating a school climate that uses data-based practices, collaboration, transformation, and advocacy (Harding-DeKam, 2014; Nadelson et al., 2020). Promoting CRE and CRP comes with responsible implementation of classroom practices, so teachers and school leaders should ensure learners' access to appropriate pedagogical tools, whether by using AI or not.

Although Reem noted that there are varieties of alternative assessment methods used, such as PBLA, she insisted on their need for specialized training, continuous support, and examples of successful CRE practices to have consistency of practices. Likewise, Wiliam (2013) posed that the use of formative assessment methods is a good way to bridge instruction and assessment. Hood et al. (2015) also noted that using qualitative methods to evaluate students rather than summative tests is a way to achieve CRE, which Reem described in relation to CRE practices at her school. Again, evaluating the process and product while assessing students can give more accurate data because learners' differences can be considered through different actions and stages. Sara also illustrated the potential of using AI in equity learning and assessment, but she argued that AI integration and culturally responsive practices applications could be still emerging because "there is growing emphasis on innovation and digital skills, explicit frameworks linking AI use with equity, cultural responsiveness, and inclusive assessment practices are less developed." Sara's comment calls educators to approach AI application with caution, so they should make themselves familiar with whatever options each platform offers before introducing it to students to reduce risk and maximize benefits.

In this regard, both participants showed awareness that CRP and CRE can be advanced through AI, and they located some challenges and recommendations as will be discussed later. This aligns with Chand's (2024) view of quality education that is inclusive and responsive, supports practical life skills, and prevents minorities from being marginalized. It is essential to note here that the Abu Dhabi Education and Knowledge department (ADEK) has a Cultural Policy that lists principals' duties in maintaining an equitable and safe cultural climate on the school level. Their overall, yet highly significant, role is to implement, document, and report school processes when and as needed. They also need to "ensure all resources and materials selected and/or developed at the school are age- and culturally appropriate," and "ensure the delivery of cultural consideration awareness induction and refresher training" (ADEK, 2026, p. 7).

Moreover, CRP was more emphasized by both principals when AI application was questioned, which validates their comments that AI is still developing, and teachers still need orientation, training, and monitoring to include meaningful equity practices. It was also noticed from both participants' responses that CRE was rather vague, and therefore, bridging CRP and CRE needs more attention. Pondering on that, the semi-structured interview tool will be improved upon this gap from the pilot sample. This means that AI-enhanced CRP and CRE should be designated separate sections, and another section for bridging both practices through AI. More emphasis will also be given to school policies regarding these issues in the UAE.

ISSUES AND CHALLENGES WITH AI APPLICATION FOR EQUITY

School principals discussed several issues that hinder AI application from enhancing CRP and CRE learning environments. Both participants described their public schools as less diverse than international and private schools because the majority of students are Emiratis (locals). One major issue both principals mentioned is the lack of meaningful and relevant training to properly implement AI to enhance CRP, which was similarly stated by Villegas and Lucas (2007). Sara asserted that AI requires proper "intentional planning and design" and recommended that teachers' professional development should be formative, structured, relevant, and individualized on how to use AI in culturally responsive ways to anticipate possible risks and benefits. Another issue is that AI resources and materials may lack neutrality as they are designed based on dominant international culture, and that might threaten equity practices. In this regard, there is a challenge for teachers to be critical and conscious about equity and diversity as Cross (2005) suggested to find neutral AI resources and contexts, which points to finding platforms closely related to Emirati, Arab, and Middle East students in the UAE context.

In addition, the results show that there are no developed AI frameworks that explicitly link AI to equity, cultural responsiveness, and inclusive assessment practices. This may lead teachers to experiment with AI and CRP in classrooms and respond to cultural and linguistic differences on their own. Doing so might have various benefits, but it does not necessarily grant effectiveness to students, especially if teachers do not get sufficient training, or they use random and risky tools. Likewise, Umoke et al. (2025) called for analyzing and regulating AI educational policies and implications to ensure equity in accessing leverage AI opportunities and challenges for diverse students. Ladson-Billings (2023) urged that CRP should be part of teachers' training programs, curriculum, and school policies. Besides, students might not have equal opportunities to access AI due to different factors like the lack of devices, family support, readiness, and academic levels. This can result in having students who benefit from AI, while others do not, and this adds extra pressure on teachers to further support students and tailor learning resources to match students' diverse needs. This also raises questions whether AI can provide equitable access and implications to bridge gaps, divisions, and inequalities that exist among diverse students (Li, 2023; Murari & Parmar, 2025). Hariharan (2025) noted that unequal access to AI can make students feel disadvantaged.

Regarding bridging equitable pedagogical and assessment practices, both principals did not specify CRE challenges and issues with aligning CRP and CRE. This could be because the participants do not have a clear conception about these specific processes. A more likely explanation is that teachers and school leadership teams are still experimenting with AI, which was indicated through the need for more relevant AI platforms and workshops. Tailored AI programs "should focus on the skills students need to work with AI now and in the future, such as critical thinking, evaluation and analysis, and really, how to ask good questions [Sara]." This way, AI can meaningfully participate in student development, which aligns with AI advantages stated by Lata (2024) and Xu (2024). As such, teachers should be well trained because "teachers lack the experience or confidence to extensively use AI [Reem]" which is a major barrier to meaningful and efficient implementation. Other overall challenges Reem included are the "over-reliance on smart tools, limited time for training and preparation, technical problems or unequal access to devices, and AI's lack of accurate understanding of the cultural or linguistic context." This leads educators to question the feasibility of using any AI tool, and whether it will add positively to their students, or instead, make them feel alienated. That's why AI should be carefully and authentically used by decision makers (Umoke et al., 2025) to avoid possible concerns and negative impact on teaching and other educational practices in the future (Barbu & Sbughea, 2024).

PRACTICAL IMPLICATIONS

The available findings include practical suggestions and recommendations to meaningfully include AI in CRP and CRE. Reem, for example, suggested having more practical workshops like *Jahiz* platform, "establishing clear guidelines for the ethical and safe use of technology, sharing successful examples from other grades, [and] using tools suitable for students with limited exposure to the English language." This was similarly suggested by Xu (2024) as AI encourages personalized learning and increases students' enthusiasm and motivation to learn. It was clear that Reem insisted on the importance of teachers' attendance to all issues through "balancing technology support with direct instruction from the teacher without replacing them and focusing on using AI to promote equitable learning and assessment, not as a substitute for human guidance." Therefore, it is essential to mentor teachers and students to use AI in ways that support their learning rather than replace their work. Through quality education (Chand, 2024) and SEL aspects (Bin Rashed & Mahmoud, 2023), equity practices that serve both pedagogy and assessment would be more sustained. Further, Sara outlined detailed guidelines to properly implement AI in education at policy makers level to clearly state relevant frameworks, at school level to conduct action research, at teachers' level to receive relevant training, and at the students' level to orient them on ethical and equitable educational practices. Likewise, fair and equitable assessment should be considered by all stakeholders (Henning & Lundquist, 2022; Henning et al., 2023). It is key to note that using AI was generally commended for CRP, CRE, and bridging both, which showed openness to adapting new approaches and technological tools in the UAE educational system. However, having clear policies and directions stated by the MOE and monitored through the school leadership remains pivotal in all means.

LIMITATIONS AND FUTURE RESEARCH DIRECTIONS

This study is not without limitations. First, it only included the results obtained from the pilot sample. Therefore, it should be further investigated and expanded to a larger sample, including different school systems, and at different locations. In addition, the instrument was designed for principals, yet surveying involved leadership, social workers, and supervisors to understand their perceptions can give triangulated data on current situations. Moreover, it is important to ask participants to share their experiences in managing training sessions, solving issues, making decisions, and facing implementation challenges through real examples. Future research can also include comparative studies to highlight differences between CRP and CRE practices in urban and rural areas, or between public schools and private schools, which have more diverse students. This can lead to important curricular recognition to get teachers and educators more involved in equity practices. Finally, document (and tools) analysis research can be conducted to check the efficiency of AI applications to guide school inclusion and cultural policy to be culturally responsive.

CONCLUSION

This study investigated school leaders' perceptions of using AI to enhance learning environments and embrace equity pedagogical and assessment practices. It used a qualitative case study and interviewed two participants for the piloting stage.

The results show that the MOE, school principals, and teachers are motivated to implement AI in the classroom to further enhance the learning environments. There are directions, guidelines, training, and professional development sessions provided by the MOE on practical AI implementation in the classroom. It was found that AI has the tendency to simplify learning and customize it based on learners' needs and academic levels to resonate long with learners. AI also has the potential to bridge educational gaps, learners' academic achievements, readiness, and competencies that could happen due to various factors. However, the school principals noticed that the PD sessions conducted by the MOE were less relevant to current needs, and they lack meaningful directions, which could be due to the continuous emergence of AI applications. More importantly, AI applications are not directly tailored to Arab learners in the UAE and the Gulf region, which highlights the risks of using tools that are not culturally responsive. This adds more responsibility to teachers to find suitable AI resources that are customized to their learners' needs, other than the effort, time, and cost this might require. The participants experienced various challenges of implementing AI mainly because teachers are not fully prepared for CRP and CRE. There is still no clear policy or framework for teachers on AI implementation to support CRP and CRE. In addition, there is a need to conduct further studies to make AI resources and contexts tailored for UAE students through pedagogy and evaluation. School principals and teachers should be culturally responsive educators with sufficient knowledge and skills to make CRP and CRE practices embedded in their classrooms. Overall, promoting equity requires responsible application of classroom practices, so educators have a collective responsibility for safe cultural inclusion by ensuring appropriate and equitable access to learning resources.

REFERENCES

Aceves, T. C., & Orosco, M. J. (2014). *Culturally responsive teaching*. University of Florida.

ADEK. (2026). Department of Education and Knowledge Webpage. Retrieved January 20, 2026, from https://www.adek.gov.ae/en/Education-System/Education-Policies/School-Policies

Al-Tarawneh, A. M., & AlOmoush, R. A. ul Islam, T., Janjua, J. I., Abbas, T., & Ihsan, A. (2024, December). Current Trends in Artificial Intelligence for Educational Advancements. I*n 2024 International Conference on Decision Aid Sciences and Applications* (DASA) (pp. 1-6). IEEE. DIO:DOI: 10.1109/DASA63652.2024.10836340

Alderson, J. C., Brunfaut, T., & Harding, L. (2017). Bridging assessment and learning: A view from second and foreign language assessment. *Assessment in Education: Principles, Policy & Practice*, *24*(3), 379–387. DOI: 10.1080/0969594X.2017.1331201

Allen, A., Hancock, S. D., Starker-Glass, T., & Lewis, C. W. (2017). Mapping culturally relevant pedagogy into teacher education programs: A critical framework. *Teachers College Record, 119*(1), 1-26. DIO: DOI:DOI: 10.1177/016146811711900107

Anchal, A. A. D. A. (2025). The Future of Commerce Education: Preparing Students for a Globalized, Technology-Driven Economy. *Innovative Journal for Advances in Education, Science. Commerce & Multidisciplinary Learning*, *1*(1), 49–59.

Barbu, C., & Sbughea, C. (2024). Artificial Intelligence in Education: Global Trends, Clusters, and Perspectives. *Economics and Applied Informatics*, (3), 265–274. DOI: 10.35219/eai15840409452

Bernard, H. R., Wutich, A., & Ryan, G. W. (2017). Analyzing qualitative data: Systematic approaches. *Sage (Atlanta, Ga.).*

Bin Rashed, F. M., & Mahmoud, E. Y. (2023). Transforming Teacher Professional Identity Through Social Emotional Learning: Two Narrative Case Studies. In Stephen, J. S., Kormpas, G., & Coombe, C. (Eds.), *Global Perspectives on Higher Education* (Vol. 11, pp. 381–393). Springer International Publishing., DOI: 10.1007/978-3-031-31646-3_25

Boutte, G. S. (2012). Urban schools: Challenges and possibilities for early childhood and elementary education. *Urban Education*, *47*(2), 515–550. DOI: 10.1177/0042085911429583

Brown-Jeffy, S., & Cooper, J. E. (2011). Toward a conceptual framework of culturally relevant pedagogy: An overview of conceptual and theoretical literature. *Teacher Education Quarterly, 38*(1), 65–84.

Buchholtz, N., Stuart, A., & Frones, T. S. (2021). Equity, equality and diversity—Putting educational justice in the Nordic model to a test. In *Equity, equality and diversity in the Nordic model of education* (pp. 13–41). Springer International Publishing.

Burbules, N. C., Lord, B. T., & Sherman, A. L. (1982). Equity, equal opportunity, and education. *Educational Evaluation and Policy Analysis, 4*(2), 169-187. DOI:-DOI: 10.3102/0162373700400

Chand, S. P. (2024). Bridging the gaps in quality education. *The Educational Review, USA, 8*(2), 202–210. DOI: 10.26855/er.2024.02.001

Chen, N. S., Smyrnova-Trybulska, E., Morze, N., Ślósarz, A., Glushkova, T., Przybyła-Kasperek, M., ... & Gubo, Š. (2024). Education in the era of AI, enhancing skills, challenges and perspectives–International context and national experience. *International Journal of Research in E-learning, 10*(2), 1-30. DOI: DOI: 10.31261/IJREL.2024.10.2.06

Chiang, Y. H. V., Chang, M., & Chen, N. S. (2024). Can generative AI help realize the shift from an outcome-oriented to a process-outcome-balanced educational practice?. *Educational Technology & Society, 27*(2), 347-385. DOI:DOI: 10.30191/ets.202404_27(2).tp04

Creswell, J. W., & Poth, C. N. (2018). *Qualitative inquiry and research design: Choosing among five approaches*. Sage publications.

Cross, B. E. (2005). New racism, reformed teacher education, and the same people oppression. *Educational studies, 38*(3), 263–274. DOI: 10.1207/s15326993es3803_6

Eslit, E. (2024). AI-Enhanced Language Learning: Bridging Cultures and Breaking Barriers. DOI:DOI: 10.20944/preprints202411.1866.v1

Espinoza, O. (2007). Solving the equity–equality conceptual dilemma: A new model for analysis of the educational process. *Educational Research, 49*(4), 343–363. DOI: 10.1080/00131880701717198

Fahadah, A., & Thomps, J. (2025). Exploring the Role of Culturally Responsive Pedagogy in Promoting Equity Across Diverse Educational Environments. *International Journal of Post Axial: Futuristic Teaching and Learning*, 97-108. DOI:DOI: 10.59944/postaxial.v3i2.445

Farheen, S., Cheema, A. A., Ullah, R. S., & Bandeali, M. M. (2025). Equity and bias in AI educational tools: A critical examination of algorithmic decision-making in classrooms. *The Critical Review of Social Sciences Studies*, *3*(3), 67–85.

Gay, G. (2018). *Culturally responsive teaching: Theory, research, and practice*. Teachers College Press.

Harding-DeKam, J. L. (2014). Defining culturally responsive teaching: The case of mathematics. *Cogent Education*, *1*(1), 972676. DOI: 10.1080/2331186X.2014.972676

Hariharan, A. (2025). Artificial Intelligence for Optimal Learning: A Comparative Approach towards AI-Enhanced Learning Environments. *Computers and Society*. DOI:/arXiv.2510.11755DOI: 10.48550

Hassanien, A. R. M., Patwa, N., Bagheri, N., & Tabash, M. I. (2025). Ethical Implications of Artificial Intelligence Accessibility in the United Arab Emirates: Bridging the Digital Divide. *International Review of Management and Marketing*, *15*(6), 22. DOI: 10.32479/irmm.20011

Heiser, C., Schnelle, T., & Tullier, S. (2023). Defining and operationalizing equity-centered assessment. *Journal of Student Affairs Inquiry, Improvement, and Impact*, *6*, 4–17. DOI: 10.18060/27921

Henning, G., & Lundquist, A. E. (2022). Using assessment to advance equity. *New Directions for Student Services*, *2022*(178-179), 185–194. DOI: 10.1002/ss.20439

Henning, G. W., Baker, G. R., Jankowski, N. A., Lundquist, A. E., & Montenegro, E. (Eds.). (2023). *Reframing assessment to center equity: Theories, models, and practices*. Taylor & Francis.

Hernandez, A. (2022). Closing the achievement gap in the classroom through culturally relevant pedagogy. *Journal of Education and Learning*, *11*(2), 1–21. DOI: 10.5539/jel.v11n2p1

Hernandez, A., & Burrows, K. (2021). Implementing culturally relevant teaching in the classroom. *Open Journal of Leadership*, *10*(4), 338-363. DOI: DOI: 10.4236/ojl.2021.104020

Hood, S., Hopson, R. K., & Kirkhart, K. E. (2015). Culturally responsive evaluation. *Handbook of practical program evaluation*, 281-317. DOI:DOI: 10.1002/9781119171386.ch12

Howard, T. C. (2019). *Why race and culture matter in schools: Closing the achievement gap in America's classrooms*. Teachers College Press., DOI: 10.31046/wabashcenter.v2i2.2916

Ladson-Billings, G. (2023). "Yes, but how do we do it?": Practicing culturally relevant pedagogy. In *White teachers/diverse classrooms* (pp. 33–46). Routledge.

Li, H. (2023). AI in education: Bridging the divide or widening the gap? Exploring equity, opportunities, and challenges in the digital age. *Advances in Education. Humanities and Social Science Research*, *8*(1), 355–355. DOI: 10.56028/aehssr.8.1.355.2023

Mahmoud, E. Y. (2024). *The Role of Task-Based Language Assessment in English Language Learning and Learner Autonomy Enhancement in an EFL High School Context in the UAE.* [Unpublished Doctoral Dissertation, United Arab Emirates University]. https://scholarworks.uaeu.ac.ae/all_dissertations/350/

MOE. (2026). United Arab Emirates Ministry of Education. Retrieved January 28, 2026, from https://moe.gov.ae/Ar/OpenData/Pages/Home.aspx

Murari, U. K., & Parmar, H. (2025). Ethical Integration of Artificial Intelligence in Inclusive Education: Addressing Challenges and Advancing Opportunities for Equitable Learning. In *Ethics and AI Integration into Modern Classrooms* (pp. 439-470). IGI Global Scientific Publishing. DOI: DOI: 10.4018/979-8-3373-2262-9.ch015

Nadelson, L. S., Albritton, S., Couture, V. G., Green, C., Loyless, S. D., & Shaw, E. O. (2020). Principals' Perceptions of Education Equity: A Mindset for Practice. *Journal of Education and Learning*, *9*(1), 1–15. DOI: 10.5539/jel.v9n1p1

Oloyede, J. (2025). Artificial Intelligence in Education: Building Ethical and Inclusive Smart Learning Ecosystems in the UAE. *Available at SSRN* 5405420. DOI: DOI: 10.2139/ssrn.5405420

Rai, J., & Beresford-Dey, M. (2025). School leadership in the United Arab Emirates: A scoping review. *Educational Management Administration & Leadership, 53*(6), 1335-1357. DOI: DOI: 10.1177/17411432231218129

Roche, S. (2013). Equity and equality in education. *International Review of Education, 59*(1), 1-5. DOI: DOI: 10.1007/s11159-013-9356-2

Ryan, C. L., & Dixson, A. D. (2006). Review of Research: Rethinking Pedagogy to Re-center Race: Some Reflections. *Language Arts*, *84*(2), 1–9. DOI: 10.58680/la20065624

Scott, S., Webber, C. F., Lupart, J. L., Aitken, N., & Scott, D. E. (2014). Fair and equitable assessment practices for all students. *Assessment in Education: Principles, Policy & Practice*, *21*(1), 52–70. DOI: 10.1080/0969594X.2013.776943

Sibanda, L. (2023). Strategies for achieving equity-based education: Towards an equitable education system. In *Social justice and culturally-affirming education in K-12 settings* (pp. 133–152). IGI Global., DOI: 10.4018/978-1-6684-6386-4.ch007

Umoke, C. C., & Nwangbo, S. O., & Onwe. (2025). O. A. AI-Driven Educational Policy Design: Enhancing Equity and Access through. *Intelligent Data Analysis*. Advance online publication. DOI: 10.56201/ijcsmt.v11.no3.2025.pg1.19

Villegas, A. M., & Lucas, T. (2007). The culturally responsive teacher. *Educational Leadership*, *64*(6), 28.

Wiliam, D. (2013). Assessment: The bridge between teaching and learning. *Voices from the Middle*, *21*(2), 15–20. DOI: 10.58680/vm201324461

Xu, Z. (2024). AI in education: Enhancing learning experiences and student outcomes. *Applied and Computational Engineering*, *51*(1), 104–111. DOI: 10.54254/2755-2721/51/20241187

KEY TERMS AND DEFINITIONS

AI-Enhanced Learning Environment: is an educational context that integrates and uses AI tools and applications in meaningful ways to optimize teaching and learning.

Culturally Responsive Evaluation (CRE): is a comprehensive framework that structures evaluation objectives and tools on culture, in which heritage, contextual, cultural values and beliefs, and students' backgrounds are considered.

Culturally Responsive Pedagogy (CRP): is a teaching method that is culturally oriented to incorporate students' cultures, identities, backgrounds and experiences into the learning process, contents, resources and activities to make diverse students' learning optimal, meaningful and relevant.

APPENDIX

Table 1. Abbreviations

AI	Artificial intelligence
ADEK	Abu Dhabi Education and Knowledge Department
CLD	Culturally and Linguistically Diverse
CRE	Culturally Responsive Evaluation
CRP	Culturally Responsive Pedagogy
ESL	English as a Second Language
IEP	Individual Educational Plan
MOE	Ministry of Education
PBLA	Project-Based Learning and Assessment
PD	Professional Development
PLC	Professional Learning Community
SEN	Special Educational Needs
UAE	United Arab Emirates

Chapter 5

AI and Data-Informed Leadership for Inclusive Decision-Making:

Leveraging Analytics to Bridge Equity Gaps in Educational Institutions

Mohammad A. Al Adwan
http://orcid.org/0000-0002-0989-9118
United Arab Emirates University, UAE

Maram Al Hassan
United Arab Emirates University, UAE

ABSTRACT

The chapter is considered as the exploration of the transformational opportunities of artificial intelligence (AI) and the application of information analytics in creating a culture supportive of educational leadership reiterates the need to establish inclusive and fair systems of decision making. The chapter outlines principles for data-driven leadership that can overcome a key shortcoming of AI tools: their frequent inability to identify underlying systemic biases that traditional methods also miss. It involves a step-by-step analysis of the questions related to the use of algorithms, ethical aspects of the manipulation of information, and confidentiality and thus emphasizes the importance of providing balancing between automation and human control in the field of educational administration. This current study presents

DOI: 10.4018/979-8-2600-0388-6.ch005

practical recommendations on the ethical implementation of AI, the improvement of professional abilities, and transparent data behavior through the synthesis of the internationally recognized paradigms with practical case studies.

1. INTRODUCTION

1.1 Contextual Background

This growing presence of the digital transformation in the educational sphere has entirely transformed the conceptualization of roles of leadership (Mamanazarov et al., 2025). Similarly, how a decision is made within the educational settings of both the secondary school sector and in institutions of higher learning. The integration of learning analytics, artificial intelligence (AI). However, data dashboard research have over the last two decades evolved through primitive record-keeping practices to modern operations of highly systematic entities identifying trends among students in terms of performance, predict future performances, and implement strategic changes (Bocchio, 2022). Modern education leaders now have the privilege to access very detailed data eco-systems to see not just measures of academic performance but equally indicators of student engagement, health, and socio-economic inequity (Luckin, 2018). The rich informational space provides the scaffold of designing the adaptive policies to benefit equity by enhancing access to high-quality education. However, digital transformation also introduces new responsibilities (Mutawa & Sruthi, 2025). This context sets the foundation for a deeper exploration of AI as both a tool and a challenge for inclusive educational leadership.

1.2 Problem Statement

Although the data systems experience rapid development efficiency and the popularity of AI advances in education, the presence of various inequalities persist in most educational systems (Amiri et al., 2025). However, in practice, it is biassed, just as the systems they are sourced out of are flawed. As an illustration, the underrepresentation of marginalized communities in the datasets can result in algorithmic models contributing to dispensation in a disadvantaged system unintentionally (Luckin, 2018). Equally, in the low-income or rural-based schools, there might be no technological infrastructure needed to utilize the AI application, and, therefore, lacking access to the digital insights that can help those areas (Ng & Ho, 2025). Furthermore, leaders struggle to balance AI's technical advantages with ethical concerns, particularly regarding student privacy, informed consent, and data transparency (Aithal et al., 2024). In the absence of adequate balances, the misuse or lack of adequate understanding of the AI-created insights may result in making decisions, which will only favor some groups of people against others. These and other issues paint a worrying situation about the lack of technological capacity and delivering it fairly.

1.3 Purpose and Rationale

The main purpose of this chapter is to discuss the opportunity to use the artificial intelligence and data-driven analytics to support ethical and inclusive decision-making processes by the educational leaders. Similarly, the process of AI classification in this exposition presents AI not only as a technological advancement but as a tool of governance that could help institutions learn the inequity and solve it (Amiri *et al.*, 2025). Based on theoretical models and case studies, this chapter argues that a method that combines the use of artificial intelligence with crucial human judgment, moral judgment, and situational analysis is justified (Ng & Ho, 2025; Aithal *et al.*, 2024). Based on this, the current trend of informational resources dependence in the modern educational system means that leadership practice will have to be changed to include digital literacy, ethics, and sensitivity towards cultural diversity.

1.4 Objectives of the Chapter

This chapter is guided by the following objectives:

1. To evaluate the impact of AI and data-informed leadership on equitable decision-making within educational institutions.
2. To identify and examine ethical and privacy-related risks associated with AI implementation in educational contexts.
3. To propose a conceptual framework for AI-driven inclusive leadership that balances technological efficiency with human-centered values and ethical principles.

2. BACKGROUND

The unequaled forces in the world and technological changes in the world are redefining the education landscape (Ayeni *et al.*, 2024). The traditional paradigm of educational leadership that is largely focused on managerial effectiveness and problem-solving in the local scale is no longer sufficient to cope with the complex needs of the twenty-first century (Aithal *et al.*, 2024). As a result, the new paradigm of future-ready leadership is developed, and that requires a flexible, strategically-minded, and systemically-companied leader. The key feature of this development is the incorporation of Artificial Intelligence (AI), which provides a revolutionary opportunity, as well as the essential levels of ethical challenges.

2.1 Defining AI in Educational Leadership

Artificial intelligence (AI) is fast becoming a foundation of modern educational change, transforming the data collection, analysis, and conversion into useful information (Ng & Ho, 2025). Although, first, AI has also performed well in conventional automation in the field of educational leadership, predictive and adaptive decision-making can be facilitated to promote organizational efficiency and social justice (Amiri *et al.*, 2025). Leaders can use the behavioral analytics dashboard, monitoring the trends of student interactions, and adaptive assessment tools, which adjust the instruction to a particular student profile, to analyze massive datasets more accurately than ever before, which can then be used to identify previously unnoticed factors that affect institutional equity and inclusion (Williamson *et al.,* 2023). On the other hand, traditional leadership models were mostly based on intuition or experience, or the presence of anecdotes (Aithal *et al.*, 2024). Conversely, data-informed decision-making (DIDM) puts into place an evidence-based culture of reflection, with leadership decisions becoming evidence-driven, based on evidence as opposed to predictions. AI extends this method by combining intricate academic, behavioral, and socio-economic factors into models that can convey the trends of exclusion or prejudice that will otherwise stay unacknowledged (Ayeni *et al.*, 2024).

Figure 1. Framework for AI-driven inclusive leadership

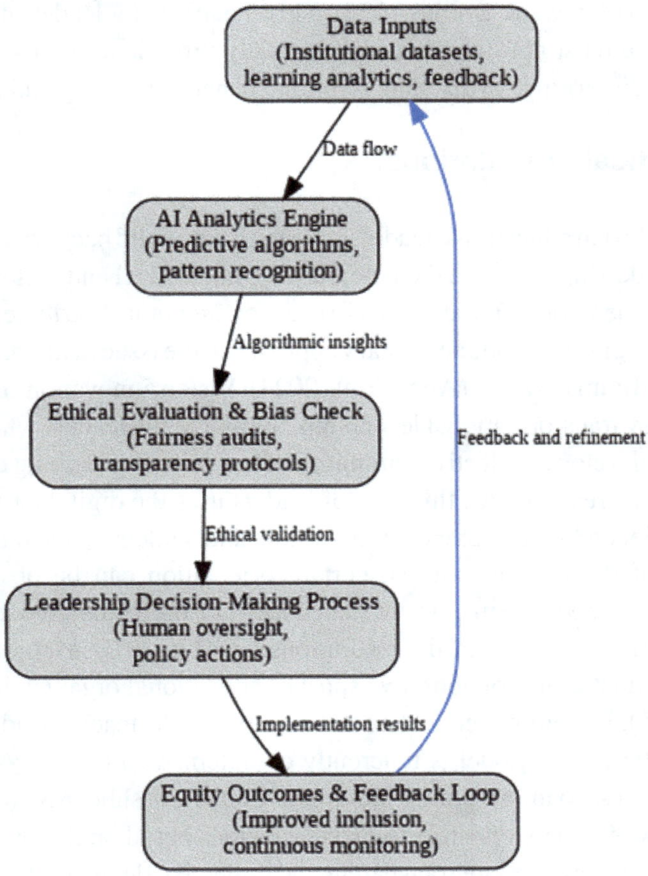

Figure 1 illustrates a model that can transform data into fair results using ethical AI filters and collaborative leadership to enhance fairness and unceasing improvement. The current section identifies the key constructs of future-ready leadership and AI in the education sector, challenges their theoretical foundations, and generalizes the current literature on the matter to place the game changer in the area of leadership preparation. As an example, the learning management and School Information Systems (SIS) currently combine both academic and demographic data to create insights that are predictive in relation to the support needs of students. AI-based analytics solutions are also used to streamline the process of resources distribution, teacher placement, and monitor the performance of students (Bocchio, 2022). However, AI does not replace leadership, it complements it. Effective AI implementation requires human control, situational consciousness and moral consideration. When educational leaders use AI in the decision-making process, they should consider its two-fold nature, the ability to democratize the use of data and the risk of increasing bias at the same time (Mutawa & Sruthi, 2025). This means that a leader in the artificial intelligence age must not only be technologically proficient but also morally and interpretively discerning, so that data is used to benefit humanity and not control it.

2.2 Theoretical Foundations

A review of AI in educational leadership must have a solid background of existing theories of leadership that have the potential to guide ethical and inclusive practice. There are four theoretical frames (transformational, servant, distributed, and ethical leadership) that give us a complementary approach to the issue of alignment between technology and human values (Aithal et al., 2024). Vision, innovation and motivation are predicted by transformational leadership, Similarly, the leaders who work under this paradigm develop a collective commitment to change by fostering creativity and flexibility. In the realm of AI, this type of leaders uses the digital tools not only to promote efficiency but also empower educators and students (Ayeni *et al.*, 2024).

In terms of the adoption of AI, certain orientation can be observed in the decision-making mechanisms, where the concern of the vulnerable learners takes preference over the comfort of the institutions. In its turn, Distributed Leadership is a representation of the collaborative spirit of educational organizations (Mutawa & Sruthi, 2025). It promotes collective action between the teachers, administration, and other parties. This model is inherently complemented by AI systems, which democratize access to information (Aithal e*t al.*, 2024); dashboards and shared data platforms allow a variety of actors to make decisions based on the shared evidence base and thus encourage more transparent and collective decisions (Luckin, 2018). The non-hierarchical nature of the distributed leadership process means the data-driven reforms are not forced down the pyramid but are instead co-constructed with the participation of the communities.

All AI implementation undertakings are anchored on Ethical Leadership (Mutawa & Sruthi, 2025). Ethical leaders are in support of fairness, transparency, and accountability, which are critical when dealing with algorithm systems that have the potential to have a direct impact on the lives of people. Ethical leaders can protect the risk of the existence of latent bias and obscure decision-making about AI-driven decisions by making them auditable and explainable (Mutawa & Sruthi, 2025). As a result, Data-Informed Decision-Making (DIDM) model provides a realistic model of combining these leadership theories (Ayeni *et al.*, 2024). The DIDM cycle consists of four repetitive steps, namely, data collection, data interpretation, action, and reflection. However, even advanced AI systems can be misleading without the human criticality and reflection (Boccio, 2022). In this regard, the DIDM model should be in harmony with a sound ethical background and professional judgment.

2.3 Literature Review (2020–2025)

Scholarship on artificial intelligence, educational leadership, and inclusion is becoming an increasingly popular topic, which suggests a greater sensitivity to the ethical implications of technology (Mutawa & Sruthi, 2025). The UNESCO (2023) AI Competency Framework of Educators highlights the necessity of developing technical skills and ethical literacy in teachers and leaders. It suggests that even the implementation of the Sustainable Development Goal 4 quality education to all can only be promoted by artificial intelligence, provided that the principles of transparency, fairness, and inclusiveness are implemented (Boccio, 2022). In line with this point of view, the OECD (2022) policy brief on artificial intelligence in school governance highlights that leaders are central to balancing information progress with values in humanities.

Empirical research has found out opportunities as well as risks of AI adoption (Williamson *et al.,* 2023). An example is predictive algorithms used in the admission of students or grading their performance, which were found to recreate social inequalities, especially where the algorithms were trained on unfair samples (Holmes *et al.*, 2022). These examples demonstrate the fact that there is need of algorithm transparency and periodic human auditing. On the contrary, effective applications represent how AI can be used to make decisions less biassed (Ng & Ho, 2025). The Ministry of Education in Singapore has introduced AI-based analytics to assist in personalization of learning journeys, which would inform Losers early and take necessary measures to maintain high-quality data protection.

Other projects like those launched in Finland link ethical AI systems to the national education strategy and, by doing this, would make sure that technological advances are in accordance with the concepts of inclusivity and civic responsibility (OECD, 2022). Although these developments have been made, there are still huge gaps. Most organizations lack explicit indicators to measure the effects of AI on the outcomes of inclusion (Mutawa & Sruthi, 2025). Also, code of ethics is often divided, and leadership education programs rarely include elements of AI literacy or data ethics (UNESCO, 2023). Furthermore, the existing literature focuses on the technological opportunities of AI, and not its social implications. Luckin (2021) and Williamson (2023) are among the scholars that suggest shifting to a new paradigm of critical AI literacy, where leaders and educators can fully understand the abilities and the limitations of algorithmic systems (Ifenthaler *et al.*, 2024; Williamson *et al.*, 2023). The literature reviewed makes it clear that there is one basic rule: AI can only become an impressive contributor to the fair decision-making process when it is guided by informed and ethically based leadership (Manda *et al.,* 2025).

The upcoming leadership paradigm shift, with the global issue and technological upheaval, introduces a set of complex dilemmas (Ifenthaler *et al.*, 2024). Although the previous section outlines the theoretical viability of a new leadership model, this chapter presents a critical analysis of the contentious matters, controversies, and possible challenges that can be encountered in the implementation process (Boccio, 2022). One of the main arguments consists of the fact that an imperfect preparatory system, institutional parochialism based on established managerial paradigms, and emergent ethical concerns presented by artificial intelligence all have contributed to the barrier to the achievement of adaptive, equity-based leadership (Ng & Ho, 2025). In addition, the chapter argues that, with AI becoming institutionalized, it is also able to both promise to combat educational inequities and present the risk of perpetrating causal patterns that continue to perpetuate inequality and discrimination by creating algorithmic bias and data governance failures (Ifenthaler *et al.*, 2024).

3. POINTS OF CONTENTION

3.1 Issues, Controversies, and Problems

The trend of developing future-ready leadership can be described as the confrontation of several contradictions that arise between the aspirational preparatory paradigms and the reality of practicalities.

3.1.1 Algorithmic Bias and Educational Inequality

Despite the constant promise of artificial intelligence as a neutral instrument, empirical studies show that the outputs of artificial intelligence are often in most cases a re-creation of existing social stratifications. The algorithms are trained on historical data that can contain hidden biases based on race, gender, disability or social economic status (Ng & Ho, 2025). Similarly, proxies used in the context of early-warning systems are often attendance, and in such a way, they may not consider contextual variables like socioeconomic hardships of a student or his multilingual status (Holmes *et al.*, 2019). Another complication can be explained by the fact that many AI decision-making is unclear. Many machine-learning models are more or less black boxes, which might not give much interpretability to decision-makers (Ifenthaler *et al.*, 2024).

3.1.2 Leadership Dilemmas

The spectrum of ethical and professional dilemmas in educational leaders who participated in the integration of artificial intelligence includes both extremes (van der Vlies, 2020). Although data-driven tools are also supposed to increase accuracy and responsibility, they can also be described as a source of danger to the retention of empathy, intuition, and contextual understanding (Ifenthaler *et al.*, 2024). Oversight of quantitative measures can simplify complex social phenomena to quantitative abstractions, and in the process, promote a management style in which technicality is prioritized over human-focused visions. In this respect, Holmes *et al.* (2022) states that analytic support is inadequate to make a decision; such interpretation must be supported with ethics. An example is that a low score of engagement does not always indicate that a student does not face outside adversities but instead, he or she may have an internal challenge (Wang et al., 2025).

As a result, this gap makes the institutions more dependent on vendors or technical specialists whose interests can be functional rather than the principles of equity and fairness (Ifenthaler *et al.*, 2024). Therefore, integrating the concept of ethical AI literacy into the management of leadership development programs is of utmost priority (Ifenthaler *et al.,* 2024).

3.1.3 Data Privacy and Governance

Van der Vlies, (2020) explored that academic institutions house some of the most sensitive information, which includes academic history, health and behavioral statistics and thus the reason behind the urgent need to establish effective governance systems. Even though the critical provisions are outlined in the international regulatory frameworks like the General Data Protection Regulation (GDPR) in Europe and the Children Online Privacy Protection Act (COPPA) in the United States, their application in the educational setting is unfair (OECD, 2022). Transparency enables the stakeholders to understand data collection, storage, and analysis processes. On the other hand, confidentiality can ensure that the individuals are not misused and illegally disclosed (Okada *et al.*, 2025).

This balancing between these imperatives is even more complex when AI devices constantly enlarge behavioral data through web-based applications or biosensors. UNESCO (2023) promotes privacy-by-design approach, which incorporates ethical protection directly into the structure of systems and, therefore, eliminates the necessity of retroactive changes. The implementation of such protocols is a critical mandate of educational leaders who are required to evaluate the compliance of vendors, obtain informed consent, and administer ethical impact assessment (Ifenthaler *et al.*, 2024). These vulnerabilities are further worsened by the digital divide experienced around the world, with schools struggling to meet their technical capacity. Similarly, it attracted to cost-effective or non-transparent AI offering not strong privacy-related features at risk of vulnerable groups (Mutawa & Sruthi, 2025). Inclusive leadership, therefore, requires active lobbying of data justice, which involves respect to digital rights on both sides of socio-economic lines with fairness.

3.1.4 Policy Fragmentation and Access Inequality

The adoption of artificial intelligence in education is performed unevenly in the world. Institutions that have advanced infrastructure and are very wealthy can easily integrate analytics in a smooth way (Ng & Ho, 2025; Mutawa & Sruthi, 2025). However, the case of schools that are not well resourced, in most cases they are left out of such developments. This disparity leads to the so-called AI elitism, whereby biased systems enjoy the fruits of predictive analytics and individualized learning, as the underprivileged systems fail to gain (Bulathwela *et al.,* 2024). In addition, there are significant differences in policy frameworks by region (Bocchio, 2022). Some nations, as the examples of Finland and Singapore, have developed holistic approaches that ensure that AI innovation is combined with moral concerns and fair distribution. Conversely, the other nation-states are characterized by the lack of coherent policy guidelines, which prompts the growth of the independent one-off initiatives, which are neither sustainable nor accountable. Disunified systems of governance mean duplicative work and lack of standardized data and minimal cross-institutional transfer of knowledge (Okada *et al.*, 2025). Therefore, equity-oriented leadership should go beyond institutions. However, a collaboration between ministries, universities, and private developers can promote harmonization of standards and promote open-source solutions to be available to the under-resourced setting (Ifenthaler *et al.,* 2024). Without this kind of systemic cooperation, artificial intelligence will end up contributing to educational inequalities instead of reducing them.

3.2 Case Studies and Comparative Analysis

3.2.1 Case 1: Singapore Ministry of Education (MOE) AI Integration

The education system in Singapore provides a good example of guided and ethics-oriented AI implementation (Gianni et al., 2022). The MOE has launched analytics systems that can create personalized learning profiles, which monitor student progress on different subjects (Okada *et al.*, 2025). Such data dashboard can help identify academic or emotional issues sooner in order to help implement specific interventions. The clear policy congruency between the government and innovation, as well as inclusion, serves as the example of how AI may be used in terms of efficiency and equity in case of clear governance (Al Mokdad, 2025). There are still obstacles, especially how to find the balance between high-stakes accountability and student autonomy (Holmes *et al.*, 2019). However, the example of Singapore shows that AI can be responsible in the framework of a consistent national vision with the focus on fairness, consent, and professional competence.

3.2.2 Case 2: United States District Predictive Models for Equity

Several U.S. school districts have adopted predictive analytics in order to detect students at risk of either academic failure or dropping out (Tanksley, 2023). These models are based on the attendance records, grade trends as well as behavioral indicators to cause early-warning interventions (Gianni et al., 2022). Theoretically, such systems make schools proactively distribute support (Eden *et al.*, 2024). Nonetheless, there has been controversy surrounding the issues of algorithmic bias and trust in the communities. Research showed that predictive risk models did not always adequately represent minority students as high-risk students in some cases because of the biased historical data (Holmes *et al.*, 2019). There was increased pressure on community advocacy groups to ensure more transparency and consent of the parents regarding the use of data (Gianni et al., 2022). However, reaction to this some districts have formed Data Ethics Review Boards, with Educationists, parents, and technologists. Such boards monitor design of algorithms and fairness metrics (Holmes *et al.*, 2019). The U.S. case reveals the significance of participatory governance and having an influencing force that will make AI adoption a matter of open discussion and not a top-down action.

3.2.3 Case 3: OECD and UNESCO Policy Frameworks

On a global scale, organizations like the OECD and UNESCO have provided recommendations according to which AI innovation is associated with human-centered values (Saha, 2025). The OECD (2022) framework puts three components of trustworthy AI as non-negotiable: transparency, accountability, and human oversight. In the same way, another UNESCO (2023) Recommendation on the Ethics of Artificial Intelligence that has been ratified by almost 200 countries promotes inclusivity, gender equality, and the rights of learners. However, it urges governments to come up with capacity-building programs that would train teachers and administrators to engage with AI not passively (Eden *et al.,* 2024). The overall implication of varying circumstances is that artificial intelligence can become a source of increased inclusivity; however, the achievement of these results depends on the nature and abilities of leadership (Tanksley, 2023).

The examples of empirical research of the integrated system in Singapore and the participatory bodies in the United States (Gianni *et al.,* 2022). Moreover, the policy coherence which the OECD advocates proves reliably that fair results are obtained with the help of conscious human management (Holmes *et al.*, 2019). On the other hand, a system with AI deployed without proper attention to cultural contexts and without consulting stakeholders is bound to continue to increase inequality (Okada *et al.*, 2025). Inclusive leadership, therefore, should be unified on three dimensions, which include technical literacy, ethical rationale, and socio-cultural sensitivity. These are the main components of the conceptual framework that is developed in the next part of this chapter.

4. SOLUTIONS AND RECOMMENDATIONS

On the other hand, the challenge of dealing with the complicated aspects of algorithmic bias, leadership dilemma, and the preparation-practice gap requires a holistic and proactive approach (DeGregory *et al.*, 2025). In addition, this section suggests a tangible list of solutions and recommendations focused on an extreme overhaul of the leadership education and the creation of a solid ethical framework that would govern the introduction of AI (Bocchio, 2022). The aim is to narrow the gap between theory and practice by empowering leaders with adaptive knowledge, moral strength, and long-term encouragement that can be necessary to traverse the complexities of the twenty-first century educational environment.

4.1 Framework for AI-Driven Inclusive Leadership

Considering the issues mentioned above, the part in question presents an ethically consistent artificial intelligence as an extension of, and not a replacement of human decision-making (Holmes *et al.*, 2019). The offered framework is supported by four operational principles transparency, accountability, human oversight, and fairness, and stipulates particular operational activities that the executive systems are expected to implement in order to bring the specified principles to life (Akinsola, 2025).

1. ***Transparency***: Educational applications of artificial intelligence need to reveal the logic and data provenance and decision-making parameters, which guide their predictive results. Open communication with teachers, parents, and students leads to trust-building and allows subjecting the results of algorithms to strong criticism (Holmes *et al.*, 2019). Administrators can also initiate AI Disclosure Statements summarizing the data collected, data processing procedures, and the retention periods.
2. **Accountability:** School administrators are encouraged to implement AI Ethics Charters, which outline the duties of the accuracy of data, its interpretation, and follow-up measures (Tanksley, 2023). With accountability chains in place, mistakes can easily be fixed without transferring responsibility to the vague system.
3. **Human Oversight:** Automated recommendations are always prone to professional judgement. Decision dashboards may also include a human verification

point whereby leadership approves the interventions before deploying data-based ones (Assumang et al., 2025).

4. **Fairness:** Before implementing, leaders should use Equity Impact Assessments (EIA) to test the algorithms against samples that represent the various gender, socioeconomic, and linguistic groups. Continuous fairness checks eliminate the possibility of bias that occurs over long term.

4.2 Data Equity Practices

The power of AI is anchored on the integrity and inclusivity of the information it is processing (Rehan, 2023). However, it is possible to establish data equity practices to ensure that technology benefits the learning community, as opposed to special groups. Inclusive data representation needs to include the diversity of student experiences, such as those learners with disabilities, refugees or language minorities (Okada *et al.,* 2025). The leaders are able to work with the local authorities in integrating demographic, behavioral, and contextual data and thus the leaders will create a more complex view of student well-being. Participatory data governance in which educational institutions can create Data Equity Councils. Similarly, teachers, parents, and students and discuss the data-collection policies and suggest improvements (Holmes *et al.,* 2019). This participatory model transforms data into property that is owned by the community and establishes the community representation in the analytics that affect them.

Guard-railed Open-Data Culture in which publication of anonymized knowledge (engagement patterns at schools' level) fosters cross-district learning and protects privacy (Okada *et al.,* 2025). Openness should be accompanied by strict anonymization and consent measures by leaders in line with the 2023 Recommendation on the Ethics of Artificial Intelligence offered by UNESCO. Similarly, adaptive system learning can be achieved by putting in place feedback schemes to allow educators to signal abnormal algorithmic performance (Okada *et al.*, 2025). There should be contracts between AI vendors to respond to such reports within specified timelines.

4.3 Capacity Building

On the one hand, it requires professional learning to produce leaders who can handle AI in a responsible manner (Tanksley, 2023). Capacity building is the redesign of curricula, nurturing the adaptive expertise, and sustaining cross-cultural competence. Leadership preparation curricula should also be completely redesigned to meet the challenges of the contemporary world (Okada *et al.*, 2025; Holmes *et al.*, 2019). Education should change the pedagogy to that of problem-based learning, and expose the future leaders to real-life scenarios, like algorithmic bias.

Besides, the implementation of AI simulation tools will enable trainees to analyze the implication of the data-driven decision-making process safely, thus, proactively developing ethical reflexivity that a responsible leader need (Okada *et al.*, 2025).

Leaders need to develop adaptive expertise to deal with the complexity and ambiguity of AI-based learning settings (Okada *et al.*, 2025). This is attained by applying an experiential learning model in addition to the technical problem solving (Mutawa & Sruthi, 2025). Design workshops help innovators to solve problems in an iterative, human-oriented way, whereas scenario-planning activities equip leaders with disruptive problem-solving. Thus, leadership laboratories or residencies located in varied environments, such as under-resourced schools to highly technological campuses, are necessary in expanding the scope of thought and essential to build the empathy that drives inclusive decision-making.

The use of cross-cultural and global competence in professional development paradigms is the perfect requirement of effective leadership in the digital age (Okada *et al.*, 2025). Considering the fact that it is impossible to introduce digital inclusion without cultural inclusion, capacity-building projects ought to be clear in creating global literacy (Holmes *et al.*, 2019).

The preliminary capacity-building activities do not enable ethical artificial-intelligence leadership in the long-term; instead, the development of supportive systems that need a robust sustaining support is necessary (Mutawa & Sruthi, 2025). The long-term professional community can help to overcome the issue of isolation and burnout among leaders by creating special mentorship teams that would unite novices with experienced experts around AI ethics (Lam, 2025). In addition, it supports Professional Learning Community (PLC) in which practitioners can collectively explore sustained equity challenges, and it provides action-research grants by which practitioners can be a critical and reflective change agent (Okada *et al.*, 2025). The idea of such grants is to enable the empirical evaluation of the inclusive AI practices in a single university and further the sharing of the research findings.

4.4 Governance and Accountability

The ethical principles of artificial intelligence need to be transformed into concrete, fair results in the educational systems; this should be done with the help of strong governance and accountability frameworks (Okada *et al.*, 2025). This should require a multi-layered solution, starting with institutional governance where each education authority creates a multidisciplinary AI Ethics Committee (Holmes *et al.*, 2019). The committee of administrators, data scientists, teachers, parents, and legal experts is a crucial inspection point since it reviews algorithms before purchasing them and regularly updates web effects and making the transparency report to maintain social trust (Mutawa & Sruthi, 2025).

Moreover, the key to community accountability is the provision of AI Literacy Dialogues. Where the parents and community members can be demystified about technology and change their positions as passive subjects to the active ones (Carolus *et al.*, 2023). However, it can offer feedback on the perceived risks, which will reinforce the democratic legitimacy of the digital transformation (Eden *et al.*, 2024). To formalize such initiatives, leaders should put in place stringent monitoring and evaluation systems where the indicators are measurable and quantifiable e.g. the achievement gaps are reduced (Tanksley, 2023). Thus, the heterogeneity of datasets and frequency of ethical audits, whose periodic publication not only strengthens accountability, but also develops a culture of learning and constant improvement at the sector level is also important factors. Table 1 illustrates a comparison between traditional and AI-driven inclusive leadership preparation models, focusing on key dimensions such as pedagogy, content, assessment methods, technology use, and global perspective.

Table 1. Comparing traditional and AI-driven inclusive leadership preparation models

Dimension	Traditional Model	AI-Driven Inclusive Model
Pedagogy	Lecture-based, theory heavy	Experiential, data-informed, problem-based learning
Content Focus	Managerial efficiency, policy compliance	Global systems, digital ethics, climate and social justice
Assessment	Exams and written reflections	Performance portfolios, simulations, and ethical audits
Learning Context	Localized, institution-specific	Cross-cultural, collaborative, globally networked
Leadership Skillset	Technical administration and supervision	Adaptive expertise, critical AI literacy, ethical reasoning
Stakeholder Engagement	Top-down communication	Co-creation with teachers, parents, and students
Equity Orientation	Reactive addressing issues post-occurrence	Proactive use predictive analytics to prevent inequities
Support Structures	Isolated mentoring programs	Continuous coaching, global peer learning, and PLC networks
Use of Technology	Treats technology as a peripheral administrative tool rather than leadership competency. Limited exposure to AI, analytics, or data visualization.	Integrates AI-enabled platforms, learning analytics dashboards, and decision-support systems to enhance evidence-based leadership and transparency in school governance (Tanksley, 2023).

continued on following page

Table 1. Continued

Dimension	Traditional Model	AI-Driven Inclusive Model
Ethical Framework	Ethical training is often theoretical and compliance-oriented, focusing on policy adherence rather than critical reflection.	Embeds ethical AI frameworks, emphasizing data justice, algorithmic fairness, and responsible innovation. Leaders engage in ethical scenario analysis and algorithm audits.
Support Structures	Professional development tends to be episodic, mentor-dependent, and limited to national boundaries. Peer collaboration is minimal.	Establishes continuous coaching, global peer-learning communities, and Professional Learning Communities (PLCs) dedicated to ongoing reflection on equity and AI ethics.
Global Perspective	Narrow focus on national or regional systems; lacks integration of international frameworks such as UNESCO or OECD guidelines.	Aligns leadership training with global educational frameworks (e.g., UNESCO AI Ethics Recommendation 2023, OECD AI in Education Policy Framework 2022) to ensure global relevance and transferability.

Source: Developed by the author based on synthesis of OECD (2022), UNESCO (2023)

4.5 Integrating Solutions into Policy and Practice

To implement these recommendations, educational systems should pursue a *phased implementation strategy:*

1. **Short-Term (1 year):** Conduct equity audits of existing data systems and train senior administrators in AI ethics and privacy law.
2. **Medium-Term (2–3 years):** Integrate ethical-AI modules into national leadership certification programs and establish Data Equity Councils at institutional levels.
3. **Long-Term (4–5 years):** Mandate transparent algorithmic reporting in national education policy and evaluate AI's impact on inclusion through longitudinal studies.

Sustained political commitment and funding are prerequisites for scaling these reforms. Partnerships with universities, technology companies, and civil-society organizations can pool expertise while maintaining public accountability (Holmes *et al.*, 2019). The pathway to inclusive, AI-driven educational leadership is not technological but human. Algorithms can process information faster, but leaders must still define what counts as fair, just, and meaningful within their contexts (Okada *et al.*, 2025).

FUTURE RESEARCH DIRECTIONS

The use of Artificial Intelligence (AI) in educational leadership is a new area of research, where the innovation is quick, and longitudinal data is scarce (Tanksley, 2023). The development of artificial intelligence as a simulator of leadership or reflective systems as seen in current studies of the generative application of artificial intelligence, including ChatGPT, Claude, or Gemini, is promising. These technologies have the potential to create simulation learning environments which determine the complex decision-making processes, hence giving potential leaders a chance to address decision making based on ethical reasoning, communication strategies, and crisis management, which are part of digitalized computer systems.

CONCLUSION

The chapter examined the role of Artificial Intelligence (AI) and data-based leadership in the potential to be an effective driver of equity, inclusion, and ethical change in education. This discussion has revealed that although the artificial intelligence field has enormous potential in taking the decision-making processes to the next level, the attainment of the benefits connected to it relies on the inclination of sound human values, awareness to the environment around them, and excellent leadership. Practitioners are recruited to go beyond interpreting dashboards or analytics; they are expected to ask questions of what is absent in their data sets, who is underrepresented and how recommendations generated by algorithms affect those students. The chapter also supports a paradigm shift in the perception of leadership preparation no longer as teaching compliance-oriented administrators but as instilling visionary, globally minded, leaders prepared to grapple with complexity and faced with a grey moral judgement. Such leaders should be adaptively knowledgeable, interculturally competent and digitally fluent in the process of balancing between innovation and justice. They, therefore, ought not to embrace artificial intelligence in the learning process because it cannot replace human judgement but it can give support. Similarly, the future of inclusive education depends on human-AI partnerships that embed empathy, justice, and transparency into every algorithmic process. Hence, the effectiveness of nascent cohort groups of leaders in present-day efforts at global notions of equity will depend on ethical data stewardship, compassionate leadership, and co-design of educational systems that represent authentic stewardship to all learners.

REFERENCES

Aithal, P. S., Prabhu, S., & Aithal, S. (2024). Future of higher education through technology prediction and forecasting. *Poornaprajna International Journal of Management, Education, and Social Science (PIJMESS), 1*(1), 01-50. https://papers.ssrn.com/sol3/Delivery.cfm?abstractid=4901474

Akinsola, K. (2025). Legal Compliance in Corporate Governance Frameworks: Best Practices for Ensuring Transparency, Accountability, and Risk Mitigation. *Accountability, and Risk Mitigation (January 31, 2025).*

Al Mokdad, A. (2025). Inclusive and Intelligent Governance: Enabling Sustainability Through Policy and Technology. In *Social System Reforms to Achieve Global Sustainability* (pp. 173-238). IGI Global Scientific Publishing. https://www.igi-global.com/chapter/inclusive-and-intelligent-governance/380524

Amiri, S. M. H., Islam, M. M., & Akter, N. (2025). Rethinking Education Policy: Pathways to Equitable and Future-Ready Learning. *SSRN, 5194153*, •••. https://papers.ssrn.com/sol3/Delivery.cfm?abstractid=5194153

Assumang, D. K., Umah, E., Vincent, M. M., Abolade, B. I., & Shasere, B. E. (2025). A Data-driven Dashboard Framework for Employee Mental Health and Organisational Decision-making. *Journal of Scientific Research and Reports, 31*(7), 979–1000. DOI: 10.9734/jsrr/2025/v31i73315

Ayeni, O., Eden, C., Ayeni, O. O., & Eden, C. A. (2024). Equity and access in higher education: Legal perspectives and management strategies. *International Journal of Science and Research Archive, 11*(2), 199–206. DOI: 10.30574/ijsra.2024.11.2.0391

Boccio, R. (2022). Race After Technology: Abolitionist Tools for the New Jim Code by Ruha Benjamin. *Configurations, 30*(2), 236–238. https://muse.jhu.edu/pub/1/article/853611/summary

Bulathwela, S., Pérez-Ortiz, M., Holloway, C., Cukurova, M., & Shawe-Taylor, J. (2024). Artificial intelligence alone will not democratise education: On educational inequality, techno-solutionism and inclusive tools. *Sustainability, 16*(2), 781. https://www.mdpi.com/2071-1050/16/2/781

Carolus, A., Augustin, Y., Markus, A., & Wienrich, C. (2023). Digital interaction literacy model–Conceptualizing competencies for literate interactions with voice-based AI systems. *Computers and Education: Artificial Intelligence, 4*, 100114. https://www.sciencedirect.com/science/article/pii/S2666920X22000698

DeGregory, C., LaCelle-Peterson, M., Lowenstein, K., & Schneider, S. (Eds.). (2025). *Locating Quality in the Dynamic Educator Preparation Landscape: Creating Quality in Context*. Stylus Publishing, LLC.

Eden, C. A., Chisom, O. N., & Adeniyi, I. S. (2024). Harnessing technology integration in education: Strategies for enhancing learning outcomes and equity. *World Journal of Advanced Engineering Technology and Sciences, 11*(2), 001-008. https://doi.org/DOI: 10.30574/wjaets.2024.11.2.0071

Holmes, W., Bialik, M., & Fadel, C. (2019). *Artificial intelligence in education promises and implications for teaching and learning*. Center for Curriculum Redesign. https://discovery.ucl.ac.uk/id/eprint/10139722/

Ifenthaler, D., Majumdar, R., Gorissen, P., Judge, M., Mishra, S., Raffaghelli, J., & Shimada, A. (2024). Artificial intelligence in education: Implications for policymakers, researchers, and practitioners. *Technology, Knowledge and Learning, 29*(4), 1693-1710. https://link.springer.com/content/pdf/10.1007/s10758-024-09747-0.pdf

Lam, Y. F. (2025). *From Isolation to Collaboration: Promoting Teacher Wellness Through Professional Learning Communities* (Doctoral dissertation, The University of Western Ontario). https://uwo.scholaris.ca/server/api/core/bitstreams/6125bfc3-217b-45c2-9e00-80568bfb454a/content

Luckin, R. (2018). *Machine Learning and Human Intelligence. The future of education for the 21st century*. UCL institute of education press. https://discovery.ucl.ac.uk/id/eprint/10178695/1/Machine%20Learning%20and%20Human%20Intelligence.pdf

Mamanazarov, S., Khajiyeva, M., Abdullaeva, D., Yuldasheva, G., Azkhodjaeva, R., Pirnazarov, A., & Xamedova, N. (2025). Innovating Human Capital Development: The Role of Education, Law, and Economics Through Digital Transformation. *Qubahan Academic Journal, 5*(3), 78-113. https://journal.qubahan.com/index.php/qaj/article/download/1698/426

Manda, V. K., Christy, V., & Jitta, M. R. (2025). Ethical AI and decision-making in management leadership. In *Ethical dimensions of AI development* (pp. 197–226). IGI Global., DOI: 10.4018/979-8-3693-4147-6.ch009

Mutawa, A. M., & Sruthi, S. (2025). UNESCO's AI Competency Framework: Challenges and Opportunities in Educational Settings. *Impacts of Generative AI on the Future of Research and Education*, 75-96. https://www.igi-global.com/chapter/unescos-ai-competency-framework/358768

Ng, S. L., & Ho, C. C. (2025). Generative ai in education: Mapping the research landscape through bibliometric analysis. *Information (Basel), 16*(8), 657.

Okada, A., Sherborne, T., Panselinas, G., & Kolionis, G. (2025). Fostering transversal skills through open schooling supported by the CARE-KNOW-DO pedagogical model and the UNESCO AI competencies framework. *International Journal of Artificial Intelligence in Education*, •••, 1–46. https://link.springer.com/content/pdf/10.1007/s40593-025-00458-w.pdf

Rehan, H. (2023). Shaping the future of education with cloud and AI technologies: Enhancing personalized learning and securing data integrity in the evolving edtech landscape. *Australian Journal of Machine Learning Research & Applications*, *3*(1), 359–395.

Saha, A. (2025). Human-centred innovation in Society 5.0. *Society 5.0: A Transformation towards Human-Centered. Artificial Intelligence*, •••, 143.

Tanksley, T. (2023). Employing an Abolitionist, Critical Race Pedagogy in CS: Centering the Voices, Experiences and Technological Innovations of Black Youth. *Journal of Computer Science Integration*, *6*(1), 9. https://digitalcommons.chapman.edu/cgi/viewcontent.cgi?article=1020&context=jcsi

van der Vlies, R. (2020). Digital strategies in education across OECD countries: Exploring education policies on digital technologies. *OECD Education Working Papers*, (226), 0_1-45. https://www.proquest.com/openview/e0a555e60c7bd27fbf409c465d41896a/1?pq-origsite=gscholar&cbl=54479

Wang, Y., Wu, H., & Wang, Y. (2025). Engagement and willingness to communicate in the L2 classroom: Identifying the latent profiles and their relationships with achievement emotions. *Journal of Multilingual and Multicultural Development*, *46*(8), 2175–2191. DOI: 10.1080/01434632.2024.2379534

Williamson, B., Komljenovic, J., & Gulson, K. (Eds.). (2023). *World yearbook of education 2024: digitalisation of education in the era of algorithms, automation and artificial intelligence*. Taylor & Francis. Gianni, R., Lehtinen, S., & Nieminen, M. (2022). Governance of responsible AI: From ethical guidelines to cooperative policies. *Frontiers of Computer Science*, *4*, 873437.

Chapter 6
Reframing School Leadership for Innovation, Technology, and Inclusion

Ayesha Mujeer
http://orcid.org/0009-0007-8629-4175
United Arab Emirates University, UAE

ABSTRACT

School leaders face rapid change. They manage the spread of artificial intelligence and digital technologies, climate-related disruption, and shifting enrolment linked to migration. At the same time, persistent gaps in access, participation, and outcomes remain. Many leadership approaches address innovation, technology, and equity as separate priorities, which fragments action. This chapter presents ITEQ Leadership—Innovation, Technology, and Equity—as a single, integrated playbook for school leaders. The chapter brings together equity-focused leadership, responsible technology use, and disciplined innovation so principals and leadership teams act with clarity. It is written for principals, deputy heads, and researchers working in diverse contexts, including low-resource, multilingual, and crisis-affected settings. The chapter translates research into leader competencies, an 18-month implementation roadmap, practical tools, and global vignettes. The aim is to support innovation that advances equity in ways that are measurable, sustainable, and grounded in community voice.

DOI: 10.4018/979-8-2600-0388-6.ch006

INTRODUCTION

School leadership now operates in a world where change is not occasional-it is routine. Principals and leadership teams manage new technologies and AI tools entering classrooms, rising expectations for digital learning, climate-related disruption, and shifting enrolment patterns linked to migration and displacement. At the same time, leaders remain accountable for closing gaps in access, participation, and outcomes for students who experience disadvantage due to disability, language, poverty, geography, race, gender, or migration status (UNESCO, 2020; UNESCO, 2019; UNICEF, 2021; World Bank, 2019). These pressures do not arrive one at a time. They overlap and amplify each other. A school that loses learning time because of extreme heat or flooding, for example, also faces higher risk of dropout, learning loss, and widening inequities-especially when families lack the resources to recover quickly (UNICEF, 2021). In this environment, leadership that treats innovation, technology, and equity as separate tracks creates confusion and slows action.

Many improvement efforts in schools still follow a split logic. One stream focuses on innovation and improvement: redesigning instruction, strengthening assessment, and building professional learning. Another stream focuses on technology: devices, platforms, data systems, cybersecurity, and AI. A third stream focuses on equity and inclusion: barriers to participation, cultural and linguistic responsiveness, disability access, and fair outcomes. Each stream offers useful tools, but schools rarely have the time, staffing, or expertise to run three major agendas in parallel. The result is often "initiative overload," with uneven implementation and limited impact (Bryk et al., 2015). Leaders need an integrated approach that recognises a basic reality: technology choices are equity choices, and equity goals require disciplined innovation.

Key Terms and Context

Co-design: Joint planning, testing, and refinement with those most affected (students, families, teachers, and inclusion staff).

Plan-Do-Study-Act (PDSA) cycle: A short improvement loop: plan a small change, do it, study evidence of impact, and act by adapting, scaling, or stopping.

Human-in-the-loop: People review and can override AI outputs before decisions are made; there is a clear route to question, appeal, and correct errors.

Equity and equality: In this chapter, equity means fairness tailored to need. Different learners may need different resources, time, or supports to reach high standards. Equality gives everyone the same input; equity gives each learner what they need to succeed. International reviews emphasise that systems which combine quality with equity achieve better outcomes overall and reduce the link between background and achievement (OECD, 2012; UNESCO, 2020). To track gaps, we refer to indicators such as learning poverty—the share of 10-year-olds unable to read and understand a simple text (World Bank, 2019).

Inclusion: Inclusion means full access, participation, and a sense of belonging for all learners—across disability, language, gender, migration, and socioeconomic status. We use *Universal Design for Learning* (UDL) as a design anchor: plan for learner variability from the start so fewer students need retrofitted accommodations (CAST, 2018). UDL highlights multiple ways to engage, represent content, and allow action and expression. In practice this means accessible materials, assistive technology where needed, and multilingual communication with families.

Innovation, technology, and leadership: Innovation refers to disciplined testing and improvement of ideas in real school settings. It is not novelty for its own sake; it is a structured way to learn what works, for whom, and under what conditions. Technology covers digital infrastructure, data systems, and classroom tools, including AI. When leadership and organisational work are mediated by information and communication technologies, we draw on the literature on e-leadership (Avolio, Kahai, & Dodge, 2000), which studies how digital tools shape influence and decision-making. Responsible use of technology in this chapter means accessibility by design, privacy and data protection, and checks for algorithmic bias.

Future-ready leadership: We use future-ready to describe leaders who can integrate equity, technology, and innovation in everyday routines. They organise improvement as a cycle: define the problem clearly, co-design solutions with those most affected, run small pilots, use evidence to adapt, then scale or stop. This draws on improvement science, which provides practical methods for disciplined inquiry and measurement (Bryk, Gomez, Grunow, & LeMahieu, 2015).

This chapter responds to that practical need by offering **ITEQ** (Innovation, Technology, Equity) Leadership, a single-leadership playbook that brings these three agendas together. ITEQ Leadership frames innovation as purposeful change that improves learning and well-being, technology as a tool that must be governed responsibly, and equity as the moral and practical compass that guides decisions about design, resources, and outcomes (Khalifa, 2018; Shields, 2017). The aim is not to add another initiative. The aim is to simplify decision-making so leadership teams can act with clarity, protect students' rights, and produce measurable improvement.

Why Integration Matters Now?

Three "global drivers" make integration urgent.

First, *inclusion* remains unfinished work. Despite decades of reform, many systems still exclude or marginalise learners through inaccessible environments, low expectations, biased discipline, weak language support, and uneven resourcing (UNESCO, 2020). Equity-focused leadership therefore requires more than goodwill. It requires leaders to identify patterns, confront structural barriers, and create conditions where every learner can participate meaningfully and succeed (Khalifa, 2018; Shields, 2017).

Second, *technology and AI* reshape schooling faster than governance keeps up. Digital tools can expand learning opportunities and support differentiation, but they also introduce risks: privacy breaches, surveillance, commercial exploitation, biased algorithms, inaccessible design, and widening digital divides. These risks affect students unevenly. Learners with disabilities, multilingual learners, and students from low-income households are often the first to experience harm when technology is adopted without accessibility standards, clear procurement rules, and strong data ethics (World Wide Web Consortium [W3C], 2024). Responsible technology leadership therefore requires leaders to ask not only "Does it work?" but also "For whom does it work, under what conditions, and at what cost?" (Anderson & Dexter, 2005).

Third, systems face disruption from climate and migration that directly affects *equity*. Climate hazards increasingly interrupt schooling and deepen vulnerability for children, particularly in low-resource settings (UNICEF, 2021). Migration and displacement also create rapid enrolment shifts and new language and trauma-related needs, requiring schools to build welcoming cultures and responsive learning supports rather than deficit narratives (UNESCO, 2019). In disrupted contexts, leaders need approaches that remain effective even when staffing, infrastructure, and budgets are constrained.

What ITEQ Leadership Draws From?

ITEQ Leadership builds on three-leadership knowledge bases.

1. *Equity-focused and transformative-leadership*

Equity-focused leadership centres fairness, inclusion, and social justice as core-leadership work rather than as "add-ons." It directs leaders to examine whose knowledge counts, whose needs are prioritised, and how school routines reproduce advantage or disadvantage (Khalifa, 2018; Shields, 2017). In this chapter, equity is treated as measurable and actionable: leaders define equity goals, remove participation barriers, and track progress using disaggregated indicators.

2. *Digital and technology leadership*

Technology leadership focuses on the conditions that allow technology to support learning: clear vision, staff capacity, reliable infrastructure, and effective governance. Empirical work shows that leadership is a key factor in whether technology investments translate into meaningful school improvement (Anderson & Dexter, 2005). In this chapter, digital leadership includes procurement and implementation discipline, accessibility, privacy protections, and data governance as core responsibilities.

3. *Adaptive and complexity-informed leadership*

School improvement rarely follows a straight line. Schools operate as complex systems, where small changes can produce unexpected effects. Complexity perspectives therefore emphasise experimentation, feedback loops, and learning-oriented leadership (Uhl-Bien et al., 2007). Adaptive-leadership also highlights that many challenges require changes in beliefs, habits, and relationships—not only technical fixes (Heifetz, 1994). In this chapter, those insights translate into a practical stance: leaders run short cycles, learn quickly, and scale only what works without harm.

Responsible AI and "Do No Harm" Safeguards

ITEQ Leadership treats responsible AI and responsible data use as non-negotiable. Schools increasingly encounter automated decision tools (for learning platforms, monitoring systems, translation tools, or analytics). These systems can introduce bias, obscure how decisions are made, and threaten privacy unless schools apply clear safeguards. This chapter aligns school-level governance with widely used public frameworks for trustworthy AI, including the OECD Recommendation on Artificial Intelligence (OECD, 2019), UNESCO's Recommendation on the Ethics of Artificial Intelligence (UNESCO, 2021), and the NIST AI Risk Management Framework (National Institute of Standards and Technology, 2023). The practical implication is straightforward: leaders build checks for transparency, fairness, privacy, security, and human oversight into procurement, implementation, and review. Accessibility is also treated as an equity baseline, guided by WCAG standards (World Wide Web Consortium, 2023).

Guiding Questions for the Chapter are Threefold

1. How can school leaders integrate innovation, technology, and equity into one decision model that fits real school routines?
2. What competencies make this integration visible in practice, and how can they be developed?
3. What step-by-step process enables schools to move from baseline diagnosis to pilots, evaluation, and scale within an 18-month window?

Purpose and Contribution of This Chapter

The purpose of this chapter is to help principals, deputy heads, and researchers move from fragmented advice to a single, usable model. The chapter closes a practical gap by offering:

- a clear ITEQ Leadership model that connects innovation, technology, and equity;
- leader competencies such as inclusive design, cultural and linguistic responsiveness, data ethics, responsible AI, and disciplined innovation;
- an 18-month action roadmap grounded in improvement cycles (Bryk et al., 2015);
- ready-to-use tools that support schools with limited research capacity, including an Equity and Tech Readiness Audit, an equity dashboard with disaggregated indicators, and decision rules for scaling or stopping initiatives.

LITERATURE REVIEW

This literature review brings together three research strands that are often discussed separately: (a) equity-focused leadership and inclusion, (b) digital leadership and technology governance, and (c) adaptive and complexity-informed leadership for change under uncertainty. It also includes research on improvement science and co-design, because integrated models require disciplined ways to test, learn, and scale practice. Together, these strands support the chapter's ITEQ Leadership model.

Table 1. Major knowledge domains that support ITEQ leadership (overview for practitioners)

Knowledge domain	What it contributes to ITEQ	Key sources
Equity-focused leadership	Sets equity aims; removes barriers; strengthens belonging and outcomes for priority learner groups.	Khalifa (2018); Shields (2017); Theoharis (2007)
Culturally relevant pedagogy and care	Supports cultural/linguistic responsiveness and relational safety.	Ladson-Billings (1995); Noddings (2013)
Digital leadership and edtech governance	Aligns tools to learning; builds capacity; manages procurement and support routines.	Anderson & Dexter (2005); ISTE (2018)
Accessibility and inclusive design	Plans for learner variability; reduces barriers in digital and non-digital materials.	CAST (2018); World Wide Web Consortium (2023)

continued on following page

Table 1. Continued

Knowledge domain	What it contributes to ITEQ	Key sources
Responsible AI and data ethics	Builds safeguards for privacy, fairness, transparency, and human oversight.	OECD (2019); UNESCO (2021); National Institute of Standards and Technology (2023)
Improvement science and implementation	Uses PDSA cycles, practical measures, and implementation supports to learn and sustain change.	Bryk et al. (2015); Durlak & DuPre (2008); Fixsen et al. (2005)

Equity-Focused Leadership for Inclusion and Justice

Equity-focused leadership positions fairness and inclusion as core-leadership work rather than an optional program. Transformative-leadership frames equity as both an ethical responsibility and a practical requirement for school improvement, especially in complex and uncertain conditions (Shields, 2017). Culturally responsive school leadership adds that equity requires leaders to honour community histories and cultural knowledge, challenge deficit narratives, and strengthen relationships with families and local communities as partners in learning (Khalifa, 2018). Social justice-leadership research shows that leaders who improve outcomes for marginalised students often change multiple parts of the school at once—culture, curriculum, pedagogy, and routines—and they also face resistance while doing so (Theoharis, 2007). This literature suggests that equity is not achieved through isolated interventions; it is built through consistent leadership decisions that remove barriers and expand participation across the whole school.

Inclusive-leadership literature complements this view by focusing on who participates in leadership and decision-making. Inclusive-leadership emphasises shared responsibility and practical structures that increase the voice and influence of teachers, students, and communities in school improvement (Ryan, 2007). A related synthesis of the principal's role in inclusive schools highlights three-leadership tasks: fostering new meanings about diversity, promoting inclusive cultures and instructional programs, and building relationships between schools and communities (Riehl, 2000). These tasks align with equity work in multilingual and high-mobility settings, where belonging, language access, and trust become essential conditions for learning.

A consistent message across equity-focused leadership research is that equity becomes achievable when leaders translate values into routines. This includes setting explicit inclusion goals, allocating time and resources to support learners who face barriers, strengthening staff learning on bias and culturally responsive practice, and using data carefully to identify gaps without blaming students or communities

(Khalifa, 2018; Shields, 2017; Theoharis, 2007). In this view, leadership is not only about vision; it is about the daily design of conditions that make equitable participation possible.

Digital Leadership and Technology Governance in Schools

Digital leadership research shows that technology does not improve learning automatically; leadership decisions shape whether technology investments become meaningful teaching and learning practices. School technology leadership is associated with the success of technology-related programs, because leaders influence vision, staff capacity, and implementation coherence (Anderson & Dexter, 2005). Standards-based frameworks also emphasise the leader's role in aligning technology use with equity, digital citizenship, professional learning, and continuous improvement (International Society for Technology in Education [ISTE], 2018). This work positions technology leadership as a system-level function: leaders coordinate infrastructure, teaching practice, professional learning, and governance rather than treating technology as a technical add-on.

At the same time, critical research on educational technology warns that digital tools can produce new forms of inequality when adoption outpaces safeguards. Technology adoption often amplifies existing gaps when learners have unequal access to devices, connectivity, assistive tools, or language supports (Selwyn, 2017). Research on datafication (the expansion of data collection and analytics in education) highlights risks such as surveillance, commercial influence, and decision-making that becomes driven by metrics rather than learning needs (Williamson, 2017). When schools adopt platforms that shape assessment, communication, and behaviour monitoring, governance choices affect whose privacy is protected, whose learning is valued, and whose identities become visible or vulnerable in data systems (Williamson & Eynon, 2020). This scholarship strengthens the case for integrating technology leadership with equity leadership rather than treating them as separate tracks.

Digital leadership research therefore supports a shift from "devices and tools" toward "technology governance." Governance includes procurement rules, privacy protections, cybersecurity basics, accessibility checks, and clarity about what data are collected, why they are collected, and who can access them. This perspective aligns with ITEQ Leadership because it treats technology decisions as educational and ethical decisions, not only operational ones.

Responsible AI, Data Ethics, and Accessibility as Equity Requirements

AI-enabled tools spread quickly, so school leaders need a small set of clear governance anchors. In this chapter, responsible AI and data governance align to the principles in the OECD AI Recommendation, UNESCO guidance, and the NIST AI Risk Management Framework (Organisation for Economic Co-operation and Development [OECD], 2019; UNESCO, 2021; National Institute of Standards and Technology, 2023). A practical requirement is human-in-the-loop decision-making: people review AI outputs, can override them, and can explain decisions, with a clear route to question, appeal, and correct errors (Baker & Hawn, 2022; UNESCO, 2021).

Accessibility is a foundational equity requirement, because technology becomes inequitable when learners cannot access content or demonstrate learning through multiple pathways. This chapter uses UDL and WCAG 2.2 as practical anchors for inclusive design in curriculum, assessment, and digital platforms (CAST, 2018; World Wide Web Consortium, 2023).

This strand of research also reframes data ethics as an equity issue. When schools collect data through learning platforms or behaviour systems, leaders need basic principles for data minimisation (collect only what is needed), purpose limitation (use data for clear learning goals), transparency (explain data use), and accountability (monitor risks and respond to concerns) (OECD, 2019; National Institute of Standards and Technology, 2023; UNESCO, 2021). Responsible AI and data ethics therefore operate as practical leadership competencies, not only technical concerns.

Adaptive and Complexity-Informed Leadership for Disruption and Change

Schools face conditions where technical solutions alone are insufficient. Adaptive-leadership describes challenges that require changes in beliefs, relationships, routines, and shared responsibility, not only new tools or policies (Heifetz, 1994). This is especially relevant for equity and inclusion, where progress often requires shifts in adult practice, expectations, and school culture. Complexity leadership theory adds that schools function as complex adaptive systems, where outcomes emerge through interactions among people, structures, and context (Uhl-Bien et al., 2007). In complex systems, leaders support learning and adaptation by enabling collaboration, experimentation, and feedback rather than relying only on top-down control.

This perspective supports two practical implications for ITEQ Leadership. First, leaders use short cycles of inquiry and improvement, because long-term planning without feedback often fails under changing conditions. Second, leaders distribute-leadership, because complex challenges exceed the capacity of any one person.

Distributed leadership frames leadership as stretched across formal and informal roles and enacted through interactions among people and routines (Spillane, 2006). This approach aligns with inclusive-leadership and equity goals, because it creates shared ownership and opens more pathways for student, teacher, and family voice in improvement work.

From Evidence to Action: Improvement Science and Co-Design

A central problem in school change is not a lack of ideas, but weak mechanisms for learning what works in context and for sustaining improvement. Improvement science addresses this problem by treating improvement as disciplined inquiry: leaders define a clear aim, use practical measures, test changes in short cycles (often through Plan-Do-Study-Act [PDSA] cycles), learn from variation, and adapt based on evidence (Bryk et al., 2015). This approach fits equity-focused work because disaggregated indicators make inequities visible and allow leaders to monitor whether changes benefit learners who face barriers. Improvement science also fits technology adoption because it supports piloting and evaluation before scaling. Co-design research strengthens implementation by positioning users-students, teachers, families, and community partners, as contributors to solution design. Co-creation literature describes a shift from designing "for" users to designing "with" users, especially when needs are diverse and solutions require local fit (Sanders & Stappers, 2008). In education, design-based implementation research (DBIR) extends this logic by focusing on innovations that are effective, sustainable, and scalable through partnerships between researchers and practitioners and attention to implementation conditions (Fishman et al., 2013; Penuel et al., 2011). Co-design and DBIR approaches align with equity goals because they elevate community voice and reduce the risk that well-intended innovations reproduce exclusion or mismatch local realities.

Overall, the literature supports an integrated leadership model that links equity aims with technology governance and disciplined innovation. Equity-focused leadership clarifies what fairness requires in routines and outcomes (Khalifa, 2018; Shields, 2017; Theoharis, 2007). Digital leadership clarifies the system conditions that make technology support learning rather than distraction or harm (Anderson & Dexter, 2005; ISTE, 2018). Accessibility and responsible AI frameworks clarify safeguards for inclusion, privacy, and accountability (CAST, 2018; Organisation for Economic Co-operation and Development [OECD], 2019; UNESCO, 2021; World Wide Web Consortium, 2023). Adaptive and complexity-informed leadership clarifies how leaders act under uncertainty through distributed capacity and learning loops (Heifetz, 1994; Spillane, 2006; Uhl-Bien et al., 2007). Improvement science and co-design provide practical methods to test, learn, and scale safely (Bryk et al.,

2015; Fishman et al., 2013; Penuel et al., 2011; Sanders & Stappers, 2008). Table 1 summarises these knowledge domains in a single view for practitioner use.

- Start with a named equity gap and track disaggregated indicators so improvement benefits priority learners.
- Treat technology as a governance decision: accessibility, privacy, interoperability, and bias risk are checked before adoption.
- Use short PDSA cycles with co-design so changes fit the local context and can be scaled safely.
- Build trust and distribute roles so improvement work remains realistic and sustainable.

THE ITEQ LEADERSHIP MODEL

Definition: ITEQ Leadership is defined as the coordinated leadership practice that integrates equity aims, responsible technology governance, and disciplined improvement methods to produce measurable and sustainable gains in access, participation, and outcomes. The framework includes three elements that operate together:

- Innovation: purposeful change that improves learning and well-being through disciplined cycles of testing and refinement (Bryk et al., 2015; Fullan, 2011).
- Technology: digital tools and data systems governed through accessibility, privacy, security, and implementation coherence (Anderson & Dexter, 2005; ISTE, 2018; Selwyn, 2017).
- Equity: the-leadership commitment to remove barriers, expand participation, and improve outcomes for learners who experience marginalisation (Khalifa, 2018; Shields, 2017).

Purpose: The model gives school leaders one clear way to bring these three strands together. Equity is the goal. Innovation is the method for learning what works. Technology is a means that must be used with care. The model is simple by design so principals and teams can use it in routine decisions.

Core principles:

1. "Equity first"- Fairness tailored to learner need. Plan for variability from the start using Universal Design for Learning (CAST, 2018).
2. "Evidence before scale"- Test ideas in small cycles and expand only when results for priority learner groups improve (Bryk, Gomez, Grunow, & LeMahieu, 2015).

3. “Community participation”- Students and families most affected help define problems and shape solutions.
4. “Digital safeguards”- Accessibility, privacy, and checks for algorithmic bias are built in, not added later (Baker & Hawn, 2022; World Wide Web Consortium, 2023).
5. “Context fit”- Decisions respect policy, finance, staffing, and local culture.

ITEQ LEADERSHIP MODEL

Figure 1. ITEQ leadership model

ITEQ domains:

- “Innovation”-Learn through disciplined change. Use short cycles to test ideas, reduce risk, and build will (Bryk et al., 2015).
- “Technology”-Build capacity in infrastructure, data use, and responsible AI. Leadership in digital contexts draws on e-leadership and school technology leadership (Avolio et al., 2000; Anderson & Dexter, 2005).
- “Equity”- Keep access, participation, opportunity to learn, and outcomes at the centre. Use disaggregated data to see who benefits and who is left out.

The Equity Lens: What "Equity" Requires in Practice

ITEQ treats equity as a measurable-leadership aim rather than a slogan. Equity-focused leadership emphasises that barriers often sit inside school routines and structures, not only inside learners. Leaders therefore examine how policy, pedagogy, assessment, discipline, language supports, and access to learning opportunities shape participation and outcomes (Khalifa, 2018; Shields, 2017). Culturally relevant pedagogy adds that equity includes valuing diverse cultural knowledge and reshaping learning so it connects meaningfully to students' identities and lived realities (Ladson-Billings, 1995). Ethics of care strengthens this point by positioning relationships, dignity, and responsiveness as central conditions for learning—especially for students who experience vulnerability (Noddings, 2013).

In ITEQ, equity is reflected through three "equity checks" that leaders apply repeatedly:

1. *Access*: Do learners have real access to learning opportunities, resources, and supports?
2. *Participation and belonging*: Do learners participate meaningfully and experience safety and belonging?
3. *Outcomes*: Do learning outcomes improve, and do gaps reduce when data are disaggregated?

A Six-Step Decision Cycle for Balanced Approach, Responsible Implementation, Inclusive Outcomes

The leaders should use this cycle for curriculum, assessment, scheduling, procurement, staff learning, and student support.

Step 1. *Diagnose the equity problem.*

Define a specific gap for a named group.

Example: "Multilingual learners have lower progression in Grade 6 science." Review access, experience, opportunity, and outcome indicators, disaggregated by group.

Step 2. *co-design responses.*

Plan with those most affected: students, families, teachers, inclusion staff. Combine practice knowledge with research.

Step 3. *Choose the minimum viable change.*

Select a small test with clear safeguards. For technology choices, check accessibility, privacy, interoperability, and potential bias. Use e-leadership criteria for roles and communication (Avolio et al., 2000; Anderson & Dexter, 2005; World Wide Web Consortium, 2023; Baker & Hawn, 2022).

Step 4. *Run the pilot and learn.*

Implement for four to eight weeks. Collect simple measures: reach, fidelity, early outcome signals, and user experience.

Step 5. *Decide to scale, adapt, or stop.*

Use plain rules:

- Scale if priority learners improved and no harm signals appeared.
- Adapt if results are mixed or access is uneven.
- Stop if results are negative or safeguards failed.

Step 6. *Codify and support.*

If scaling, write simple guidance, train staff, align timetable and budget, and include the change in school policy. Monitor with disaggregated indicators each term.

Figure 2. Six-step decision cycle for curriculum, assessment, scheduling, procurement, staff learning, and student support

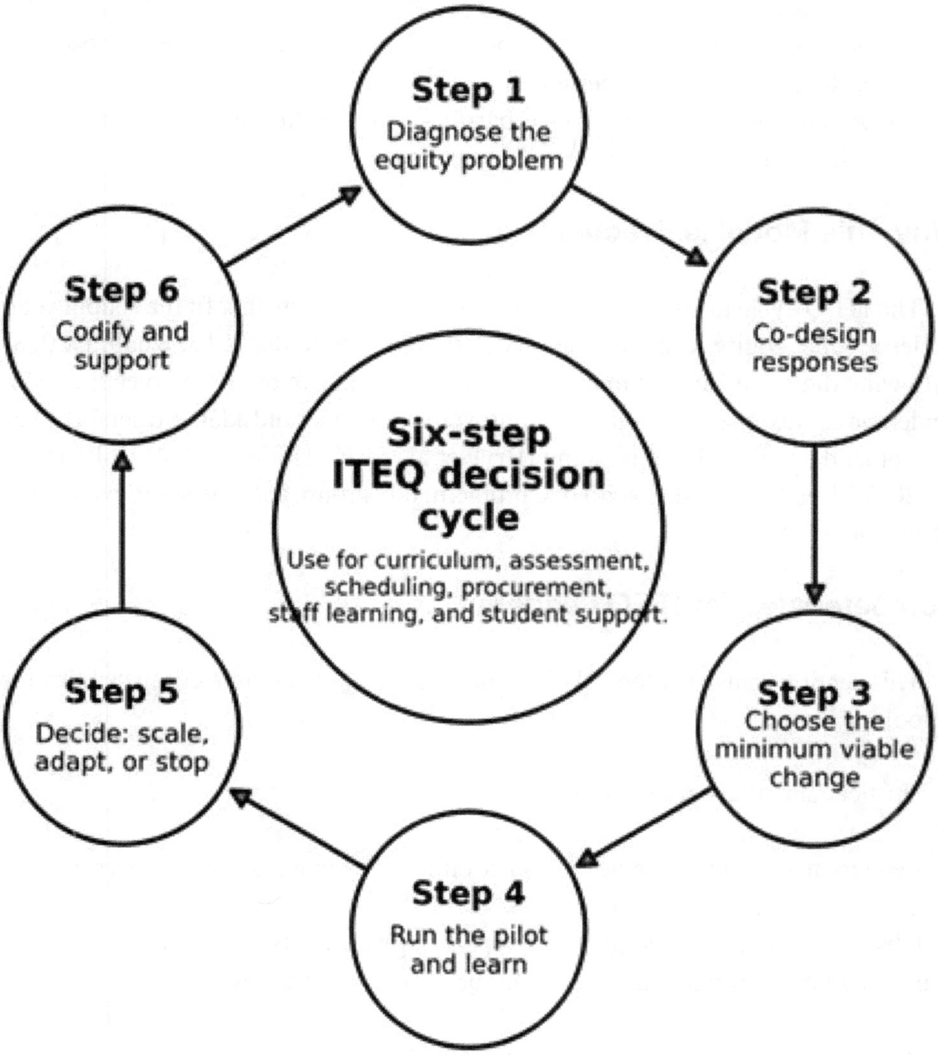

Role Clarity

- *Principal and senior team*: Set the equity aim, choose pilots, and protect time for cycles.
- *Inclusion lead*: Ensure UDL, accommodations, and language access are present in design and review.

- *Data and IT leads*: Manage data quality, privacy, interoperability, and bias checks; support staff with training (Anderson & Dexter, 2005; Baker & Hawn, 2022).
- *Teachers and student leaders*: co-design and run tests; share feedback on workload and learner experience.
- *Families and partners:* Surface barriers, validate fit, and advise on culture and language.

Why This Model is Practical

The ITEQ cycle turns broad ideas into steps and artifacts that fit the school year. It blends what equity leadership names as the goal (Shields, 2017; Khalifa, 2018) with what digital leadership requires for safe and effective use (Avolio et al., 2000; Anderson & Dexter, 2005) and what improvement science and adaptive perspectives recommend for disciplined learning (Bryk et al., 2015; Heifetz, 1994; Uhl-Bien et al., 2007). Leaders can start with one problem, one group, and one short cycle, then build from there.

Competencies for ITEQ Leaders

This section translates the ITEQ frame into clear, observable competencies for school leaders.

1) Justice and ethics orientation

Leaders make equity the goal and act on it. They name structural barriers and align resources to learner need.

Observable practices: Equity aims appear in plans; decisions consider who benefits and who is left out; staff use equity protocols in meetings.

2) Cultural and linguistic responsiveness and inclusion

Leaders honour community knowledge, languages, and identities and ensure participation in decisions.

Observable practices: Leaders co-design initiatives with students and families; interpretation at meetings; bias-aware discipline and admissions; accessible communication.

3) Data and evidence literacy

Leaders use evidence to learn, not to label. They build routines to define problems precisely, test change ideas, and study variation.

Observable practices: Clear problem statements; small tests with measures; regular reviews; attention to subgroup effects.

4) Responsible technology and AI

Leaders treat technology to widen access and improve decisions, while protecting rights.

Observable practices: Leaders establish checks for accessibility and assign clear roles for data stewardship; Practice human-in-the-loop decisions.

5) Inclusive design and UDL

Leaders plan for learner variability from the start. UDL guides curriculum, assessment, and technology choices so fewer supports need to be retrofitted (CAST, 2018).

6) Innovation discipline

Leaders help staff learn under uncertainty.

Observable practices: Time is protected for tests of change; decision rules are explicit; small wins are codified.

7) Systems navigation and partnerships

Leaders align policy, staffing, funding, and partnerships to sustain change.

Observable practices: Roles are shared; partnerships with health, social services, and community groups support targeted needs.

8) Wellbeing, trust, and crisis leadership

Leaders protect the conditions that make improvement possible: trust, psychological safety, and clear routines during disruption.

Observable practices: Presence of Staff forums; student support pathways; crisis playbooks for continuity of learning; reflection on workload and feasibility in every pilot.

METHOD FOR BUILDING THE MODEL

Overview

The chapter uses two complementary methods: an integrative literature review to map and synthesise what is known, and a design-science approach to specify and operationalise the ITEQ framework into usable components. Using both ensures conceptual breadth and practical specificity (Torraco, 2005, 2016; Hevner, March, Park, & Ram, 2004; Peffers, Tuunanen, Rothenberger, & Chatterjee, 2007).

Integrative Review

An integrative review allows inclusion of diverse evidence—theoretical papers, empirical studies, and credible practice reports—and aims to generate new frameworks rather than only summarise findings (Whittemore & Knafl, 2005; Torraco, 2005). We followed common guidance to ensure rigour:

1. Problem framing: clarify the gap—leadership guidance for innovation, technology, and equity remains siloed (Webster & Watson, 2002; Snyder, 2019).
2. Search and selection: scan peer-reviewed scholarship and major agency publications across six strands: equity-oriented leadership, culturally responsive-leadership, e-leadership/technology leadership, data use and privacy, improvement science/innovation, and inclusive design (UDL). We applied inclusion criteria that prioritised conceptual clarity, relevance to K–12, and methodological quality (vom Brocke et al., 2009; Whittemore & Knafl, 2005).
3. Analysis and synthesis: build a concept matrix by concepts and outcomes, compare findings across strands, and identify complementary mechanisms and gaps (Webster & Watson, 2002; Torraco, 2016).
4. Output: propose an integrated model where equity is the goal, innovation provides the learning process, and technology is a means used with safeguards.

Design-Science

Design-science focuses on producing and evaluating artifacts—constructs, models, methods, and instantiations—that address a real problem with clear utility and grounding in prior knowledge (Hevner et al., 2004; Gregor & Hevner, 2013).

We used the Design Science Research Methodology (DSRM) steps to operationalise ITEQ:

1. Problem identification and objectives: define the-leadership integration gap and set design objectives (coherent, school-ready, equity-first).
2. Design and development: specify the ITEQ model, eight competencies, a six-step decision cycle, and four tools (audit, procurement/privacy checklist, dashboard, scale/stop rules).
3. Demonstration: show applicability through short global vignettes in varied contexts.
4. Evaluation: align each component with criteria from the literature (e.g., UDL accessibility, privacy and bias checks, improvement-science measures). The chapter proposes feasible use-in-practice checks—reach, early outcomes for named groups, workload feasibility—consistent with formative evaluation in design research (McKenney & Reeves, 2012).
5. Communication: present the artifact and its use cases in practitioner-friendly language, with citations that link each step to the knowledge base.

Transparency and Reproducibility

An appendix will include the search logic (databases, exemplar terms), inclusion criteria, the concept matrix template, and the evaluation rubric. This makes the approach auditable and open to extension in future studies (Whittemore & Knafl, 2005; Peffers et al., 2007).

18-Month Implementation Roadmap

This roadmap shows how a school can move from diagnosis to sustainable practice in 18 months. It combines short improvement cycles with shared roles so change is feasible and owned across the school (Bryk et al., 2015; Spillane, 2006). Each phase lists objectives, key activities, roles, outputs, and resourcing notes. Equity is the goal; innovation is the method; technology is a means used with accessibility, privacy, and bias checks (CAST, 2018; World Wide Web Consortium, 2023).

Phase 0 (Months 0–2): Baseline Equity and Tech Readiness Audit

Objective- Establish a clear problem and a fair starting line.
Key activities:

- Disaggregate core indicators: access, participation/belonging, opportunity to learn, and outcomes (Bryk et al., 2015).
- Map digital capacity, data governance, accessibility, and interoperability (Anderson & Dexter, 2005; World Wide Web Consortium, 2023).

- Identify 1–2 priority learner groups and 1–2 target subjects or processes

Roles:

- Principal/senior team: name the priority group and approve scope.
- Inclusion lead: check fit with UDL and language access (CAST, 2018).
- Data & IT leads: run audits for privacy, data quality, and infrastructure.

Phase 1 (Months 3–6): Co-Design and Pilot Setup

Objective- Design change ideas with the people most affected and prepare safe tests.

Key activities:

- Hold co-design sessions with students, families, teachers, and support staff (Khalifa, 2018).
- Specify 2–3 "minimum viable changes" for an 8-week trial (e.g., UDL-aligned lesson routines; multilingual family communication; bias-aware early-warning supports).
- Apply a simple selection rubric: equity fit, accessibility, privacy, bias risk, capacity, interoperability, and evidence (Baker & Hawn, 2022; World Wide Web Consortium, 2023).
- Build data collection plans (few measures, disaggregated) and workload checks (Bryk et al., 2015).

Roles:

- Design team (teachers + inclusion + data): write the pilot charters and lesson/resource templates.
- Students/families panel: validate relevance and usability.
- Procurement/finance: confirm total cost of ownership and exit clauses.

Phase 2 (Months 7–12): Run Pilots and Evaluate

Objective- Learn quickly and decide with evidence.

Key activities:

- Implement 2–3 pilots for 8 weeks each; run two Plan–Do–Study–Act cycles (Bryk et al., 2015).
- Track reach, fidelity, early outcomes, and experience

- Conduct accessibility checks (UDL), privacy reviews, and a basic bias screen for any algorithmic tool (CAST, 2018; World Wide Web Consortium, 2023; Baker & Hawn, 2022).
- Hold monthly learning huddles to compare results across subgroups and contexts.

Roles.

- Heads of department/grade leads: coach teachers; remove timetable obstacles.
- Data & IT leads: automate simple reports; ensure secure, minimal data flows (Anderson & Dexter, 2005; Marsh, Pane, & Hamilton, 2006).
- Principal/senior team: apply decision rules—scale, adapt, or stop.

Phase 3 (Months 13–18): Scale and Codify

Objective- Make what works routine and sustainable.
Key activities:

- Scale only the pilots that improved results for priority learners.
- Codify changes: short playbooks; assessment and timetable adjustments; on-boarding modules for new staff.
- Align structures: budget lines, procurement standards (accessibility, privacy, interoperability), vendor SLAs, and data stewards.
- Build a simple equity dashboard; review termly with staff, students, and families.
- Plan for spread to a second subject or year group; document adaptations (Coburn, 2003).

Roles:

- Senior team: policy updates; budget reallocation; performance development alignment.
- Teacher leaders: run peer coaching; maintain examples and resource banks.
- Community partners: support targeted needs (e.g., translation, health, social services).

TOOLS AND INSTRUMENTS

This section offers four practical tools, each tied to research-based criteria. Use them together with short improvement cycles so choices are safe, feasible, and focused on equity.

1. Equity & Tech Readiness Audit (Weeks 1–6)

Purpose. Establish a fair starting line before acting.

How to use: Form a small team (principal or deputy, inclusion lead, data/IT lead, two teachers). In three short meetings, complete the checks below and produce one page of priorities.

Checks and criteria

- Access and participation. Do all learners reach core teaching, supports, and devices? Disaggregate by disability, language, gender, migration, and socio-economic status (UNESCO, 2020).
- Opportunity to learn. Are curriculum time, pathways, and accommodations equitably available (Bryk, Gomez, Grunow, & LeMahieu, 2015)?
- Technology capacity. Infrastructure reliability, staff digital confidence, and support routines; research links leadership attention to these factors with better edtech outcomes (Anderson & Dexter, 2005).
- Accessibility by design. Materials and platforms align with UDL principles and the Web Content Accessibility Guidelines from the World Wide Web Consortium (CAST, 2018; World Wide Web Consortium, 2023).
- Data protection. Purpose limitation, data minimisation, security, and clear roles for stewardship (Marsh, Pane, & Hamilton, 2006).

2. Bias-Aware Procurement and Privacy Checklist

Purpose. Choose tools that extend access and protect rights.

How to use: Apply at three points: (1) pre-market scan, (2) shortlist evaluation, (3) contract finalisation.

Criteria drawn from research and standards.

- Accessibility. Conformance with WCAG 2.1/2.2 and support for assistive tech, captions, and multilingual interfaces (World Wide Web Consortium, 2023; CAST, 2018).

- Privacy and security. Data inventory (what, why, where), consent/notice, retention, deletion, encryption, role-based access; minimal data by design (Marsh et al., 2006).
- Algorithmic fairness and risk. For tools that recommend, flag, classify, or grade, require a basic bias assessment (e.g., disparate error rates by subgroup), human-in-the-loop decisions, and an appeal route. Align with the AI risk principles in the National Institute of Standards and Technology (NIST) AI Risk Management Framework and education-specific reviews (Baker & Hawn, 2022; National Institute of Standards and Technology, 2023).
- Interoperability and exit. Ability to export data in standard formats and contract clauses that avoid lock-in (Anderson & Dexter, 2005).
- Evidence and workload. Prior studies or a feasible in-school pilot; support and training for staff (Bryk et al., 2015).

3. Simple Equity Dashboard With Disaggregation

Purpose: See quickly who is benefiting and who is not.

How to use: Track a small set of indicators in four lenses; show trends by group and by programme/class.

Lenses and research anchors:

- Access. Attendance, device/connectivity access, receipt of accommodations (UNESCO, 2020).
- Participation and experience. Course participation, student voice and belonging surveys (Bryk & Schneider, 2002).
- Opportunity to learn. Time on task, curriculum pathways (advanced courses, language supports), tutoring receipt (Bryk et al., 2015).

Table 2. Example equity dashboard display with disaggregation (illustrative data)

Lens & indicator	All students	Multilingual learners	Students of determination	Equity signal (gap)
Access: Attendance rate (%)	92	88	85	Lower attendance for priority groups
Access: Device/connectivity access (%)	95	90	92	Connectivity gap for multilingual learners
Participation: Belonging survey (% agree)	74	60	58	Belonging gap; review inclusion supports

continued on following page

Table 2. Continued

Lens & indicator	All students	Multilingual learners	Students of determination	Equity signal (gap)
Opportunity: Grade 6 science progression (% meeting expected)	62	48	40	Achievement gap; adjust supports and pedagogy
Outcomes: Progression to advanced science pathway (%)	32	18	12	Opportunity gap; review pathways and advisement

Figure 3. Example dashboard visual: Grade 6 science progression, disaggregated (illustrative)

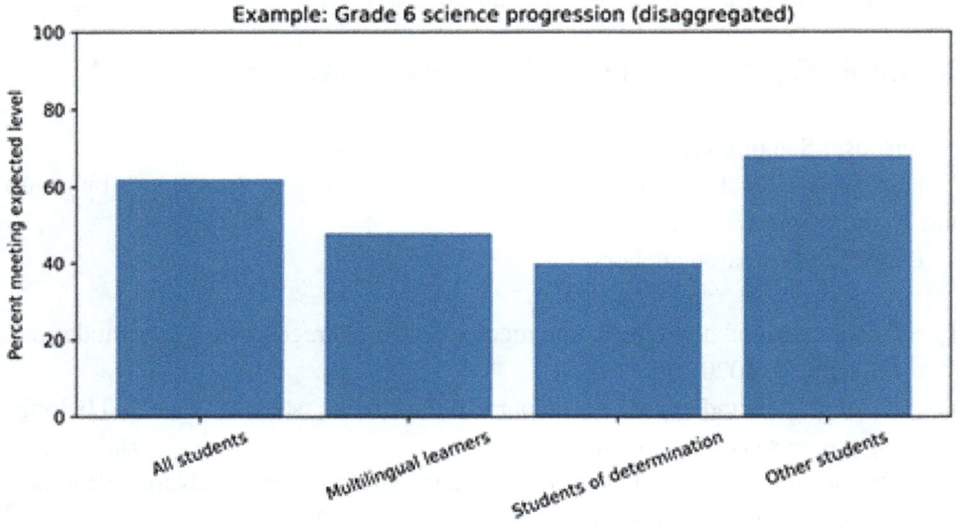

Ethical practice:

- Protect privacy.
- Explain the purpose to staff and families; use data to improve support, not to label students (Marsh et al., 2006).
- Align visuals to UDL (clear language, multiple representations) so information is usable for more people (CAST, 2018).

4. Decision rules for scaling or stopping (Used after each 6–8 week pilot)

Purpose. Make clear choices with evidence, not intuition.

How to use: After an 8-week pilot, apply the rules below with the team that ran the work and a student/family representative.

Rules tied to scholarship.

- Scale when:
  - Priority learners show improvement on agreed measures, and
  - Accessibility checks and privacy requirements are met, and
  - No disparate harms are detected in bias screens (Bryk et al., 2015; World Wide Web Consortium, 2023; Baker & Hawn, 2022).
- Adapt when:
  - Results are mixed or benefits are uneven across groups, or
  - Implementation burden is high. Decide one change and run another short cycle (Bryk et al., 2015).
- Stop when:
  - Outcomes are negative or inequitable, or
  - Safeguards fail or costs exceed benefits. Document learning and retire the tool or approach (Fixsen et al., 2005).

GLOBAL VIGNETTES

Vignette 1 — Kenya: Low-resource literacy improvement with disciplined pilots

A headteacher in a mixed rural–urban zone uses the ITEQ cycle to close early-grade reading gaps. The diagnosis shows Grade 1–2 learners in low-income schools reading well below benchmarks. With teachers and parents, the school co-designs two minimum-viable changes: tighter lesson routines and weekly coaching using the Tusome tablets already issued to instructional coaches. The technology is simple—offline lesson guides, observation tools, and quick feedback loops—backed by clear privacy rules. Two 8-week pilots run in Kiswahili and English. Disaggregated checks track reach and progress for girls, boys, and multilingual learners. Results improve, teacher workload is manageable, and the school scales and codifies routines across Grades 1–3. This mirrors evidence from Kenya's national Tusome program: structured materials plus coaching can raise early-grade reading at scale when leadership clarifies expectations and feedback routines (Piper, Jepkemei, & Kibukho, 2018; Marsh, Pane, & Hamilton, 2006).

Lesson. Low-bandwidth tech, clear routines, and short cycles can deliver equitable gains when leaders protect time for coaching and use data for learning, not labeling (Bryk, Gomez, Grunow, & LeMahieu, 2015).

Vignette 2 — Jordan: Refugee-responsive schooling with privacy and language access

In a double-shift public school hosting Syrian and Jordanian students, the principal diagnoses barriers: afternoon-shift attendance dips, families lack information in Arabic dialects, and some learners hesitate to share data. The team co-designs fixes with student representatives and a parent council linked to a nearby UNICEF Makani center. The technology choices are modest: a bilingual messaging system, consent-based data collection aligned to ministry guidance, and an offline repository of UDL-aligned materials. Two pilots—translated family outreach and small-group learning support—run for 8 weeks. Attendance and progression improve in the afternoon shift, without privacy complaints. The school scales the approach and documents adaptations for neighboring schools. This pattern reflects evidence that double-shift arrangements and community hubs can expand access when combined with targeted supports and data practices that respect rights (Culbertson et al., 2016; UNICEF Jordan, 2022; World Bank, 2023).

Lesson. In crisis-affected settings, equity moves fast when leaders pair language access with careful data practices and simple, low-cost tools.

Vignette 3 — Uruguay: Inclusive digital learning with accessibility by design (Plan Ceibal)

A suburban school plugs into Uruguay's Plan Ceibal infrastructure but diagnoses uneven participation among learners with low vision and emerging readers. The staff co-designs adjustments: UDL lesson planning, screen-reader-friendly materials, captions in Spanish and English, and a weekly help desk for families. Technology is treated as a means, not the goal: devices are configured for accessibility, platforms use open formats, and teachers receive short, just-in-time PD. After two 8-week pilots, participation and task completion rise for Students of Determination and multilingual learners. The school codifies accessibility checks in procurement and shares its playbook with the district. This aligns with research showing Plan Ceibal's role in widening digital access and participation, and with findings that device programs show stronger results when paired with pedagogy and teacher support (Yanguas, 2020; Pittaluga, 2012).

Lesson. Equity gains from edtech depend on design choices—accessibility, teacher support, and clear routines—more than on devices alone.

CONCLUSION AND FUTURE DIRECTIONS

This chapter proposed ITEQ Leadership—a single, school-ready model that aligns innovation, technology, and equity. It translated the idea into practical components: clear competencies, a six-step decision cycle, an 18-month roadmap, and four tools (readiness audit, procurement and privacy checklist, equity dashboard, and scale/stop rules). The model keeps equity as the goal, uses innovation as the method for disciplined learning, and treats technology as a means that must be accessible, private, and fair.

Future research.

1. Validation studies. Test the reliability and usefulness of the competency rubric and dashboard indicators across contexts and learner groups.
2. Impact and mechanisms. Use quasi-experimental or stepped-wedge designs to estimate the effects of ITEQ adoption on access, participation, opportunity to learn, and outcomes; study how effects vary by subgroup and school conditions.
3. Implementation costs and feasibility. Track time, training, and budget required to run short cycles, and examine workload trade-offs for teachers and leaders.
4. Responsible AI in practice. Evaluate bias-screening routines, human-in-the-loop decisions, and appeal pathways for common school tools (early-warning systems, automated translation, grading aids).
5. Comparative and regional studies. Compare adaptations of ITEQ in low-resource, multilingual, and crisis-affected settings; identify design features that travel well.

Integrated leadership matters because principals make many small decisions every day—and a single, coherent model keeps those decisions aligned so innovation and technology reliably serve equity.

REFERENCES

Anderson, R. E., & Dexter, S. L. (2005). School technology leadership: An empirical investigation of prevalence and effect. *Educational Administration Quarterly*, *41*(1), 49–82. DOI: 10.1177/0013161X04269517

Avolio, B. J., Kahai, S. S., & Dodge, G. E. (2000). e-leadership: Implications for theory, research, and practice. *The Leadership Quarterly*, *11*(4), 615–668. DOI: 10.1016/S1048-9843(00)00062-X

Baker, R. S., & Hawn, A. (2022). Algorithmic bias in education. *International Journal of Artificial Intelligence in Education*, *32*, 1052–1092. DOI: 10.1007/s40593-021-00285-9

Bryk, A. S., Gomez, L. M., Grunow, A., & LeMahieu, P. G. (2015). *Learning to improve: How America's schools can get better at getting better*. Harvard Education Press.

Bryk, A. S., & Schneider, B. (2002). *Trust in schools: A core resource for improvement*. Russell Sage Foundation.

CAST. (2018). Universal Design for Learning (UDL) guidelines (Version 2.2). http://udlguidelines.cast.org

Coburn, C. E. (2003). Rethinking scale: Moving beyond numbers to deep and lasting change. *Educational Researcher*, *32*(6), 3–12. DOI: 10.3102/0013189X032006003

Culbertson, S., Ling, T., Henham, M.-L., Corbett, J., Karam, R., Pankowska, P., Saunders, C., Bellasio, J., & Baruch, B. (2016). Evaluation of the Emergency Education Response for Syrian Refugee Children and Host Communities in Jordan (RR-1203). RAND Corporation. https://www.rand.org/pubs/research_reports/RR1203.html

Durlak, J. A., & DuPre, E. P. (2008). Implementation matters: A review of research on the influence of implementation on program outcomes and the factors affecting implementation. *American Journal of Community Psychology*, *41*(3–4), 327–350. DOI: 10.1007/s10464-008-9165-0

Fishman, B. J., Penuel, W. R., Allen, A.-R., Cheng, B. H., & Sabelli, N. (2013). Design-based implementation research: An emerging model for transforming the relationship of research and practice. In B. J. Fishman & W. R. Penuel (Eds.), Yearbook of the National Society for the Study of Education (Vol. 112, No. 2, pp. 136–156). Teachers College Record.

Fixsen, D. L., Naoom, S. F., Blase, K. A., Friedman, R. M., & Wallace, F. (2005). *Implementation research: A synthesis of the literature*. University of South Florida.

Fullan, M. (2011). *Change leader: Learning to do what matters most*. Jossey-Bass.

Gregor, S., & Hevner, A. R. (2013). Positioning and presenting design science research for maximum impact. *Management Information Systems Quarterly*, *37*(2), 337–355.

Heifetz, R. A. (1994). *Leadership without easy answers*. Harvard University Press.

Hevner, A. R., March, S. T., Park, J., & Ram, S. (2004). Design science in information systems research. *Management Information Systems Quarterly*, *28*(1), 75–105.

International Society for Technology in Education. (2018). ISTE standards for education leaders. https://iste.org/standards/education-leaders

Jordan, U. N. I. C. E. F. (2022). Final report: Summative impact evaluation of the UNICEF Jordan Makani programme [Report]. https://www.unicef.org/jordan/media/11671/file/Makani%20summative%20impact%20evaluation_English.pdf

Khalifa, M. A. (2018). *Culturally responsive school leadership*. Harvard Education Press.

Khalifa, M. A., Gooden, M. A., & Davis, J. E. (2016). Culturally responsive school leadership: A synthesis of the literature. *Review of Educational Research*, *86*(4), 1272–1311. DOI: 10.3102/0034654316630383

Ladson-Billings, G. (1995). Toward a theory of culturally relevant pedagogy. American Educational Research Journal, 32(3), 465–491. Marsh, J. A., Pane, J. F., & Hamilton, L. S. (2006). Making sense of data-driven decision making in education: Evidence from recent RAND research (OP-170). RAND Corporation. https://www.rand.org/pubs/occasional_papers/OP170.html

McKenney, S., & Reeves, T. C. (2012). *Conducting educational design research*. Routledge.

. National Institute of Standards and Technology. (2023). Artificial intelligence risk management framework (AI RMF 1.0) (NIST AI 100-1). https://doi.org/DOI: 10.6028/NIST.AI.100-1

Noddings, N. (2013). *Caring: A relational approach to ethics and moral education* (2nd ed.). University of California Press. (Original work published 1984)

Organisation for Economic Co-operation and Development. (2012). *Equity and quality in education: Supporting disadvantaged students and schools*. OECD Publishing., DOI: 10.1787/9789264130852-

Organisation for Economic Co-operation and Development. (2019). Recommendation of the Council on Artificial Intelligence. https://legalinstruments.oecd.org/en/instruments/oecd-legal-0449

Peffers, K., Tuunanen, T., Rothenberger, M. A., & Chatterjee, S. (2007). A design science research methodology for information systems research. *Journal of Management Information Systems*, *24*(3), 45–77.

Penuel, W. R., Fishman, B. J., Cheng, B. H., & Sabelli, N. (2011). Organizing research and development at the intersection of learning, implementation, and design. *Educational Researcher*, *40*(7), 331–337. DOI: 10.3102/0013189X11421826

Piper, B., Jepkemei, E., & Kibukho, K. (2018). Kenya's Tusome national literacy program: Impacts, sustainability, and scale. *Journal of Educational Change*, *19*(3), 293–321.

Pittaluga, L. (2012). *One Laptop per Child and bridging the digital divide: The case of Plan Ceibal in Uruguay*. Agencia Nacional de Investigación e Innovación.

Riehl, C. J. (2000). The principal's role in creating inclusive schools for diverse students: A review of normative, empirical, and critical literature on the practice of educational administration. *Review of Educational Research*, *70*(1), 55–81. DOI: 10.3102/00346543070001055

Ryan, J. (2007). Inclusive-leadership: A review. *Journal of Educational Administration and Foundations*, *18*, 92–125.

. Sanders, E. B.-N., & Stappers, P. J. (2008). Co-creation and the new landscapes of design. co-design, 4(1), 5–18. https://doi.org/DOI: 10.1080/15710880701875068

Selwyn, N. (2017). *Education and technology: Key issues and debates* (2nd ed.). Bloomsbury Academic.

Shields, C. M. (2017). *Transformative-leadership in education: Equitable, inclusive, and quality education in an uncertain and complex world* (2nd ed.). Routledge.

Snyder, H. (2019). Literature review as a research methodology: An overview and guidelines. *Journal of Business Research*, *104*, 333–339.

Spillane, J. P. (2006). *Distributed leadership*. Jossey-Bass.

Theoharis, G. (2007). Social justice educational leaders and resistance: Toward a theory of social justice-leadership. *Educational Administration Quarterly*, *43*(2), 221–258. DOI: 10.1177/0013161X06293717

Torraco, R. J. (2005). Writing integrative literature reviews: Guidelines and examples. *Human Resource Development Review*, *4*(3), 356–367.

Torraco, R. J. (2016). Writing integrative literature reviews: Using the past and present to explore the future. *Human Resource Development Review*, *15*(4), 404–428.

Uhl-Bien, M., Marion, R., & McKelvey, B. (2007). Complexity leadership theory: Shifting leadership from the industrial age to the knowledge era. *The Leadership Quarterly*, *18*(4), 298–318. DOI: 10.1016/j.leaqua.2007.04.002

United Nations International Children's Emergency Fund. (2021). The climate crisis is a child rights crisis: Introducing the Children's Climate Risk Index (CCRI). https://www.unicef.org/media/105376/file/UNICEF-climate-crisis-child-rights-crisis.pdf

United Nations Educational, Scientific and Cultural Organization. (2019). Global education monitoring report 2019: Migration, displacement and education—Building bridges, not walls. https://unesdoc.unesco.org/ark:/48223/pf0000265866

United Nations Educational, Scientific and Cultural Organization. (2020). Global education monitoring report 2020: Inclusion and education—All means all. https://unesdoc.unesco.org/ark:/48223/pf0000373718

United Nations Educational, Scientific and Cultural Organization. (2021). Recommendation on the ethics of artificial intelligence. https://unesdoc.unesco.org/ark:/48223/pf0000380455

vom Brocke, J., Simons, A., Riemer, K., Niehaves, B., Plattfaut, R., & Cleven, A. (2009). Reconstructing the giant: On the importance of rigour in documenting the literature search process. In *Proceedings of the 17th European Conference on Information Systems* (pp. 2206–2217).

Webster, J., & Watson, R. T. (2002). Analyzing the past to prepare for the future: Writing a literature review. MIS Quarterly, 26(2), xiii–xxiii. Whittemore, R., & Knafl, K. (2005). The integrative review: Updated methodology. *Journal of Advanced Nursing*, *52*(5), 546–553. DOI: 10.1111/j.1365-2648.2005.03621.x

Williamson, B. (2017). Big data in education: The digital future of learning, policy and practice. *Sage (Atlanta, Ga.)*.

Williamson, B., & Eynon, R. (2020). Historical threads, missing links, and future directions in AI in education. *Learning, Media and Technology*, *45*(3), 223–235. DOI: 10.1080/17439884.2020.1798995

World Bank. (2019). Ending learning poverty: What will it take? https://documents1.worldbank.org/curated/en/395151571251399043/pdf/Ending-Learning-Poverty-What-Will-It-Take.pdf

. World Bank. (2023). Jordan education—Evidence from the Syrian inflow to Jordan [Slide deck].

World Wide Web Consortium. (2023). Web Content Accessibility Guidelines (WCAG) 2.2 (W3C Recommendation; updated December 12, 2024). https://www.w3.org/TR/WCAG22/

Yanguas, M. L. (2020). Technology and educational choices: Evidence from a one-laptop-per-child program. *Economics of Education Review*, *77*, 101997.

APPENDIX

Appendix I

Equity & Tech Readiness Audit

Team (names/roles): Principal/Deputy · Inclusion Lead · Data/IT Lead · 2 Teachers · Student/Family Rep

Date: ___/___/____ Focus group(s): __________ Subject/area: __________

A. Equity baseline (tick/short notes)
   - Access (devices/assistive tech/transport): Yes Partial No → Notes: __________
   - Participation & experience (belonging/voice/discipline fairness): Yes Partial No → Notes: __________
   - Opportunity to learn (curriculum time, advanced pathways, accommodations): Yes Partial No → Notes: __________
   - Outcomes (progression/mastery, disaggregated): Visible Patchy Not available → Notes: __________

B. Technology capacity & governance
   - Infrastructure reliability & support routines: Strong Mixed Weak
   - Staff digital confidence (self-report/PD logs): High Medium Low
   - Data protection (purpose, minimisation, retention, deletion): Clear Needs work
   - Accessibility by design (UDL + WCAG checks): In place Partial Not in place (CAST; World Wide Web Consortium)

C. Priority problem (single sentence, precise, disaggregated)

Example: "Multilingual learners in Grade 6 science have lower unit-test mastery and lower participation in lab tasks."

Baseline indicators (with groups):

1. __________ 2) __________ 3) __________

Immediate constraints/risks (privacy, bias, workload): __________

Decision: We will target _________ learners in _________ with an 8-week pilot on __________.

Appendix II

Bias-Aware Procurement & Privacy Checklist

Tool/vendor: __________ Use case: __________
Decision stage: Scan Shortlist Contract
Accessibility & inclusion (UDL)

- Works with screen readers/keyboard navigation/captions/multiple languages: Yes No
- Student/parent accessibility needs addressed in onboarding/training: Yes No

Privacy & security (purpose limitation; data minimisation)

- Data inventory (what, why, where stored, who accesses, how long): Attached
- Consent/notice texts in plain language: Attached
- Encryption at rest/in transit; role-based access; deletion on exit: Confirmed
- Contract includes data-processing addendum & audit rights: Yes No

Algorithmic risk (if recommending/flagging/classifying/grading)

- Bias assessment (error rates by subgroup) reviewed: Yes No
- Human-in-the-loop and appeal route defined: Yes No (Baker & Hawn; National Institute of Standards and Technology (NIST))
- Clear explanations available to staff/families: Yes No

Interoperability & exit

- Open exports (format listed) and vendor SLA with uptime/support & exit clause: Yes No

Decision: Proceed Pilot with safeguards Do not adopt Notes: __________

Appendix III

Table 3. Equity dashboard

Lens	Indicator	Definition	Source	Cadence	Owner	Disaggregation
Access	% students with device+connectivity	Device issued and home connectivity verified	SIS/Survey	Monthly	Data lead	Disability · Language · Gender · SES · Migration
Participation	% reporting "I feel I belong"	Share of students responding agree/ strongly agree	Climate survey	Termly	Inclusion lead	As above
Opp. to learn	% in advanced pathways / language supports	Enrolled in AP/IB/ advanced math; enrolled in ELL	SIS	Termly	HoD	As above
Outcomes	Unit mastery in Grade 6 science	% meeting mastery threshold	LMS	Monthly	HoD	As above

Appendix IV

Scale/Adapt/Stop Decision Note (after each 6–8-week pilot)

Pilot title: __________ Dates: __________ Priority group: __________
Change tested (minimum viable change): __________
Evidence summary

- Reach (% of target group engaged): ____
- Fidelity (core steps done as planned): ____
- Early outcomes (named indicators, with comparison): ____
- Experience (teacher workload, student/family feedback): ____
- Safeguards Accessibility Passed Fix needed · Privacy Passed Fix needed · Bias screen Clear Concern

Decision (tick one) — with reasons

- Scale (evidence of benefit for priority group + safeguards passed)
- Adapt (mixed/uneven results or high workload; one change to test next)
- Stop (negative/inequitable effects or safeguard failure)

Next steps & owners (2–3 bullets, with dates):

- __________

- ________________
- ________________

Chapter 7
Leading for Wellbeing and Equity in School

Asma Abdallah
http://orcid.org/0000-0003-1028-7618
Sharjah Education Academy, UAE

Ahmed Alkaabi
http://orcid.org/0000-0001-7220-8087
United Arab Emirates University, UAE

Mohammed Borhandden Musah
http://orcid.org/0000-0003-4572-8348
Emirates College for Advanced Education (ECAE), UAE

ABSTRACT

The chapter discusses the role of school leaders in promoting educational equity through a whole-school approach to wellbeing focused on emotional safety, inclusivity, and support of all students. Also, with the ongoing escalation of issues related to student mental health, student belonging, and school climate, the concept of well-being is now a leadership imperative and no longer on the fringes of the initiative. This chapter discusses how emotionally safe and supportive learning environments are part of the equitable outcomes, especially among students with marginalized or vulnerable backgrounds. It examines the major issues in realizing whole-school wellbeing, such as uneven awareness, a lack of resources, and cultural opposition, and highlights the need to have coherent leadership and community involvement. The chapter is based on research and practice and describes strategic approaches that combine social-emotional learning, restorative practices, supportive structures, that are inclusive and positive school culture.

DOI: 10.4018/979-8-2600-0388-6.ch007

INTRODUCTION

In modern education, the problem of student well-being has become one of the primary priorities of school leaders due to the increased awareness of emotional security, sense of belonging, and mental health as the key pillars of learning and equity. Well-being in Finland is not perceived as a support service to education, but rather an inherent aspect thereof, where education has traditionally been viewed as a public good based on the principles of trust, inclusion, and holistic development (Bashir & Francis, 2024). The Finnish education policy and practice highlight the concept that schools not only have the role of academic learning but are also responsible for the social, emotional, and psychological growth of the students in the inclusive communities. This view places wellbeing as a leadership role that determines the daily life of schools and the experiences of learners (Carroll et al., 2022).

This leadership demand has been escalated due to the growing visibility of the mental health issues facing students. The increased anxiety, stress, and disengagement in children and youths brought about by social change, digitalization, and the latest global upheavals have led to a reevaluation of the role of the school as an emotional and social place (Abdallah & Abdallah, 2023) . Studies have always revealed that the ability of students to learn is highly associated with their sense of security, belonging, and support in schools. Learners will be more inclined to participate and then continue and succeed when they feel valued and emotionally secure. On the contrary, school conditions where students feel locked out, are fearful or neglected, deter wellbeing and academic performance(Lehtonen & Kuuskorpi, 2023).

Comprehensive schooling traditions of equity and preventive support have encoded this linkage between wellbeing and learning in Finland. Another characteristic of the Finnish system that is worth mentioning is that it focuses on early intervention, multi-professional cooperation, and student welfare services that are part of the daily life in a school. Instead of using high-stakes accountability or punitive discipline, Finnish schools have traditionally placed more emphasis on guidance, care, and trust-based relationships. The fact that Finland is a nation with this orientation makes it a relevant context to look into whole-school wellbeing as the leadership approach towards equity promotion (Wyn et al., 2000).

A whole-school approach to wellbeing is a systemic and coordinated attempt to entrench emotional safety, support, and inclusion throughout the life of the school. This practice is not limited to single programs or individual interventions but to leadership practices, school culture, curriculum, relationship and community engagement (Abdallah & Alkaabi, 2023). Whole-school models do not support the idea that well-being is the task of one counselor or one support unit, but rather a collective endeavor, which includes leaders, teachers, support staff, students, and families. This method is quite compatible with the educational beliefs held by Finnish people, i.e., collaboration, collective responsibility, and professional agency of teachers (Browne, 2017).

There is also the equity dimension of whole-school wellbeing, which is especially important. School environments are not uniformly experienced among the students. Students with less disadvantaged socioeconomic backgrounds, students with disabilities, students in migrant and minority groups, and students with trauma experience are more prone to facing obstacles to emotional safety and belonging (Abdallah & Musah, 2023). Lack of targeted leadership can result in wellbeing programs being created to support already the most advantaged students, and vulnerable populations being underserved. In this respect, well-being is not a neutral idea but a highly equity-sensitive area. There are four aspects of student access to leadership decisions that discipline, support services, student voice, and school climate may decrease or increase existing inequalities (Beatty, 2007).

This dimension of equity has gained acceptance in the Finnish education policy. Universal support with specific interventions to address the needs of students, irrespective of their backgrounds, is a priority in student welfare frameworks, where all students are provided with basic well-being support, whilst those with more needs are given the appropriate support. This stratified approach is indicative of a larger Nordic concept of equity as something proportional and not something uniform(Abdallah, et al., 2024) . Nevertheless, these principles have not been translated into the uniform practice within schools, and this is a leadership challenge, especially as schools are increasingly exposed to mounting pressures surrounding the workload, resources, and evolving student needs (McGrath & Noble, 2010).

Although there are generalized rhetoric commitments to wellbeing, the actual meaning of whole-school wellbeing is not actually clear. Without developing consistent strategies and mutual understanding among employees, schools can use well-being language in their mission statements. Well-being initiatives, in certain instances, are not unified but rely on the interests of separate individuals instead of institutionalized leadership (Fang et al., 2024). There can also be a conflict between academic and well-being priorities where some of the stakeholders view emotional support as less important than academic rigor (Alqodsi & Abdallah, 2024). These tensions demonstrate the necessity of a leadership that has the capacity to make wellbeing not a competing agenda but rather the condition upon which learning and equity can be achieved (Roffey, 2008).

These issues are also influenced by the Finnish trust-related system within the context. Professional autonomy on a large scale places a great burden on the school leaders to decipher the policy, align provision, and foster cultures of inclusivity (Abdallah, 2023) . On the one hand, this autonomy allows context-sensitive solutions, but on the other hand, it implies that the standard of well-being leadership may differ in schools. It is thus imperative to be in a position to learn how the leaders can create a systematic way of establishing emotionally safe and supportive environments to maintain equity throughout the system (Mugabekazi & Mukanziza, 2025).

These concerns are discussed in this chapter as the author considers how school leaders can develop and manage whole-school wellbeing programs that enhance equity and inclusion. It takes a critical and book-based orientation that places the concept of wellbeing in a wider discussion of educational leadership, social justice, and school culture, as opposed to a technical intervention. Based on research, policy frameworks, and examples of good practice, the chapter examines the difficulties leaders go through as well as the options they can adopt (Mugabekazi & Mukanziza, 2025).

The chapter has three goals that proceed one after another. First, it theorizes the idea of whole-school wellbeing as an equity-driven leadership practice and specifies some of the most important concepts, including emotional safety, supportive learning environments, and inclusive school climate. Second, it critically evaluates the barriers that do not promote successful implementation, such as cultural resistance, resource constraints, and disproportionate support of marginalized students (Alqodsi & Abdallah, 2024). Third, it presents leadership-based solutions that show the extent to which well-being can be integrated throughout the school structures, relations, and community partnerships (Goldberg et al., 2018).

The chapter is structured in the following way. The background section describes the background concepts and studies that connect wellbeing, school climate, and equity with specific reference to whole-school models and Finnish school culture (Abdallah, Ismail, & Alkaabi, 2024) . The body of analysis takes a closer look at some of the problematic areas and debates in leading wellbeing with equity, explaining why implementation is still a challenge despite the investment in policy. The solutions and recommendations section outlines practical solutions on leadership approaches that allow the construction of emotionally safe, supportive, and inclusive learning environments. The chapter ends by looking at what the concept of whole-school wellbeing leadership can imply for educational equity and the overarching growth of inclusive school societies (Barrett & Twycross, 2020).

This chapter suggests that emotional safety and supportive school environments cannot be considered additional items but are requirements of equitable education by placing wellbeing central to leadership. Leading whole-school wellbeing, in the Finnish context where inclusion, trust, and holistic development are central ideals, signifies tradition and a necessary reaction to modern circumstances (Abdallah, 2024).

BACKGROUND

The notion of whole-school wellbeing has become a significant part of educational research and policy, with schools being viewed as significant arenas of facilitating not just academic learning but also, in terms of emotional, social, and psychological wellbeing. This cognition has been entrenched within the traditions of the Finnish education system, which aims education as a comprehensive, inclusive, and welfare-oriented system. To discuss whole-school wellbeing as the leadership strategy of equity, there is a need to clarify major conceptual assumptions and place them in the context of the available research and policy-making models that underlie Finnish schooling (Abdallah et al., 2023).

Whole-School Wellbeing

Whole-school wellbeing is a systemic and integrated approach where the well-being is incorporated in all aspects of school life instead of being solved through individual intervention programs or by a single approach (Abdallah & Awad, 2026). It includes leadership practices, school culture, teaching and learning, relationships, support services, and interaction with families and communities. Within this model, well-being is not a limited set of counseling services or extra-curricular activities but an element that is incorporated in day-to-day activities, policies, and interactions. The studies have always shown that disjointed or add-on methods of wellbeing are not adequate, as they do not focus on the structural and cultural factors that determine the experiences of safety, belonging, and support of students (Whitley, 2010).

In Finland, the whole-school wellbeing movement is confined to the comprehensive school model, the focus of which is prevention, early assistance, and inclusiveness (Alkaabi et al., 2025). The Finnish schools have a system that includes the services of student welfare in the daily activities of schools, e.g., the services of school psychologists, social workers, and health professionals. This integration is evidence of the interpretation that well-being cannot be isolated from learning and that schools have a role to play in caring for the entire child. Whole-school wellbeing is thus not a new or imported idea in Finland and is rather a continuation and formalization of the values of an existing education (Eleftheriades et al., 2020).

Emotional Safety and Supportive Learning Environments

Well-being depends on the fundamental aspect of emotional safety as a condition that preconditions the meaningful learning. It is a perception of the students that they are no longer bullied, discriminated, humiliated, or fearful of the possibility of being excluded or punished, and they can freely express themselves (Al-Qodsi et al., 2024) . The emotional safety facilitates students to take intellectual and social risks, to seek assistance when necessary, and to participate in school life. A friendly learning environment is based on the concept of emotional safety, where the social and emotional requirements of the students are identified and met along with the academic requirements (Rowe & Stewart, 2009).

Trust-based relationships between students and teachers have traditionally been the focus of Finnish educational research and practice. Lack of standardized testing, little application of punitive accountability actions, and powerful teacher autonomy also help create environments where relational trust may prosper. Research has revealed that those environments are correlated with increased student engagement, reduced levels of stress, and improved school climates. Nevertheless, emotional safety is not something that can be thought to be homogeneous among all students (Jadalhaq et al., 2023) . The issue of leadership is important in determining whose security is at stake and in determining the policy and practice that would accommodate the issue of exclusion and marginalization (Wells et al., 2003).

Equity in Wellbeing

Equity as related to the school's well-being can be defined as the intentional action in order to make sure that every student, no matter his or her background, identity, or need, gains access to emotional support and considers himself or herself part of the school community (Alqodsi, 2021). This view acknowledges the fact that different students have well-being variants and that certain groups are more vulnerable to existing risks of emotional safety and belonging. Students with disabilities, migrant and minority students, students living in poverty, and students with previous trauma are disproportionately impacted by bullying and exclusion as well as mental health issues (Konu & Rimpela, 2002).

The Finnish education policy has always addressed the issue of equity by offering universal provision and special support (Alqodsi & Abdallah, 2024) . This practice can be seen in the student welfare systems, which offer minimum services to every student and special services to students with special needs. Leadership-wise, equality in wellbeing involves leaving behind homogenous practices to differentiated strategies addressing divergent experiences. In the absence of purposeful leadership, well-being programs can unintentionally reproduce inequality by giving students who are already advantaged an additional advantage (Storrie et al., 2010).

School Climate and Leadership

This is an effective instrument as it examines the atmosphere in schools and the degree of leadership that administrators are capable of providing. School climate is directly connected with whole-school wellbeing and includes norms, relationships, values, and expectations that define the day-to-day life in schools. Mutual respect, helpful relations, and a common dedication to inclusion are related to a positive school climate (Ismail & Ismail, 2024). Studies have shown that the school climate has a great impact on well-being and academic achievement and that it mediates the impact of the socioeconomic background and other risk factors (Jones & MacDonald, 2012).

It has been established that leadership is one of the important determinants of school climate. The decentralization and trust-based system in Finland ensures that the influence of principals and leadership teams on the interpretation of policies, allocation of resources, and building of relationships is quite significant (Ismail, 2024). The practice of leadership that focuses on collaboration, care, and shared responsibility is more likely to create climates where well-being is prioritized. On the other hand, a narrow-minded leadership that is keen on academic achievement or compliance with administrative regulations might overlook the emotional aspect of schooling, despite the existence of a system of holistic values (Higgins & Booker, 2023).

Frameworks Informing Whole-School Wellbeing

International and national systems are another context that is useful in the analysis of wellbeing in schools as a whole. International social-emotional learning programs, trauma-informed education programs, and inclusive schooling programs highlight the significance of school-wide efforts to promote the mental health and emotional growth of students (Ismail, 2024). The frameworks have regularly emphasized leadership, professional learning, and community engagement as essential facilitators of sustainable wellbeing practices (Hoare et al., 2017).

In Finland, student well-being, participation, and inclusion are educational objectives identified as national curriculum guidelines. Wellbeing is presented as a process that is embedded in teaching, assessment, and school culture in addition to an outcome (Abdallah et al., 2024). This learning focus supports the notion that well-being is a communal issue that demands coherent leadership as opposed to individual interventions (Lewallen et al., 2015).

From Policy to Practice

Although conceptually and policy-based, research suggests that it is still not easy to convert whole-school wellbeing into a consistent practice. Inequality in the implementation can be caused by differences in leadership capacity, availability of resources, and school culture. Some schools have been able to entrench wellbeing in structures and relationships, and also those that have not been able to get past rhetoric (Ramadan & Ismail, 2023). This policy-experience disconnect presents the necessity to study the topic of well-being within the framework of leadership. This background section forms the basis of critical analysis since it draws the foundation of whole-school wellbeing on the basis of previously known research, Finnish educational traditions, and equity-based frameworks (Aldous & Ismail, 2024). The next section investigates the practical and theoretical issues school heads struggle with when trying to implement the idea of emotionally safe, conducive, and inclusive learning environments into practice, which explains the importance of well-being leadership as both a necessity and a complication (Roper, 2013).

MAIN FOCUS OF THE CHAPTER

Issues, Controversies, and Problems

Although Finland has a high policy approach to the welfare of students and inclusive education, the provision of whole-school wellbeing in the equity approach is fraught with a series of complex and under-recognized challenges. Such challenges are not only operational but are truly cultural, structural, and ethical in nature as they represent the strains between the historic schooling practices, the changing needs of students, and the growing demands being placed on school leaders (Ismail & Aldous, 2024). This part of the book critically reviews the major problems and scandals that make the provision of emotionally safe, supportive, and inclusive learning conditions in Finnish schools complex (Wu et al., 2024).

Conceptual Ambiguity and Uneven Commitment to Wellbeing

A key difficulty in the field of leading whole-school wellbeing is the absence of common and accurate practices defining what wellbeing is in practice. Despite the high visibility of the concept of wellbeing in the discourse of Finnish education policy and curriculum, it can serve as an umbrella term that covers mental health, social-emotional learning, student welfare services, school climate, and inclusion (Ismail & Aldous, 2025). This conceptual breadth, though useful, may bring in ambiguity as well. The various stakeholders, such as teachers, leaders, support staff, and policymakers, might have different interpretations of wellbeing, and their implementation may be patchy or partial (Ruch & Coll, 2022).

In a number of schools, well-being is more likely to be linked to the personal services of an individual, whether through counseling or psychological intervention, rather than being a shared task incorporated in day-to-day pedagogy and leadership.

In other ones, well-being is viewed as an additional initiative, which is only engaged in times of crises, but which is left behind when the academic pressure takes place (Aldous & Ismail, 2025). This disproportionate dedication has the potential to undermine whole-school coherence and wellbeing as a rhetorical ideal, rather than a school life principle (Ismail & Aldous, 2025). To school leaders, it is a matter of going beyond a symbolic approval and endeavoring to develop a shared and working vision of wellbeing to guide decision-making across all fields of schooling (Enos, 2019).

Resource Constraints and Professional Capacity

Finland has a relatively high level of investment in education and student welfare, but the lack of resources is a long-term problem, especially concerning time, personnel, and professional growth. Coordination, collaboration, and reflection activities, which are part of leading whole-school wellbeing, are often limited by heavy workloads and conflicting priorities. Teachers and leaders can be aware of the role of wellbeing but find it difficult to meaningfully incorporate it into daily practice because they do not have time to plan, talk about, and learn about it (Kitzrow, 2009).

The professional capacity is also different in schools. Although the Finnish educators are well trained, not all of them feel as competent to tackle complex mental health needs, behaviors that are related to trauma, or culturally responsive wellbeing practices (Aldous & Ismail, 2025). Social-emotional learning training, restorative practices, or trauma-informed learning can lack balance and lead to unequal support of students. Where wellbeing initiatives are based excessively on the individual competence of an individual, but not on structures of shared work, inequities may arise both within and between schools (Watkins et al., 2011).

These capacity gaps are of great concern as far as equity is concerned. Schools with a larger percentage of students with additional needs might have more challenges with their well-being and, at the same time, demand more staff (Ibrahim, 2020). The scarcity of resources is a threat to increase, rather than decrease, inequalities in emotional safety and support without specific support and coordination of leadership (Gregg et al., 2025).

Cultural Resistance and Competing Educational Priorities

Another scandal surrounding the whole-school wellbeing leadership is concerning the deeply rooted cultural practices in schooling where academic success, order, and productivity are valued above emotional and relationship aspects (El Zaatari & Ibrahim, 2021). Even though the academic expectations and the discourses of performance are normally contrasted with high-pressure and test-driven models of education, Finland has an influence on academic expectations and performance discourses (El Zaatari & Ibrahim, 2021). A heavy emphasis on well-being can be seen by some educators and stakeholders as a deviation from "core" academic activity or as the loss of standards (Ehrnstrom et al., 2022).

This has been especially clear in the controversy of discipline and behavior management. Conventional punitive strategies like excluding students or enforcing strict rules can be justified as a means of safeguarding the state of order, even when the data indicates that they are harming emotional security and targeting disadvantaged students more. The transition to the restorative or supportive is a potentially resisting step since it needs a shift in perceptions of authority, responsibility, and student behavior (Soini et al., 2010).

These cultural tensions are delicate for school leaders. Unless it is strategically directed by management, well-being programs can be shallow or controversial, thus restricting their ability to change the school climate (Ibrahim, 2013). The difficulty is to redefine well-being as not an opposition to academic rigor, but as the state that allows all students to be engaged and learn over the long term (Cădariu & Rad, 2025).

Equity Gaps and Differential Experiences of Safety

The continuity of disproportionate experiences of emotional safety and belonging, perhaps, is the most serious concern of whole-school wellbeing leadership. Although Finnish schools report positive climates generally, research and practice show that not every student group in a school is experiencing the positive climates equally. Learners with disabilities, migrant or minority students, LGBTQ +, and students with a History of trauma or socio-economic disadvantage face more risks of being bullied, excluded, or marginalized (Bashir & Francis, 2024).

Without clear equity-based initiatives, whole-school wellbeing initiatives may not solve these differences. Universal programs that fail to consider the differences in needs would only benefit those students who already feel safe, leaving behind those students. In particular, some general activities in social-emotional learning might be ineffective in addressing the particular problems of students who have to overcome cultural exclusion or institutional prejudice (Carroll et al., 2022).

The choices about the distribution of resources, the concept of student voice, and support structures are leadership decisions that predetermine the well-being of whom. In a situation when equity considerations are explicitly defined but not evident, wellbeing projects may reproduce existing disparities and contradict their intentions (Lehtonen & Kuuskorpi, 2023).

Fragmentation of Responsibility and Coordination Challenges

The entire school's well-being needs to be organized among various players, such as teachers, administrative teams, student welfare officers, and third parties. This coordination is, in practice, hard to attain. Wellbeing accountabilities can be shared without having a leader or collaborative responsibility, disintegrating. The support services might work side by side with the teaching instead of being incorporated into the classroom practice and school culture (Wyn et al., 2000).

Because Finland has a decentralized system, with a significant degree of autonomy in schools, the differences in capacity and coordination among leaders can lead to disparities in implementation. Some schools build robust, holistic wellbeing systems, and those that are ad hoc, based on personal commitment (Ibrahim, 2010). This inconsistency creates equity issues on the system-wide level because access to emotionally safe and permissive conditions can be contingent upon the school that the student enrolls in, instead of uniform national standards (Beatty, 2007).

Emotional Labor and Leadership Sustainability

Being a role model of wellbeing across the school also makes the school leader subject to profound emotional and moral pressure. Principals and leadership teams are supposed to be role models of caring, dealing with the complex needs of students, supporting the well-being of staff, and dealing with crises, all without leading to an institution that is not stable. This is the emotional work that is not always noticeable and is not always supported enough, which leads to more burnout of the leader (Goodman, 2017).

Without proper support, supervision, or systemic support, the sustainability of the wellbeing initiative is threatened when leaders are not well supported. Wellbeing leadership that is based on equity needs to care about both the students, as well as the care about the wellbeing of educators and leaders, whose ability to be caring is predetermined by their working conditions (McGrath & Noble, 2010).

The problems described show that promoting whole-school wellbeing as equitably as possible is not a simple task and that it is not a universally agreed idea, even at a system as highly regarded as Finland. The ambiguities in concepts, limited resources, cultural conflicts, unfair student experience, and leadership pressures interact to complicate the implementation. These difficulties cannot be solved without conscious, knowledgeable, and values-based leadership. The section below details solutions and proposals addressing these complexities, which illustrate how whole-school wellbeing can be converted into a principle into sustainable practice that can propel emotional safety, inclusion, and equity (Roffey, 2008).

SOLUTIONS AND RECOMMENDATIONS

To address the challenges mentioned above, a leadership strategy should focus on making wellbeing not a separate program but a governance and equity role of schooling. Whole-school wellbeing in the Finnish case, in which the normative base of education is trust, professional autonomy, and inclusion, should be championed by consistent vision-building, moral judgment, and stable institutional alignment. The section progresses along a series of strategies that are interconnected and support each other in implementing the concepts of emotional safety, support, and inclusion into long-term leadership approaches that can help to solve not only daily demands but also structural inequalities as well (Kennedy, 2019).

Establishing a Shared Vision and Coherent Wellbeing Framework

One of the key initial actions in driving whole-school wellbeing is to achieve an organizational, school-based vision of wellbeing that is clearly connected to equity and inclusion. In Finland, student welfare policies and national curriculum give a general mandate on the promotion of wellbeing, yet the school-level leadership decides how these mandates are to be implemented. The best leaders define wellbeing as a shared task that is integrated in teaching, assessment, discipline, relationships, and decision-making (Enos, 2019).

This necessitates the shift of the disjointed efforts of initiatives to a coherent structure that integrates values, policies, and practices. This type of framework must explain what emotional safety, inclusion, and support entail within the local school setting, but at the same time, it must align with national values. Notably, the way of creating this framework must be participatory. The dialogue with teachers, students, parents, and student welfare professionals assists in the development of shared ownership and minimizes ambiguity. Trust and legitimacy are strengthened through this participatory approach in Finnish schools, where collaborative cultures are firmly established (Kitzrow, 2009).

A well-defined wellbeing framework is also used as a guideline when making decisions. In the case of dilemmas (choosing between academics and emotional needs or dealing with a behavioral problem), leaders can rely on common values instead of snap-shots. This consistency is especially significant to equity, where it is important to make sure that the practice of wellbeing is not solely tied to personal judgment but is informed by the shared agreement of promises (Watkins et al., 2011).

Cultivating a Positive and Inclusive School Culture

One of the main mechanisms of wellbeing being practiced in everyday practice is through school culture. The role of relational trust, respectful interaction, and student participation in establishing positive school climates is always emphasized in Finnish research. The leaders can be a decisive factor in creating these conditions because they can model inclusive values and express their expectations regarding respectful behavior, and make the student voice heard (Chong, 2016).

Fastening school cultures can also be defined as inclusive ones with explicit norms that do not accept bullying, discrimination, and exclusion, and inclusive school cultures encourage belonging and respect. The behavior of leadership, including the manner in which conflict situations are managed, the way diversity is respected, and the role of the student in the school activities, are all indicators of whose well-being is considered. These cues have a special implication for marginalized students (Ehrnstrom et al., 2022).

Practically, the creation of an inclusive culture is based on the long-term observation of the daily interactions as opposed to the symbolic ones. Periodical opportunities to discuss, mentoring, peer support systems, and solving problems together reinforce social connections and diminish loneliness. Leaders in Finnish schools can take advantage of this relational proximity to create environments where students feel visible, listened to, and appreciated because in Finnish schools, the level of hierarchical distance between students and staff is relatively low (Watkins et al., 2011).

Integrating Social-Emotional Learning and Mental Health Support

Systematic implementation of social-emotional learning (SEL) and mental health support throughout grade levels of a whole-school wellbeing approach is needed. The delivery of SEL is implicit in Finland through curriculum objectives based on participation, self-regulation, and interaction skills as opposed to being taught as a discrete subject. Leadership plays an important role in making sure that these competencies are carefully built and maintained (Gregg et al., 2025).

Leaders can reinforce the integrations of SEL by promoting cross-curricular approaches, teacher collaboration, and aligning assessment practices with well-being objectives. No less significant is the provision of access to mental health resources. Schools in Finland have the advantage of integrated student welfare teams, but leadership defines the efficacy of implementing these services in coordination with classroom practice (Kitzrow, 2009).

Equity-wise, leaders should make sure that mental health support can be available and responsive to various needs. Universal provision might not adequately meet the needs of students who have experienced stress due to migration, students with learning problems, and students who have encountered trauma. Successful leaders analyze data, professional knowledge, and partnership with welfare professionals to understand such gaps in support to act proactively and not reactively (Watkins et al., 2011).

Adopting Restorative and Supportive Approaches to Discipline

Punitive actions represent a serious challenge to the emotional safety and fairness of a school. Punitive strategies based on exclusion or humiliation destroy trust and target vulnerable students disproportionately. The Finnish education policy has given more focus on restorative and supportive responses to behavior, but the application of these responses to behavior amongst schools is different (Gregg et al., 2025).

Restorative practices focus on learning, responsibility, and repairing relationships, as well as on punishment. In case of conflicts, students are instructed to reflect, learn, and regain trust in the community. These approaches require leadership to justify them, offer professional growth, and ensure consistency between the staff (Chong, 2016).

Restorative practices lower the chances of marginalization in terms of equity by acting upon the behavior in the social and emotional circumstances of the behavior. The champions of restorative leaders help to create emotionally safe spaces where errors are seen as learning opportunities and not reasons to be excluded.

Building Inclusive Support Structures and Multi-Professional Collaboration

Effective coordination is needed between professionals working in student welfare and educators to achieve whole-school wellbeing. The Finnish schools do not lag in this respect, as there are some psychologists, social workers, and health professionals at school systems. Nevertheless, it is the leadership that makes the difference between the resources being integrated as support structures or siloed services (Kennedy, 2019).

Leaders may reinforce coordination by introducing routines of regular collaboration, defining roles, and making sure that the considerations of well-being are used to make pedagogical decisions. The concepts of inclusive support structures also imply that attention should be paid to the areas of transition, including entering the school, changing grades, or moving to the next level of education, where the perception of security and belonging can be very fragile in students. The equity-based approach to leadership makes the support systems receptive to the needs of different students instead of being standardized to the average learner. This can include options of differentiated instruction with students with disabilities, language support of multilingual students, or culturally sensitive work with families (Gregg et al., 2025).

Engaging Families and Communities as Wellbeing Partners

Well-being is not something that is in the school walls. Students have emotional experiences and abilities to learn within the context of the family and the community. The Finnish tradition of working with schools and families has always been an important part of Finnish education, but whole-school wellbeing needs to explore a further level of collaboration between schools and families, which can be achieved through informational communication (Kitzrow, 2009).

The dialogue, joint problem-solving, and involvement of the families in the well-being initiatives can help leaders engage with the families. Trust and alignment are reinforced by providing the space where parents can raise their concerns, know about school practices, and make a contribution to the decisions. In families with marginalized backgrounds, the active outreach is especially significant in order to overcome exclusion and miscommunication. Community partnerships- including working with the youth services, mental health providers, and the local organizations- expand the ability to support wellbeing of the school. Whether leaders develop such networks increases emotional safety and equity, and the needs of students are treated as a whole (Chong, 2016).

Using Data Ethically to Support Wellbeing and Equity

Data-informed leadership has the potential of reinforcing whole-school wellbeing ethically and reflectively. The patterns of attendance, climate surveys, and student feedback may assist leaders in determining which areas of concern and tracking the progress. Nevertheless, data should be analyzed with a degree of care to prevent labeling or surveillance (Mugabekazi & Mukanziza, 2025).

Under the trust-based system in Finland, ethical use of data (data mining, data analytics) must be transparent, proportional, and take into account the student voice. Leaders ought to engage staff and students in data interpretation and the determination of how the information is used to take action. Once data are deployed to shed light on injustices and support intervention instead of dominating them, they will be instruments of justice, not marginalization (Rowe & Stewart, 2009).

Table 1. Safe and inclusive school wellbeing checklist (optional)

Domain	Key Leadership Questions
Emotional Safety	Do all student groups report feeling safe and respected?
Inclusion	Are marginalized students receiving targeted support?
School Culture	Are restorative practices used consistently?
Support Services	Are welfare services integrated into daily practice?
Community Engagement	Are families and students meaningfully involved?

Synthesis

A combination of these strategies shows that whole-school wellbeing as a systemic leadership task, as opposed to a set of isolated interventions, is an equity-focused initiative. Whole-school wellbeing leadership, in the Finnish context, which is based on the values of trust, inclusion, and professional responsibility, is a continuation of tradition and also a reaction to modernity. Incorporating emotional safety, support, and a sense of belonging into the organization and culture of schools, leaders will be able to provide the environment in which even those students not the most privileged can succeed academically, socially, and emotionally (Wyn et al., 2000).

FUTURE RESEARCH DIRECTIONS

Though the whole-school wellbeing has emerged as a leading goal in Finnish education policy and practice, there exist notable gaps in the research foundation that is required to promote equity-oriented leadership in the area. The literature suggests a high level of evidence of the relationship between well-being and school climate and the learning outcomes, although the majority of studies are cross-sectional, program-specific, or short-term in their outcomes. To enhance future studies on the theoretical and practical basis of whole-school wellbeing leadership, studies should be more longitudinal, systematic, and context-sensitive (Enos, 2019).

The long-term equity effects of whole-school wellbeing initiatives are one of the important areas of future research. Although Finnish schools are often found to be well ahead of international levels in the manifestation of student well-being, less is known about how the sustained leadership on well-being has any effect on the educational pathways of various student groups in the long term. Longitudinal studies of samples of cohorts of students through full schooling would enlighten us on whether environments that are emotionally safe and supportive help close achievement gaps based on socioeconomic status, migration origin, disability, or mental health susceptibility. This research would assist in establishing whether wellbeing programs only widen the general climate or act as equity mechanisms (Chong, 2016).

Another crucial direction is to study the field of leadership practices and capacities that are related to well-being. Although leadership has been broadly acknowledged to be the centerpiece of school climate, empirical studies have seldom disaggregated which leadership practices, forms, or decision-making mechanisms are the most effective in instilling well-being in schools. Comparative analyses across municipalities and school types may help understand the role of leadership capacity, collaboration, and governance structures in depth and the sustainability of wellbeing practices in the Finnish context, which is characterized by decentralized leadership and is based on professional trust. This research question would also be of great use in informing leadership preparation and professional development (Gregg et al., 2025).

Another aspect of sustainability that has not been well studied is the well-being of educators and school leaders themselves, which would be of value in future research efforts. The impact of teacher and leader emotional health is straightforward in their ability to support students and maintain inclusive practices. In Finland, where people anticipate care, inclusion, and individualized assistance, the emotional labor linked to wellbeing leadership should be paid a bit more attention. Research into the ways schools can reconcile the needs put on employees and the supportive work environments might inform more comprehensive wellbeing frameworks, which consider the school at the level of the whole (Chong, 2016).

The other promising field of research is associated with culturally responsive and inclusive practices of wellbeing. With the growing diversity of Finnish schools, there is a necessity to learn how the wellbeing initiatives can be tailored so that they have a reflection of various cultural interpretations of emotional expression, support, and belonging. The qualitative study with students and families of migrant and minor backgrounds would help to further understand the experience of wellbeing and where the existing strategies might fail to meet the expectations. This kind of work would assist in ensuring that whole-school wellbeing somehow does not unintentionally favor dominant cultural norms (Kennedy, 2019).

The contribution of digital tools and technology to wellbeing is also worth close research. The application of technology to wellbeing monitoring, communication, or even offering a mental health assistant should be viewed with ethical and equity concerns, even though Finland has high scores in digital integration in the education sector. Further studies are needed on how the digital wellbeing tools can be applied responsibly so as to increase support without compromising the values such as trust, privacy, and relational care, which are at the core of Finnish education (Enos, 2019).

Lastly, policy-based research on the correspondence between national wellbeing models and the school-level practice could be studied. Although Finnish school policies on student welfare and their curricula are well-articulated in terms of commitment to wellbeing and inclusion, inconsistency in their implementation remains. Comparative policy research would be able to find out enabling conditions (e.g., funding models, intersectoral collaboration, or accountability mechanisms) that would be used to support wellbeing leadership across schools in a consistent manner and to be equity-focused (Goldberg et al., 2018).

Combined, these research directions highlight the fact that whole-school wellbeing is a dynamic and changing area of study and not a body of practice. Further development of knowledge in this field is possible through the interdisciplinary cooperation of education researchers, psychologists, sociologists, and policy researchers. Further studies can help Finnish school leaders to improve the current wellbeing strategies not only to be effective but also to be fair, sustainable, and sensitive to the needs of the students and communities that continuously evolve (Carroll et al., 2022).

CONCLUSION

The chapter has discussed the concept of whole-school wellbeing as one of the key building blocks of equitable education, which is no longer a peripheral issue but a core-value area of school leadership in modern Finland. Based on the Finnish values of trust, inclusion, and professional autonomy, the discussion has revealed that emotionally safe and supportive learning conditions are the key to ensuring that not only the most advantaged students, but also others, have the opportunity to engage in schooling to the fullest and reach their potential.

The discussion has proved that there is a strong interconnection between well-being and equity. In Finnish schools, where the academic achievement is already perceived to be rather good on a system level, the differences begin to appear in the form of mental health differences, feelings of belonging, and access to support. Students with backgrounds of socioeconomic disadvantage, migrant or minority identity, and students with special educational needs are overrepresented when wellbeing is approached in a disjointed or incoherent manner. One way of responding to these inequities in a systematic and sustainable way is to have a whole-school approach, where wellbeing becomes a part of leadership practices, school culture, pedagogy, and systems of student welfare.

The chapter has also indicated that there is more than just the introduction of individual programs or curricular supplements to be a leading factor for well-being. Rather, it requires a leadership change of direction: not to tackle problems in re-activity, but explicitly to culture-building; not to individual responsibility, but to collective responsibility; not to the narrow academic measurements, but to more comprehensive notions of success such as emotional safety, relationships, and inclusion. The Finnish school leadership system, with its professional trust and professional collaboration as central elements, offers a solid background to such an approach, but it is also confronted by the issues of resource pressure, staff wellbeing, and growing student diversity.

Leading us by critically addressing the lack of shared understanding, cultural resistance, and disproportionate capacity across schools, the chapter has highlighted the fact that the notion of well-being leadership is complex and value-oriented in nature. Discipline, support structures, and student voice decisions are not neutral because they determine the well-being that is prioritized and whose needs are marginalized. This results in the fact that equity-oriented wellbeing leadership necessitates moral judgment, self-reflectivity, and the readiness to challenge the existing norms that could be unintentionally exclusionary of vulnerable students.

The policies proposed in this chapter, such as creating a shared vision of well-being, incorporating social-emotional learning, applying restorative practices, and enhancing supportive learning environments, are purposeful, systematic, and supportive of inclusive learning techniques, which prove that emotionally safe and supportive schools are a possibility. The Finnish examples and the context of the policies demonstrate that the aspect of well-being can be integrated into the entire school in order to improve not only the student performance but also teacher retention, school climate, and the trust of the community.

To conclude, the notion of whole-school wellbeing should be perceived as a long-term investment in the equity of education and social cohesion. In the case of Finland, the key to maintaining its dedication to inclusive and high-quality education in the time of increasing complexity lies in the hands of leaders who prioritize wellbeing as the core of school leadership. As schools become emotionally secure communities, where all students feel noticed, nurtured, and cherished, they become quite potent learning spaces as well as justice spaces. Whole-school wellbeing is not simply a concern of care; thus, it is a strategic, ethical necessity of the future of equitable education.

REFERENCES

Abdallah, A. K. (2023). Teacher-led, student-focused, and unleashing the power of teacher empowerment for school improvement and success. In *Restructuring leadership for school improvement and reform*. IGI Global., DOI: 10.4018/978-1-6684-7818-9.ch001

Abdallah, A. K. (2024). The impact of gender, psychology, and cultural dimensions on leadership development in distance education. *Scientific Reports*, *14*(1), 68495. Advance online publication. DOI: 10.1038/s41598-024-68495-4

Abdallah, A. K., & Abdallah, R. K. (2023). Achieving academic excellence: The intersection of teacher development, quality education, and entrepreneurship. In *Innovations in teacher development, personalized learning, and upskilling the workforce*. IGI Global., DOI: 10.4018/978-1-6684-5518-0.ch007

Abdallah, A. K., & Alkaabi, A. A. M. (2023). *Restructuring leadership for school improvement and reform*. IGI Global., DOI: 10.4018/978-1-6684-7818-9

Abdallah, A. K., Ismail, L. S., & Alkaabi, A. M. (2024). Green careers: Educating for the future of sustainability. In *Legal frameworks and educational strategies for sustainable development*. IGI Global., DOI: 10.4018/979-8-3693-2987-0.ch017

Abdallah, A. K., Ismail, L. S., & Ismail, O. A. S. (2024). Foundations of sustainability education: Concepts and contexts. In *Legal frameworks and educational strategies for sustainable development*. IGI Global., DOI: 10.4018/979-8-3693-2987-0.ch011

Abdallah, A. K., & Musah, M. B. (2023). Principal and teacher licensing as a tool to school improvement. In *Restructuring leadership for school improvement and reform*. IGI Global., DOI: 10.4018/978-1-6684-7818-9.ch014

Abdallah, R. K., Al Maktoum, S. B., & Al Mansoori, M. K. (2023). The road to lesson observation as a tool to school improvement: Accountability vs. perfunctory. In *Restructuring leadership for school improvement and reform* (pp. 222–252). IGI Global., DOI: 10.4018/978-1-6684-7818-9.ch012

Abdallah, R. K., Aljuburi, A. H., & AlKhasawneh, T. N. (2023). School improvement in culturally diverse schools: Valuable insights of successful components. In *Restructuring leadership for school improvement and reform* (pp. 105–124). IGI Global., DOI: 10.4018/978-1-6684-7818-9.ch006

Abdallah, R. K., & Awad, M. J. (2026). Integrating artificial intelligence and technology into UAE teacher licensing systems for global education reforms. In *Building a unified teacher licensing system: Policies, education reforms, and cultural integration* (pp. 211–250). IGI Global. https://doi.org/. Barrett, D., & Twycross, A. (2020). Student mental health and well-being: are universities doing enough? *Evid Based Nurs, 23*(2), 33-34. https://doi.org/DOI: 10.4018/979-8-3373-0837-1.ch008

Al-Qodsi, E. M., Jadalhaq, I. M., & El-Maknouzi, M. E. H. (2024). The place of UAE's food security in the national legislation and its role in supporting global food security. *Cogent Social Sciences, 10*(1), 2319379. Advance online publication. DOI: 10.1080/23311886.2024.2319379

Aldous, S. M., & Ismail, G. A. (2025). AI for sustainable emergency preparedness and response in schools. In *Convergence of AI, education, and business for sustainability*. IGI Global., DOI: 10.4018/979-8-3373-1917-9.ch003

Alkaabi, A. M., Abdallah, A. K., Abdallah, R., Al Hasan, M., & Mohamed, A. (2025). Principal engagement in the teacher evaluation process in remote schools: A narrative inquiry of language teachers. *Forum for Linguistic Studies, 7*(3), 209–230. DOI: 10.30564/fls.v7i3.8502

Alqodsi, E. M. (2021). Analyzing the implementation of usufruct rights and obligations in the UAE Civil Transactions Law. *International Journal of Criminal Justice Sciences, 16*(1), 95–109.

Alqodsi, E. M., & Abdallah, A. K. (2024). *Legal frameworks and educational strategies for sustainable development*. IGI Global., DOI: 10.4018/979-8-3693-2987-0

Barrett, D., & Twycross, A. (2020). Student mental health and well-being: Are universities doing enough? *Evidence-Based Nursing, 23*(2), 33–34.

Bashir, H. A., & Francis, J. (2024). The College Campus, a Place of Learning, and a Place of Healing. *Advances in Social Sciences Research Journal, 11*(7), 31–41. DOI: 10.14738/assrj.117.17246

Beatty, B. (2007). Going through the Emotions: Leadership That Gets to the Heart of School Renewal. *Australian Journal of Education, 51*(3), 328–340. DOI: 10.1177/000494410705100309

Browne, V. (2017). Under the Radar: The Mental Health of Australian University Students. *The Australian and New Zealand Student Services Association, 25*(2), 51–62. DOI: 10.30688/janzssa.2017.16

Cădariu, I.-E., & Rad, D. (2025). Mapping the Whole School Approach in social and emotional learning and wellbeing: A bibliometric review with implications for social work and education. *Technium Social Sciences Journal*, *72*, 169–188. DOI: 10.47577/tssj.v72i1.12872

Carroll, A., Bower, J. M., Chen, H., Watterston, J., & Ferguson, A. (2022). School-wide Approaches for Promoting Social and Emotional Well-Being in Australian School Contexts: Focus Group Interviews with System and School Stakeholders. *American Journal of Education*, *129*(1), 109–138. DOI: 10.1086/721798

Chong, P. W. (2016). The Finnish "Recipe" Towards Inclusion: Concocting Educational Equity, Policy Rigour, and Proactive Support Structures. *Scandinavian Journal of Educational Research*, *62*(4), 501–518. DOI: 10.1080/00313831.2016.1258668

Ehrnstrom, C., Blankenheim, A., Bottiglio, M., Tomatz, M., West, A., Bryant, T., LaHoda, R., & Gerberich, S. (2022). Embedding counselors within departments across campus can meet increased demand. *Student Affairs Today*, *25*(3), 6–7. DOI: 10.1002/say.31083

El Zaatari, W., & Ibrahim, A. (2021). What promotes adolescent students' school belonging? Students' and teachers' convergent/divergent views. *Cogent Education*, *8*(1), 1–20. DOI: 10.1080/2331186X.2021.1984628

Eleftheriades, R., Fiala, C., & Pasic, M. D. (2020). The challenges and mental health issues of academic trainees. *F1000 Research*, *9*, 104. DOI: 10.12688/f1000research.21066.1

Enos, G. (2019). College takes multilayer approach to addressing student mental health. *Mental Health Weekly*, *29*(42), 1–8. DOI: 10.1002/mhw.32115

Fang, M., Abdallah, A. K., & Vorfolomeyeva, O. (2024). Collaborative AI-enhanced digital mind-mapping as a tool for stimulating creative thinking in inclusive education for students with neurodevelopmental disorders. *BMC Psychology*, *12*(1), 1975. Advance online publication. DOI: 10.1186/s40359-024-01975-4

Goldberg, J. M., Sklad, M., Elfrink, T. R., Schreurs, K. M. G., Bohlmeijer, E. T., & Clarke, A. M. (2018). Effectiveness of interventions adopting a whole school approach to enhancing social and emotional development: A meta-analysis. *European Journal of Psychology of Education*, *34*(4), 755–782. DOI: 10.1007/s10212-018-0406-9

Goodman, L. (2017). Mental Health on University Campuses and the Needs of Students They Seek to Serve. *Building Healthy Academic Communities Journal*, *1*(2), 31–44. DOI: 10.18061/bhac.v1i2.6056

Gregg, E. A., Ohlson, M., Dominguez, A. R., & Steele, S. (2025). A Proposal for Improving Student-Athletes' Mental Health Through Leadership Training. *Sport Management Education Journal, 19*(1), 59–61. DOI: 10.1123/smej.2023-0002

Higgins, E., & Booker, R. (2023). What are the main factors that are thought to impact upon the implementation of a whole school approach to student mental health and wellbeing in schools? A systematic review. *International Journal of Wellbeing, 13*(2), 77–94. DOI: 10.5502/ijw.v13i2.2833

Hoare, E., Bott, D., & Robinson, J. (2017). Learn it, Live it, Teach it, Embed it: Implementing a whole school approach to foster positive mental health and wellbeing through Positive Education. *International Journal of Wellbeing*, *7*(3), 56–71. DOI: 10.5502/ijw.v7i3.645

Ibrahim, A. (2010). Education in the UAE: A socio-cultural analysis. In Zhao, Y. (Ed.), *Handbook of Asian education: A cultural perspective* (pp. 327–344). Routledge., DOI: 10.4324/9780203816318

Ibrahim, A. (2020). *What hurts or helps teacher collaboration? Evidence from UAE schools. Prospects: Comparative Journal of Curriculum.* Learning, and Assessment., DOI: 10.1007/s11125-019-09459-9

Ibrahim, A. S. (2013). The learning needs of beginning teachers in the United Arab Emirates. *Journal of Education for Teaching: International Research and Pedagogy, 39*(5), 491–506. DOI: 10.1080/02607476.2013.739791

Ismail, G. A., & Aldous, S. M. (2024). Digital innovation in green learning: Ensuring safety while fostering environmental stewardship. In *Legal frameworks and educational strategies for sustainable development*. IGI Global., DOI: 10.4018/979-8-3693-2987-0.ch016

Ismail, G. A., & Aldous, S. M. (2025). AI-driven health and safety management in school facilities. In *Convergence of AI, education, and business for sustainability*. IGI Global., DOI: 10.4018/979-8-3373-1917-9.ch002

Ismail, L. S., & Ismail, O. A. S. (2024). Adaptive strategies for success: Monitoring and evaluating blue-green infrastructure in urban development. In *Integrating blue-green infrastructure into urban development*. IGI Global., DOI: 10.4018/979-8-3693-8069-7.ch001

Ismail, O. A. S. (2024). Sustainable automotive engineering: Empowering the next generation of eco-conscious engineers. In *Legal frameworks and educational strategies for sustainable development*. IGI Global., DOI: 10.4018/979-8-3693-2987-0.ch019

Jadalhaq, I. M., Abdulhay, I. E., Alqodsi, E. M., & El Maknouzi, M. E. H. (2023). A systematic review and meta-analysis of interruption of the statute of limitations for civil claims: A comparative study of Arab legislations. *Heliyon*, *9*(9), e16756. DOI: 10.1016/j.heliyon.2023.e16756

Jones, H., & MacDonald, G. (2012). Promoting Mental, Emotional and Social Health, a Whole School Approach. *International Journal of Mental Health Promotion*, *4*(1), 24–25. DOI: 10.1080/14623730.2002.9721851

Kennedy, K. (2019). Centering Equity and Caring in Leadership for Social-Emotional Learning: Toward a Conceptual Framework for Diverse Learners. *Journal of School Leadership*, *29*(6), 473–492. DOI: 10.1177/1052684619867469

Kitzrow, M. A. (2009). The Mental Health Needs of Today's College Students: Challenges and Recommendations. *NASPA Journal*, *46*(4), 646–660. DOI: 10.2202/1949-6605.5037

Konu, A., & Rimpela, M. (2002). Well-being in schools: A conceptual model. *Health Promotion International*, *17*(1), 79–87. DOI: 10.1093/heapro/17.1.79

Lehtonen, S., & Kuuskorpi, M. (2023). Towards Typological and Spatial Diversities Learning from the typological solutions of the Finnish comprehensive public-school buildings. *Architectural Research in Finland*, *6*(1). Advance online publication. DOI: 10.37457/arf.130449

Lewallen, T. C., Hunt, H., Potts-Datema, W., Zaza, S., & Giles, W. (2015). The Whole School, Whole Community, Whole Child model: A new approach for improving educational attainment and healthy development for students. *The Journal of School Health*, *85*(11), 729–739. DOI: 10.1111/josh.12310

McGrath, H., & Noble, T. (2010). Supporting positive pupil relationships: Research to practice. *Educational and Child Psychology*, *27*(1), 79–90. DOI: 10.53841/bpsecp.2010.27.1.79

Mugabekazi, J. C., & Mukanziza, J. (2025). Educational Leadership, Mental Health, and Equity: A Review of Effective Interventions in Schools. *European Journal of Educational Management*, *8*(1), 49–62. DOI: 10.12973/eujem.8.1.49

Ramadan, R. S., & Ismail, O. A. S. (2023). Building a better future: The role of school inspection in driving educational excellence. In *Restructuring leadership for school improvement and reform*. IGI Global., DOI: 10.4018/978-1-6684-7818-9.ch011

Roffey, S. (2008). Emotional literacy and the ecology of school wellbeing. *Educational and Child Psychology*, *25*(2), 29–39. DOI: 10.53841/bpsecp.2008.25.2.29

Roper, L. D. (2013). Breaking the Silence Surrounding Mental Health on Campus. *Journal of College and Character, 14*(1), 75–78. DOI: 10.1515/jcc-2013-0010

Rowe, F., & Stewart, D. (2009). Promoting connectedness through whole-school approaches: A qualitative study. *Health Education, 109*(5), 396–413. DOI: 10.1108/09654280910984816

Ruch, C. P., & Coll, K. (2022). Presidents and the Campus Mental Health Crisis: Challenges, Options, and Strategy. *Journal of Research on the College President, 6*. Advance online publication. DOI: 10.54119/jrcp.2022.603

Soini, T., Pyhältö, K., & Pietarinen, J. (2010). Pedagogical well-being: Reflecting learning and well-being in teachers' work. *Teachers and Teaching, 16*(6), 735–751. DOI: 10.1080/13540602.2010.517690

Storrie, K., Ahern, K., & Tuckett, A. (2010). A systematic review: Students with mental health problems—a growing problem. *International Journal of Nursing Practice, 16*(1), 1–6. DOI: 10.1111/j.1440-172X.2009.01813.x

Watkins, D. C., Hunt, J. B., & Eisenberg, D. (2011). Increased demand for mental health services on college campuses: Perspectives from administrators. *Qualitative Social Work: Research and Practice, 11*(3), 319–337. DOI: 10.1177/1473325011401468

Wells, J., Barlow, J., & Stewart-Brown, S. (2003). A systematic review of universal approaches to mental health promotion in schools. *Health Education, 103*(4), 197–220. DOI: 10.1108/09654280310485546

Whitley, J. (2010). The Role of Educational Leaders in Supporting the Mental Health of All Students. *Exceptionality Education International, 20*(2). Advance online publication. DOI: 10.5206/eei.v20i2.7663

Wu, F., Freeman, G., Wang, S., & Flores, I. (2024). The Future of College Student Mental Health: Student Perspectives. *Journal of College Student Mental Health, 38*(4), 975–1010. DOI: 10.1080/28367138.2024.2400612

Wyn, J., Cahill, H., Holdsworth, R., Rowling, L., & Carson, S. (2000). MindMatters, a whole-school approach promoting mental health and wellbeing. *The Australian and New Zealand Journal of Psychiatry, 34*(4), 594–601. DOI: 10.1080/j.1440-1614.2000.00748.x

Chapter 8
Leading Resilient Schools:
Safety, Continuity, and Equity in Times of Crisis

Ghaith Ismail
http://orcid.org/0009-0007-2705-6011
Madar International School, UAE

Sara Aldous
http://orcid.org/0009-0006-4806-9076
Liwa International School for Girls, UAE

ABSTRACT

In this chapter, we discuss the role of resilient. The recent global upheavals, such as pandemics, natural disasters, armed conflict, and climate-related emergencies, have revealed vulnerabilities in the systems of education that led to loss of learning, psychosocial damage, and increased inequalities. Based on existing international models like Education in Emergencies, the INEE Minimum Standards, and UNESCO models, the chapter examines the main leadership issues that emerge during crises, like gaps in preparation, safety and well-being issues, unfairness in terms of access to marginalized learners, and socio-emotional pressure existing in school communities. It is a compilation of evidence-based approaches and global practices that show how adaptive, equity-focused leadership can be used to contribute to crisis preparedness, learning continuity, and trust and resilience. The chapter concludes that resilient leadership is critical towards safeguarding educational systems and making sure that the responses to the crisis do not strengthen any existing inequalities.

DOI: 10.4018/979-8-2600-0388-6.ch008

INTRODUCTION

New patterns of crisis are becoming defining of education systems all over the world, disrupting schooling, endangering the safety of learners, and aggravating structural inequalities. COVID-19 pandemic, massive natural catastrophes, climate emergencies, military conflict, and forced migration have all demonstrated the weakness of the education systems under strain (Smith & Riley, 2012). The shutdown of schools, infrastructure destruction, interrupted school routines, and the lack of access to the most vital services have become the new elements of the modern educational context. Such disruptions have not just halted academic education, but they have undermined physical, psychological, and access to essential social resources, which schools used to offer (Akkari & Lauwerier, 2014).

Crises do not often hit all the learners in the same way. Socio-economically disadvantaged students, rural and marginalized students, refugee students, and students with disabilities are disproportionately affected in the case of an emergency. Low access to digital technologies, precarious living conditions, food insecurity, and lack of psychosocial support contribute to educational exclusion in situations where schools have to be closed or work in restrictive conditions(Abdallah & Abdallah, 2023) . Schools in most settings serve not only as locations of education, but as places of safety, food, stability, and social intimacy (Anderson et al., 2011). In case such institutions are broken or unable to react properly to the crises, the aftermath of these effects is not simply in terms of the loss of learning, but in the framework of more serious risks to child safety and neighborhood stability (Angwas, 2025).

School leadership is of critical importance within this framework. School leaders must be able to cope with uncertainty, pressured decision-making, and juggle between the conflicting priorities linked to health, safety, academic continuity, and equity(Abdallah & Alkaabi, 2023). The situation of crisis requires the ability to adapt, moral judgment, and emotional intelligence, along with administrative skills, and this is challenging the traditional model of leadership(Abdallah & Alkaabi, 2023). During the crisis, leaders need to know how to continue to learn when they cannot meet in person, how they can protect their staff and students in the face of an emergency, and whether they can prevent the further marginalization of vulnerable learners by the crisis measures. Such duties place leadership not only as a managerial role but as one of the key mechanisms by which educational resiliency is exercised (Angwas, 2025).

Resilience in education does not just mean the ability to withstand shock, but it is also the ability to adjust, recover, and even improve in the wake of disruption. Strong schools foresee dangers, put in place preparedness systems, respond well during crises, and bring lessons learnt to long-term development plans (Abdallah & Musah, 2023). Notably, resilience should be seen to be inseparable from equity.

A school system that maintains continuity for a group of learners and leaves out a group of learners cannot be classified to be resilient (Atillo et al., 2025). Equity-based leadership makes sure that the responses to crises are based on the needs of the vulnerable individuals and that structural obstacles hindering access to safe learning systems, teaching continuity, and access to psychosocial support are mitigated (Bromley & Andina, 2010).

The chapter focuses on resilient school leadership, which is analyzed in the interdependent categories of safety, continuity, and equity. It discusses how leaders can make schools crisis-ready, safeguard their well-being, learning throughout the crises, and recovery efforts that enhance future preparedness (Abdallah, et al., 2024). The chapter uses the international literature and global best practices, including Education in Emergencies, INEE Minimum Standards, and UNESCO guidelines, to contextualize school leadership in the context of wider initiatives to create crisis-responsive education systems (Brooks & Ezzani, 2021).

The chapter goes ahead to initially lay down important conceptual bases of resilience, school safety, continuity planning, and educational equity during crises (Fang et al., 2024). It subsequently examines the key challenges and dilemmas encountered by school leaders in emergencies, such as gaps in preparedness, safety, disproportionate effects, and socio-emotional pressure among school communities. Based on this analysis, the chapter provides evidence-based approaches and best practices on how to be a leader of resilient and inclusive schools both during and after crises (Alqodsi & Abdallah, 2024). Through an integrative effort to derive universal lessons and strategies of leadership, the chapter posits that resilient leadership with equity at the core is necessary to secure the future of education under the conditions of continuous turmoil (Brown et al., 2001).

BACKGROUND

A conceptual background of resilient school leadership during crisis should be based on a clear understanding of the interrelationship between resilience, school safety, continuity planning, and educational equity. The ideas have been discussed in great detail within the sphere of education policy, disaster risk management, and humanitarian response, which is especially relevant to situations where instability and uncertainty are the norm (Abdallah, 2023). The two of them together offer a framework through which one can analyze how schools can prepare, respond, and recover in the event of a crisis and still be able to carry out their basic educational and social processes (Chatzipanagiotou & Katsarou, 2023).

The resilient education systems are usually said to be education systems with the ability to foresee risk, absorb shock, adjust to changing circumstances, and remain able to provide equitable learning opportunities both before and after disruption (Alqodsi & Abdallah, 2024). Educational resilience does not just come down to infrastructure or emergency operations; it consists of leadership practices, institutional culture, and governance structures, as well as community relationships (Abdallah, Ismail, & Alkaabi, 2024). The studies and literature have always stressed that resilience is dynamic and not a static process, and depends on the efficiency with which schools learn the lessons of the previous crisis and apply them to future planning. In this respect, the resilience could be viewed as a reflection of the short-term response to the crisis and the long-term learning on the institutional level (Cunningham, 2025).

The notion of resilience is closely connected with that of school safety, which can be described as protecting students, personnel, and school communities against physical, health, and emotional harm. School safety, however, does not only include information building security, or a disaster-sensitive system, but also health guidelines, protective measures, and emotional comfort (Abdallah, 2024). The issues of safety escalate when schools are faced with threats like the spread of diseases, environmental risks, violence, or displacement during the crisis. The literature highlights that learning is not sustainable when there is a breakdown of safety, and the relationship between schools and communities becomes worse. Consequently, it makes safety a central task of school administration in an emergency (Elliott et al., 2022).

Continuity planning is another important aspect of crisis leadership, and it considers how education should be maintained in cases of disrupted schooling. Continuity planning is a process that involves the foresight of probable interruption and the creation of alternative ways of instruction, communication, and assessment. This encompasses readiness for remote/hybrid instruction, adaptable educational schedules, responding to emergency curriculum changes, as well as systems to monitor student activities (Friesen & Bell, 2006). Evidence studies conducted after the mass closure of schools, especially during the COVID-19 pandemic, show that systems that had continuity plans in place were in a better position to reduce learning losses and retain student-teacher relationships. On the other hand, the lack of continuity planning was likely to lead to disengagement, especially in younger learners and those with a disadvantaged background (Fu & Zhang, 2024).

Educational equity is central to everything that goes on in crisis leadership. Equity during crises can be described as the equal allocation of resources, assistance, as well as opportunities in a manner that every learner, irrespective of their vulnerability, would receive an opportunity to access education during crisis periods (Abdallah et al., 2023). Crises are likely to increase existing inequalities in poverty, disability, gender, migration status, and geographic isolation. Disproportional impact is on students who are not able to access digital devices, stable housing, healthcare, and psychosocial support in case of closures and switches to alternative learning models. The academic literature of crisis education has consistently indicated that equity-free resilience can promote structural disadvantage (Abdallah et al., 2023). A school system that continues to sustain some learners at the expense of others cannot be viewed in any meaningful way as resilient (Gontang).

These are the underpinnings of various powerful international concepts that inform educational leadership during times of crisis. The Education in Emergencies (EiE) model is the result of humanitarian and development practice that focuses on the human right to education in emergencies and makes schooling a stabilizing experience for children and the community. EiE principles emphasize safe learning conditions, quick reaction systems, and nonjudgmental approaches, which put vulnerable groups into focus (Abdallah & Awad, 2026). Education is considered a process of learning, as well as a kind of protection, psychosocial support, and community healing (Hayes & Derrington, 2023).

To supplement this strategy, the INEE Minimum Standards of Education offer a popular guideline on quality, safety, and equity in the provision of education systems in states of crisis. The standards characterize key areas which include safe learning conditions, access and continuity of learning, teacher support, and stakeholder coordination (Kamaruddin, 2024). Noteworthy, the INEE framework focuses on preparedness and mitigation of risks, which requires the education systems to embed crisis planning into the daily governance of the system, as opposed to regarding the emergencies as unusual phenomena. According to research, those schools that are based on the principles of INEE are better prepared to react to the crisis situation and be able to recover faster after it (Karakose, 2021).

Guidelines on education system resilience, disaster risk reduction, and inclusive recovery are also added to this body of knowledge by UNESCO and other international organizations. The efforts of UNESCO emphasize that the policy on education, preparedness to disasters, health systems, and mechanisms of social protection must be coordinated at the systemic level (Alkaabi et al., 2025). This point of view supports the concept that school leadership functions as a part of a more general institutional ecosystem and that the ability to respond well to a crisis requires the coordination of other sectors (Al-Qodsi et al., 2024). The leadership capacity should then extend beyond the school level decision-making to include the interaction with the outside world through the agencies, families, and community organizations (Kolehmainen et al., 2022).

Literature on crisis leadership in education highlights the unique requirements of school leaders in times of emergencies. Crisis leadership, in contrast to everyday administrative leadership, involves quick sense-making, ethical judgment, emotional intelligence, and adaptive problem-solving (Jadalhaq et al., 2023). Leaders need to act on incomplete information, address increased anxiety levels among employees and relatives, and make decisions that have serious health, safety, and equity implications. Research has always indicated that open leaders who are empathetic and who care more about the common good tend to have a higher chance of sustaining trust and organizational unity in times of disruption (Landa et al., 2021).

Simultaneously, tensions and dilemmas are realized by crisis leadership. Leaders also have conflicting demands, including balancing public health measures and academic expectations or limited resources distributed among unequal needs (Alqodsi, 2021). These dilemmas cannot be solved only by the help of technical solutions; they need value-based decisions that are based on the notions of equity and care. As a result, modern research is gradually defining crisis leadership as an ethical and interpersonal, but not purely managerial, practice (Leithwood, 2021).

MAIN FOCUS OF THE CHAPTER

Issues, Controversies, and Problems

The strengths and weaknesses of education systems are unusual in the way that crises bring them to light. As much as schools are expected to be places of stability and protection, emergencies can often expose the lack of preparedness, leadership capacity, and coordination within the institutions (Ismail & Ismail, 2024). The problems of school leaders in a crisis are complex, as they go beyond the practical issues of operations to the more profound issues of safety, persistence, justice, and emotional health. This part will investigate the most significant problems and scandals that influence the leadership in schools during crises, explaining why resilience should be defined as a structural and moral obligation (Morgan, 2014).

Among the most enduring problems has to be the gaps in preparedness and continuity. Most of the schools find themselves in a crisis without detailed emergency plans and strategic procedures on how to go about the business of education in times of crisis. Preparedness is regarded as a marginal administrative activity as opposed to a part and parcel of school governance. Consequently, crisis responses are usually reactive, hasty, and uneven (Ismail & Ismail, 2024). In the case of the COVID-19 pandemic, schools that did not have a well-developed contingency plan were unable to switch to other learning approaches, which resulted in an extended teaching hiatus and teenage disconnection (Naidu, 2021). Continuity planning is often poorly developed, even in situations that are likely to experience frequent natural disasters, and very little is invested in scenario-based planning, employee training, or redundancy systems. Lack of strong preparedness structures frustrates the effectiveness of leaders to take decisive and consistent action during crises(Özen & Yavuz, 2024).

Closely connected to preparedness is the problem of providing safety and well-being. The crises pose direct risks to physical health and safety, such as the spread of disease, environmental risks, violence, and damage to infrastructure (Ismail, 2024). Meanwhile, they produce a strong psychological stress among the students, the teachers, and even the school leaders themselves. School communities during an emergency are usually tinged with fear, uncertainty, and grief, which impacts concentration, motivation, and interpersonal relationships (Pastor et al., 2024).

School leaders have to work in a multifaceted environment, where safety at the physical level and mental health issues are equally pressing. It has been stated in the literature that the lack of perceived safety or inconsistency in the implementation of safety protocols leads to a loss of trust in school leadership, which only exacerbates the learning conditions (Ismail, 2024). On the other hand, extreme defensive safety reactions can reduce access to education or social interaction, posing a conflict between safety and engagement (Raffo & Gunter, 2008).

One of the most controversial aspects in crises is the struggle between the safety and the continuity of learning. Issues such as the choice of the school closing, reopening a school, or using remote teaching can often become a point of a heated discussion among policy makers, teachers, families, and communities. Such choices are hardly value-neutral; they are based on conflicting interests dealing with health, academic achievement, economic demands, and social depression (Radd et al., 2021). The issue of the relative risks of face-to-face teaching and the long-term effects of learning loss and social isolation created disagreements during the pandemic. School leaders were often put in the role of reconciling such conflicts as they issued orders that were at times inconsistent or fast-changing (Abdallah et al., 2024). These circumstances underline the ethical intricacy of crisis leadership, in which leaders have to make judgments in the face of uncertainty, with insufficient information, as well as substantial impacts(Raffo & Gunter, 2008).

Crises further amplify unequal effects on the student population, which is also one of the biggest problems for robust leadership. The poor socio-economic background and students with disabilities, refugees and displaced children, and those in remote or conflict-ridden regions are disproportionately impacted during emergencies. Their access to digital devices, dependable internet connectivity, secure housing, health, and positive learning environments limits the possibility of engaging in other learning modalities (Ramadan & Ismail, 2023). The experience of massive school shutdowns shows that better-equipped students, both in material and social terms, have an easier time adjusting, and marginalized students are disadvantaged further. Unless there is an equity component to the use of technology in responding to a crisis, then the education gaps become more diverse instead of becoming narrower (Rørstad Welle & Gunnulfsen, 2025).

Such inequalities bring to the fore some basic questions concerning fairness and accountability in crisis leadership. Although most leaders aim to promote continuity among all learners, they are at times constrained by the structure to manage the situation of unequal starting conditions. The process of resource allocation is a controversial one, especially when schools have to choose how to allocate scarce devices, learning resources, or support services. In the absence of clear equity frameworks that direct the decision-making process, crisis reactions are likely to favor already advantaged populations. Consequently, the concept of resilience will have to be critically reviewed: resilience that maintains learning among certain people but not all recreates inequality instead of alleviating it (Sahlberg, 2021).

The other notable problem is the socio-emotional stress and the loss of social connectedness in school communities. Schools serve as significant platforms of social and emotional support as well as of identity (Aldous & Ismail, 2024). Crises that affect normal schooling affect students in isolation, anxiety, and deprivation of routine. The school personnel and teachers are also exposed to more work, emotional burnout, and moral fatigue in an effort to help learners cope in demanding situations. Studies on trauma-informed education indicate that socio-emotional needs remain unaddressed and can lead to a long-term impact on learning, behavior, and well-being. However, psychosocial support is often underfunded in the response to the crisis as a secondary factor to academic recovery, but not an element of resilience (Smith & Riley, 2012).

A combination of these pressures imposes astronomical demands on school leaders. The crisis leadership style is distinguished by increased visibility, a high level of responsibility, and emotional work (Ismail & Aldous, 2024). The leaders need to communicate effectively even in times of uncertainty, maintain staff welfare, calm families, and liaise with outside agencies, while they handle their stress, and limitations and limitations themselves. Literature records that unprepared or poorly supported leaders face higher chances of burnout, hence compromising organizational stability and recovery ability. This brings to focus the fact that resilience in the student is not the only aspect that needs to be put into consideration, but the resilience of leadership itself (Sterling, 2013).

Crisis leadership also has controversies that make these issues even more difficult. One such debate is related to the extent to which school leaders should have autonomy in times of an emergency (Ismail & Aldous, 2025). Decentralization can be centralized to encourage consistency and alignment with public health, and when over-centralized, it might make leaders fail to respond to the surrounding situation. On the other hand, decentralized strategies provide school-level flexibility but create a quality and accountability imbalance. The other controversy is associated with the use of technology in crisis response (Radd et al., 2021).

Although the digital platforms have facilitated the continuity of learning in most settings, their fast usage has also revealed inequity in the state of teachers, data privacy, and inequitable access. These discussions make it clear that crisis leadership does not have any universal solutions; the responses should be specific to the situation and based on the real principles (Aldous & Ismail, 2025). Collectively, these problems represent that the process of taking the lead in times of crisis is rife with a thick knot of operational issues, ethical conundrums, and structural imbalances. The gaps in preparedness, safety issues, unequal effects, and socio-emotional burdens are not independent issues but rather dimensions of system vulnerability related to each other (Tarricone et al., 2021a). They illustrate that technical solutions can never be resilient. Rather, the resilience needs an anticipatory, adaptive, and equity-oriented leadership. These challenges are the basis of finding solutions and strategies, as discussed in the next section on solutions and recommendations on how to lead the resilient, safe, and inclusive schools during crisis periods (El Zaatari & Ibrahim, 2021).

SOLUTIONS AND RECOMMENDATIONS

To overcome the issues that have been mentioned in the previous section, a multifaceted approach to leadership, incorporating preparedness, adaptability, and equity into the schooling functions, is needed. Successful leadership in crises is not spontaneous or situational, and it is based on a system of planning, building up relationships, and a clear dedication to the protection of the most vulnerable members of the school community (Tarricone et al., 2021b). The ideas presented in this part are strategic plans that are based on empirical findings in global practice and studies and are used to describe how school leaders can foster safety, continuity, and equity amidst disruptions (Ismail & Aldous, 2025). Resilient leadership is based on crisis preparedness. Schools that react well to emergencies have usually been able to do so due to their prior planning and reacting to emergencies instead of proactively responding (Virella, 2023).

Preparedness entails the formulation of clear emergency response plans, covering various situations, such as health emergencies, natural disasters, as well as security threats. These plans define the roles and responsibilities, communication procedures, and decision-making lines and minimize confusion during the event of a crisis. Safety drills, risk assessment, and employee training are regular and help in achieving institutional preparedness as well as strengthening a common sense of the procedures (Vu Nguyen, 2025).

Notably, preparedness planning works best when it is inclusive, and teachers, support staff, students, families, and local authorities contribute to such planning.

Such an integrated strategy not only enhances the quality of plans, but it also increases trust and adherence in case of an emergency. Other than technical preparedness, adaptive leadership is a major factor in maneuvering through crises. Crises upset a set routine and usually leave the existing policies inadequate, so leaders have to make decisions using incomplete information in time. Adaptive leadership lays emphasis on flexibility, situational awareness, and responsiveness to changing circumstances. Leaders who are sincere in their communication, do not mind that they cannot be sure, and show empathy are better placed to maintain morale and unity within the organization (Walls, 2017).

The scholarly evidence suggests that in times of crisis, relational trust is a valuable asset; when school communities regard leaders as trustworthy and caring, they tend to approach difficult changes in constructive ways (Ibrahim, 2018) . This is also adaptive leadership, which incorporates distributed decision-making and allows the teams to react at all levels effectively and not just to the central authority. The ability to ensure continuity of learning is another crucial aspect of resilient leadership. Schools should be capable of moving to other forms of teaching when they are forced to of physical attendance. Remote or hybrid learning platforms, flexible academic calendars, and contingency curricula that emphasize key learning outcomes are some of the effective continuities planning strategies (Walls, 2017). The recent experience in the world shows that continuity works best in cases where schools have already adopted digital devices and blended learning as a standard educational practice.

Continuity is, however, not just limited to technological offerings; continuity also needs to be done through continuity of meaningful teacher-student relationships, continuity of engagement, and continuity of feedback. Leaders are very important in organizing teaching expectations, assisting teachers to work together, and aligning assessment practices with the crisis circumstances. Equity-based support should also be provided, which is equally important. Crises worsen already existing imbalances, and it is urgent that the response of leaders should specifically cover the problems of inequality in access to resources and opportunities (Williams & Liou, 2023).

Interventions such as equity-based distribution of devices and connections support among students due to the digital divide, delivery of learning resources to students who cannot access the internet, and liberal policies that accommodate different home situations can be considered equity-oriented. Students living with disabilities, language barriers, and caring typically need special arrangements to keep up with the disruption (Atillo et al., 2025). Instead of treating the entire student body as equal, effective leaders can use data and local expertise to determine the people who are at greatest risk and provide assistance to them first. Simultaneously, resilient leadership focuses on psychosocial well-being as a fundamental element of addressing the crisis. The emergencies cause stress, anxiety, and trauma that can impair learning long after the immediate disruptions have subsided(Anderson et al., 2011).

Trauma-informed schools will be more effective in aiding emotional recovery and restoring the feeling of safety. These involve training employees to identify distress, having access to counseling services, and developing a routine that promotes stability and belonging. The commitment of the leadership to wellbeing is an indication that the consideration of care and compassion is part of educational continuity rather than an auxiliary consideration. In addition, it is also crucial to support the well-being of the staff members, as it is frequently seen that teachers and school personnel are put under increased emotional stress during crises (Bromley & Andina, 2010).

Community engagement and intersectoral collaboration are another factor that reinforces a resilient response. Schools do not act on their own in case of an emergency; they are effective only when they are coordinated with health services, social protection agencies, community organizations, and families. Those leaders who build strong relationships before the occurrence of the crisis are likely to mobilize resources and exchange information during the time of disruption. The community engagement increases the legitimacy, culturally responsive responses, and enhances the school's capacity to respond to multifaceted needs. International practice shows that when education systems are structured to provide the school-level of leadership with the national level of emergency structures and with local support networks, the school-level outcomes are more coherent and equitable (Hayes & Derrington, 2023).

All these strategies are grounded in the need to develop a safety and trust culture. The culture of the organization influences the reaction of the schools to pressure. By making safety, transparency, and inclusion part of the day-to-day practice, crisis responses will be viewed as valid and successful. Leaders can add to these cultures by setting an example of ethical decision-making, promoting openness and transparency, and strengthening collective accountability. A Trust culture does not remove conflict or uncertainty, but it gives a platform on which people can solve problems and recover (Vaccari & Gardinier, 2019).

Figure 1. Components of a resilient school system in times of crisis

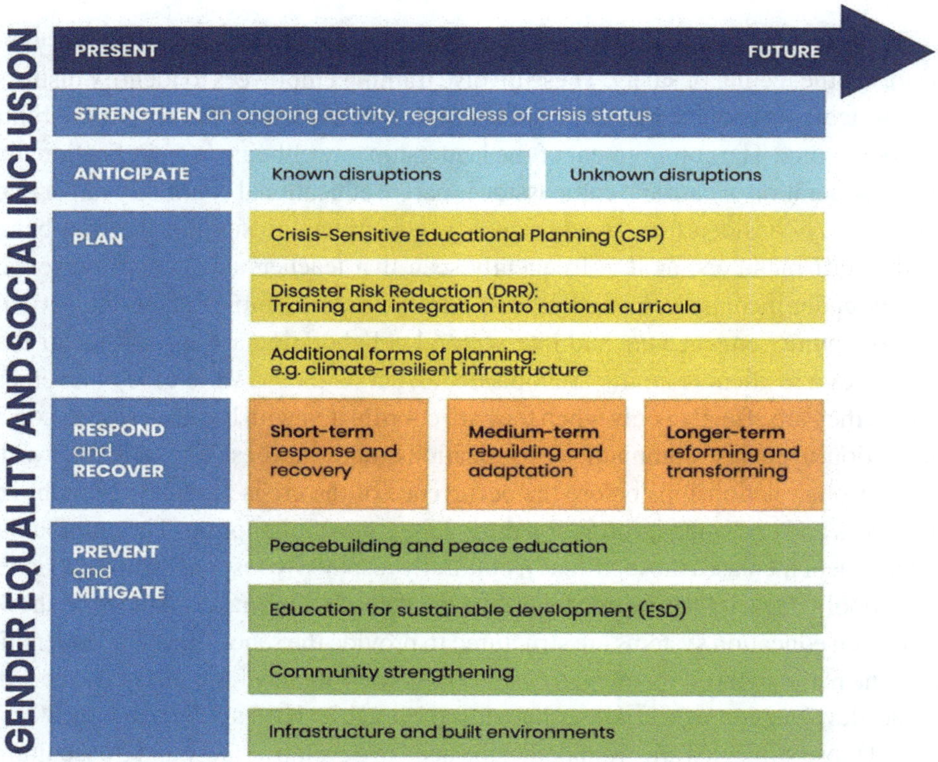

Figure 1 presents the interaction between safety, learning continuity, psychosocial well-being, leadership, and equity within a resilient education system responding to crisis conditions.

These measures highlight the notion that strong leadership is a strategic and relational approach. Those that are interdependent in an effective crisis response include preparedness planning, adaptive decision-making, learning continuity, equity-focused support, psychosocial care, and community collaboration(Ibrahim, 2013) . By becoming part of everyday governance, as opposed to measures that are only invoked in the case of emergencies, they improve the ability of schools to endure disruption and to become even better than they were before crises. The next section dwells on future research hypotheses that can further enhance the knowledge and practice in this important area of educational leadership (Williams & Liou, 2023).

LEADERSHIP DECISION-MAKING UNDER UNCERTAINTY: GOVERNANCE, ETHICS, AND POWER IN CRISIS CONTEXTS

Crises essentially change the circumstances of operation of educational leadership. Nobody can have concrete rules, routines, and accountability mechanisms that guide decision-making in stable contexts when systems are suddenly disrupted. Under these circumstances, school administrators must operate under uncertainty, partial facts, and conflicting ethical propositions. Crisis decision-making thus goes beyond technical problem-solving, and it becomes a process of ethical judgment, governance, and power bargaining. These dimensions are imperative to understand what resilient leadership is and how it may be applied responsibly. Epistemic uncertainty is one of the typical features of a crisis context. There is often a need for leaders to make decisions with little to no dependable data, without definite timeframes, and with no unified policy direction (Atillo et al., 2025).

In the case of a public health crisis, such as information about the risk of transmission, protection measures, or the reopening criteria, they can change very quickly and may even conflict with previous guidance. In much the same way, in conflict or disaster environments, there is a loss of access to correct situational awareness due to communication failures and damage to infrastructure (Ibrahim, 2012) . With such circumstances, one cannot depend on evidence-based models only, which are traditionally linked with rational planning, to make leadership decisions. Instead, leaders are expected to be involved in sense-making, which requires the use of professional judgment, ethical reasoning, and background-related knowledge to make sense of uncertain signals and take action (Angwas, 2025).

This ambiguity makes the ethical aspect of leadership more pronounced. Crisis decisions frequently imply trade-offs between competing goods, e.g., between physical and mental health, or between academic standards and access and inclusion. School closures, assessment policies, attendance requirements, or disciplinary enforcement in emergency times are not neutral administrative decisions, but they anchor their own interests whose needs take precedence and whose risks are acceptable. Leadership ethics in a crisis thus demand that justice, care, as well as proportionality are brought into explicit focus. The leaders have to look beyond the aggregate outcomes and focus on the differentiated impacts of decisions on various student groups (Sterling, 2013).

Ethical leadership in crisis should not be taken as an ordinary concept because it goes against the old traditional accountability systems that focus on adherence to set standards. When faced with an emergency, strict compliance with the standard operating procedures may only serve to make matters worse instead of alleviating them. Such as requiring students to attend or be assessed uniformly during wholesale disruption will be disproportionately harmful to those students who may have been displaced, ill, or required to care for someone. The ethical crisis leadership is rather contextually responsive, and the rules are interpreted with flexibility against the realities of their lives. It does not mean that there is no accountability, but just a change towards responsibility based on professional ethics and the trust of the people. The governance structures are decisive in how the leaders manage such ethical issues (Özen & Yavuz, 2024).

The extent of autonomy that school leaders are accorded is very different in the education systems, especially in emergencies. In very centralized systems, the power of decision-making is mostly vested in the ministerial or district levels, where the schools are supposed to follow the directives unanimously (Ibrahim, 2010) . Although centralization can bring about coherence and alignment of health to the people, it also acts as a constraint to viewing leaders as limited in reacting to local circumstances. Decentralized systems, on the other hand, provide more discretion to the leadership but threaten to deliver unequal quality and unfair results when the resources and capacity differ dramatically across schools (Pastor et al., 2024).

This central and local control is a long-standing government predicament in crisis leadership. It has been shown that sometimes a balance between school-level adaptability and system-level coordination is a key to successful crisis response. Mobilization of resources and minimum standards of safety, as well as equity between regions, need centralized authorities. Meanwhile, school leaders have contextual knowledge about their communities that is essential to match responses to such needs (Tarricone et al., 2021b).

Institutional structures that facilitate dialogue, feedback, and adaptive execution will hence be more likely to achieve resilient results compared to strict hierarchical forms. The issue of power and legitimacy in the educational institutions is also revealed in crisis leadership. Emergency decisions are highly criticized by families, employees, the media, and politicians. The authority of leaders cannot be based on the formal position only, but on assumed legitimacy, which is created by transparency, consistency, and moral credibility (Vaccari & Gardinier, 2019).

Leaders who speak frankly about uncertainty, recognize the limitations, and justify why tough choices are being made will be in a better position to preserve trust even during conflict. On the other hand, a lack of transparency or unstable decision-making processes erodes trust and may create resistance, which further disrupts schools. Aspects of power are especially noticeable when decision-making is concerned with marginalized groups (Vu Nguyen, 2025).

The failure of leadership to ask these questions is because it may recreate structural inequalities by emergency necessity. Such practices as inclusive governance can help to balance unfair powers and make crisis responses more representative. The other important aspect of decision-making in uncertain situations entails trade-offs in time. The crisis leaders need to strike a balance between the short-term emergency response and the education implications. Interventions aimed at stabilizing systems during the short-term after disruption can have unintended consequences that can result in long-term effects of normalized loss of learning, weakened accountability, or student disengagement. Indicatively, the sustained use of emergency remote learning in the absence of proper support systems may entrench inequalities and destroy the quality of instruction (Smith & Riley, 2012).

Strong leadership thus necessitates forward-thinking, whereby immediate possession is taken into account as well as future restoration and reinforcement of the system. This time complexity highlights the significance of learning-oriented leadership. Crises create new knowledge on the vulnerabilities of the system, institutional capacity, and social inequalities. Leaders who view crises as learning moments, but not merely disruptions to be survived, will have a greater ability to institutionalize the lessons in policy and practice (Sahlberg, 2021).

This involves updating continuity plans, investing in staff capacity, fortifying data systems, and reassigning presumptions about schooling. The governance systems, which institutionalize reflection and post-crisis assessment, lead to resilience over time and not a repetition of fragility. The emotional stress on a leader during decision-making under crisis is also very high. Responsibility, social pressure, and uncertainty are added to the stress and burnout (Pastor et al., 2024). However, the resiliency of leadership is mostly assumed and not reinforced. It has also been theorized that decision fatigue, decreased effectiveness, and attrition occur more frequently in leaders who do not have access to peer networks, mentoring, or psychological support. The implication of this is on the governance on system level: resilience should be fostered not only at the level of students and schools but also at the level of the leaders through the professional support systems (Özen & Yavuz, 2024).

Figure 2. Leadership decision-making under uncertainty in crisis contexts

Figure 2 depicts how school leaders navigate incomplete information, ethical dilemmas, governance constraints, and equity considerations when making high-stakes decisions during crises.

Notably, the crisis leadership undermines the leading discourses of leadership as heroism. Charismatic leadership might be reassuring in the short term, but long-term resilience lies in shared leadership ability. The models of distributed leadership which empower teams, distribute decision making, and enable a variety of expertise alleviate the cognitive and emotional load on individual leaders and enhance the flexibility of the organization. Collective leadership helps resolve issues at a faster rate, is more legitimate, and more inclusive in crises. Decision-making under uncertainty has an analytical value since it reveals the normative basis of education systems. Crises are the events that require leaders to answer some inherent questions regarding schooling purpose, equity meaning, and institutional responsibility (Walls, 2017).

The value structures of education systems are expressed in the value that is given to examination performance versus student well-being versus social protection in times of crisis or vice versa. Leadership decisions, hence, serve as moral clues that create institutional culture even after the crisis has already over. In this regard, strong school administration cannot be narrowed down to a list of established preparedness measures or technical skills. It is a practice of governance that is instilled in ethical reasoning, power relations, and expectations in society. Leaders have to walk a fine line between not compromising principles on ambivalence, not compromising inclusion on authority, and not compromising dissent on decisiveness (Atillo et al., 2025).

This is a set of tensions that characterize the nature of crisis leadership and why resilience should be conceptualized as a technical and normative accomplishment. This section supports the chapter by anticipating decision-making in the context of uncertainty, which strengthens the main argument of this chapter: resilience in education cannot be achieved without the policies of leadership ethics, governance design, and equity promises. Crises do not just put systems to the test, but they expose their values. The question of how leaders make decisions in the face of pressure is a determinant of the survival of schooling as well as the legitimacy and fairness of education systems during periods of great uncertainty (Landa et al., 2021).

FUTURE RESEARCH DIRECTIONS

Despite the recent crises that have produced an increasing number of studies on education system resilience, there are still substantial gaps in the knowledge regarding the role of school leadership in protecting safety, continuity, and equity in the circumstances of long-term disruption. It is important that further studies be conducted in order to provide insight into the theory, enhance empirical research, and guide policy and leadership practice in various educational environments. Among the critical future research opportunities is the long-term educational and psychosocial effects of persistent disruptions. Although the negative impact of temporary academic losses and health-related issues has been most extensively reported, the impact of repeated or prolonged crises on the academic career of students, their mental health, and social growth in the long term is less well-known (Virella, 2023).

Longitudinal studies of learners during periods of crisis and subsequent crisis would be useful in providing evidence on recovery patterns and in informing leadership approaches that facilitate both academic engagement and emotional stability. A second priority would be comparative studies of crisis leadership models in the various national and institutional settings. The education systems are diverse in terms of the governance structures, availability of resources, and cultural expectations of the leaders. Comparative studies of the crisis response of centralized and decentralized arrangements, or the ways leadership practices vary in high-income and low-income contexts, would help clarify the contexts in which a particular response to crisis is most effective (Tarricone et al., 2021b).

Such studies would go into the creation of context-sensitive leadership models as opposed to the generic models. Equity-based crisis interventions are also a subject of research that needs further exploration. Though it has been demonstrated consistently that the crisis tends to impact marginalized learners out of proportion, there is little empirical work done to understand which specific strategies will do the best job in addressing these inequities. Scholarship investigating the effectiveness of device distribution programs, flexible assessment policies, inclusive remote learning designs, and specific psychosocial supports would assist leaders in making more effective choices regarding resource allocation. Students with disabilities, displaced students, and the poor are also worthy of special consideration in the context of research on crisis, since their experiences are frequently overlooked (Sterling, 2013).

A different line of enquiry is in the aspect of the utilization of technology and data systems in disaster preparedness and disaster management. The role of digital platforms in continuity in learning has been vital, but the success of this depends greatly on infrastructure and the capacity of teachers, as well as the access of students. Leadership preparation and professional learning in the context of crisis should be analyzed. Although crisis leadership requires adaptive, relational, and ethical skills, several leadership development programs pay minimal or no attention to emergency preparedness, trauma-informed leadership, or making equitable decisions in the midst of pressure (Vu Nguyen, 2025).

The studies that measure leadership training models and professional development interventions may help to redesign the preparation programs to help school leaders be more prepared to live in an era of repeated disruption. Altogether, these research lines support the idea that resilient school leadership is a dynamic area that needs long-term academic consideration. Increasing the knowledge in such spheres will allow policymakers, educators, and leaders to cease crisis management as a reaction model and adopt proactive equity-based resilience-building methods (Williams & Liou, 2023). This kind of research is important in the fortification of education systems and making sure that schools are safe, inclusive, and productive even in the uncertainty of the future.

CONCLUSION

This chapter has explored how resilient school leadership is critical in maintaining safety, continuity of learning, and promoting educational equity during a crisis. With education systems facing a period of constant upheaval - caused by pandemics, climatic crises, war, and social-economic instability - the institutional ability of schools to act responsibly has become a key determining factor in the quality of education and social safety. It has been shown that crises not only reveal the weaknesses in operations but also systemic injustices that define the experiences and performance of learners. The chapter has discussed resilience in education as not merely physical preparedness or an emergency response framework by basing the discussion on the known global frameworks and recent studies. The practices of leadership that constitute resilience are anticipatory, adaptive, and ethically focused and are able to respond to immediate risks and long-term impacts. School leaders stand in the middle of policy, community expectations, and the needs of students, having to make complex decisions when they are uncertain about them and being trusted, legitimate, and inclusive.

As demonstrated in the chapter, issues like a lack of preparedness, safety and well-being consideration, inequality of effects, and socio-emotional burden are not independent of each other. To overcome these difficulties, there is a need to integrate leadership strategies that entail crisis preparations, adaptive decision-making, continuity planning, equity-based support, and psychosocial well-being concerns. These elements should be considered as fundamental dimensions of school governance and not interim solutions because the schools are better placed to resist disruption and recuperate in a manner that will enhance future capacity.

The key idea that is presented by the argument throughout this chapter is that resilience is not something that can be decoupled from equity. The responses to the crisis that protect the learning and safety of certain students and not others are likely to reinforce structural disadvantage and demoralize the social purpose of education. Fair leadership also makes sure that the most vulnerable learners are considered, the distribution of resources represents the differentiated needs, and the crisis action helps build more inclusive systems, and not just stabilize the situation. Being a resilient school leader is not an accidental or periodic-only task but a key aspect of modern educational leadership. It takes a long-term leadership dedication, knowledgeable policy assistance, and a shared awareness that securing education in times of turmoil is the cornerstone of securing societies as well.

REFERENCES

Abdallah, A. K. (2023). Teacher-led, student-focused, and unleashing the power of teacher empowerment for school improvement and success. In *Restructuring leadership for school improvement and reform*. IGI Global., DOI: 10.4018/978-1-6684-7818-9.ch001

Abdallah, A. K. (2024). The impact of gender, psychology, and cultural dimensions on leadership development in distance education. *Scientific Reports*, *14*(1), 68495. Advance online publication. DOI: 10.1038/s41598-024-68495-4

Abdallah, A. K., & Abdallah, R. K. (2023). Achieving academic excellence: The intersection of teacher development, quality education, and entrepreneurship. In *Innovations in teacher development, personalized learning, and upskilling the workforce*. IGI Global., DOI: 10.4018/978-1-6684-5518-0.ch007

Abdallah, A. K., & Alkaabi, A. A. M. (2023). *Restructuring leadership for school improvement and reform*. IGI Global., DOI: 10.4018/978-1-6684-7818-9

Abdallah, A. K., & Alkaabi, A. A. M. (2023). Preface: Shaping the future – The essential role of school leaders in driving education improvement. In *Restructuring leadership for school improvement and reform*. IGI Global.

Abdallah, A. K., Ismail, L. S., & Alkaabi, A. M. (2024). Green careers: Educating for the future of sustainability. In *Legal frameworks and educational strategies for sustainable development*. IGI Global., DOI: 10.4018/979-8-3693-2987-0.ch017

Abdallah, A. K., Ismail, L. S., & Ismail, O. A. S. (2024). Foundations of sustainability education: Concepts and contexts. In *Legal frameworks and educational strategies for sustainable development*. IGI Global., DOI: 10.4018/979-8-3693-2987-0.ch011

Abdallah, A. K., & Musah, M. B. (2023). Principal and teacher licensing as a tool to school improvement. In *Restructuring leadership for school improvement and reform*. IGI Global., DOI: 10.4018/978-1-6684-7818-9.ch014

Abdallah, R. K., Al Maktoum, S. B., & Al Mansoori, M. K. (2023). The Road to Lesson Observation as a Tool to School Improvement: Accountability vs. Perfunctory. In Abdallah, A., & Alkaabi, A. (Eds.), *Restructuring Leadership for School Improvement and Reform* (pp. 222–252). IGI Global Scientific Publishing., DOI: 10.4018/978-1-6684-7818-9.ch012

Abdallah, R. K., & Awad, M. J. (2026). Integrating Artificial Intelligence and Technology Into UAE Teacher Licensing Systems for Global Education Reforms. In Massouti, A., & Abdallah, A. (Eds.), *Building a Unified Teacher Licensing System: Policies, Education Reforms, and Cultural Integration* (pp. 211–250). IGI Global Scientific Publishing., DOI: 10.4018/979-8-3373-0837-1.ch008

Akkari, A., & Lauwerier, T. (2014). The education policies of international organizations: Specific differences and convergences. *Prospects*, *45*(1), 141–157. DOI: 10.1007/s11125-014-9332-z

Al-Qodsi, E. M., Jadalhaq, I. M., & El-Maknouzi, M. E. H. (2024). The place of UAE's food security in the national legislation and its role in supporting global food security. *Cogent Social Sciences*, *10*(1), 2319379. Advance online publication. DOI: 10.1080/23311886.2024.2319379

Aldous, S. M., & Ismail, G. A. (2024). Safeguarding the future: Integrating student safety into sustainable education practices. In *Legal frameworks and educational strategies for sustainable development.* IGI Global., DOI: 10.4018/979-8-3693-2987-0.ch018

Aldous, S. M., & Ismail, G. A. (2025). Crisis management and teacher preparedness: Embedding health and safety in teacher education programs. In *Building a unified teacher licensing system: Policies, education reforms, and cultural integration.* IGI Global., DOI: 10.4018/979-8-3373-0837-1.ch013

Alkaabi, A. M., Abdallah, A. K., Abdallah, R., Al Hasan, M., & Mohamed, A. (2025). Principal engagement in the teacher evaluation process in remote schools: A narrative inquiry of language teachers. *Forum for Linguistic Studies*, *7*(3), 209–230. DOI: 10.30564/fls.v7i3.8502

Alqodsi, E. M. (2021). Analyzing the implementation of usufruct rights and obligations in the UAE Civil Transactions Law. *International Journal of Criminal Justice Sciences*, *16*(1), 95–109.

Alqodsi, E. M., & Abdallah, A. K. (2024). *Legal frameworks and educational strategies for sustainable development.* IGI Global., DOI: 10.4018/979-8-3693-2987-0

Anderson, A., Hyll-Larsen, P., & Hofmann, J. (2011). The Right to Education for Children in Emergencies. *Journal of International Humanitarian Legal Studies*, *2*(1), 84–126. DOI: 10.1163/187815211x586151

Angwas, R. O. (2025). School Heads' Emergency Management Competencies: Its Influence on Continuity of Teaching and Learning During Emergency Situations in the Division of Agusan Del Sur, Philippines. *International Journal of Scientific and Research Publications*, *15*(6), 203–207. DOI: 10.29322/IJSRP.15.06.2025.p16225

Atillo, F. F., Batao, H. S., Giger, V. M. D., & Elesio, J. M. (2025). School Heads' Crisis Leadership: Experiences in Managing Natural Disasters and School Emergencies. *School Heads'. Crisis Leadership: Experiences in Managing Natural Disasters and School Emergencies*, *165*(1), 14–14.

Bromley, P., & Andina, M. (2010). Standardizing chaos: A neo-institutional analysis of the INEE Minimum Standards for Education in Emergencies, Chronic Crises and Early Reconstruction. *Compare: A Journal of Comparative Education*, *40*(5), 575–588. DOI: 10.1080/03057920903254972

Brooks, M. C., & Ezzani, M. D. (2021). Islamic school leadership: Advancing a framework for critical spirituality. *International Journal of Qualitative Studies in Education : QSE*, *35*(3), 319–336. DOI: 10.1080/09518398.2021.1930265

Brown, J. H., D'Emidio-Caston, M., & Benard, B. (2001). *Resilience education*. Corwin Press.

Chatzipanagiotou, P., & Katsarou, E. (2023). Crisis management, school leadership in disruptive times and the recovery of schools in the post COVID-19 era: A systematic literature review. *Education Sciences*, *13*(2), 118.

Cunningham, A. E. (2025). *A Qualitative Study Exploring How School And District Education Leaders Respond To Critical Organizational Crisis And Change Events*. Franklin University.

Elliott, K. E., Mathew, K. A., Fan, Y., & Mattson, D. (2022). Educating during a Health Emergency: An Integrative Review of the Literature from 1990 to 2020. *Journal on Education in Emergencies*, *8*(3). Advance online publication. DOI: 10.33682/85qf-kr51

Fang, M., Abdallah, A. K., & Vorfolomeyeva, O. (2024). Collaborative AI-enhanced digital mind-mapping as a tool for stimulating creative thinking in inclusive education for students with neurodevelopmental disorders. *BMC Psychology*, *12*(1), 1975. Advance online publication. DOI: 10.1186/s40359-024-01975-4

Friesen, K., & Bell, D. (2006). Risk Reduction and Emergency Preparedness Activities of Canadian Universities. *International Journal of Mass Emergencies and Disasters*, *24*(2), 223–249. DOI: 10.1177/028072700602400204

Fu, Q., & Zhang, X. (2024). Promoting community resilience through disaster education: Review of community-based interventions with a focus on teacher resilience and well-being. *PLoS One*, *19*(1), e0296393. https://journals.plos.org/plosone/article/file?id=10.1371/journal.pone.0296393&type=printable

Gontang, M. G. Leadership Resiliency and Adaptability: Effect on Crisis Management in Multigrade Schools. *International Journal of Open-Access, Interdisciplinary & New Educational Discoveries of ETCOR Educational Research Center*, *4*(1), https://etcor.org/storage/iJOINED/Vol.%20IV(1),%20168-180.pdf

Hayes, S. D., & Derrington, M. L. (2023). School leadership in uncertain times: Identifying dimensions of effective principal leadership. *School Leadership & Management*, *43*(4), 330–347. DOI: 10.1080/13632434.2023.2171002

Ibrahim, A. (2010). *Education in the UAE: A socio-cultural analysis.* In Y. Zhao et al., *Handbook of Asian Education: A Cultural Perspective* (pp. 327-344). Routledge. https://doi.org/DOI: 10.4324/9780203816318

Ibrahim, A. (2018). *Directive, collaborative, or non-directive? Supervision perceptions of UAE thesis/dissertation approaches.* Issues in Educational Research, 28(3), 679–700. https://www.iier.org.au/iier28/ibrahim.pdf

Ibrahim, A. S. (2012). Induction and mentoring of novice teachers: A scheme for the United Arab Emirates. *Teacher Development*, *16*(2), 235–253. DOI: 10.1080/13664530.2012.688676

Ibrahim, A. S. (2013). The learning needs of beginning teachers in the United Arab Emirates. *Journal of Education for Teaching: International Research and Pedagogy*, *39*(5), 491–506. DOI: 10.1080/02607476.2013.739791

Ismail, G. A., & Aldous, S. M. (2024). Digital innovation in green learning: Ensuring safety while fostering environmental stewardship. In *Legal frameworks and educational strategies for sustainable development*. IGI Global., DOI: 10.4018/979-8-3693-2987-0.ch016

Ismail, G. A., & Aldous, S. M. (2025). AI-driven health and safety management in school facilities. In *Convergence of AI, education, and business for sustainability*. IGI Global., DOI: 10.4018/979-8-3373-1917-9.ch002

Ismail, L. S., & Ismail, O. A. S. (2024). Adaptive strategies for success: Monitoring and evaluating blue-green infrastructure in urban development. In *Integrating blue-green infrastructure into urban development*. IGI Global., DOI: 10.4018/979-8-3693-8069-7.ch001

Ismail, O. (2024). Digital transformation in education: Navigating the challenges and opportunities of remote learning. In *Building resilient education models post crisis*. IGI Global., DOI: 10.4018/979-8-3693-8125-0.ch007

Ismail, O. A. S. (2024). Sustainable automotive engineering: Empowering the next generation of eco-conscious engineers. In *Legal frameworks and educational strategies for sustainable development*. IGI Global., DOI: 10.4018/979-8-3693-2987-0.ch019

Jadalhaq, I. M., Abdulhay, I. E., Alqodsi, E. M., & El Maknouzi, M. E. H. (2023). A systematic review and meta-analysis of interruption of the statute of limitations for civil claims: A comparative study of Arab legislations. *Heliyon*, *9*(9), e16756. DOI: 10.1016/j.heliyon.2023.e16756

Kamaruddin, S. A. (2024). Disaster Preparedness Design in Secondary School Environment. *JUPE: Jurnal Pendidikan Mandala*, *9*(4). Advance online publication. DOI: 10.58258/jupe.v9i4.7821

Karakose, T. (2021). Emergency remote teaching due to COVID-19 pandemic and potential risks for socioeconomically disadvantaged students in higher education. *Educational Process International Journal*, *10*(3). Advance online publication. DOI: 10.22521/edupij.2021.103.4

Kolehmainen, J., Kurikka, H., Keerberg, A., & Raagmaa, G. (2022). Being resilient between the region and the higher education system? Views on regional higher education institutions in Estonia and Finland. *Towards resilient organizations and societies: A cross-sectoral and multi-disciplinary perspective*, 249-276.

Landa, N., Zhou, S., & Marongwe, N. (2021). Education in emergencies: Lessons from COVID-19 in South Africa. *International Review of Education*, *67*(1-2), 167–183. DOI: 10.1007/s11159-021-09903-z

Leithwood, K. (2021). A Review of Evidence about Equitable School Leadership. *Education Sciences*, *11*(8). Advance online publication. DOI: 10.3390/educsci11080377

Morgan, H. (2014). Review of research: The education system in Finland: A success story other countries can emulate. *Childhood Education*, *90*(6), 453–457.

Naidu, S. (2021). *Building resilience in education systems post-COVID-19* (Vol. 42). Taylor & Francis.

Özen, H., & Yavuz, P. (2024). A theoretical analysis for resilience: Developing a complex adaptive leadership model in schools. *Anadolu Eğitim Liderliği ve Öğretim Dergisi*, *12*(1), 49–72.

Pastor, M. J. D., Acosta, R. L., & Aquino, M. U. (2024). Resiliency practices in educational crisis management among school administrators. *International Journal of Education, 17*(1), 71–78.

Radd, S. I., Generett, G. G., Gooden, M. A., & Theoharis, G. (2021). *Five practices for equity-focused school leadership*. ASCD.

Raffo, C., & Gunter, H. (2008). Leading schools to promote social inclusion: Developing a conceptual framework for analysing research, policy and practice. *Journal of Education Policy, 23*(4), 397–414. DOI: 10.1080/02680930801923799

Ramadan, R. S., & Ismail, O. A. S. (2023). Building a better future: The role of school inspection in driving educational excellence. In *Restructuring leadership for school improvement and reform*. IGI Global., DOI: 10.4018/978-1-6684-7818-9.ch011

Rørstad Welle, K. B., & Gunnulfsen, A. E. (2025). School leadership: Dilemmas in dealing with crises. *Educational Management Administration & Leadership*. Advance online publication. DOI: 10.1177/17411432251325099

Sahlberg, P. (2021). *Finnish lessons 3.0: What can the world learn from educational change in Finland?* Teachers College Press.

Smith, L., & Riley, D. (2012). School leadership in times of crisis. *School Leadership & Management, 32*(1), 57–71. DOI: 10.1080/13632434.2011.614941

Sterling, S. (2013). Learning for resilience, or the resilient learner? Towards a necessary reconciliation in a paradigm of sustainable education. In *Resilience in social-ecological systems* (pp. 45–62). Routledge.

Tarricone, P., Mestan, K., & Teo, I. (2021a). https://doi.org/DOI: 10.37517/978-1-74286-639-0

Tarricone, P., Mestan, K., & Teo, I. (2021b). Building resilient education systems: A rapid review of the education in emergencies literature.

Vaccari, V., & Gardinier, M. P. (2019). Toward one world or many? A comparative analysis of OECD and UNESCO global education policy documents. *International Journal of Development Education and Global Learning, 11*(1). Advance online publication. DOI: 10.18546/ijdegl.11.1.05

Virella, P. M. (2023). Introducing the pillars of equity-oriented crisis leadership: A conceptual framework. *School Leadership & Management, 43*(4), 390–410. DOI: 10.1080/13632434.2023.2186848

Vu Nguyen, V. H. (2025). *Finnish Students' Educational Provision Experience Towards Resilience*. Recovery and Renewal of Education Systems.

Walls, T. E. (2017). *Race, resilience, and resistance: A culturally relevant qualitative examination of how black women school leaders advance racial equity and social justice in US schools*. University of Nevada.

Williams, T., & Liou, Y.-H. (2023). Framing K-12 School Leaders' Roles and Competencies in Times of Crisis. *Journal of School Leadership*, *34*(1), 26–46. DOI: 10.1177/10526846231187576

Chapter 9
Smart Learning and Smart Schools:
Transforming Indian Education Through AI-Enabled NEP 2020 Implementations

Nasir Ahmad Ganaie
http://orcid.org/0000-0001-6781-834X
University of Kashmir, India

Irfat Jan
http://orcid.org/0009-0003-7156-7362
University of Kashmir, India

Senthil Kumar A. V.
http://orcid.org/0000-0002-8587-7017
Nehru Institute of Information Technology and Management, India

Nagakishore Bhavanam S.
http://orcid.org/0000-0003-3798-6945
Mangalayatan University, Jabalpur, India

Tavseef Ahmad Mir
http://orcid.org/0000-0002-6354-1520
University of Kashmir, India

Sambasiva Rao K. R. S.
http://orcid.org/0000-0002-0061-8754
Mangalayatan University, India

ABSTRACT

India's National Education Policy 2020 integrates Artificial Intelligence to address educational disparities across heterogeneous contexts—rural-urban divides, resource-constrained government schools, and technologically advanced academies. The chapter employs qualitative policy examination, institutional readiness assessments, and critical synthesis of empirical research on intelligent tutoring systems and learning analytics within Indian educational ecosystems. Analysis reveals AI's multifaceted potential: personalised learning pathways, augmented teacher capacity in under-resourced contexts, and equitable access in geographically dispersed communities. The 2026-27 mandatory AI curriculum presents developmental oppor-

DOI: 10.4018/979-8-2600-0388-6.ch009

tunities; success requires substantial investment in teacher preparation and critical AI literacy. Realising transformative potential demands balanced integration of technological innovation with institutional capacity building, teacher empowerment, and transparent governance, prioritising educational equity and resource allocation.

INTRODUCTION: THE INFLEXION POINT: INDIA'S EDUCATIONAL MOMENT IN THE AGE OF ARTIFICIAL INTELLIGENCE

The face of education in the twenty-first century is at a critical inflexion of extraordinary challenges and extraordinary opportunities. The combination of technological innovation, demographic dynamism and changing demands of the labour market, along with the changing expectations of the changing society, has restructured the playing field on which educational systems operate on a very fundamental level (Gopali & Shetty, 2019). For India, our country of over 1.4 billion people, a country which is marked by an extremely high degree of socio-economic heterogeneity, linguistic diversity and significant educational disparities, this moment has a certain vertige to it. The pace at which Artificial Intelligence (AI) is being implemented in educational systems is a revolutionary development which has implications not only within the walls of schools and colleges, but also includes involvement of the fabric of social mobility, economic opportunity and democratic participation (Ngo et al., 2024).

The potential of AI for education is resounding in powerful ways in policy circles, philanthropy organisations, educational technology entrepreneurs, and among policymakers. Narratives of AI-enabled personalisation, democratic access to education and pedagogical innovation are bouncing all around these days, and in the wake of being oftentimes imbued with things as techno-optimism: that technological solutions to problems have the capacity to overcome deeply seeded inequalities in the educational world (Desai & Desai, 2023). At the same time, counternarratives about risks (algorithmic bias, digital divides, teacher displacement, privacy violations) provide counsel of caution on the undiluted deployment of technology. Between these polarised positions is a complex reality of how educational systems might strategically, thoughtfully and equitably place AI technologies in a broader transformative agenda (David et al., 2020).

The National Education Policy 2020: Recalibrating Educational Vision and Systemic Transformation

National Education Policy 2020 (NEP 2020) is of the most far-reaching nature in terms of educational reform in India since the National Education Policy 1986 (Rahman, 2022). As a policy document, NEP 2020 is a transcendence of the traditional statements of academic goals; it is an ambitious blueprint of the re-conceptualisation of India's educational ecosystem, across a range of dimensions, almost simultaneously (Singh, 2025). The policy lays out a vision of transformation articulated along three foundational pillars, which are access, ensuring that educational opportunities are accessible to all citizens regardless of their geographical, economic or social circumstances; equity, ensuring that educational systems actively address and interrupt existing patterns of stratification and discrimination and excellence, fostering the highest standards of pedagogical quality, institutional performance and learning outcomes (Aynul Bari & Goswamee, 2024).

In the framework of this comprehensive policy set up, technology innovation and more specifically, Artificial Intelligence does not play the peripheral role of an add-on but contrives itself to play a central enabling role. NEP 2020 recognises the fact that India's challenges in education, like chronic teacher shortages, inadequacies in infrastructure, regional disparities, differences in quality and access gaps, are not problems that are to be solved through traditional efforts of systemic reform alone. Technology, if properly used and integrated, provides the basis of the transcendence of these constraints at least to a certain extent. The intelligent tutoring of systems with AI may provide personal learning help in situations where there are not many teachers (Venkata et al., 2025). Data-bound wealth resource allocation in an institution which struggles with resources may be made possible through learning analytics platforms. There is a generative AI tool that may assist in content generation in the different languages of the country. The usage of digital delivery mechanisms may be able to reach out to communities in the field of education that are far. Yet the policy document itself is a recognition of the complexity and challenges attendant to integrating technology. NEP 2020 is focused on the use of technology to be explicit for the stated educational values, and not as an end in and of itself. The policy point is that technological systems have to not prevail over the pedagogical vision, institutional and more importantly, commitments to equity and human development (Chowdhury & Hanumanthu, 2023). This penumbral positioning, acknowledgement of possible limitations to the implementation of such technological resolutions, forms the intellectual location for the critical examination of the ways in which AI may contribute in authentic ways to the transformation of education.

The Implementation Reality: Bridging the Policy Practice

Despite the visionary articulation of NEP 2020 and the broad policy consensus of the need for educational reform, the process of translating aspirational policy language to institutional practice is enormously complex. The policy-implementation gap, the chasm between what the policy documents envision and what the institutions do, is a feature which is conspicuous in the educational landscape in India and, indeed, stands out firmly (Chaudhari, 2023). Multiple factors contribute to this gap, including a lack of adequate resources and consistent institutional capacity based on these resources; inadequate teacher preparation; unclear governance models; entrenched organisational cultures and competing policy priorities; and the sheer complexity of the systemic change itself.

Specifically in terms of the integration of AI, this implementation gap is played out on multiple dimensions. While elite urban private schools have been trying out AI-powered learning systems, intelligent tutoring platforms and complex analytics infrastructure, government schools catering to the majority of India's learners often have little access to basic technological infrastructure, stable electricity supply and internet connectivity. Teacher preparation isn't there yet. Most teacher education programs don't focus on teacher preparation in technology integration or understanding artificial intelligence (Sutar, 2024). Governance frameworks for the proper use of AI in education spaces are underdeveloped. Data protection policies are also not yet good enough. Curricular synchronisation of integration of AI and a more extensive educational vision is yet to find expressiveness in the majority of situations. Understandably, understanding this policy implementation gap proves to be key to realistically evaluating the potential contribution that AI can make to educational transformation. So instead of taking for granted that policy articulation leads to institutional changes, there needs to be a critical analysis of specific conditions, investments and systemic reforms, which would make possible meaningful integration of AI (Das et al., 2023).

India's Educational Heterogeneity: Context for AI Integration

India's educational system is a reflection of India's linguistic plurality, geographical diversity, economic, social and religious and cultural diversity of the country and contains extraordinary diversity in the education system (Singh & Narayanan, 2023). This diversity implies that an implementation framework of an AI should be sensitive to the diversity of the 'context' and should not face a standardisation of the technological solutions. Although considering the heterogeneity of the educational institutions in India, Urban metropolitan centres are seen as the elite private schools with state-of-the-art physical infrastructure, highly qualified teachers, comprehensive learning resources and access to advanced technologies (Kulal et al., 2024). These are the educational institutions which cater primarily to the affluent families, which prepare students for the competitive level of higher education and the professional routes. Simultaneously, rural government schools in geographically remote locations, and minimum infrastructural environments with chronic vacancies of teachers and paucity of learning materials, as well as no assurance of access to any technology (Manodamrongsat et al., 2022). Students in these types of contexts often come from agricultural families or work in the informal sector, with low levels of, as well as significant barriers to education access and attainment.

This is a dramatic institutional homogeneity that carries over to the learning needs and student population. India's education system is confronted with the challenges of students with disability, students from disadvantaged castes and religious groups, who are subjected to a system of discrimination in education, students confronted by gender-constructed constraints, students that originate from less well-off economic families and economically disadvantaged backgrounds, and students that have different language backgrounds (Vigoda-Gadot & Mizrahi, 2024). Additionally, there are twenty-two recognised languages of India, and scores of regional languages in the country's educational system, which cause challenges to a standardised curriculum and pedagogy.

Effective implementation of AI has to be sensitised to this diversity. Solutions that are appropriate for urban private schools involving sophisticated technological infrastructure, high-cost systems and English medium instruction may turn out to be totally inappropriate to rural government schools, geographically remote communities or institutions serving marginalised populations. Rather than assuming that technology implementations will occur in all contexts, contextually responsive implementations frameworks take no position on AI implementation occurring in the same way in all contexts, but instead require that AI implementation be variable according to context in institutions, available resources, teacher capacity, student need, and educational vision.

The Dual Promise and Peril of Educational Technology: Theoretical Considerations

Educational technology adoption is always accompanied by an equivalent number of opportunities and risks. Technological optimists have their eyes on the transformational potential of how technology can scale access, make learning more personalised, pedagogically effective and democratise educational opportunity (Tian et al., 2025). Technological pessimists look for risks that technology will produce more unequal, rather than more equal, societies; to give way to concentrations of power and wealth; to anthropocentric limitations on our agency; to dishearten us from the questions of basic material allocation, of equity.

Neither is an obscure representation of reality. Technology is not emancipatory or oppressive in itself but is fundamentally dependent on those institutions that conceive, apply, control and evaluate their technological use in one context or another. A system based on learning analytics could be used to support an early identification of at-risk learners and targeted intervention, or sow the seeds of damaging stereotypes and limit learner expectations through deterministic labelling. Intelligent tutoring systems could provide individual access to learning (even extended access to education) for the disadvantaged, or educational augmentation to technologically privileged populations. AI-generated content might help make access to quality learning materials more democratic in more than one language or hardcode bias, misinformation and cultural insensitivity (Sethuramalingam, 2020). The actual outcomes depend upon the way it is implemented (implementation decisions), governance arrangements, concern for ethics and the considered context of systems. This recognition has a role in the approach given in an analytic manner in this chapter. Instead of some techno optimism or techno pessimism, there is some real distance of critical analysis, which analyses both the real opportunities and real dangers, and identifies the conditions that can maximise the benefits and minimise the harms.

Objectives of the Study

The basic objective of this chapter is to construct and use the Multi-dimensional Framework for Equitable AI Integration (MAE-AI) as a hard analytical tool to determine the complex process of adoption of Artificial Intelligence in the educational ecosystem of India, with its diversity. This study aims to look beyond the simplistic adoption metric associated with technology by critically looking at the role of AI vis-a-vis the normative aims of access, equity and quality as provided in the National Education Policy 2020 (NEP 2020). The first specific objective is that, by mapping systematically the existing and emerging applications of AI, including Intelligent Tutoring Systems (ITS) and Generative AI (GenAI) vis-a-vis the NEP 2020 framework, the implications of the challenges in implementation (i.e. chronic shortcomings of digital infrastructures and resources) for the spread of substantive capabilities of students in heterogeneous learning contexts are analysed. The second objective is to measure the algorithmic equity using the rigorous framework of Data Justice, which measures the role of potential algorithmic bias in the learning analytics and assessment systems that can potentially continue or exacerbate the existing inequalities of a stratified society on the basis of socio-economic and caste disparities in the absence of comprehensive fairness audits. The third primary objective is the identification of institutional pre-requisites for sustainable and equitable integration of AI that can be considered in particular in terms of infrastructural and governance reforms to be developed in order to facilitate the transition from the restrictive "school factory model" to effective Smart Learning Ecosystems (SLEs). This objective is centred around institutional capacity building that is needed to help manage digital data in a secure and ethically responsible manner and develop sensitive, enabling and engaging phygital spaces that help promote student well-being. Finally, the aim of the study is to bring out articulation of actionable governance and pedagogical pathways by proposing Co-Agency Model of Teacher-AI Collaboration (TAC) in order to enable the augmentation of technology, instead of its displacement in order to preserve the autonomy and professional capacity of the teachers, while further proposing robust ethical framework of accountability, and strategies for critical AI literacy development.

Theoretical Frameworks: Understanding Technology in Educational Contexts

Multiple theoretical frameworks provide a light to understand the relative role of technology in the educational systems. Constructivist learning theory has focused on the role that technology can play as a cognitive tool to support learner agency, critical thinking and knowledge construction (K., 2021). Instead of the technology as the means of transmitting fixed knowledge in constructivist approaches, the learner is an agent in the process of meaning-making processes, and the technology is a tool, a mediation for cognitive development. Socio-cultural perspectives using Vygotskian traditions consider learning as essentially a social phenomenon, as well as a cultural one (Nagpal, 2023). Within this framework, technology is conceived as a tool which is a bridge between the individual cognitive capacity and social construction of knowledge, and that learning is an outcome of interaction with other people and cultural artefacts.

Situated cognition frameworks put an emphasis on the idea that learning is basically based on meaningful location. Technology, when separated from learning situations in the real world, often leads to inert knowledge - facts and skills are separated from a meaningful application. Effective use of technology and technological tools pedagogy requires technology integration: effective use of technological tools in authentic learning activities, meaningful problems and relevant context (Upadhya & Saraf, 2025). Equity-focused frameworks have been informed by the traditions of critical pedagogy and social justice and ask about the questions of whose interests are served in technology, how technological systems potentially reproduce or interrupt inequality, and what conditions would allow for technology to serve emancipatory educational purposes.

The capability approach that has been developed by Amartya Sen and expounded by Martha Nussbaum provides a fruitful framework to analyse the implications of educational technology. This framework's human rights analytical focus, instead of inputs of resources and technology deployment, focuses on substantive freedoms and capabilities to be developed by people (Bapte, 2022). Applied to AI in Education, the Capability approach gives rise to the following questions: Is Artificial Intelligence implementation widening substantive capabilities of learners, teachers and educational institutions? Or does it restrict capabilities, supercharged surveillance or algorithmic-bias or digital divides? This question brings a focus on the effects on real-life human flourishing, and not just those of the adoption of technology (Soni, 2022).

The Pedagogical Engine: Teacher AI Collaboration

Effective integration of AI is dependent on the definition of the role of human and machine in teaching, pedagogical. This framework draws upon Socio-cultural Theory, and most specifically upon Vygotsky's concept of the Zone of Proximal Development (ZPD) and looks at AI systems as "more knowledgeable others" (MKO) who are capable of scaffolding and providing just-in-time aid to learners. This is the explicit view of AI, in configuring a pedagogical support role for AI, and looking to support human capability with AI and not totally supplant the teacher role (Dustker et al., 2022). The foundation for the framework is the Co-Agency Stance for Teacher-AI Collaboration TAC. This model is based on the notion that man and Generative AI (GenAI) are co-agents and their roles are unearthed dynamically. The principle that they use to guide this collaboration is "design as delegation of constrained agency", keeping the teacher in the critical position of interpretation and the accountable decision maker in the classroom. Ethics, as it relates to this collaborative environment, is interpreted to mean "care", being the governance of the relationship between teacher and technology. However, the successful implementation of co-agency is very strongly conditional on the level of readiness of the institutions, particularly in the Global South (Raj, 2025). Challenges such as infrastructural limitations, lack of trust, barriers to usability (e.g. long response times, lack of vernacular content), and uneven levels of faculty capacity are stymying sustained and practical TAC. Suppose AI systems are created with their primary function as being efficient, as a tool to encourage a model of displacement, then destroying Teacher agency. This erosion has been found to reduce the teacher's investment in ethical stewardship and adaptation that may lead to poor uptake and ineffective implementation, which is documented in the empirical research globally (Pathak & Pathak, 2021). Therefore, in order to abide by the ethical principle of Respect for Autonomy, there ought to be proactive investment into institutional capacity building and competency development processes in order to prepare the teachers to utilise AI in an ethical and effective manner (Cosens et al., 2020).

The Infrastructural Paradigm: Smart Learning Ecosystems (Sles) and Institutional Capacity

The last level is the evolution of learning environments that are expected to support the normative and pedagogical objectives in the framework. A Smart Learning Ecosystem (SLEs) is a transformation from being stuck in a 200 + years old and rigid 'school factory model' to a flexible and digitally enabled 'phygital spaces. The cultural paradigm for the design of these future environments is the 'people in place centred design.' This view sees the individual as a unique individual being as having an intrinsic connection between their own well-being and their environment and the dynamics of the relationship (Das, 2024). Phygital spaces that are both the physical and the digital elements should be sensitive, allowing, interesting, encouraging, the functional specificity, flexibility and centrality in the territory of reference. Functionally specific spaces make possible pedagogy such as 'learning by being', Problem-Project-Process Based Learning (P3BL) and encourage competencies over and above knowing rote knowledge. Through a deliberate functional creation of an environment of functional specificity, the SLE is an institutional conversion mechanism which has the ability to transform technological resources into valuable skills, such as the ability of critical inquiry, as well as cross-boundary collaboration. Furthermore, governance of such augmented phygital spaces will require frameworks that go beyond data protection (e.g. Privacy by Design) towards including features of an 'ethics of interactions' which deal with collective dynamics and vulnerabilities, e.g., peer surveillance and control of platforms (Somani, 2024). The realisation of the vision of SLE requires a layered approach, including national standardisation, institutional investment in ethical governance and capacity building and mandatory shift to outcomes - no inputs or adoption rates. This commitment to sound implementation capacity is an operationalisation of the moral and ethical principle of Beneficence in that integration of AI will serve a meaningful purpose of bringing about the good of the community.

The Mandate for Critical Examination: Research Questions and Analytical Objectives

Against this contextual background, a number of critical questions need to be examined to determine how it is possible for AI technologies to make a meaningful contribution in solving some of the most pressing educational problems of India, such as inequitable access, teacher shortage, quality disparity, inequalities of outcomes, and the purview of NEP 2020 (Sharma et al., 2023). This question needs to go far beyond techno-utopian narratives, however, if it is to deal with specific mechanisms through which AI might address particular challenges and conditions to make such contributions. Where are the pre-requisites and investments for taking AI to the institution's heterogeneous environment? Landscape of India? Addressing this question requires paying special attention to infrastructures, human capacity, governance and conditions for the systemic integration of AI in order to ensure that it brings educational benefits and not perpetuates inequality (Dasgupta, 2025). The questions that come up now are: What are the dangers involved in bringing AI into education, and what, if anything, can be done about it? This question calls for frank admission of the possibility of harms - e.g. algorithmic bias or violations of privacy, replacement of teachers, perpetuation of the digital divide - as well as consideration of governance frameworks, ethical protocols and protections which could avoid or mitigate harms. How can the integration of AI pave the way for a mandatory AI curriculum to be implemented in 2026-27? Under what circumstances can a mandatory curriculum be helpful in building critical AI literacy and ethical consciousness, and not just technical skills? This question aims to bridge and to make connections between the two issues of the deployment of AI technology and innovation of curriculum, and asks how the two issues may potentially reinforce each other in efforts to prepare learners for meaningful engagement in AI-shaped futures (Sarkar & Sarkar, 2021). What is the role that teachers need to play in the integrated education system that involves AI, and how can the integration of AI empower and not replace the teaching professionals? This is a question which rejects narratives of the obsolescence of teachers and instead asks how AI could be used to augment teaching capacity and support teacher professional development.

LITERATURE REVIEW: THE DUAL MANDATE OF AI IN EDUCATIONAL EQUITY

This chapter offers a critical review of the current body of scholarly literature around the incorporation of Artificial Intelligence (AI) in education through the dialectic between the possibilities AI has to transform education for the purpose of personalisation, and the systemic risks of AI within the framework of massive structural inequality (Mishra & Mishra, 2024). The review is organised to provide the conceptual linking along with the efficacy of AI and the empirical challenges of the implementation, bias and institutional readiness in developing economies with the help of evidence from India.

The Promise of Individual Learning and Capability Development

The foundation literature indicates that AI is a possible mechanism for removing pervasive disparities in learners as well as moving towards inclusive education through better accessibility, personalisation and higher-quality instruction. AI technologies, in particular Intelligent Tutoring Systems and adaptive personalised learning (AIPL), are proven to be able to dynamically adapt to a student's pace and learning style and give students greater understanding and retention from directed feedback. From the case studies in India, in rural areas, the functional benefits of AIPL in the areas of basic academics were focused on by means of empirical evidence (Smitha, 2020). The emergence of Generative AI (GenAI) and chatbot tutors in particular is a new paradigm of technology as a dynamic new partner that will encourage skillsets ranging from prompt engineering to critical thinking. This provides for teaching that is very skill-adaptive and can be drastically implemented on a scale far beyond the level of traditional teaching practices, and that is therefore pointing to a way of bridging complex educational gaps in large class educational settings. While the prospects of AI favouring in an objective fashion what students with low baselines, makes the prospect of a powerful alignment with development goals focused on the improvement of individual functioning entirely dependent on equity of access, and unbiased data (Acharya & Vagdal, 2023). The great potential for upscaling has to be critically analysed vis-a-vis the potential for structural barriers, for example, the digital divide, which can wash out personalised gains through exclusion at the system level.

Algorithmic Bias, Equality and Stratified Context

The aspirational benefits of AI are set against a worry that swirls about the ethical implications with regard to algorithmic bias, especially when speaking in terms of deep structural inequality. A major deficit in the literature has been that significant dimensions of social identity which exist at the level of the world are understudied, and identities central to stratification in South Asia, such as caste, are almost entirely ignored in fairness literature in the mainstream (Saini et al., 2021). This is not just theoretical, as empirical studies done to implement the Machine Learning (ML) models on public health data in India confirmed the existence of fairness gaps across socio-economic and caste-groups. Narrowly, it was seen that the performance models had been reduced for scheduled tribes, as well as for the low socio-economic stratum. Algorithmic bias, such as in the form of assessment systems or curation, has the potential to contribute to or perpetuate existing educational disparities. Policy recommendations that can be drawn from this literature are an emphasis on the need to have ethical guidelines that emphasise the need for fairness, transparency, accountability and data privacy so as to minimise the possibility of bias. Arriving at equitable results is complicated, since even sophisticated solutions for mitigating the effect, like Equalised Odds Post-processing, were shown to limit subgroup differences but, at times, came with the trade-off of a moderate loss of overall model performance (Kar Sharma, 2020). The reporting of a specific caste-based performance deterioration suggests the lack of a global standard of unfairness in dealing with the localised and chronic forms of stratification. If the biases are structurally hard-wired into social systems, if such biases are manifested in the training data set, then adequate mitigation will require more than generalised technical fixes. Require a governance context that requires transparency of sourcing of training data, as well as local audit of fairness before deployment. In addition, there must be a certain level of AI literacy amongst staff, as highlighted by international frameworks, to ensure that there is an ability on the part of those deploying to appreciate and acknowledge potential inequities in the practical implementation process (K C, 2022).

Teacher-AI Collaboration and the Challenge of Contextualization

The integration of AI involves significant changes in the workflow of teachers and the transition to cooperative pedagogical models. One of the great struggles in linguistically diverse situations is the provision of quality, culturally as well as vernacular. Systems like Shiksha Copilot, which is a Human-in-the-Loop (HIL) or HIL, artificial intelligence (AI) system that is designed for use in the low-resourced Indian classrooms, bring about the need for HIL system design for technology-enhanced support of the bilingual lesson plan (Bora, 2024). There is empirical evidence to support the idea that teachers should be active within evaluation and adapting and situating AI-generated content with a focus on limitations that exist in current Large Language Models (LLMs) as they are utilised in isolation. While on the one hand, the promise of AI is the promise of efficiency in the instructional and administrative tasks, though, as the usage patterns indicate, the promise comes with a great tension. A large proportion of teachers (60.8%) are using these tools in one single session for the reason of creating lesson plans for a more extended period (e.g. 10 weeks). This pattern suggests to us that oftentimes, AI efficiency is being used to ensure administrative compliance because of increased time demands, in place of additional time for sustained pedagogical engagement or reflective practice. When teachers are short of time, they say that they struggle with the challenge of getting GenAI to align with pedagogical goals (Dr. Dharmendra Kumar Dubey et al., 2023). This leads to a risk of AI with an increased efficiency (quantity) and, at the same time, to a decreased quality of pedagogical (contextual depth and relevance by passing through the crucial HIL stages of cultural significance and adaptation). Sustained adoption of AI is thus extremely contingent upon systematic support and the use of focused professional development (PD) that goes beyond mere use of GenAI to address issues such as assessment of misalignment to enable teachers to integrate GenAI in a pedagogy-driven manner (Tiwari, 2022).

Institutional Capacity and the Transition to Phygital Ecosystems

The successful scale of AI EdTech is fundamentally constrained by the systemic capacity of institutions, and requires profound transformation in terms of infrastructure, governance and pedagogy. Institutional capacity deficits are endemic to low-income situations such as weak infrastructure, no funds, outdated training programs, overcrowded classrooms and overburdened staff (Sudhagar & Mary Binu, 2022). This is aggravated by a widening digital divide across the world and a lack of institutional capacity in terms of digital data management and strategy to prevent the effective governance of data, which is needed to enable intelligent systems. The digital divide poses a challenge in the process of hybrid learning implementation, where some of the problems include network connectivity and the absence of "facilitating conditions" which are necessary for the process to function (MHRD, 2020).

Sustainable integration of AI is developed based on the paradigm shift from the classical "school factory model" to Smart Learning Ecosystems (SLEs). SLEs ensure that there is a centred design which enables the well-being of students and emulates the use of technology in sensitive, encouraging and engaging ways, with a focus. This transformation implies the physical transformation of spaces that have "functional specificity" and flexibility, and is associated with the configuration of the classroom space with the use of digital technologies (Betsurmath & Chidambaram, 2024). The Unified Theory of Acceptance and Use of Technology (UTAUT) provide an interesting theoretical framework for the study of sustainability, which is crucial to note that acceptance of technology by staff and students crucially depends on: performance expectancy and, critically, facilitating conditions (such as adequate infrastructural support, quality training, etc).

Crucially, institutional capacity development is defined according to the need to increase organisational effectiveness by changing the formal and informal rules organising the organisational interactions. This view is possible because the place is not simply a question of filling up the data strategy gaps and outmoded pedagogical frameworks (the factory model), but also involves making an investment in hardware. If the institutions are not able to successfully generate the "facilitating conditions" which are essential for UTAUT to work successfully in spite of the technical success in the systems for an AI, they will be rejected or fail because of the friction in operation (Soni, 2023a). Therefore, the move towards sustainable AI is, at the same time, a move towards institutional modernisation and an act of reforming government.

Re-Imagining Smart Learning: From Digital Tools To Adaptive Learning Ecosystems

Instead, in its strict conceptualisation, innovative learning goes far beyond the presence of the digital tools, online platforms and classrooms made possible by technology. It means the building of adaptive learning ecosystems where pedagogy, technology, institutional governance and learner diversity are integrated in an informed and dynamic environment (Aswal & Chandra, 2025). In the Indian context, innovative learning will have to be taken to be a systemic response to long prevailing structural deficits in access, quality and equity rather than a cosmetic layer of digital over fragile educational foundations.

At the bottom of the concept of innovative learning is the capability of the system to be smart and respond constantly to the needs of the learners. This includes the gathering and interpretation of granular data of learning; the adaptation of content, pace and modality on the basis of learner progress; and the integration of multiple sources of feedback (including teacher observation, learner reflection and peer collaboration). Artificial intelligence-powered tools - knowledgeable tutoring systems, recommendation engines, learning analytics dashboards and generative Artificial intelligence-based content curation systems are the computational infrastructure for such responsiveness. However, absent coherent pedagogical intent and institutional capacity, there is a risk that these tools will be of the wisdom of the most balkanised vendor-driven interventions, not anchored in deep learning processes. Indian schools and institutions of higher education need, therefore, a re-conceptualisation of innovative learning, which puts human development, critical thinking and equity over digital efficiency. It is one which is able to provide inclusive, learner-centred environments where AI is used to support differentiated instruction, multi-lingual pedagogies, diagnostic assessment and teacher professional judgement. In this extended understanding, technological sophistication is, needless to say, a necessary but hardly sufficient condition for educational transformation.

Intelligent Tutoring Systems and Personalised Pathways in Indian Classrooms

Among the most visible innovations made possible by Artificial Intelligence (AI) in the Indian education system is intelligent tutoring systems (ITS), adaptive learning platforms, many of them being developed by private ed-tech companies, which are increasingly being integrated in the school ecosystem, as well as in after-school ones. These systems contained the promise to make learning more personalised, being able to diagnose the strengths and weaknesses of learners and make recommendations regarding learning paths and feedback on the spot (Das, 2023). Their pedagogical logic is a break from homogeneous, teacher-centred teaching that upholds the textbook to individual modulated trajectories, which in principle are able to adapt on the basis of the various learning paces and past knowledge profiles.

In the Indian situation, where the teacher is using an overcrowded classroom with forty to sixty students, the use of the ITS platforms seems to be very attractive. In theory, they can make possible additional practice for struggling learners, enrichment for the advanced students, and remediation for the students who have fallen behind in the foundation levels. For government schools that suffer from chronic shortcomings of teachers, these systems are sometimes in the form of compensatory mechanisms that can fill in some of the gaps in instruction. Yet realities of implementation confound such an upbeat story. The design of many ITS platforms is still very examination-focused, focused on high-stakes board exams and competitive tests on a board exam basis over and above the greater learning outcomes that are envisaged in NEP 2020, including creativity, critical thinking, socio-emotional competencies and ethical reasoning. Many of the systems emphasise drill and practice formats that maximise performance on the test but run the risk of narrowing the curriculum and crowding out reflective, dialogic and project-based learning (Alok & Rajesh, 2023). Moreover, the algorithms behind the classification and evolution of students are often secret and hence raise the question of fairness and perpetuating stereotypes and long-term consequences of a first labelling by algorithms.

The potential of equitable ITS in India is dependent on deliberative choices of its integration. If deployed in only fee-paying schools and urban centres, they may increase learning gaps as they empower those who are already privileged with better infrastructural, parental support, and digital familiarity with tools, but if they are deployed in the government schools without adequate preparation in terms of the training of the teachers and the infrastructure, they may be presently underutilised or abused (Gong & Wen, 2023). Their successful use of ITS requires thoughtful policies to help make the stage for the possibilities of ITS as adjunct scaffolding chaperoned by teachers, as opposed to as a replacement for pedagogical relationships. Teachers do need to be prepared not only to use technology but also to be able to interpret the product of algorithms in a critical manner, put recommendations into their context and integrate digital information with their own deep understandings of the socio-cultural realities of their learners (Kumar et al., 2025).

Learning Analytics and the Datafication of Educational Decision-Making

The proliferation of AI in education has been accompanied by the proliferation of learning analytics platform that aims to translate large amounts of educational data, such as attendance records, assessment results, engagement metrics, and click-streams, into actionable learning insights. In theory, such datafication will enable the Indian academic institutions to have powerful tools to track learning outcomes and identify early warning signs of disengagement, or dropouts, successful pedagogical strategies, or to plan the allocation of resources where they are needed the most (Kumar et al., 2021). The promise around learning analytics is granular and real-time visibility into the trajectory of the learners for a so-far characterised system with fragmented and delayed data flows. At an individual classroom level, analytics dashboards have the ability to highlight which students are struggling with a particular concept, and targeted intervention can be given. At the institutional level, aggregated data might be used to inform how curricula are redesigned, priorities for staff development and policy decisions (Soni, 2023b). At the system level, the administrators of the state and national level may know the regional imbalances with respect to learning outcomes potentially and give priority to the capacity building endeavours appropriately.

However, the way that the data is used for analysis is not necessarily fairer for education decisions. Data is always partial, subject to construction and valuing, what measures and what system chooses not to measure and what to do with the measured indicators. Over-reliance on quantifiable metrics may result in the marginalisation of forms of learning that may be more difficult to measure, such as critical thinking, civic engagement, creativity or socio-emotional competencies (Mir, 2023). This, further, makes predictive models of some learners in some category (e.g. "at risk"), based on patterns of the past, which further (reinforce) unconsciously held social stratifications (caste, gender, class, language or geography).

In the potential Indian context in which the educational disadvantage is deeply interwoven with historical and structural inequalities, learning analytics needs to be handled with caution in terms of methodology and ethics. Institutions, therefore, need the ability to ask questions about the data and disaggregate the results along categories of social differences and resist easy interpretations which naturalise underperformance in marginalised communities. Data should be perceived as an instrument on the structures of challenging and not viewed as an object of essentialising difference. Governance frameworks have to ensure that analytics are used for supportive intervention as opposed to punitive surveillance tools and that both students and communities are afforded dignity and agency regarding their educational data.

Generative AI and Multi-Lingual Content Curation in a Diverse Polity

One of the most significant potential promises of the generative AI technology to the field of Indian education is the potential of being able to cater to multi-lingual, culturally responsive and contextual content creation. Given the extraordinary linguistic diversity of India and recognition in the Constitution of the country of various languages, the presence in the linguistic communities, as well as high-quality learning materials, were formidable challenges in the past (Mukherjee, 2024). Generative AI models, which have the potential to generate explanations, examples, stories, assessments and more in a variety of languages, are ostensibly a powerful tool to fill this gap (Syafhendry et al., 2025).

Well-designed AI tools can be utilised by teachers for the support of: The generation of differentiated materials for learning with learners with different competency levels, the translation of content into local languages, and offering different representations of complex concepts which are suited to different cognitive styles (Sahu & Behera, 2022). For those learners who are in marginalised communities, who may not be able to access education in a language other than the language of instruction, such tools may help in overcoming the linguistic barriers which serve as a barrier, thus keeping them away from understanding and participating. For those schools that do not have many resources, the production of content through an AI might help to minimise the time spent on static textbooks and create more dynamic and more frequently updated curriculum resources.

But, once again, all it takes is potential, where there is a risk. Generative systems which have been trained mainly on the English language or Global North corpora may contain biases in terms of culture, epistemological hierarchies and representational omissions which are out of congruence with the local knowledge traditions and Indian socio-cultural realities (More, 2023). This is a potential in the absence of careful curation and oversight from educators for AI-generated content to perpetuate stereotypes or make implicit judgments in one worldview over another. Furthermore, ease of creating content can be a temptation to the institutions taking the cheap and fast route to a high volume (and high volume is tempting), which favours quantity over quality and obliterates the deliberate and reflective labour of curriculum design.

For generative AI to make a real contribution to NEP 2020's ambitions of multilingual, inclusive and culturally grounded education, it needs to be embedded into participative structures for content governance. Teachers, local scholars, language experts and community representatives need to play central roles in evaluating the accuracy of materials that AI have generated and correcting opportunities and inaccuracies, as well as consider ensuring that the materials reflect local context and constitutional values (Pavan Ramchandra Manurkar, 2023). Generative AI need to be viewed in the valuable tools space for an overall schema of humanism in knowledge production, not an education pedagogical Czar.

Smart Schools as Institutional Innovations: Beyond Hardware and Bandwidth

The discourse on smart schools in India is increasingly running the risk of collapsing institutional transformation under an inventory of devices, connectivity and digital platforms. Classrooms being equipped with interactive boards, distribution of tablets and learning management systems are often pronounced as the attainment of 'smartness'. Such techno-centric conceptions are a cover for more pedestrian institutional changes, which are needed if there is going to be sustainable reform. A really smart school is a school which is defined not by the procurement of hardware, but by its organisational intelligence - its ability to learn from data, think about practices, innovate in pedagogies and reorganise structures to meet the needs of diverse learners (Gupta & Gupta, 2022). This organisational intelligence is indispensable from the professional agency of teachers, the quality of leadership, the involvement of communities and the clarity of educational purpose. But AI can assist these capacities with analytic tools, communication channels and pedagogical resources, but it cannot substitute these. In terms of practical manifestations, smart schools in India would have to undergo a change in the routines and cultures of the institutions. Decision-making processes require balancing between the evidence coming from the learning analytics and the insights of the teachers and students. Timetables as well as classroom practices need to be flexible enough to meet the needs of blended modalities where teachers have the chance to flexibly combine modalities of face-to-face interaction, AI-supported individualised practice, group projects and reflection-based learning. Assessment system needs to change from high-stakes examination being considered as the only source of assessment and start offering continuous multi-dimensional assessment, formative and not with AI tools, where applicable, but with a human eye for interpretation (Sharma & Singh, 2023). In government schools and resource-constrained situations, smartness would then have to be 'redefined' in reference to feasibility and sustainability. Low-tech and Hybrid solutions - e.g. models of shared devices, community digital hubs and offline capable AI tools - are potentially pedagogically more meaningful than expensive, complex and fragile infrastructures that can't be maintained. Institutional smartness in this context is hence about the ability to strategically choose what kinds of technology should be adopted, adapted and controlled, and how they can relate to local realities, but it is not about efforts to replicate high-end models where there is no fit with the context.

Teacher–AI Collaboration: From Automation Anxiety to Augmented Pedagogy

The shift of AI into the educational space always raises the subject of how the role of the teacher is going to be reconfigured. Popular narratives lean in different directions, namely, on the one hand, predictions on replacing human teachers with AI systems; on the other hand, teachers are being described as insurmountable barriers to the progress of technology. They both have intellectually mindless and politically dead stands (Manizia et al., 2024).

In the context of India, where there is a paucity of teachers and a lack of consistent preparation and unfavourable working conditions, for AI systems to assist teachers logically, there is no substitute for the human functions of care and mentorship, socio-emotional support and contextual judgement that teachers bring. Instead of this, a more productive lens is that of teacher-AI collaboration, whereby AI augments, not replaces, pedagogical labour. Intelligent tuition systems can take care of the repetitive drill practices so that there is more room left for the teacher to get involved in more conceptual explaining, discussion and individual support. Learning analytics can be used to identify which students need attention, such that in the process of determining the students, the teachers would want to focus their limited time in a strategic way. Generative tools can be used to assist teachers in creating differentiated assignments or assessments, and they can be instrumental in the multi-lingual or heterogeneous classroom.

Such augmentation is, however, not an automatic process. It needs teachers who are sure of themselves, who are critically literate, and professionally empowered in relation to technology. If teachers encounter AI in terms of rigid and non-negotiable systems which have more authority than the authority of teachers themselves, this causes problems for teachers to either fight the adoption of AI or give in on specific ways to destroy and reduce the professional identity of teachers. If, on the other hand, teachers are involved in the design, adaptation and governance of the AI tools, their knowledge, which comes from their own experience, can add significantly to a better match between the technological affordances and the reality of the class (Bora & Mathew, 2024).

Teacher education policy, therefore, needs to foreground as an aspect of critical professional formation no less than AI literacy itself as a technical competency. To address this, pre-service teacher education programmes need to ensure that they have modules on AI concepts, including educational applications, ethical issues and critical data literacy, and in-service professional development needs to include sustained practice, rather than a one-off professional development opportunity. Such an approach makes teachers the co-designers and reflective practitioners in an artificial intelligence (AI) enabled ecosystem and not as passive takers of externally designed systems.

Equity at the Core: AI, The Digital Divide and the Politics of Access

Any discussion of AI in Indian education, focused on questions of equity to one side, runs the risk of being complicit in the reproduction of structural injustice. The digital divide in India, therefore, is multifaceted, and is not just about differences in internet connectivity and device access, but about differences in digital literacy, at-home learning environment, parental support and language proficiency as well as institutional capability. As AI systems move even more to the centre of educational processes, these divides are more risky for the risk of naturalisation and deepening (Bholane, 2025).

The students in the wealthy urban households with consistent access to the internet, their own personal devices, and digitally literate parents are in a position to benefit disproportionally from enhanced platforms in the form of both formal schooling as well as the growing ed-tech marketplace, particularly from applications after school. For them, artificially intelligent tools would be, possibly, used for enhancing the advantages already existing, in terms of reinforcing success in examinations subject to high stakes and access to elite institutions. By comparison, learners living in rural areas, informal settlements, conflict-affected areas or marginalised communities don't have access to basic connectivity or space for digital learning, which means high-end AI tools are largely irrelevant or inaccessible (Sharma et al., 2022).

In the event that AI is going to function as a tool of education of justice as a concoction against the vectors of stratification, access has to be regarded as a question of rights, of public policy, not supply of markets. This includes public investment into the digital infrastructure in underserved areas, as well as subsidised or free access to quality AI-enabled learning platforms to those who could not afford to use them and integration of AI tools into public schooling rather than having to rely primarily on private markets. It also requires explicit monitoring of the deployment and outcomes of AI on the basis of social categories such as caste, gender, disability and language in ensuring that interventions do not drive upstream inequalities.

The politics of access to the infrastructure of AI is not only on the visible terrain of the infrastructure of AI, but it takes place on the less-visible terrain of epistemic inclusion. If AI systems, content and analytics are not created with representation from marginalised communities, then they could inadvertently hard-code cultural bias and normative assumptions in an attempt to marginalise particular identities and knowledges. Equity-oriented AI in Indian education must thus involve participation of the historically 'left out' in the conceptualisation, designing, evaluation and governing (Jolly & Kaur, 2025).

Data, Power and Protection: Governance of AI and Educational Privacy

AI-enabled educational systems are effectively data-dependent - continuous data streams of learner interaction, assessment results, behavioural metrics and demographic indicators. Whilst in turn such data is necessary for personalisation and analytics, it at the same time opens up vulnerabilities in the form of problems relating to privacy, surveillance and possible misuse. In an Indian educational scenario, which does not have a legal and institutional architecture aggregating data protection in place, but is in a state of evolution, the possibilities and growth of data-intensive educational technologies are a cause of serious concern (Lissen & Bautista, 2021). Educational data is special because it is sensitive. They can tell us not only about academic performance, but about the cognitive profiles, behavioural tendencies and the socio-economic contexts as well. When coupled with identifiers such as caste, religion and region or the disabled status, they can become powerful tools to discriminate, profile or stigmatise if not dealt with properly. Commercialisation of education data on the basis of targeted advertising or the use of algorithmic profiling or third-party sharing, especially if minors are involved, is a particularly acute issue in ethics (Mehrotra, 2023).

Robust AI governance frameworks in education would therefore need to have clear principles and guidelines about how to work. These are informed and meaningful consent; data minimisation and purpose limitation; data secure storage and data transmission; prohibition of exploitative monetisation of data; allowing transparency over algorithms and data flows; and grievance redress and accountability mechanisms. Students and parents should have the right of access, error correction and, in particular, a request for deletion of student data. Educational institutions need to have internal policies about who in the institution can access what data for what purposes, which is all about stopping the use of data in punitive or exclusionary ways.

Beyond the context of institutional policies, regulatory authorities, at the state and national level, for example, would have to define norms relating to educational data, under sector-wide data protection regimes. Public guidelines on the use of AI education should investigate the need for thinking around the fairness of algorithms, explain and redress situations in which algorithmic AI-driven decisions lead to harm or disadvantage (Mitra & Sinha, 2023). Without such safeguards, the growth of AI in Indian education runs the risk of catalysing a culture of surveillance which is antithetical to the development of free, critical and autonomous learners envisaged in NEP 2020.

The 2026–27 AI Curriculum: From Digital Skill to Critical Ai Literacy

One of the most consequential aspects in the process of educational reform, which is currently underway in India, is the introduction of an AI curriculum from 2026-27 onwards on a compulsory basis. Properly implemented, this initiative has the potential to democratise literacy for AI and prepare the learners in a way that will enable them to participate in a meaningful fashion in AI-influenced economies, and also to promote critical understanding of ethical, social and political dimensions of intelligent systems. Poorly implemented, there would be a danger that this would degenerate to a narrow technicist syllabus with privilege towards coding skills, but ignoring the bigger implications of algorithmic decision-making in society (Kakodkar et al., 2024).

For the transformational potential of the AI curriculum to take hold, however, it will have to unacquaint itself with AI as a set of technical tools or vocational competencies. While foundational understanding of algorithms, data structures, machine learning basics and computational thinking are essential, equally important are capacities to critically interrogate the extent to which AI systems affect employment, governance, social interaction, identity formation and democratic processes. Learners should be asked to consider who's making the AI systems, whose interests are being served by it, who's left out of their considerations and how they may be reconfigured in the service of social justice and ecological sustainability (Panigrahi & Gupta, 2021).

This kind of curriculum also has to be in the foundation that it is developmental and pedagogical enough. At the school level, appropriate age of the students, algorithmic thinking, recognition of patterns, bias of decision making and limitation of automation can be introduced through unplugged activities, games and real-life examples rather than exclusively with the use of screen-based instruction. At the higher secondary and the tertiary levels, more advanced technical content could be used with case studies, debates and project-based learning, looking into the role AI can play in sectors such as health, agriculture, finance, policing and education itself (Vyas, 2020). The introduction of AI as a subject to be taught in schools can not be based on a small group of people, technically trained specialists, but on wide sections of the teaching workforce, demanding upskilling. Moreover, the concepts of AI should not be relegated to computer science classes but a part of social studies, ethics, political science and humanities classrooms, which question of power, rights, democracy and ethics - already centre. This cross-curricular integration is appropriate in the emphasis on a holistic approach to education, in the context of an interdisciplinary approach, in NEP 2020, protection against marginalisation of

AI education, which may be on narrow technical skills without a critical reflection (Kawale, 2024).

Learning From Elsewhere, Rooting in the Indian Context

While the challenges and the opportunities around educational needs are unique to India, there are many lessons from the experience of integration of AI in other systems, some of which are comparative: Some of the high income countries have invested a lot in AI based adaptive platforms and national data infrastructures, while some of the smaller countries have been able to address critical issues of digital literacy and participatory governance, rather than being too quick to implement the technology. Multilateral organisations have also created frameworks and guidelines about ethical AI in education. But such blind imitation of the international models in the Indian environment is bound to do no good. Differences in infrastructures, institutional capacity, social stratification and linguistic diversity, as well as political economy, are of course differences to be sensitively adapted. Nevertheless, there are comparative perspectives to be aware of in that recurring patterns: Recurring patterns are that technology initiatives that have been successful in the long run are often those that have been included in sustained, well-resourced reform programmes with a focus on teacher development, curriculum redesign and governance reform in addition to the deployment of hardware (Naik et al., 2024). An example of this is the fact that projects which are driven by vendor incentives or short-term funding cycles will often crumble when the support from outside the project is gone. For India, it is a discussion not to integrate or to synthesise the learning that takes place all over the world with the local wisdom. Indigenous pedagogical traditions, practices of community-based learning traditions, and a diversity of epistemologies are rich resources for imagining what AI-enhanced education might represent other than as conventional models of education centred around Western educational models (Saharia & Mazumdar, 2024). Rather than educational modernisation, modernisation must follow trajectories that are global north, so that Indian educational communities can imagine educational models which AI tools can help them to support multilingualism, community participation, ecological awareness and constitutional values.

Toward a Transformative Synthesis: Technology, Capacity and Democratic Governance

The general argument that emerges out of this analysis is that effective contribution of AI in the Indian educational scenario depends upon transformative synthesis of three overlapping domains, namely technological innovation, institutional capacity and democratic governance. Technological innovation, however sophisticated, is not in a position to deal with the structural inequalities and is not able to guarantee educational justice. Institutional capacity in the form of able teachers and reflective leadership, effective infrastructural and adaptive organisational cultures is indispensable (Arun, 2022). Democratic governance with transparency, accountability, participation and protection of rights is the normative and regulatory basis for ensuring that technological power is not used to entrench inequality.

On this triadic synthesis, innovative learning and smart schools made possible by AI are instrumental to a larger educational democratisation project rather than being an end in themselves. When implemented in systems that prioritise equity and empower the priorities of teachers whilst being respectful of the dignity of the learner, and which engage the community, AI can help to support more responsive and inclusive education and more effective learning (Mir et al., 2025). Taken to systems which do not take account of such foundations, on the other hand, AI threatens to be yet one more layer through which existing hierarchies are reproduced and legitimised.

The way forward for Indian education is therefore neither unquestioningly welcoming and mindlessly rejecting AI nor some interaction with AI being critical, strategic and ethical. This doesn't mean just making sudden big choices; rigorous evaluation; being comfortable with abandoning failure and harm-causing ways of doing things; investing for the long term in people and institutions (Ganaie et al., 2025). It makes it a requirement that we are absolutely sure that decisions concerning technology are analysed in the light of educational purpose: Would they extend or restrict substantive abilities among learners and teachers, would they concretise or extend the distance, or would they enrich or lessen democratic participation? If the above questions remain at the centre of the policy and practice, then innovative learning and smart schools powered by AI can contribute to a constitutional promise of equality and dignity and opportunity for all learners in India (Dar & Ganaie, 2021). And if they're sidelined to the short on the basis of the imperatives of the market, or the spectacle of technology, with the grave risk that the country will have lost some of its chance in history, as well as the anger of the very inequalities education is supposed to address.

DISCUSSION AND LIMITATIONS OF THE STUDY

Discussion: Synthesising the Dual Mandate of AI Integration

The Multi-dimensional Framework for Equitable AI Integration (MAFE-AI) developed in this study expose a deep tension on the heart of the transformation of education policy in India between, on the one hand, the way on which AI seem to give a technological unique grip over the NEP 2020 (national education policy) 2020, particularly the goals of equity and access, and, on the other hand, the way had fundamentally limited efficacy is deft profound seated institutional deficits and structural inequalities. This is a double mandate, and it is reflected in the way in which the normative, the critical, the pedagogical and the infrastructural levels are synthetically combined. From the normative perspective, the promise of AI to increase student capabilities has been shown to be so, especially in the case of rural case studies, where AIPL systems showed more powerful gains for those students who were from lower baselines in terms of foundational literacy and numeracy. This, therefore, shows the possibilities of AI to work as a potent conversion factor to turn into concrete educational freedoms of technology resources. However, this is subjectively threatened on a structural level, given a critical constraint of Data Justice. Algorithmic Fairness literature provides the fact that the performance of the models goes down drastically for structurally disadvantaged groups like scheduled tribes and lower socio-economic strata. Since existing fairness seems inclined to ignore identities that are central to the South Asian stratification system, like castes, the "black box" nature of algorithms is a direct violation of the ethics of Justice and Transparency and paralyses the capacity of stakeholders to question embedded notions of bias.

Pedagogical layer: represented by the Co-Agency Model of Teacher-AI Collaboration (TAC), reveals with even more critical separation from the theory dream, and the reality of its implementation. At the same time, AI is intended to be a teacher augmentation tool, reci. In linguistically diverse, low-resource environments, usage trends are evidenced to show that more than 60% of teachers make use of Gen AI in single, sustained sessions to build lesson plans to cover extended periods of time. This is a tendency to efficiency, which means that the AI is most particularly presently being used for relieving an administrative compliance somewhat reflective, sustained pedagogy, plus this can lead to a 'Productivity Paradox' as such quality takes over from the contextual quality and cultural relevance. This deterioration in the quality of pedagogy is, however, further compounded by the undying problems of the production of good-quality vernacular content. In order to uphold the ethical principle of Respect for Autonomy, it will require systematic professional development. In order to help teachers move from being passive consumers of the output of AI to being critical, ethical co-designers of AI.

Finally, the materialisation of Smart Learning Ecosystems (SLEs) is dependent on overcoming chronic institutional fragility. The vision of phygital space being sensitive, enabling and engaging for the well-being of students is limited by practical barriers in terms of "pervasive network connectivity problems", and no essential "facilitating conditions". Mature sustainable adoption requires the impartial investment of hardware; however, it dangerously transforms the organisational fabric -

build up the institutional capacity for by amending the formal and informal rules by which interactions are organised. Without this kind of fundamental institutional reform - and understanding this idea - AI is peripheral input, rather than embedded systemic, as an agent of equitable transformation.

Limitations of the Study

The presented analysis, though conceptually competent, is necessarily limited by a host of empirical and methodological limitations inherent in the present stream of scholarly work produced on the topic of AI in developing educational systems. First of all, the results in the study in terms of equitable impact are limited in regard to the scope of generalizability. Although the review has based the discussion on the basis of case studies derived from India (eg rural AIPL interventions and collaborative systems in low-resource classrooms), numerous of the basic theory in regards to implementation models are based on more generic conditions from the Global South or western-centres, or derived from a particular level of education eg in postgraduate settings, as well as in terms of infrastructural requirements (eg UTAUT and institutional capacity development). Consequently, there is a need for careful contextual validation of the application of such frameworks across the considerable heterogeneity that exists within India (from metropolitan universities to remote tribal schools), which haven't even started (as of now), based on the available literature.

Second, inconsistency in the empirical evidence that underlies the research in terms of measuring and methodologies is a limitation in the study. A common criticism of the literature that has been published in this area is that too often it has focused on tracking adoption rates (inputs) with little to no attention to student learning outcomes or expanded capacity (impacts). Poorly developed programs that waste time and rob students of learning opportunities, and will often be disguised by mere measures of use and do intravariate cycles of procrastination. Furthermore, there are methodological inconsistencies between different research studies, especially regarding the implementation of the long-term retention and subtle changes in the quality of pedagogy, which is more important to confirm the model of the TAC. The call, in this instance, for long-term studies into measuring sustainability and end-lasting capability expansion run by AI is most unsolved in the current body of work done on this.

Third is a considerable drawback due to the lack of scholarship on the issue of structural stratification. Although the MAFE-AI model requires the need for Data Justice as an essential filter, the mainstream literature on algorithmic fairness ignores identities which are central to the social stratification of South Asia, for example, caste, virtually completely. While there is clear evidence from the empirical research to establish that there is a decline in performance among scheduled tribes and among lower socioeconomics, the theories in which such effects from caste-based bias can be mitigated have not been developed enough. This gap constitutes a serious shortfall in the implementation of the Data Justice pillar as a whole, with the analysis regressing to more general principles of non-discrimination, whereas solutions to the context of the nation are urgently needed.

Finally, the part of the study dealing with a pedagogical transformation of is currently constraining since it is focused on specific applications of AI - that is, intelligent tutoring system (AIPL) and GenAI for lesson planning. The bigger implication of AI by admin governance, admissions or high-stakes assessment systems, all critical areas, can chips often decrease in India, as revealed by an empirical dive deep inside the reviewed literature. Future research needs to increase the length of observation and the variety of AI applications studied, in order to have a more holistic evaluation of the MAFE-AI framework.

CONCLUSION

AI in Indian Education: Choosing Justice Over Technological Determinism

The culmination of this chapter makes it an intricate theory-based view of the integration of artificial intelligence in the change of education in India. Rather than taking AI as a self-evident cure or seeing AI as an actor in the field of technology, the study puts AI in the context of educational reform in general as a contingent, contested, deeply politicised actor. The argument in the chapter has been that the value of AI-enabled innovative learning and smart schools is not to be judged in terms of the density of devices, the sophistication of algorithms or the scale of adoption. Instead, what seems to be really important around AI is its potential to augment and or diminish substantive freedoms and capabilities of learners, teachers and communities, in the Indian context.

At the centre of this argument is the argument to be informed and influenced by normative commitment to equity, justice and human dignity in its educational reform. AI systems, regardless of how good they are, can't think up these values on their own. At best, they are tools which can supplement or subvert pre-existing social relations, pedagogical practices and institutional structures. The chapter has therefore insisted on the need for subjecting the adoption of AI to clearly stated educational purposes, which itself have to be determined through democratic deliberations and participatory processes. In these lights, the central question then is not if AI will be used in education in India, but how its deployment will be governed and how it will be deployed in a way that its deployment contributes to the more general goals of access, equity and excellence.

A further basic knowledge is the role of the teacher needed and should be reinvented in the age of AI. Instead, realign out that they are being displaced as well as deskilled with algorithmic systems (teachers need to enable as critical interpreters, ethical gatekeepers and co-designers of AI empowered learning environments). Their professional expertise, contextual knowledge and pedagogical judgement are still indispensable to the development of critical thinking, ethical reasoning and democratic participation. The chapter has, thus, advocated for a model of a collaboration between teachers and AI that has a role of teacher augmentation rather than teacher replacement and one in which the teacher autonomy is structurally protected and supported in a pedagogical diversity.

The ethical and governance of AI education has also been discussed in front of, along with, the analysis. There is a huge gathering and exploitation of educational data, which opens the chances of surveillance and profiling, closing in and discriminating against individuals in such a way that cannot be solved with technical solutions alone. Instead, robust and participatory governance frameworks are needed to ensure that data practices are transparent, accountable and in line with the rights and dignity of learners. These frameworks need to be embedded in a larger democratic process with input from teachers, students, parents and civil society so that decisions around AI in education are not handed over to technocratic elites or commercial interests.

Finally, the chapter has attempted to make an argument that the emerging artificial intelligence (AI) curriculum is a historical opportunity to develop the critical AI literacy of the Indian learners. This literacy must not only be technical, but social, political and ethical: there needs to be dimensions surrounding the social, political and moral dimensions of algorithmic systems. By introducing the idea of AI education in the social science subjects, humanities and ethics curriculum and grounding it in the Indian realities of caste, gender, religion and regional inequality, the curriculum can help learners to become not only users of AI, but informed citizens who can interrogate and change the technologies that shape their lives.

In conclusion, in the mentioned chapter, though it is not said that the fate of the artificial intelligence in the education system of India is a technical inevitability, it is a political choice. The direction this choice will take, however, will be a determining factor as to whether AI will be a force for democratisation and justice or among the mechanisms for the deepening of existing inequalities. The challenge is to ensure it is not only technologically advanced, but also substantively fair, human-centred, and democratically ruled AI-enabled innovative learning and smart schools. Only then can AI add a meaningful contribution to the broader vision of the education aspiration of India.

REFERENCES

Acharya, S. K., & Vagdal, T. (2023). The role of academic libraries in the context of national education policy (NEP)-2020. *IP Indian Journal of Library Science and Information Technology*, *8*(1). Advance online publication. DOI: 10.18231/j.ijlsit.2023.006

Alok, P. D., & Rajesh, G. A. (2023). A Comparative Study on National Education Policy 1986 and 2020. *International Research Journal of Human Resources and Social Sciences, 10*(1).

Arun, D. P. (2022). Perceived Opportunities of National Education Policy-2020. *Indian Research Journal of Extension Education*, *22*(3). Advance online publication. DOI: 10.54986/irjee/2022/jul_sep/145-149

Aswal, D. K., & Chandra, A. (2025). Leveraging the Aswal Model to Understand and Amplify the Impact of India's National Education Policy. *Mapan - Journal of Metrology Society of India, 40*(3). https://doi.org/DOI: 10.1007/s12647-025-00840-y

Aynul Bari, M., & Goswamee, G. (2024). The Impact of National Education Policy 2020 On Teacher Training Institutions. *Theory into Practice*, *2024*(5).

Bapte, V. D. (2022). Libraries in the context of the National Education Policy. *Annals of Library and Information Studies*, *69*(3). Advance online publication. DOI: 10.56042/alis.v69i3.63666

Betsurmath, C. G., & Chidambaram, S. B. (2024). National Education Policy 2020, India: A planned change management requisite for higher education institutions. *Journal of Infrastructure. Policy and Development*, *8*(9). Advance online publication. DOI: 10.24294/jipd.v8i9.3020

Bholane, K. (2025). National Education Policy 2020: A Catalyst for Skill-Based Education. SSRN *Electronic Journal*. https://doi.org/DOI: 10.2139/ssrn.5093645

Bora, D., & Mathew, S. (2024). Reshaping Higher Education: A Comparative Study of India's National Education Policies. *International Journal for Multi-dimensional Research Perspectives*, *2*(5). Advance online publication. DOI: 10.61877/ijmrp.v2i5.149

Bora, I. (2024). The Status of Life Skill Education in the National Education Policy 2020. [JETIR]. *Journal of Emerging Technologies and Innovative Research, 11*(7).

Chaudhari, Y. S. Mr. (2023). National Education Policy 2020 and Changing Role of Libraries. *Library Philosophy and Practice*, (7860).

Chowdhury, A. R., & Hanumanthu, P. (2023). Analysing India's National Education Policy from the Angle of Research, IP, Innovation, and Entrepreneurship. *Journal of Intellectual Property Rights*, *28*(3). Advance online publication. DOI: 10.56042/jipr.v28i3.1616

Cosens, B. A., Ruhl, J. B., Soininen, N., & Gunderson, L. (2020). Designing Law to Enable Adaptive Governance of Modern Wicked Problems. *Vanderbilt Law Review*, *73*(6).

Dar, R. A., & Ganaie, N. A. (2021). Importance Of Nep 2020 For Changing the Role of Teacher Educators. *Elementary Education Online*, *20*(1), 8289–8301. DOI: 10.17051/ilkonline.2021.01.847

Das, P. (2023). Recommendations And Challenges of Teacher Education In National Education Policy (Nep) 2020. *International Journal of Research Publication and Reviews*, *4*(8). Advance online publication. DOI: 10.55248/gengpi.4.823.51490

Das, P. (2024). Redefining College Libraries in Today's "Digital India": A Special Reference to the National Education Policy 2020. *RAY. International Journal of Multidisciplinary Studies*, *9*(1).

Das, P., Das, G., & Barman, P. (2023). National Education Policy 2020: Current Issues and Re-imagining the Future of Higher Education. *International Journal of Indian Psychology*, *11*(3). Advance online publication. DOI: 10.25215/1103.360

Dasgupta, S. T. (2025). Strengthening Early Childhood Education in Bangladesh: Lessons from the National Education Policy (NEP)-2020 of India. *Interchange*, *56*(2). Advance online publication. DOI: 10.1007/s10780-025-09541-6

David, S., Anand, R. S., & Sagayam, M. (2020). Enhancing AI-based evaluation for smart cultivation and crop testing using agro datasets. *Journal of Artificial Intelligence and Systems*, *2*(1). Advance online publication. DOI: 10.33969/ais.2020.21010

Desai, A., & Desai, M. (2023). A Review of the State of Cybersecurity in the Healthcare Industry and Propose Security Controls. *Mesopotamian Journal of Artificial Intelligence in Healthcare, 2023.* Advance online publication. DOI: 10.58496/mjaih/2023/016

Dr. Dharmendra Kumar Dubey, Dr. Mritunjai Pandey, Er. Yukti Varshney, & Er. Shreyas Pande. (2023). The Implications of the National Education Policy, 2020, on Legal Education in India. *International Journal of Advanced Research in Science. Tongxin Jishu.* Advance online publication. DOI: 10.48175/ijarsct-8903

Smitha S. (2020). National Education Policy (NEP) 2020-Opportunities and Challenges in Teacher Education. *International Journal of Management (IJM, 11*(11).

Dustker, S., Bandi, S., & Oakes, W. (2022). Scope of Service-Learning in Accomplishing Objectives of National Education Policy 2020, India: Conceptual Analysis. *Journal of Engineering Education Transformations, 36*(Special Issue 2). https://doi .org/DOI: 10.16920/jeet/2023/v36is2/23054

Ganaie, N. A., Saikia, T., Mir, T. A., & Jan, I. (2025). *Dynamics of Public Policy and Good Governance in India: The Road to Viksit Bharat* (First). Authors Click Publishing. https://doi.org/DOI: 10.5281/ZENODO.15870017

Gong, X., & Wen, J. (2023). The Text Analysis of National Education Policy 2020. *Journal of Education. Teaching and Social Studies, 5*(1). Advance online publication. DOI: 10.22158/jetss.v5n1p95

Gopali, N., & Shetty, H. (2019). The AI Conveyor Belt. *European Conference on the Impact of Artificial Intelligence and Robotics, ECIAIR 2019*. https://doi.org/ DOI: 10.34190/ECIAIR.19.083

Gupta, P. B., & Gupta, B. (2022). Role of Strategic Human Resource Management Practices (SHRMPs) for Gearing up Higher Education Institutions to Achieve Vision of National Education Policy (NEP 2020) and Industry 4.0. *AJMR 798 Amity Journal of Management Research ADMAA Amity. Journal of Management Research, 5*(1).

Jolly, D. A., & Kaur, D. P. (2025). Integrating Artificial Intelligence into India's National Education Policy 2020: Opportunities, Challenges and Strategic Pathways. *International Journal of Engineering Research & Technology (Ahmedabad), 14*(5).

K C, T. (2022). Impact of National Education Policy 2020 on Higher Education. *SUMEDHA Journal of Management, 11*(2). https://doi.org/DOI: 10.46454/sumedha/11.2.2022.422

K., M. S. (2021). National Education Policy 1986 Vs National Education Policy 2020 – A Comparative Study. *International Research Journal on Advanced Science Hub, 2*(Special Issue ICAMET 10S). https://doi.org/DOI: 10.47392/irjash.2020.210

Kakodkar, P. V., Rishipathak, P., & Sriranga, J. (2024). Transformation in the Teachers' Role According to the National Education Policy 2020 Guidelines in the Indian Context. *The Journal of the Indian Association of Public Health Dentistry, 22*(1). Advance online publication. DOI: 10.4103/jiaphd.jiaphd_214_23

Kawale, P. R. (2024). *Current Scenario of the National Education Policy (NEP) 2020*. Gurukul International Multidisciplinary Research Journal., DOI: 10.69758/ gimrj/2409iii07v12p0008

Kulal, A. N. A., Dinesh, S., Bhat, D. C., & Girish, A. (2024). Evaluating the Promise and Pitfalls of India's National Education Policy 2020: Insights from the Perspectives of Students, Teachers, and Experts. *SAGE Open, 14*(4). Advance online publication. DOI: 10.1177/21582440241279367

Kumar, K., Prakash, A., & Singh, K. (2021). How the National Education Policy 2020 can be a lodestar to transform the future generation in India. *Journal of Public Affairs, 21*(3). Advance online publication. DOI: 10.1002/pa.2500

Kumar, N., Kumar, P., Kumar, R., Negi, A., & Kuma, B. (2025). National Education Policy 2020: A Vision for Transforming Education and Its Challenges. *IOSR Journal Of Humanities and Social Science, 30*(1).

Lissen, E. S., & Bautista, A. S. (2021). National Education Policy 2020. Building a new educational system in India. *Revista Española de Educación Comparada*, (37). Advance online publication. DOI: 10.5944/REEC.37.2021.29048

Manizia, L., Borah, T., Boruah, J., & Doley, G. (2024). The Synergy between the National Education Policy 2020 in India and STEAM Education. *Agriculture Association of Textile Chemical and Critical Reviews, 12*(3). Advance online publication. DOI: 10.21276/aatccreview.2024.12.03.48

Manodamrongsat, P., Intarachai, P., & Intarachai, C. (2022). The Impact of Artificial Intelligence on Education. *Phranakhon Rajabhat Research Journal: Humanities and Social Sciences, 17*(2).

Mehrotra, V. (2023). *Continuous professional development and teacher education post-implementation of the national education policy 2020*. Global Science Research Journals.

MHRD. (2020). National [Ministry of Human Resource Development, Government of India. *Ministry of Human Resource Development.*]. *Educational Policy*, •••, 2020.

Mir, A. A. (2023). The Scope of Technology in National Education Policy 2020: a Study. *ResearchGate.net* (April).

Mir, S. A., Saini, N., Senthil Kumar, A. V., Ganaie, N. A., Rautrao, R. R. R., Choudhary, A., Sehgal, S., & Khandelwal, A. R. R. (2025). GenAI. In *New Media Applications in Digital Education* (pp. 339–362). IGI Global Scientific Publishing., DOI: 10.4018/979-8-3373-5157-5.ch012

Mishra, S. K., & Mishra, P. (2024). National Education Policy 2020 and Multilingualism in India. *International Journal of English Literature and Social Sciences, 9*(1). Advance online publication. DOI: 10.22161/ijels.91.46

Mitra, N. L., & Sinha, M. K. (2023). National Education Policy 2020 and Challenges to the Bar Council of India. *Asian Journal of Legal Education, 10*(1). Advance online publication. DOI: 10.1177/23220058221138121

More, K. M. (2023). Reshaping Guidance and Counselling in Schools with Reference to National Education Policy (NEP 2020). *Scholarly Research Journal for Interdisciplinary Studies Online, 12*(79).

Mukherjee, S. (2024). Re-imagining Teacher Education in India: Assessing the Implications of National Education Policy 2020. *International Multidisciplinary Research Journal, 6*(1). Advance online publication. DOI: 10.54476/ioer-imrj/718522

Nagpal, P. (2023). Implementing the National Education Policy 2020: Challenges and Solutions in School Education in India. *International Journal of Creative Research Thoughts, 11*(1).

Naik, B., Chandiramani, J., & Majumdar, S. (2024). Is India's higher education system a case of elusive inclusive development? In *Cogent Education* (Vol. 11, Number 1). https://doi.org/DOI: 10.1080/2331186X.2024.2428874

Ngo, D., Nguyen, A., Dang, B., & Ngo, H. (2024). Facial Expression Recognition for Examining Emotional Regulation in Synchronous Online Collaborative Learning. *International Journal of Artificial Intelligence in Education, 34*(3). Advance online publication. DOI: 10.1007/s40593-023-00378-7

Panigrahi, S. P., & Gupta, S. (2021). National Education Policy- 2020: Rethinking Assessment in Higher Education. *Scholarly Research Journal for Humanity Science and English Language, 9*(46). Advance online publication. DOI: 10.21922/srjhsel.v9i46.1531

Pathak, R. H., & Pathak, R. (2021). National Education Policy 2020: Can It Improve Faculty Motivation and Academic Outcomes in India? *International Research Journal of Modernization in Engineering Technology and Science, 3*(4).

Pavan Ramchandra Manurkar. (2023). A Review of the National Education Policy 2020. *Journal of Legal, Ethical and Regulatory Issues, 24*(1).

Rahman, A. (2022). Review of Essential Amendments in Indian Higher Education with Special Reference to COVID-19 Pandemic and National Education Policy (NEP) 2020. *International Journal of Learning. Teaching and Educational Research, 21*(12). Advance online publication. DOI: 10.26803/ijlter.21.12.9

Raj, S. B. (2025). Pathways to inclusive higher education: Learnings from India's National Education Policy 2020. *Nordic Journal of Studies in Educational Policy, 11*(1). Advance online publication. DOI: 10.1080/20020317.2024.2382376

Saharia, G., & Mazumdar, S. (2024). Vocational Education in the Light of NEP 2020. *International Journal of Indian Psychology*, *12*(4).

Sahu, N., & Behera, H. (2022). National Education Policy 2020: A Historical Perspective. *International Journal for Research in Applied Science and Engineering Technology*, *10*(6). Advance online publication. DOI: 10.22214/ijraset.2022.44872

Saini, M., & Singh, M., Kaur, Manpreet, & Kaur, Manevpreet. (2021). Analysing the tweets to examine the behavioural response of Indian citizens over the approval of the National Education Policy 2020. *International Journal of Educational Development*, *82*. Advance online publication. DOI: 10.1016/j.ijedudev.2021.102356

Sarkar, S., & Sarkar, L. (2021). Visions of National Education Policy 2020 in School Education. *International Journal of Multidisciplinary Educational Research*, *10*(1).

Sethuramalingam, D. (2020). Digital Governance: Theory, Policy and Practice. SSRN *Electronic Journal*. https://doi.org/DOI: 10.2139/ssrn.3679639

Sharma, A., Prakash, A. R., Sharma, M. A., Ravi, A., Asst, P., Asst, R. S. S. N., & Litt, D. (2022). Reforms in higher education in India: National Education Policy-2020. *Retrieved from International Journal of Health Sciences, 6*(S5).

Sharma, G., & Mittal, R., & Zayan. (2023). Teacher Education in India's National Education Policy 2020: Knowledge Traditions, Global Discourses and National Regulations. *Contemporary Education Dialogue*, *20*(2). Advance online publication. DOI: 10.1177/09731849231168728

Sharma, G., & Singh, S. (2023). Locating Children's Right to Education in India's National Education Policy 2020. *The Journal for Critical Education Policy Studies*, *21*(2).

Sharma, Kar, Dr. J. (2020). National Education Policy 2020: Language Perspective. *International Journal of Management Research and Social Science*, *8*(1). Advance online publication. DOI: 10.30726/ijmrss/v8.i1.2021.81003

Singh, A. K. (2025). From policy to practice: Challenges and pathway for advancing multi-lingual education through India's national education policy 2020. *Policy Futures in Education*, *23*(4). Advance online publication. DOI: 10.1177/14782103251320532

Singh, A. K., & Narayanan, V. H. (2023). Can There be a Paradigm Shift in the Indian Education System? An Analysis of Socio-Economic Challenges in Implementing National Education Policy 2020. *Pertanika Journal of Social Science & Humanities*, *31*(2). Advance online publication. DOI: 10.47836/pjssh.31.2.14

Somani, R. (2024). Implementation of National Education Policy 2020 in Pharmacy Education. In the *Indian Journal of Pharmaceutical Education and Research* (Vol. 58, Number 2). https://doi.org/DOI: 10.5530/ijper.58.2s.38

Soni, M. (2023a). A Literature Survey on National Education Policy 2020 (NEP 2020) and Libraries. *Journal of Learning and Educational Policy*, (34). Advance online publication. DOI: 10.55529/jlep.34.13.23

Soni, M. (2023b). A Literature Survey on National Education Policy 2020 (NEP 2020) and Libraries. *Journal of Learning and Educational Policy*, (34). Advance online publication. DOI: 10.55529/jlep.34.13.26

Soni, R. (2022). Challenges and Issues in National Education Policy 2020. *International Research Journal of Modernization in Engineering Technology and Science*, *4*(03).

Sudhagar, D. P., & Mary Binu, T. D. (2022). Understanding stakeholders' intention to follow the National Education Policy 2020 using the theory of planned behaviour. *International Journal of Sustainable Society*, *14*(3). Advance online publication. DOI: 10.1504/IJSSOC.2022.125650

Sutar, D. B. (2024). Libraries and the National Education Policy (NEP 2020) of India in higher education. *Library Hi Tech News*, *41*(7). Advance online publication. DOI: 10.1108/LHTN-05-2024-0085

Syafhendry, S., Ganaie, N. A., & Yama, A. (2025). Smart elections or rigged algorithms: The rise of artificial intelligence in electoral governance in Southeast Asia. *Frontiers in Political Science*, *7*, 1672310. DOI: 10.3389/fpos.2025.1672310

Tian, Z., Zou, H., Yang, S., & Hou, Q. (2025). Research on Collaborative Governance of Cross-Domain Digital Innovation Ecosystems Based on Evolutionary Game Theory. *Systems*, *13*(7). Advance online publication. DOI: 10.3390/systems13070558

Tiwari, A. (2022). *National Education Policy 2020: Empowering Teacher Education*. Paripex Indian Journal of Research., DOI: 10.36106/paripex/7008072

Upadhya, A., & Saraf, M. N. (2025). Heralding a New Era for Higher Education Institutes: Moving Towards Implementation of National Education Policy 2020: A Pharmacy Undergraduate Program Perspective. In the *Indian Journal of Pharmaceutical Education and Research* (Vol. 59, Number 1). https://doi.org/DOI: 10.5530/ijper.20250760

Venkata, R. R., Bhattacharya, P., Lakhtakia, A., & Krishnasamy, S. T. (2025). Recommendations of India's National Education Policy 2020 for higher education. *Proceedings of the Indian National Science Academy*, *91*(1). Advance online publication. DOI: 10.1007/s43538-025-00386-2

Vigoda-Gadot, E., & Mizrahi, S. (2024). The digital governance puzzle: Towards an integrative theory of humans, machines, and organisations in public management. *Technology in Society*, *77*. Advance online publication. DOI: 10.1016/j.techsoc.2024.102530

Vyas, D. P. (2020). National education policy, 2020 and disability rights. *18 ~ International Journal of Research in Special Education, 1*(2).

Compilation of References

Abdallah, A. K. (2024). The impact of gender, psychology, and cultural dimensions on leadership development in distance education. *Scientific Reports*, *14*(1), 68495. Advance online publication. DOI: 10.1038/s41598-024-68495-4 PMID: 39112564

Abdallah, A. K., & Abdallah, R. K. (2023). Achieving academic excellence: The intersection of teacher development, quality education, and entrepreneurship. In *Innovations in teacher development, personalized learning, and upskilling the workforce*. IGI Global., DOI: 10.4018/978-1-6684-5518-0.ch007

Abdallah, A. K., Ismail, L. S., & Alkaabi, A. M. (2024). Green careers: Educating for the future of sustainability. In *Legal frameworks and educational strategies for sustainable development*. IGI Global., DOI: 10.4018/979-8-3693-2987-0.ch017

Abdallah, A. K., & Musah, M. B. (2023). Principal and teacher licensing as a tool to school improvement. In *Restructuring leadership for school improvement and reform*. IGI Global., DOI: 10.4018/978-1-6684-7818-9.ch014

Abdallah, R. K., Al Maktoum, S. B., & Al Mansoori, M. K. (2023). The Road to Lesson Observation as a Tool to School Improvement: Accountability vs. Perfunctory. In Abdallah, A., & Alkaabi, A. (Eds.), *Restructuring Leadership for School Improvement and Reform* (pp. 222–252). IGI Global Scientific Publishing., DOI: 10.4018/978-1-6684-7818-9.ch012

Aceves, T. C., & Orosco, M. J. (2014). *Culturally responsive teaching*. University of Florida.

Acharya, S. K., & Vagdal, T. (2023). The role of academic libraries in the context of national education policy (NEP)-2020. *IP Indian Journal of Library Science and Information Technology*, *8*(1). Advance online publication. DOI: 10.18231/j.ijlsit.2023.006

ADEK. (2026). Department of Education and Knowledge Webpage. Retrieved January 20, 2026, from https://www.adek.gov.ae/en/Education-System/Education-Policies/School-Policies

Agyeman, N. Y., & Aphane, V. (2024). Exploring school leadership styles used to improve instruction and learning in schools. *Journal of Research Initiatives*, *8*(1). https://digitalcommons.uncfsu.edu/jri/vol8/iss3/1

Aileni, A. R. (2025). AI-Driven Educational Equity: A Data Architecture for Addressing Achievement Gaps in Public Education Systems. *Journal of Computer Science and Technology Studies*, *7*(4), 535–540. DOI: 10.32996/jcsts.2025.7.4.63

Aithal, P. S., Prabhu, S., & Aithal, S. (2024). Future of higher education through technology prediction and forecasting. *Poornaprajna International Journal of Management, Education, and Social Science (PIJMESS), 1*(1), 01-50. https://papers.ssrn.com/sol3/Delivery.cfm?abstractid=4901474

Akgün, S., & Greenhow, C. (2022). Artificial intelligence in education: Addressing ethical challenges in K-12 settings. *AI and Ethics*, *2*(3), 431–440. DOI: 10.1007/s43681-021-00096-7 PMID: 34790956

Akinsola, K. (2025). Legal Compliance in Corporate Governance Frameworks: Best Practices for Ensuring Transparency, Accountability, and Risk Mitigation. *Accountability, and Risk Mitigation (January 31, 2025).*

Akkari, A., & Lauwerier, T. (2014). The education policies of international organizations: Specific differences and convergences. *Prospects*, *45*(1), 141–157. DOI: 10.1007/s11125-014-9332-z

Al Mokdad, A. (2025). Inclusive and Intelligent Governance: Enabling Sustainability Through Policy and Technology. In *Social System Reforms to Achieve Global Sustainability* (pp. 173-238). IGI Global Scientific Publishing. https://www.igi-global.com/chapter/inclusive-and-intelligent-governance/380524

Alainati, N. D. S. J., Almonawer, N. D. N. S., & Al-Hammad, N. D. F. A. (2023). Transformational Leadership in Education: Review of literature. *International Journal of Business and Management*. Advance online publication. DOI: 10.24940/theijbm/2023/v11/i2/bm2302-016

Alderson, J. C., Brunfaut, T., & Harding, L. (2017). Bridging assessment and learning: A view from second and foreign language assessment. *Assessment in Education: Principles, Policy & Practice*, *24*(3), 379–387. DOI: 10.1080/0969594X.2017.1331201

Aldous, S. M., & Ismail, G. A. (2025). AI for sustainable emergency preparedness and response in schools. In *Convergence of AI, education, and business for sustainability*. IGI Global., DOI: 10.4018/979-8-3373-1917-9.ch003

Ali, I., Nguyen, K., Ali, A. M., & Cui, T. (2025). Human–AI collaboration in knowledge ecosystems: A multidisciplinary review, integrative framework and future directions. *Journal of Knowledge Management*, •••, 1–22.

Alkaabi, A. M., Abdallah, A. K., Abdallah, R., Al Hasan, M., & Mohamed, A. (2025). Principal engagement in the teacher evaluation process in remote schools: A narrative inquiry of language teachers. *Forum for Linguistic Studies*, *7*(3), 209–230. DOI: 10.30564/fls.v7i3.8502

Allen, A., Hancock, S. D., Starker-Glass, T., & Lewis, C. W. (2017). Mapping culturally relevant pedagogy into teacher education programs: A critical framework. *Teachers College Record, 119*(1), 1-26. DIO: DOI:DOI: 10.1177/016146811711900107

Alok, P. D., & Rajesh, G. A. (2023). A Comparative Study on National Education Policy 1986 and 2020. *International Research Journal of Human Resources and Social Sciences, 10*(1).

Alqodsi, E. M. (2021). Analyzing the implementation of usufruct rights and obligations in the UAE Civil Transactions Law. *International Journal of Criminal Justice Sciences*, *16*(1), 95–109.

Al-Qodsi, E. M., Jadalhaq, I. M., & El-Maknouzi, M. E. H. (2024). The place of UAE's food security in the national legislation and its role in supporting global food security. *Cogent Social Sciences*, *10*(1), 2319379. Advance online publication. DOI: 10.1080/23311886.2024.2319379

Al-Tarawneh, A. M., & AlOmoush, R. A. ul Islam, T., Janjua, J. I., Abbas, T., & Ihsan, A. (2024, December). Current Trends in Artificial Intelligence for Educational Advancements. I*n 2024 International Conference on Decision Aid Sciences and Applications* (DASA) (pp. 1-6). IEEE. DIO:DOI: 10.1109/DASA63652.2024.10836340

Amiri, S. M. H., Islam, M. M., & Akter, N. (2025). Rethinking Education Policy: Pathways to Equitable and Future-Ready Learning. *SSRN, 5194153*, •••. https://papers.ssrn.com/sol3/Delivery.cfm?abstractid=5194153

Anchal, A. A. D. A. (2025). The Future of Commerce Education: Preparing Students for a Globalized, Technology-Driven Economy. *Innovative Journal for Advances in Education, Science. Commerce & Multidisciplinary Learning*, *1*(1), 49–59.

Anderson, A., Hyll-Larsen, P., & Hofmann, J. (2011). The Right to Education for Children in Emergencies. *Journal of International Humanitarian Legal Studies*, *2*(1), 84–126. DOI: 10.1163/187815211x586151

Anderson, R. E., & Dexter, S. L. (2005). School technology leadership: An empirical investigation of prevalence and effect. *Educational Administration Quarterly*, *41*(1), 49–82. DOI: 10.1177/0013161X04269517

Angwas, R. O. (2025). School Heads' Emergency Management Competencies: Its Influence on Continuity of Teaching and Learning During Emergency Situations in the Division of Agusan Del Sur, Philippines. *International Journal of Scientific and Research Publications*, *15*(6), 203–207. DOI: 10.29322/IJSRP.15.06.2025.p16225

Arun, D. P. (2022). Perceived Opportunities of National Education Policy-2020. *Indian Research Journal of Extension Education*, *22*(3). Advance online publication. DOI: 10.54986/irjee/2022/jul_sep/145-149

Assumang, D. K., Umah, E., Vincent, M. M., Abolade, B. I., & Shasere, B. E. (2025). A Data-driven Dashboard Framework for Employee Mental Health and Organisational Decision-making. *Journal of Scientific Research and Reports*, *31*(7), 979–1000. DOI: 10.9734/jsrr/2025/v31i73315

Aswal, D. K., & Chandra, A. (2025). Leveraging the Aswal Model to Understand and Amplify the Impact of India's National Education Policy. *Mapan - Journal of Metrology Society of India, 40*(3). https://doi.org/DOI: 10.1007/s12647-025-00840-y

Atillo, F. F., Batao, H. S., Giger, V. M. D., & Elesio, J. M. (2025). School Heads' Crisis Leadership: Experiences in Managing Natural Disasters and School Emergencies. *School Heads'. Crisis Leadership: Experiences in Managing Natural Disasters and School Emergencies*, *165*(1), 14–14.

Autio, C., Schwartz, R., Dunietz, J., Jain, S., Stanley, M., Tabassi, E., Hall, P., & Roberts, K. (2024). *Artificial intelligence risk management framework: Generative artificial intelligence profile* (NIST AI 600-1). National Institute of Standards and Technology. https://doi.org/DOI: 10.6028/NIST.AI.600-1

Avolio, B. J., Kahai, S. S., & Dodge, G. E. (2000). e-leadership: Implications for theory, research, and practice. *The Leadership Quarterly*, *11*(4), 615–668. DOI: 10.1016/S1048-9843(00)00062-X

Ayeni, O., Eden, C., Ayeni, O. O., & Eden, C. A. (2024). Equity and access in higher education: Legal perspectives and management strategies. *International Journal of Science and Research Archive*, *11*(2), 199–206. DOI: 10.30574/ijsra.2024.11.2.0391

Aynul Bari, M., & Goswamee, G. (2024). The Impact of National Education Policy 2020 On Teacher Training Institutions. *Theory into Practice*, *2024*(5).

Baker, R. S., & Hawn, A. (2022). Algorithmic bias in education. *International Journal of Artificial Intelligence in Education*, *32*, 1052–1092. DOI: 10.1007/s40593-021-00285-9

Bapte, V. D. (2022). Libraries in the context of the National Education Policy. *Annals of Library and Information Studies*, *69*(3). Advance online publication. DOI: 10.56042/alis.v69i3.63666

Baran, M. (2025). AI-augmented leadership: Redefining leaders' style and competencies. In *AI and Humanistic Management* (pp. 147–169). Routledge.

Barbu, C., & Sbughea, C. (2024). Artificial Intelligence in Education: Global Trends, Clusters, and Perspectives. *Economics and Applied Informatics*, (3), 265–274. DOI: 10.35219/eai15840409452

Barrett, D., & Twycross, A. (2020). Student mental health and well-being: Are universities doing enough? *Evidence-Based Nursing*, *23*(2), 33–34.

Barr, N., Pennycook, G., Stolz, J. A., & Fugelsang, J. A. (2015). The brain in your pocket: Evidence that Smartphones are used to supplant thinking. *Computers in Human Behavior*, *48*, 473–480. DOI: 10.1016/j.chb.2015.02.029

Bashir, H. A., & Francis, J. (2024). The College Campus, a Place of Learning, and a Place of Healing. *Advances in Social Sciences Research Journal*, *11*(7), 31–41. DOI: 10.14738/assrj.117.17246

Bass, B. M., & Avolio, B. J. (1995). Theory of transformational leadership redux. *The Leadership Quarterly*.

Bass, B. M., & Bass Bernard, M. (1985). *No. 3* (Vol. 25). Leadership and performance beyond expectations. Free press.

Beatty, B. (2007). Going through the Emotions: Leadership That Gets to the Heart of School Renewal. *Australian Journal of Education*, *51*(3), 328–340. DOI: 10.1177/000494410705100309

Bernard, H. R., Wutich, A., & Ryan, G. W. (2017). Analyzing qualitative data: Systematic approaches. *Sage (Atlanta, Ga.)*.

Betsurmath, C. G., & Chidambaram, S. B. (2024). National Education Policy 2020, India: A planned change management requisite for higher education institutions. *Journal of Infrastructure. Policy and Development*, *8*(9). Advance online publication. DOI: 10.24294/jipd.v8i9.3020

Bholane, K. (2025). National Education Policy 2020: A Catalyst for Skill-Based Education. SSRN *Electronic Journal*. https://doi.org/DOI: 10.2139/ssrn.5093645

Bin Rashed, F. M., & Mahmoud, E. Y. (2023). Transforming Teacher Professional Identity Through Social Emotional Learning: Two Narrative Case Studies. In Stephen, J. S., Kormpas, G., & Coombe, C. (Eds.), *Global Perspectives on Higher Education* (Vol. 11, pp. 381–393). Springer International Publishing., DOI: 10.1007/978-3-031-31646-3_25

Boccio, R. (2022). Race After Technology: Abolitionist Tools for the New Jim Code by Ruha Benjamin. *Configurations*, *30*(2), 236–238. https://muse.jhu.edu/pub/1/article/853611/summary

Bora, D., & Mathew, S. (2024). Reshaping Higher Education: A Comparative Study of India's National Education Policies. *International Journal for Multi-dimensional Research Perspectives*, *2*(5). Advance online publication. DOI: 10.61877/ijmrp.v2i5.149

Bora, I. (2024). The Status of Life Skill Education in the National Education Policy 2020. [JETIR]. *Journal of Emerging Technologies and Innovative Research*, *11*(7).

Boutte, G. S. (2012). Urban schools: Challenges and possibilities for early childhood and elementary education. *Urban Education*, *47*(2), 515–550. DOI: 10.1177/0042085911429583

Bromley, P., & Andina, M. (2010). Standardizing chaos: A neo-institutional analysis of the INEE Minimum Standards for Education in Emergencies, Chronic Crises and Early Reconstruction. *Compare: A Journal of Comparative Education*, *40*(5), 575–588. DOI: 10.1080/03057920903254972

Brooks, M. C., & Ezzani, M. D. (2021). Islamic school leadership: Advancing a framework for critical spirituality. *International Journal of Qualitative Studies in Education : QSE*, *35*(3), 319–336. DOI: 10.1080/09518398.2021.1930265

Browne, V. (2017). Under the Radar: The Mental Health of Australian University Students. *The Australian and New Zealand Student Services Association*, *25*(2), 51–62. DOI: 10.30688/janzssa.2017.16

Brown, J. H., D'Emidio-Caston, M., & Benard, B. (2001). *Resilience education.* Corwin Press.

Brown-Jeffy, S., & Cooper, J. E. (2011). Toward a conceptual framework of culturally relevant pedagogy: An overview of conceptual and theoretical literature. *Teacher Education Quarterly*, *38*(1), 65–84.

Bryk, A. S., Gomez, L. M., Grunow, A., & LeMahieu, P. G. (2015). *Learning to improve: How America's schools can get better at getting better*. Harvard Education Press.

Bryk, A. S., & Schneider, B. (2002). *Trust in schools: A core resource for improvement*. Russell Sage Foundation.

Buchholtz, N., Stuart, A., & Frones, T. S. (2021). Equity, equality and diversity—Putting educational justice in the Nordic model to a test. In *Equity, equality and diversity in the Nordic model of education* (pp. 13–41). Springer International Publishing.

Bulathwela, S., Pérez-Ortiz, M., Holloway, C., Cukurova, M., & Shawe-Taylor, J. (2024). Artificial intelligence alone will not democratise education: On educational inequality, techno-solutionism and inclusive tools. *Sustainability, 16*(2), 781. https://www.mdpi.com/2071-1050/16/2/781

Burbules, N. C., Lord, B. T., & Sherman, A. L. (1982). Equity, equal opportunity, and education. *Educational Evaluation and Policy Analysis, 4*(2), 169-187. DOI:-DOI: 10.3102/0162373700400

Burns, E. M., & Ward, W. D. (1978). Categorical perception—phenomenon or epiphenomenon: Evidence from experiments in the perception of melodic musical intervals. *The Journal of the Acoustical Society of America, 63*(2), 456–468. PMID: 670543

Cădariu, I.-E., & Rad, D. (2025). Mapping the Whole School Approach in social and emotional learning and wellbeing: A bibliometric review with implications for social work and education. *Technium Social Sciences Journal, 72*, 169–188. DOI: 10.47577/tssj.v72i1.12872

Carolus, A., Augustin, Y., Markus, A., & Wienrich, C. (2023). Digital interaction literacy model–Conceptualizing competencies for literate interactions with voice-based AI systems. *Computers and Education: Artificial Intelligence, 4*, 100114. https://www.sciencedirect.com/science/article/pii/S2666920X22000698

Carroll, A., Bower, J. M., Chen, H., Watterston, J., & Ferguson, A. (2022). School-wide Approaches for Promoting Social and Emotional Well-Being in Australian School Contexts: Focus Group Interviews with System and School Stakeholders. *American Journal of Education, 129*(1), 109–138. DOI: 10.1086/721798

CAST. (2018). Universal Design for Learning (UDL) guidelines (Version 2.2). http://udlguidelines.cast.org

Chand, S. P. (2024). Bridging the gaps in quality education. *The Educational Review, USA*, *8*(2), 202–210. DOI: 10.26855/er.2024.02.001

Chang, M. A., Tissenbaum, M., Philip, T. M., & D'Mello, S. K. (2025). Co-designing AI with youth partners: Enabling ideal classroom relationships through a novel AI relational privacy ethical framework. *Computers and Education: Artificial Intelligence*, *8*. Advance online publication. DOI: 10.1016/j.caeai.2025.100364

Chatzipanagiotou, P., & Katsarou, E. (2023). Crisis management, school leadership in disruptive times and the recovery of schools in the post COVID-19 era: A systematic literature review. *Education Sciences*, *13*(2), 118.

Chaudhari, Y. S. Mr. (2023). National Education Policy 2020 and Changing Role of Libraries. *Library Philosophy and Practice*, (7860).

Chen, N. S., Smyrnova-Trybulska, E., Morze, N., Ślósarz, A., Glushkova, T., Przybyła-Kasperek, M., ... & Gubo, Š. (2024). Education in the era of AI, enhancing skills, challenges and perspectives–International context and national experience. *International Journal of Research in E-learning*, *10*(2), 1-30. DOI: DOI: 10.31261/IJREL.2024.10.2.06

Chen, R., Wu, Y., Chen, Z., & Zhou, P. (2025). Advancing educational equity in rural China: The impact of AI devices on teaching quality and learning outcomes for sustainable development. *Frontiers in Psychology*, *16*, 1588047. Advance online publication. DOI: 10.3389/fpsyg.2025.1588047 PMID: 41267767

Chiang, Y. H. V., Chang, M., & Chen, N. S. (2024). Can generative AI help realize the shift from an outcome-oriented to a process-outcome-balanced educational practice?. *Educational Technology & Society*, *27*(2), 347-385. DOI:DOI: 10.30191/ets.202404_27(2).tp04

Chkheidze, S. (2024). Transformational leadership in change management in educational organizations. *International Journal of Teaching and Learning Sciences*, *2*(1). Advance online publication. DOI: 10.71010/IJTLS.2025.e110

Chong, P. W. (2016). The Finnish "Recipe" Towards Inclusion: Concocting Educational Equity, Policy Rigour, and Proactive Support Structures. *Scandinavian Journal of Educational Research*, *62*(4), 501–518. DOI: 10.1080/00313831.2016.1258668

Chowdhury, A. R., & Hanumanthu, P. (2023). Analysing India's National Education Policy from the Angle of Research, IP, Innovation, and Entrepreneurship. *Journal of Intellectual Property Rights*, *28*(3). Advance online publication. DOI: 10.56042/jipr.v28i3.1616

Coburn, C. E. (2003). Rethinking scale: Moving beyond numbers to deep and lasting change. *Educational Researcher*, *32*(6), 3–12. DOI: 10.3102/0013189X032006003

Collie, R. J., Martin, A. J., & Gasevic, D. (2024). Teachers' generative AI self-efficacy, valuing, and integration at work: Examining job resources and demands. *Computers and Education: Artificial Intelligence*, *7*, 100333. DOI: 10.1016/j.caeai.2024.100333

Cosens, B. A., Ruhl, J. B., Soininen, N., & Gunderson, L. (2020). Designing Law to Enable Adaptive Governance of Modern Wicked Problems. *Vanderbilt Law Review*, *73*(6).

Costa, J., Pádua, M., & Moreira, A. C. (2023). Leadership styles and innovation management: What is the role of human capital? *Administrative Sciences*, *13*(2), 47. DOI: 10.3390/admsci13020047

Creswell, J. W., & Poth, C. N. (2018). *Qualitative inquiry and research design: Choosing among five approaches*. Sage publications.

Cross, B. E. (2005). New racism, reformed teacher education, and the same people oppression. *Educational studies*, *38*(3), 263–274. DOI: 10.1207/s15326993es3803_6

Culbertson, S., Ling, T., Henham, M.-L., Corbett, J., Karam, R., Pankowska, P., Saunders, C., Bellasio, J., & Baruch, B. (2016). Evaluation of the Emergency Education Response for Syrian Refugee Children and Host Communities in Jordan (RR-1203). RAND Corporation. https://www.rand.org/pubs/research_reports/RR1203.html

Cunningham, A. E. (2025). *A Qualitative Study Exploring How School And District Education Leaders Respond To Critical Organizational Crisis And Change Events*. Franklin University.

Dar, R. A., & Ganaie, N. A. (2021). Importance Of Nep 2020 For Changing the Role of Teacher Educators. *Elementary Education Online*, *20*(1), 8289–8301. DOI: 10.17051/ilkonline.2021.01.847

Darvishi, A., Khosravi, H., Sadiq, S., Gašević, D., & Siemens, G. (2023). *Impact of AI assistance on student agency*. Computers & Education. *Article*, *104967*. Advance online publication. DOI: 10.1016/j.compedu.2023.104967

Dasgupta, S. T. (2025). Strengthening Early Childhood Education in Bangladesh: Lessons from the National Education Policy (NEP)-2020 of India. *Interchange*, *56*(2). Advance online publication. DOI: 10.1007/s10780-025-09541-6

Das, P. (2023). Recommendations And Challenges of Teacher Education In National Education Policy (Nep) 2020. *International Journal of Research Publication and Reviews*, *4*(8). Advance online publication. DOI: 10.55248/gengpi.4.823.51490

Das, P. (2024). Redefining College Libraries in Today's "Digital India": A Special Reference to the National Education Policy 2020. *RAY. International Journal of Multidisciplinary Studies*, *9*(1).

Das, P., Das, G., & Barman, P. (2023). National Education Policy 2020: Current Issues and Re-imagining the Future of Higher Education. *International Journal of Indian Psychology*, *11*(3). Advance online publication. DOI: 10.25215/1103.360

David, S., Anand, R. S., & Sagayam, M. (2020). Enhancing AI-based evaluation for smart cultivation and crop testing using agro datasets. *Journal of Artificial Intelligence and Systems*, *2*(1). Advance online publication. DOI: 10.33969/ais.2020.21010

DeGregory, C., LaCelle-Peterson, M., Lowenstein, K., & Schneider, S. (Eds.). (2025). *Locating Quality in the Dynamic Educator Preparation Landscape: Creating Quality in Context*. Stylus Publishing, LLC.

Desai, A., & Desai, M. (2023). A Review of the State of Cybersecurity in the Healthcare Industry and Propose Security Controls. *Mesopotamian Journal of Artificial Intelligence in Healthcare*, *2023*. Advance online publication. DOI: 10.58496/mjaih/2023/016

Dexter, S., & Richardson, J. W. (2020). What does technology integration research tell us about the leadership of technology? *Journal of Research on Technology in Education*, *52*(1), 17–36. DOI: 10.1080/15391523.2019.1668316

Dissanayake, L., & Al-Sharify, A. (2025). AI and Decision Making: How does the integration of AI influence leadership decision making within technology driven companies? In Dobrescu, P., Vladu, L., & Durach, F. (2024). INNOVATION AND EDUCATION: A CHALLENGING RELATIONSHIP. INTED2024 Proceedings, Elabied, N. (2024). Collaborative Leadership With AI: New Paradigms in University Administration. *International Research Journal of Engineering & Applied Sciences*, *12*(3), 01-06. https://doi.org/DOI: 10.55083/irjeas.2024.v12i03001

Dr. Dharmendra Kumar Dubey, Dr. Mritunjai Pandey, Er. Yukti Varshney, & Er. Shreyas Pande. (2023). The Implications of the National Education Policy, 2020, on Legal Education in India. *International Journal of Advanced Research in Science. Tongxin Jishu*. Advance online publication. DOI: 10.48175/ijarsct-8903

Dubey, P. K. (2025). Personalized Learning and Pedagogy: Harnessing AI for Tailored Education. In Wang, V. (Ed.), *Integrating AI Into Pedagogical Education* (pp. 81–102). IGI Global Scientific Publishing., DOI: 10.4018/979-8-3693-6130-6.ch004

Durães, D., Bezerra, R. M. A., & Novais, P. (2024). AI-driven educational transformation in secondary schools: Leveraging data insights for inclusive learning environments. In *Proceedings of the IEEE Global Engineering Education Conference (EDUCON)*. https://doi.org/DOI: 10.1109/EDUCON60312.2024.10578910

Durlak, J. A., & DuPre, E. P. (2008). Implementation matters: A review of research on the influence of implementation on program outcomes and the factors affecting implementation. *American Journal of Community Psychology*, *41*(3–4), 327–350. DOI: 10.1007/s10464-008-9165-0

Dustker, S., Bandi, S., & Oakes, W. (2022). Scope of Service-Learning in Accomplishing Objectives of National Education Policy 2020, India: Conceptual Analysis. *Journal of Engineering Education Transformations, 36*(Special Issue 2). https://doi.org/DOI: 10.16920/jeet/2023/v36is2/23054

Dwivedi, Y. K., Kshetri, N., Hughes, L., Slade, E. L., Jeyaraj, A., Kumar Kar, A., Baabdullah, A. M., Koohang, A., Raghavan, V., Ahuja, M., Albanna, H., Albashrawi, M. A., Al-Busaidi, A. S., & Balakrishnan, J. (2023). "So what if ChatGPT wrote it?": Multidisciplinary perspectives on opportunities, challenges and implications of generative conversational AI for research, practice and policy. *International Journal of Information Management*, *71*, 102642. Advance online publication. DOI: 10.1016/j.ijinfomgt.2023.102642

Eaton, S. E. (2023). Postplagiarism: Transdisciplinary ethics and integrity in the age of artificial intelligence and neurotechnology. *International Journal for Educational Integrity*, *19*, 23. Advance online publication. DOI: 10.1007/s40979-023-00144-1

Eden, C. A., Chisom, O. N., & Adeniyi, I. S. (2024). Harnessing technology integration in education: Strategies for enhancing learning outcomes and equity. *World Journal of Advanced Engineering Technology and Sciences, 11*(2), 001-008. https://doi.org/DOI: 10.30574/wjaets.2024.11.2.0071

Ehrnstrom, C., Blankenheim, A., Bottiglio, M., Tomatz, M., West, A., Bryant, T., LaHoda, R., & Gerberich, S. (2022). Embedding counselors within departments across campus can meet increased demand. *Student Affairs Today*, *25*(3), 6–7. DOI: 10.1002/say.31083

El Zaatari, W., & Ibrahim, A. (2021). What promotes adolescent students' school belonging? Students' and teachers' convergent/divergent views. *Cogent Education*, *8*(1), 1–20. DOI: 10.1080/2331186X.2021.1984628

Eleftheriades, R., Fiala, C., & Pasic, M. D. (2020). The challenges and mental health issues of academic trainees. *F1000 Research*, *9*, 104. DOI: 10.12688/f1000research.21066.1

Elliott, K. E., Mathew, K. A., Fan, Y., & Mattson, D. (2022). Educating during a Health Emergency: An Integrative Review of the Literature from 1990 to 2020. *Journal on Education in Emergencies*, *8*(3). Advance online publication. DOI: 10.33682/85qf-kr51

Enos, G. (2019). College takes multilayer approach to addressing student mental health. *Mental Health Weekly*, *29*(42), 1–8. DOI: 10.1002/mhw.32115

Eslit, E. (2024). AI-Enhanced Language Learning: Bridging Cultures and Breaking Barriers. DOI:DOI: 10.20944/preprints202411.1866.v1

Espinoza, O. (2007). Solving the equity–equality conceptual dilemma: A new model for analysis of the educational process. *Educational Research*, *49*(4), 343–363. DOI: 10.1080/00131880701717198

European Union. (2024). *Regulation (EU) 2024/1689 of the European Parliament and of the Council of 13 June 2024 laying down harmonised rules on artificial intelligence (Artificial Intelligence Act)*. https://data.europa.eu/eli/reg/2024/1689/oj

Fahadah, A., & Thomps, J. (2025). Exploring the Role of Culturally Responsive Pedagogy in Promoting Equity Across Diverse Educational Environments. *International Journal of Post Axial: Futuristic Teaching and Learning*, 97-108. DOI:DOI: 10.59944/postaxial.v3i2.445

Faisal, R. (2025). Ethical AI Integration in Education: Policies, Challenges, and Strategies for Bridging Digital Divides in Emerging Economies. *Crossroads of Social Inquiry*, *1*(2), 1–18. DOI: 10.64851/csi.v1i2.28

Fang, M., Abdallah, A. K., & Vorfolomeyeva, O. (2024). Collaborative AI-enhanced digital mind-mapping as a tool for stimulating creative thinking in inclusive education for students with neurodevelopmental disorders. *BMC Psychology*, *12*(1), 1975. Advance online publication. DOI: 10.1186/s40359-024-01975-4 PMID: 39289718

Farheen, S., Cheema, A. A., Ullah, R. S., & Bandeali, M. M. (2025). Equity and bias in AI educational tools: A critical examination of algorithmic decision-making in classrooms. *The Critical Review of Social Sciences Studies*, *3*(3), 67–85.

Fishman, B. J., Penuel, W. R., Allen, A.-R., Cheng, B. H., & Sabelli, N. (2013). Design-based implementation research: An emerging model for transforming the relationship of research and practice. In B. J. Fishman & W. R. Penuel (Eds.), Yearbook of the National Society for the Study of Education (Vol. 112, No. 2, pp. 136–156). Teachers College Record.

Fixsen, D. L., Naoom, S. F., Blase, K. A., Friedman, R. M., & Wallace, F. (2005). *Implementation research: A synthesis of the literature*. University of South Florida.

Florentino, B., Sestito, C., Cruz, W., de Carvalho, A., & Bonidia, R. (2025). *Artificial intelligence for all? Brazilian teachers on ethics, equity, and the everyday challenges of AI in education* (Preprint). https://doi.org//arXiv.2512.23834DOI: 10.48550

Friesen, K., & Bell, D. (2006). Risk Reduction and Emergency Preparedness Activities of Canadian Universities. *International Journal of Mass Emergencies and Disasters*, *24*(2), 223–249. DOI: 10.1177/028072700602400204

Fullan, M. (2011). *Change leader: Learning to do what matters most*. Jossey-Bass.

Fu, Q., & Zhang, X. (2024). Promoting community resilience through disaster education: Review of community-based interventions with a focus on teacher resilience and well-being. *PLoS One*, *19*(1), e0296393. https://journals.plos.org/plosone/article/file?id=10.1371/journal.pone.0296393&type=printable

Ganaie, N. A., Saikia, T., Mir, T. A., & Jan, I. (2025). *Dynamics of Public Policy and Good Governance in India: The Road to Viksit Bharat* (First). Authors Click Publishing. https://doi.org/DOI: 10.5281/ZENODO.15870017

Gao, Q., Xu, W., Pan, H., Shen, M., & Gao, Z. (2025). Human-Centered Human-AI Collaboration (HCHAC). *arXiv preprint arXiv:2505.22477*.

Gay, G. (2018). *Culturally responsive teaching: Theory, research, and practice*. Teachers College Press.

Gerlich, M. (2025). AI tools in society: Impacts on cognitive offloading and the future of critical thinking. *Societies (Basel, Switzerland)*, *15*(1), 6. Advance online publication. DOI: 10.3390/soc15010006

Gökçe, A. (2025). Revolutionizing education with AI: Ethical considerations in K–12 settings. In *IntechOpen*. https://doi.org/DOI: 10.5772/intechopen.1012230

Goldberg, J. M., Sklad, M., Elfrink, T. R., Schreurs, K. M. G., Bohlmeijer, E. T., & Clarke, A. M. (2018). Effectiveness of interventions adopting a whole school approach to enhancing social and emotional development: A meta-analysis. *European Journal of Psychology of Education*, *34*(4), 755–782. DOI: 10.1007/s10212-018-0406-9

Gong, X., & Wen, J. (2023). The Text Analysis of National Education Policy 2020. *Journal of Education. Teaching and Social Studies*, *5*(1). Advance online publication. DOI: 10.22158/jetss.v5n1p95

Gontang, M. G. Leadership Resiliency and Adaptability: Effect on Crisis Management in Multigrade Schools. *International Journal of Open-Access, Interdisciplinary & New Educational Discoveries of ETCOR Educational Research Center*, *4*(1), https://etcor.org/storage/iJOINED/Vol.%20IV(1),%20168-180.pdf

Goodman, L. (2017). Mental Health on University Campuses and the Needs of Students They Seek to Serve. *Building Healthy Academic Communities Journal, 1*(2), 31–44. DOI: 10.18061/bhac.v1i2.6056

Gopali, N., & Shetty, H. (2019). The AI Conveyor Belt. *European Conference on the Impact of Artificial Intelligence and Robotics, ECIAIR 2019*. https://doi.org/ DOI: 10.34190/ECIAIR.19.083

Gregg, E. A., Ohlson, M., Dominguez, A. R., & Steele, S. (2025). A Proposal for Improving Student-Athletes' Mental Health Through Leadership Training. *Sport Management Education Journal, 19*(1), 59–61. DOI: 10.1123/smej.2023-0002

Gregor, S., & Hevner, A. R. (2013). Positioning and presenting design science research for maximum impact. *Management Information Systems Quarterly, 37*(2), 337–355.

Guardiola, M.-A. (2025). Educational Leadership and AI in the Post-COVID-19 Era: Ethical Challenges and Opportunities in Catalonia. *Digital Citizenship and the Future of AI Engagement, Ethics, and Privacy*, 569-602.

Gupta, P. B., & Gupta, B. (2022). Role of Strategic Human Resource Management Practices (SHRMPs) for Gearing up Higher Education Institutions to Achieve Vision of National Education Policy (NEP 2020) and Industry 4.0. *AJMR 798 Amity Journal of Management Research ADMAA Amity. Journal of Management Research, 5*(1).

Harding-DeKam, J. L. (2014). Defining culturally responsive teaching: The case of mathematics. *Cogent Education, 1*(1), 972676. DOI: 10.1080/2331186X.2014.972676

Hassanien, A. R. M., Patwa, N., Bagheri, N., & Tabash, M. I. (2025). Ethical Implications of Artificial Intelligence Accessibility in the United Arab Emirates: Bridging the Digital Divide. *International Review of Management and Marketing, 15*(6), 22. DOI: 10.32479/irmm.20011

Hayes, S. D., & Derrington, M. L. (2023). School leadership in uncertain times: Identifying dimensions of effective principal leadership. *School Leadership & Management, 43*(4), 330–347. DOI: 10.1080/13632434.2023.2171002

Heenan, I. W., De Paor, D., Lafferty, N., & McNamara, P. M. (2023). The Impact of Transformational School Leadership on School Staff and School Culture in Primary Schools—A Systematic Review of International literature. *Societies (Basel, Switzerland), 13*(6), 133. DOI: 10.3390/soc13060133

Heifetz, R. A. (1994). *Leadership without easy answers*. Harvard University Press.

Heiser, C., Schnelle, T., & Tullier, S. (2023). Defining and operationalizing equity-centered assessment. *Journal of Student Affairs Inquiry, Improvement, and Impact, 6*, 4–17. DOI: 10.18060/27921

Henning, G. W., Baker, G. R., Jankowski, N. A., Lundquist, A. E., & Montenegro, E. (Eds.). (2023). *Reframing assessment to center equity: Theories, models, and practices*. Taylor & Francis.

Henning, G., & Lundquist, A. E. (2022). Using assessment to advance equity. *New Directions for Student Services*, *2022*(178-179), 185–194. DOI: 10.1002/ss.20439

Hernandez, A., & Burrows, K. (2021). Implementing culturally relevant teaching in the classroom. *Open Journal of Leadership, 10*(4), 338-363. DOI: DOI: 10.4236/ojl.2021.104020

Hernandez, A. (2022). Closing the achievement gap in the classroom through culturally relevant pedagogy. *Journal of Education and Learning*, *11*(2), 1–21. DOI: 10.5539/jel.v11n2p1

Hevner, A. R., March, S. T., Park, J., & Ram, S. (2004). Design science in information systems research. *Management Information Systems Quarterly*, *28*(1), 75–105.

Higgins, E., & Booker, R. (2023). What are the main factors that are thought to impact upon the implementation of a whole school approach to student mental health and wellbeing in schools? A systematic review. *International Journal of Wellbeing*, *13*(2), 77–94. DOI: 10.5502/ijw.v13i2.2833

Hoare, E., Bott, D., & Robinson, J. (2017). Learn it, Live it, Teach it, Embed it: Implementing a whole school approach to foster positive mental health and wellbeing through Positive Education. *International Journal of Wellbeing*, *7*(3), 56–71. DOI: 10.5502/ijw.v7i3.645

Holmes, W., Bialik, M., & Fadel, C. (2019). *Artificial intelligence in education promises and implications for teaching and learning*. Center for Curriculum Redesign. https://discovery.ucl.ac.uk/id/eprint/10139722/

Holstein, K., & Aleven, V. (2022). Designing for human–AI complementarity in K-12 education. *AI Magazine*, *43*(2), 239–248. DOI: 10.1002/aaai.12058

Hood, S., Hopson, R. K., & Kirkhart, K. E. (2015). Culturally responsive evaluation. *Handbook of practical program evaluation*, 281-317. DOI:DOI: 10.1002/9781119171386.ch12

Howard, T. C. (2019). *Why race and culture matter in schools: Closing the achievement gap in America's classrooms*. Teachers College Press., DOI: 10.31046/wabashcenter.v2i2.2916

Ibrahim, A. (2010). *Education in the UAE: A socio-cultural analysis.* In Y. Zhao et al., *Handbook of Asian Education: A Cultural Perspective* (pp. 327-344). Routledge. https://doi.org/DOI: 10.4324/9780203816318

Ibrahim, A. (2018). *Directive, collaborative, or non-directive? Supervision perceptions of UAE thesis/dissertation approaches*. Issues in Educational Research, 28(3), 679–700. https://www.iier.org.au/iier28/ibrahim.pdf

Ibrahim, A. (2020). *What hurts or helps teacher collaboration? Evidence from UAE schools*. Prospects: Comparative Journal of Curriculum, Learning, and Assessment. https://doi.org/.DOI: 10.1007/s11125-019-09459-9

Ibrahim, A. S. (2012). Induction and mentoring of novice teachers: A scheme for the United Arab Emirates. *Teacher Development, 16*(2), 235–253. DOI: 10.1080/13664530.2012.688676

Ibrahim, A. S. (2013). The learning needs of beginning teachers in the United Arab Emirates. *Journal of Education for Teaching: International Research and Pedagogy, 39*(5), 491–506. DOI: 10.1080/02607476.2013.739791

Idowu, J. A. (2024). Debiasing Education Algorithms. *International Journal of Artificial Intelligence in Education, 34*(4), 1510–1540. DOI: 10.1007/s40593-023-00389-4

Ifenthaler, D., Majumdar, R., Gorissen, P., Judge, M., Mishra, S., Raffaghelli, J., & Shimada, A. (2024). Artificial intelligence in education: Implications for policymakers, researchers, and practitioners. *Technology, Knowledge and Learning, 29*(4), 1693-1710. https://link.springer.com/content/pdf/10.1007/s10758-024-09747-0.pdf

International Society for Technology in Education & Association for Supervision and Curriculum Development. (2025). *AI in education: Professional learning and support for educators*. ISTE+ASCD. https://iste.org/ai

International Society for Technology in Education. (2018). ISTE standards for education leaders. https://iste.org/standards/education-leaders

Irawan, M. A., & Anwar, Z. (2025). Harnessing artificial intelligence for inclusive education management: Strategies for supporting students with special needs. [JEMIN]. *Journal of Educational Management and Instruction, 5*(2), 350–370. DOI: 10.22515/jemin.v5i2.11650

Ismail, G. A., & Aldous, S. M. (2025). Integrating health and safety standards in teacher licensing systems: A GCC perspective. In *Building a unified teacher licensing system: Policies, education reforms, and cultural integration*. IGI Global., DOI: 10.4018/979-8-3373-0837-1.ch015

Ismail, L. S., & Ismail, O. A. S. (2024). Adaptive strategies for success: Monitoring and evaluating blue-green infrastructure in urban development. In *Integrating blue-green infrastructure into urban development*. IGI Global., DOI: 10.4018/979-8-3693-8069-7.ch001

Ismail, O. (2024). Digital transformation in education: Navigating the challenges and opportunities of remote learning. In *Building resilient education models post crisis*. IGI Global., DOI: 10.4018/979-8-3693-8125-0.ch007

ISO. (2023). *ISO/IEC 42001:2023 Artificial intelligence management system*. https://www.iso.org/standard/81230.html

Jadalhaq, I. M., Abdulhay, I. E., Alqodsi, E. M., & El Maknouzi, M. E. H. (2023). A systematic review and meta-analysis of interruption of the statute of limitations for civil claims: A comparative study of Arab legislations. *Heliyon*, *9*(9), e16756. DOI: 10.1016/j.heliyon.2023.e16756

Jolly, D. A., & Kaur, D. P. (2025). Integrating Artificial Intelligence into India's National Education Policy 2020: Opportunities, Challenges and Strategic Pathways. *International Journal of Engineering Research & Technology (Ahmedabad)*, *14*(5).

Jones, H., & MacDonald, G. (2012). Promoting Mental, Emotional and Social Health, a Whole School Approach. *International Journal of Mental Health Promotion*, *4*(1), 24–25. DOI: 10.1080/14623730.2002.9721851

Jordan, U. N. I. C. E. F. (2022). Final report: Summative impact evaluation of the UNICEF Jordan Makani programme [Report]. https://www.unicef.org/jordan/media/11671/file/Makani%20summative%20impact%20evaluation_English.pdf

Jose, B., Cleetus, A., Joseph, B., Joseph, L., Jose, B., & John, A. K. (2025, August). Epistemic authority and generative AI in learning spaces: rethinking knowledge in the algorithmic age. In *Frontiers in Education* (Vol. 10, p. 1647687). Frontiers Media SA. https://doi.org/DOI: 10.3389/feduc.2025.1647687

Joshi, S. (2025a). Comprehensive Review of Artificial Intelligence in Management, Leadership, Decision-Making and Collaboration. *Decision-Making and Collaboration (April 15, 2025)*.

Joshi, S. (2025b). Review of Artificial Intelligence in Management, Leadership, Decision-Making and Collaboration.

K C, T. (2022). Impact of National Education Policy 2020 on Higher Education. *SUMEDHA Journal of Management, 11*(2). https://doi.org/DOI: 10.46454/sumedha/11.2.2022.422

K., M. S. (2021). National Education Policy 1986 Vs National Education Policy 2020 – A Comparative Study. *International Research Journal on Advanced Science Hub, 2*(Special Issue ICAMET 10S). https://doi.org/DOI: 10.47392/irjash.2020.210

Kakodkar, P. V., Rishipathak, P., & Sriranga, J. (2024). Transformation in the Teachers' Role According to the National Education Policy 2020 Guidelines in the Indian Context. *The Journal of the Indian Association of Public Health Dentistry, 22*(1). Advance online publication. DOI: 10.4103/jiaphd.jiaphd_214_23

Kamaruddin, S. A. (2024). Disaster Preparedness Design in Secondary School Environment. *JUPE: Jurnal Pendidikan Mandala, 9*(4). Advance online publication. DOI: 10.58258/jupe.v9i4.7821

Karakose, T. (2021). Emergency remote teaching due to COVID-19 pandemic and potential risks for socioeconomically disadvantaged students in higher education. *Educational Process International Journal, 10*(3). Advance online publication. DOI: 10.22521/edupij.2021.103.4

Kawale, P. R. (2024). *Current Scenario of the National Education Policy (NEP) 2020.* Gurukul International Multidisciplinary Research Journal., DOI: 10.69758/gimrj/2409iii07v12p0008

Kennedy, K. (2019). Centering Equity and Caring in Leadership for Social-Emotional Learning: Toward a Conceptual Framework for Diverse Learners. *Journal of School Leadership, 29*(6), 473–492. DOI: 10.1177/1052684619867469

Kgothule, R., Palmer, J., Alexander, G., & De Klerk, E. (2021). Transformative leadership in multicultural schooling contexts: A critical reflection of in-service teachers practices and school manager roles. *Education and New Developments, 620–624.* Advance online publication. DOI: 10.36315/2021end131

Khalifa, M. A. (2018). *Culturally responsive school leadership.* Harvard Education Press.

Khalifa, M. A., Gooden, M. A., & Davis, J. E. (2016). Culturally responsive school leadership: A synthesis of the literature. *Review of Educational Research, 86*(4), 1272–1311. DOI: 10.3102/0034654316630383

Khan, M., Thongnun, W., Zamani, M., Siripap, P., Channuwong, S., & Lertatthakornkit, T. (2025). Strategies for reducing educational inequality in primary schools using adaptive learning technologies. *International Journal of Environmental Sciences*, *11*(7), 416–424. DOI: 10.64252/13f8wm17

Kim, J. (2025). Perspectives on AI integration in K-12 schools: Opportunities, challenges, and strategic approaches. *Midwest Journal of Education*, *2*(1). Advance online publication. DOI: 10.69670/mje.2.1.4

Kim, J., Lee, H., & Cho, Y. H. (2022). Learning design to support student-AI collaboration: Perspectives of leading teachers for AI in education. *Education and Information Technologies*, *27*(5), 6069–6104. DOI: 10.1007/s10639-021-10831-6

Kitzrow, M. A. (2009). The Mental Health Needs of Today's College Students: Challenges and Recommendations. *NASPA Journal*, *46*(4), 646–660. DOI: 10.2202/1949-6605.5037

Klimova, B., Pikhart, M., Benites, A. D., Lehr, C., & Sanchez-Stockhammer, C. (2023). Neural machine translation in foreign language teaching and learning: A systematic review. *Education and Information Technologies*, *28*(1), 663–682. DOI: 10.1007/s10639-022-11194-2

Kolehmainen, J., Kurikka, H., Keerberg, A., & Raagmaa, G. (2022). Being resilient between the region and the higher education system? Views on regional higher education institutions in Estonia and Finland. *Towards resilient organizations and societies: A cross-sectoral and multi-disciplinary perspective*, 249-276.

Konu, A., & Rimpela, M. (2002). Well-being in schools: A conceptual model. *Health Promotion International*, *17*(1), 79–87. DOI: 10.1093/heapro/17.1.79

Kotlyar, I., & Krasman, J. (2025). Student reactions to AI versus human feedback in teamwork skills assessment. *International Journal of Educational Technology in Higher Education*, *22*, 57. Advance online publication. DOI: 10.1186/s41239-025-00555-9

Kulal, A. N. A., Dinesh, S., Bhat, D. C., & Girish, A. (2024). Evaluating the Promise and Pitfalls of India's National Education Policy 2020: Insights from the Perspectives of Students, Teachers, and Experts. *SAGE Open*, *14*(4). Advance online publication. DOI: 10.1177/21582440241279367

Kulik, J. A., & Fletcher, J. D. (2016). Effectiveness of Intelligent Tutoring Systems: A Meta-Analytic Review. *Review of Educational Research*, *86*(1), 42–78. https://www.jstor.org/stable/resrep22695

Kumar, N., Kumar, P., Kumar, R., Negi, A., & Kuma, B. (2025). National Education Policy 2020: A Vision for Transforming Education and Its Challenges. *IOSR Journal Of Humanities and Social Science, 30*(1).

Kumar, K., Prakash, A., & Singh, K. (2021). How the National Education Policy 2020 can be a lodestar to transform the future generation in India. *Journal of Public Affairs*, *21*(3). Advance online publication. DOI: 10.1002/pa.2500

Kundu, A., & Bej, T. (2025). AI policies in school education: A comparative study on China, Singapore, Finland, and the US. *Journal of Science and Technology Policy Management.*

Ladson-Billings, G. (1995). Toward a theory of culturally relevant pedagogy. American Educational Research Journal, 32(3), 465–491. Marsh, J. A., Pane, J. F., & Hamilton, L. S. (2006). Making sense of data-driven decision making in education: Evidence from recent RAND research (OP-170). RAND Corporation. https://www.rand.org/pubs/occasional_papers/OP170.html

Ladson-Billings, G. (2023). "Yes, but how do we do it?": Practicing culturally relevant pedagogy. In *White teachers/diverse classrooms* (pp. 33–46). Routledge.

Lam, Y. F. (2025). *From Isolation to Collaboration: Promoting Teacher Wellness Through Professional Learning Communities* (Doctoral dissertation, The University of Western Ontario). https://uwo.scholaris.ca/server/api/core/bitstreams/6125bfc3-217b-45c2-9e00-80568bfb454a/content

Landa, N., Zhou, S., & Marongwe, N. (2021). Education in emergencies: Lessons from COVID-19 in South Africa. *International Review of Education*, *67*(1-2), 167–183. DOI: 10.1007/s11159-021-09903-z

Lee, S. M. (2023). The effectiveness of machine translation in foreign language education: A systematic review and meta-analysis. *Computer Assisted Language Learning*, *36*(1–2), 103–125. DOI: 10.1080/09588221.2021.1901745

Lehtonen, S., & Kuuskorpi, M. (2023). Towards Typological and Spatial Diversities Learning from the typological solutions of the Finnish comprehensive public-school buildings. *Architectural Research in Finland*, *6*(1). Advance online publication. DOI: 10.37457/arf.130449

Leithwood, K. (2021). A Review of Evidence about Equitable School Leadership. *Education Sciences*, *11*(8). Advance online publication. DOI: 10.3390/educsci11080377

Létourneau, A., Deslandes Martineau, M., Charland, P., Karran, J. A., Boasen, J., & Léger, P. M. (2025). *A systematic review of AI-driven intelligent tutoring systems (ITS) in K-12 education*. npj Science of Learning, 10, Article 29. https://doi.org/ DOI: 10.1038/s41539-025-00320-7

Lewallen, T. C., Hunt, H., Potts-Datema, W., Zaza, S., & Giles, W. (2015). The Whole School, Whole Community, Whole Child model: A new approach for improving educational attainment and healthy development for students. *The Journal of School Health*, *85*(11), 729–739. DOI: 10.1111/josh.12310

LI, H., & Tian, F. (2025). Advancing decision-making through AI-human collaboration: A systematic review and conceptual framework.

Li, H. (2023). AI in education: Bridging the divide or widening the gap? Exploring equity, opportunities, and challenges in the digital age. *Advances in Education. Humanities and Social Science Research*, *8*(1), 355–355. DOI: 10.56028/aehssr.8.1.355.2023

Lim, L.-A., Dawson, S., Gašević, D., Joksimović, S., Fudge, A., Pardo, A., & Gentili, S. (2020). Students' sense-making of personalised feedback based on learning analytics. *Australasian Journal of Educational Technology*, *36*(6), 15–33. DOI: 10.14742/ajet.6370

Lissen, E. S., & Bautista, A. S. (2021). National Education Policy 2020. Building a new educational system in India. *Revista Española de Educación Comparada*, (37). Advance online publication. DOI: 10.5944/REEC.37.2021.29048

Luckin, R. (2018). *Machine Learning and Human Intelligence. The future of education for the 21st century*. UCL institute of education press. https://discovery.ucl.ac.uk/id/eprint/10178695/1/Machine%20Learning%20and%20Human%20Intelligence.pdf

Mahmoud, E. Y. (2024). *The Role of Task-Based Language Assessment in English Language Learning and Learner Autonomy Enhancement in an EFL High School Context in the UAE.* [Unpublished Doctoral Dissertation, United Arab Emirates University]. https://scholarworks.uaeu.ac.ae/all_dissertations/350/

Mamanazarov, S., Khajiyeva, M., Abdullaeva, D., Yuldasheva, G., Azkhodjaeva, R., Pirnazarov, A., & Xamedova, N. (2025). Innovating Human Capital Development: The Role of Education, Law, and Economics Through Digital Transformation. *Qubahan Academic Journal, 5*(3), 78-113. https://journal.qubahan.com/index.php/qaj/article/download/1698/426

Manda, V. K., Christy, V., & Jitta, M. R. (2025). Ethical AI and decision-making in management leadership. In *Ethical dimensions of AI development* (pp. 197–226). IGI Global., DOI: 10.4018/979-8-3693-4147-6.ch009

Manizia, L., Borah, T., Boruah, J., & Doley, G. (2024). The Synergy between the National Education Policy 2020 in India and STEAM Education. *Agriculture Association ofTextile Chemical and Critical Reviews*, *12*(3). Advance online publication. DOI: 10.21276/aatccreview.2024.12.03.48

Manodamrongsat, P., Intarachai, P., & Intarachai, C. (2022). The Impact of Artificial Intelligence on Education. *Phranakhon Rajabhat Research Journal: Humanities and Social Sciences, 17*(2).

Mariyono, D., Hidayatullah, A. N. A., & Kamila, A. N. A. (2025). Integrating Artificial Intelligence in Inclusive Leadership: Transforming Educational Management for a Globalized Future. *Authorea Preprints.*

Martin, F., Zhuang, M., & Schaefer, D. (2024). Systematic review of research on artificial intelligence in K–12 education (2017–2022). *Computers and Education: Artificial Intelligence*, *6*, 100195. DOI: 10.1016/j.caeai.2023.100195

Ma, W., Adesope, O. O., Nesbit, J. C., & Liu, Q. (2014). Intelligent tutoring systems and learning outcomes: A meta-analysis. *Journal of Educational Psychology*, *106*(4), 901. DOI: 10.1037/a0037123

McGrath, H., & Noble, T. (2010). Supporting positive pupil relationships: Research to practice. *Educational and Child Psychology*, *27*(1), 79–90. DOI: 10.53841/bpsecp.2010.27.1.79

McKenney, S., & Reeves, T. C. (2012). *Conducting educational design research.* Routledge.

Mehrotra, V. (2023). *Continuous professional development and teacher education post-implementation of the national education policy 2020*. Global Science Research Journals.

Melo-López, V.-A., Basantes-Andrade, A., Gudiño-Mejía, C.-B., & Hernández-Martínez, E. (2025). The impact of artificial intelligence on inclusive education: A systematic review. *Education Sciences*, *15*(5), 539. DOI: 10.3390/educsci15050539

METWALLI, M. M. A. S. (2024). *ARTIFICIAL INTELLIGENCE IN EDUCATIONAL LEADERSHIP: CHALLENGES AND OPPORTUNITIES* LIVERPOOL JOHN MOORES UNIVERSITY].

MHRD. (2020). National [Ministry of Human Resource Development, Government of India. *Ministry of Human Resource Development.*]. *Educational Policy*, •••, 2020.

Michopoulou, K. (2025). The principle of equality in education: Exploring the legal aspects of the right to inclusive and equitable quality education for achieving the development of a democratic citizenship. *European Journal of Education and Pedagogy*, *6*(2), 64–69.

Michopoulou, K., & Chin Gan, J. K. (2025). Ethical leadership in AI-enabled schools: Navigating human rights, equity, and justice in education. *European Journal of Education and Pedagogy*, *6*(5), 988. Advance online publication. DOI: 10.24018/ejedu.2025.6.5.988

Mir, A. A. (2023). The Scope of Technology in National Education Policy 2020: a Study. *ResearchGate.net* (April).

Mir, S. A., Saini, N., Senthil Kumar, A. V., Ganaie, N. A., Rautrao, R. R. R., Choudhary, A., Sehgal, S., & Khandelwal, A. R. R. (2025). GenAI. In *New Media Applications in Digital Education* (pp. 339–362). IGI Global Scientific Publishing., DOI: 10.4018/979-8-3373-5157-5.ch012

Mishra, S. K., & Mishra, P. (2024). National Education Policy 2020 and Multilingualism in India. *International Journal of English Literature and Social Sciences*, *9*(1). Advance online publication. DOI: 10.22161/ijels.91.46

Mitra, N. L., & Sinha, M. K. (2023). National Education Policy 2020 and Challenges to the Bar Council of India. *Asian Journal of Legal Education*, *10*(1). Advance online publication. DOI: 10.1177/23220058221138121

MOE. (2026). United Arab Emirates Ministry of Education. Retrieved January 28, 2026, from https://moe.gov.ae/Ar/OpenData/Pages/Home.aspx

More, K. M. (2023). Reshaping Guidance and Counselling in Schools with Reference to National Education Policy (NEP 2020). *Scholarly Research Journal for Interdisciplinary Studies Online, 12*(79).

Morgan, H. (2014). Review of research: The education system in Finland: A success story other countries can emulate. *Childhood Education*, *90*(6), 453–457.

Moundridou, M., Matzakos, N., & Doukakis, S. (2024). Generative AI tools as educators' assistants: Designing and implementing inquiry-based lesson plans. *Computers and Education: Artificial Intelligence*, *7*, 100277. Advance online publication. DOI: 10.1016/j.caeai.2024.100277

Mugabekazi, J. C., & Mukanziza, J. (2025). Educational Leadership, Mental Health, and Equity: A Review of Effective Interventions in Schools. *European Journal of Educational Management*, *8*(1), 49–62. DOI: 10.12973/eujem.8.1.49

Mukherjee, S. (2024). Re-imagining Teacher Education in India: Assessing the Implications of National Education Policy 2020. *International Multidisciplinary Research Journal*, *6*(1). Advance online publication. DOI: 10.54476/ioer-imrj/718522

Mukhtarkyzy, K., Smagulova, L., Tokzhigitova, A., Serikbayeva, N., Sayakov, O., Turkmenbayev, A., & Assilbayeva, R. (2025). A systematic review of the utility of assistive technologies for SEND students in schools. *Frontiers in Education*, *10*, 1523797. Advance online publication. DOI: 10.3389/feduc.2025.1523797

Murari, U. K., & Parmar, H. (2025). Ethical Integration of Artificial Intelligence in Inclusive Education: Addressing Challenges and Advancing Opportunities for Equitable Learning. In *Ethics and AI Integration into Modern Classrooms* (pp. 439-470). IGI Global Scientific Publishing. DOI: DOI: 10.4018/979-8-3373-2262-9.ch015

Mutawa, A. M., & Sruthi, S. (2025). UNESCO's AI Competency Framework: Challenges and Opportunities in Educational Settings. *Impacts of Generative AI on the Future of Research and Education*, 75-96. https://www.igi-global.com/chapter/unescos-ai-competency-framework/358768

Nadelson, L. S., Albritton, S., Couture, V. G., Green, C., Loyless, S. D., & Shaw, E. O. (2020). Principals' Perceptions of Education Equity: A Mindset for Practice. *Journal of Education and Learning*, *9*(1), 1–15. DOI: 10.5539/jel.v9n1p1

Nagpal, P. (2023). Implementing the National Education Policy 2020: Challenges and Solutions in School Education in India. *International Journal of Creative Research Thoughts*, *11*(1).

Naidu, S. (2021). *Building resilience in education systems post-COVID-19* (Vol. 42). Taylor & Francis.

Naik, B., Chandiramani, J., & Majumdar, S. (2024). Is India's higher education system a case of elusive inclusive development? In *Cogent Education* (Vol. 11, Number 1). https://doi.org/DOI: 10.1080/2331186X.2024.2428874

Ngo, D., Nguyen, A., Dang, B., & Ngo, H. (2024). Facial Expression Recognition for Examining Emotional Regulation in Synchronous Online Collaborative Learning. *International Journal of Artificial Intelligence in Education*, *34*(3). Advance online publication. DOI: 10.1007/s40593-023-00378-7

Ng, S. L., & Ho, C. C. (2025). Generative ai in education: Mapping the research landscape through bibliometric analysis. *Information (Basel)*, *16*(8), 657.

Noddings, N. (2013). *Caring: A relational approach to ethics and moral education* (2nd ed.). University of California Press. (Original work published 1984)

Obed, B., & Bright, B. (2025). Algorithmic bias in educational systems: Examining the impact of AI-driven decision making in modern education. *World Journal of Advanced Research and Reviews*, *25*(1), 2012–2017. DOI: 10.30574/wjarr.2025.25.1.0253

OECD. (2021). *OECD digital education outlook 2021: Pushing the frontiers with artificial intelligence, blockchain and robots*. OECD Publishing. https://www.oecd.org/content/dam/oecd/en/publications/reports/2021/06/oecd-digital-education-outlook-2021_0f1487d9/589b283f-en.pdf

OECD. (2023). *Digital education outlook 2023: Towards an effective digital education ecosystem*. OECD Publishing., DOI: 10.1787/c74f03de-

Okada, A., Sherborne, T., Panselinas, G., & Kolionis, G. (2025). Fostering transversal skills through open schooling supported by the CARE-KNOW-DO pedagogical model and the UNESCO AI competencies framework. *International Journal of Artificial Intelligence in Education*, •••, 1–46. https://link.springer.com/content/pdf/10.1007/s40593-025-00458-w.pdf

Oloyede, J. (2025). Artificial Intelligence in Education: Building Ethical and Inclusive Smart Learning Ecosystems in the UAE. *Available at SSRN* 5405420. DOI: DOI: 10.2139/ssrn.5405420

Organisation for Economic Co-operation and Development. (2012). *Equity and quality in education: Supporting disadvantaged students and schools*. OECD Publishing., DOI: 10.1787/9789264130852-

Organisation for Economic Co-operation and Development. (2019). Recommendation of the Council on Artificial Intelligence. https://legalinstruments.oecd.org/en/instruments/oecd-legal-0449

Ouedraogo-Thomas, R. (2025). From Tool to Digitized Co-Conspirator: A Reflective Analysis of GPT-Based Engagement with Educational Equity. *American Journal of STEM Education*. https://doi.org/DOI: 10.32674/jxz8hn16

Özen, H., & Yavuz, P. (2024). A theoretical analysis for resilience: Developing a complex adaptive leadership model in schools. *Anadolu Eğitim Liderliği ve Öğretim Dergisi*, *12*(1), 49–72.

Panigrahi, S. P., & Gupta, S. (2021). National Education Policy- 2020: Rethinking Assessment in Higher Education. *Scholarly Research Journal for Humanity Science and English Language*, *9*(46). Advance online publication. DOI: 10.21922/srjhsel.v9i46.1531

Papa, R., & Jackson, K. M. (2021). *Artificial intelligence, human agency and the educational leader*. Springer Nature.

Pastor, M. J. D., Acosta, R. L., & Aquino, M. U. (2024). Resiliency practices in educational crisis management among school administrators. *International Journal of Education, 17*(1), 71–78.

Pathak, R. H., & Pathak, R. (2021). National Education Policy 2020: Can It Improve Faculty Motivation and Academic Outcomes in India? *International Research Journal of Modernization in Engineering Technology and Science*, *3*(4).

Paulienė, R. (2012b). Transforming Leadership Styles and Knowledge Sharing in a Multicultural Context. *Business Management and Education*, *10*(1), 91–109. DOI: 10.3846/bme.2012.08

Pavan Ramchandra Manurkar. (2023). A Review of the National Education Policy 2020. *Journal of Legal, Ethical and Regulatory Issues, 24*(1).

Peffers, K., Tuunanen, T., Rothenberger, M. A., & Chatterjee, S. (2007). A design science research methodology for information systems research. *Journal of Management Information Systems*, *24*(3), 45–77.

Penuel, W. R., Fishman, B. J., Cheng, B. H., & Sabelli, N. (2011). Organizing research and development at the intersection of learning, implementation, and design. *Educational Researcher*, *40*(7), 331–337. DOI: 10.3102/0013189X11421826

Peterson, S. (2025). Addressing student use of generative AI in schools and higher education: Academic integrity and assessment design challenges. *Frontiers in Education*, *10*, 1610836. DOI: 10.3389/feduc.2025.1610836

Piper, B., Jepkemei, E., & Kibukho, K. (2018). Kenya's Tusome national literacy program: Impacts, sustainability, and scale. *Journal of Educational Change*, *19*(3), 293–321.

Pittaluga, L. (2012). *One Laptop per Child and bridging the digital divide: The case of Plan Ceibal in Uruguay*. Agencia Nacional de Investigación e Innovación.

Puerta-Beldarrain, M., Gomez-Carmona, O., Sanchez-Corcuera, R., Casado-Mansilla, D., Lopez-de-Ipina, D., & Chen, L. (2025). A multifaceted vision of the Human-AI collaboration: A comprehensive review. *IEEE Access : Practical Innovations, Open Solutions*.

Radd, S. I., Generett, G. G., Gooden, M. A., & Theoharis, G. (2021). *Five practices for equity-focused school leadership*. ASCD.

Raffo, C., & Gunter, H. (2008). Leading schools to promote social inclusion: Developing a conceptual framework for analysing research, policy and practice. *Journal of Education Policy, 23*(4), 397–414. DOI: 10.1080/02680930801923799

Rahman, A. (2022). Review of Essential Amendments in Indian Higher Education with Special Reference to COVID-19 Pandemic and National Education Policy (NEP) 2020. *International Journal of Learning. Teaching and Educational Research, 21*(12). Advance online publication. DOI: 10.26803/ijlter.21.12.9

Rai, J., & Beresford-Dey, M. (2025). School leadership in the United Arab Emirates: A scoping review. *Educational Management Administration & Leadership, 53*(6), 1335-1357. DOI: DOI: 10.1177/17411432231218129

Raj, S. B. (2025). Pathways to inclusive higher education: Learnings from India's National Education Policy 2020. *Nordic Journal of Studies in Educational Policy, 11*(1). Advance online publication. DOI: 10.1080/20020317.2024.2382376

Ray, P. P. (2023). ChatGPT: A comprehensive review on background, applications, key challenges, bias, ethics, limitations and future scope. *Internet of Things and Cyber-Physical Systems, 3*, 121–154. DOI: 10.1016/j.iotcps.2023.04.003

Rehan, H. (2023). Shaping the future of education with cloud and AI technologies: Enhancing personalized learning and securing data integrity in the evolving edtech landscape. *Australian Journal of Machine Learning Research & Applications, 3*(1), 359–395.

Research on School Culture and Multicultural Education in Indonesia. (2025). *The influence of school's culture on multicultural education in Indonesia*. ResearchGate.

Revolusi, P., & Febriandy, R. K. (2025). Human-AI Educational Collaboration: Facing Learning Challenges in the Digital Age. *International Journal of Management, Entrepreneurship. Social Science and Humanities, 8*(2), 289–312. DOI: 10.31098/ijmesh.v8i2.3229

Riehl, C. J. (2000). The principal's role in creating inclusive schools for diverse students: A review of normative, empirical, and critical literature on the practice of educational administration. *Review of Educational Research, 70*(1), 55–81. DOI: 10.3102/00346543070001055

Risko, E. F., & Gilbert, S. J. (2016). Cognitive offloading: How the mind extends itself. *Trends in Cognitive Sciences, 20*(9), 676–688. DOI: 10.1016/j.tics.2016.07.002 PMID: 27542527

Roche, S. (2013). Equity and equality in education. *International Review of Education, 59*(1), 1-5. DOI: DOI: 10.1007/s11159-013-9356-2

Roffey, S. (2008). Emotional literacy and the ecology of school wellbeing. *Educational and Child Psychology, 25*(2), 29–39. DOI: 10.53841/bpsecp.2008.25.2.29

Roper, L. D. (2013). Breaking the Silence Surrounding Mental Health on Campus. *Journal of College and Character, 14*(1), 75–78. DOI: 10.1515/jcc-2013-0010

Rørstad Welle, K. B., & Gunnulfsen, A. E. (2025). School leadership: Dilemmas in dealing with crises. *Educational Management Administration & Leadership*. Advance online publication. DOI: 10.1177/17411432251325099

Rowe, F., & Stewart, D. (2009). Promoting connectedness through whole-school approaches: A qualitative study. *Health Education, 109*(5), 396–413. DOI: 10.1108/09654280910984816

Ruch, C. P., & Coll, K. (2022). Presidents and the Campus Mental Health Crisis: Challenges, Options, and Strategy. *Journal of Research on the College President, 6*. Advance online publication. DOI: 10.54119/jrcp.2022.603

Ryan, C. L., & Dixson, A. D. (2006). Review of Research: Rethinking Pedagogy to Re-center Race: Some Reflections. *Language Arts, 84*(2), 1–9. DOI: 10.58680/la20065624

Ryan, J. (2007). Inclusive-leadership: A review. *Journal of Educational Administration and Foundations, 18*, 92–125.

Saha, A. (2025). Human-centred innovation in Society 5.0. *Society 5.0: A Transformation towards Human-Centered. Artificial Intelligence*, •••, 143.

Saharia, G., & Mazumdar, S. (2024). Vocational Education in the Light of NEP 2020. *International Journal of Indian Psychology, 12*(4).

Sahlberg, P. (2021). *Finnish lessons 3.0: What can the world learn from educational change in Finland?* Teachers College Press.

Sahu, N., & Behera, H. (2022). National Education Policy 2020: A Historical Perspective. *International Journal for Research in Applied Science and Engineering Technology, 10*(6). Advance online publication. DOI: 10.22214/ijraset.2022.44872

Sai Rama Krishna, M., Monika Singh, T., Karuna, D., Divya, R., & Shuaib, M. (2025). Synergic Thinking: A New Era of Human-AI Decision-Making. In *The Power of Agentic AI: Redefining Human Life and Decision-Making: In Industry 6.0* (pp. 139-150). Springer.

Saini, M., & Singh, M., Kaur, Manpreet, & Kaur, Manevpreet. (2021). Analysing the tweets to examine the behavioural response of Indian citizens over the approval of the National Education Policy 2020. *International Journal of Educational Development, 82*. Advance online publication. DOI: 10.1016/j.ijedudev.2021.102356

Sarfraz, M., Bhutta, M., & Ivascu, L. (2024). Leadership in Cross-Cultural Contexts: Strategies for Global success. *International Journal of Organizational Leadership, 13. First, 2024*(Special Issue), 1–5. DOI: 10.33844/ijol.2024.60410

Sargiotis, D. (2025). Fostering Ethical and Inclusive AI: A Human-Centric Paradigm for Social Impact. *International Journal of Research Publication and Reviews, 6*(1), 3754–3779. DOI: 10.55248/gengpi.6.0125.0529

Sarkar, S., & Sarkar, L. (2021). Visions of National Education Policy 2020 in School Education. *International Journal of Multidisciplinary Educational Research, 10*(1).

Scott, S., Webber, C. F., Lupart, J. L., Aitken, N., & Scott, D. E. (2014). Fair and equitable assessment practices for all students. *Assessment in Education: Principles, Policy & Practice, 21*(1), 52–70. DOI: 10.1080/0969594X.2013.776943

Selwyn, N. (2017). *Education and technology: Key issues and debates* (2nd ed.). Bloomsbury Academic.

Selwyn, N. (2024). On the limits of artificial intelligence (AI) in education. *Nordisk Tidsskrift for Pedagogikk og Kritikk, 10*(1), 3–14. DOI: 10.23865/ntpk.v10.6062

Semwaiko, G. S., Chao, W.-H., & Yang, C.-Y. (2024). Transforming K–12 education: A systematic review of AI integration. *International Journal of Educational Technology and Learning, 17*(2), 43–63. DOI: 10.55217/101.v17i2.847

Sethuramalingam, D. (2020). Digital Governance: Theory, Policy and Practice. SSRN *Electronic Journal*. https://doi.org/DOI: 10.2139/ssrn.3679639

Sharma, A., Prakash, A. R., Sharma, M. A., Ravi, A., Asst, P., Asst, R. S. S. N., & Litt, D. (2022). Reforms in higher education in India: National Education Policy-2020. *Retrieved from International Journal of Health Sciences, 6*(S5).

Sharma, G., & Mittal, R., & Zayan. (2023). Teacher Education in India's National Education Policy 2020: Knowledge Traditions, Global Discourses and National Regulations. *Contemporary Education Dialogue, 20*(2). Advance online publication. DOI: 10.1177/09731849231168728

Sharma, G., & Singh, S. (2023). Locating Children's Right to Education in India's National Education Policy 2020. *The Journal for Critical Education Policy Studies, 21*(2).

Sharma, Kar, Dr. J. (2020). National Education Policy 2020: Language Perspective. *International Journal of Management Research and Social Science*, *8*(1). Advance online publication. DOI: 10.30726/ijmrss/v8.i1.2021.81003

Shields, C. M. (2017). *Transformative-leadership in education: Equitable, inclusive, and quality education in an uncertain and complex world* (2nd ed.). Routledge.

Sibanda, L. (2023). Strategies for achieving equity-based education: Towards an equitable education system. In *Social justice and culturally-affirming education in K-12 settings* (pp. 133–152). IGI Global., DOI: 10.4018/978-1-6684-6386-4.ch007

Sikander, N., Zeeshan, A., Muhammad Nouman, S., Muhammad Mudaber, J., & Ahmed, H. (2024). Ai for Inclusive Educational Governance and Digital Equity Examining the Impact of Ai Adoption and Open Data on Community Trust and Policy Effectiveness. *Contemporary Journal of Social Science Review*, *2*(04), 2557–2567. DOI: 10.63878/cjssr.v2i04.1502

Singh, A. K. (2025). From policy to practice: Challenges and pathway for advancing multi-lingual education through India's national education policy 2020. *Policy Futures in Education*, *23*(4). Advance online publication. DOI: 10.1177/14782103251320532

Singh, A. K., & Narayanan, V. H. (2023). Can There be a Paradigm Shift in the Indian Education System? An Analysis of Socio-Economic Challenges in Implementing National Education Policy 2020. *Pertanika Journal of Social Science & Humanities*, *31*(2). Advance online publication. DOI: 10.47836/pjssh.31.2.14

Smitha S. (2020). National Education Policy (NEP) 2020-Opportunities and Challenges in Teacher Education. *International Journal of Management (IJM, 11*(11).

Smith, L., & Riley, D. (2012). School leadership in times of crisis. *School Leadership & Management*, *32*(1), 57–71. DOI: 10.1080/13632434.2011.614941

Snyder, H. (2019). Literature review as a research methodology: An overview and guidelines. *Journal of Business Research*, *104*, 333–339.

Soini, T., Pyhältö, K., & Pietarinen, J. (2010). Pedagogical well-being: Reflecting learning and well-being in teachers' work. *Teachers and Teaching*, *16*(6), 735–751. DOI: 10.1080/13540602.2010.517690

Somani, R. (2024). Implementation of National Education Policy 2020 in Pharmacy Education. In the *Indian Journal of Pharmaceutical Education and Research* (Vol. 58, Number 2). https://doi.org/DOI: 10.5530/ijper.58.2s.38

Soni, M. (2023a). A Literature Survey on National Education Policy 2020 (NEP 2020) and Libraries. *Journal of Learning and Educational Policy*, (34). Advance online publication. DOI: 10.55529/jlep.34.13.23

Soni, R. (2022). Challenges and Issues in National Education Policy 2020. *International Research Journal of Modernization in Engineering Technology and Science*, *4*(03).

Southgate, E., Naghizade, E., Corman, A., & Atherton, M. (2025). Towards a governance roadmap for educational technology in Australian schools. *Journal of Educational Technology & Society*, *28*(4). Advance online publication. DOI: 10.1007/s13384-025-00916-3

Sperling, K., Stenberg, C. J., McGrath, C., Åkerfeldt, A., Heintz, F., & Stenliden, L. (2024). In search of artificial intelligence (AI) literacy in teacher education: A scoping review. *Computers and Education Open*, *6*, 100169. Advance online publication. DOI: 10.1016/j.caeo.2024.100169

Spillane, J. P. (2006). *Distributed leadership*. Jossey-Bass.

Sterling, S. (2013). Learning for resilience, or the resilient learner? Towards a necessary reconciliation in a paradigm of sustainable education. In *Resilience in social-ecological systems* (pp. 45–62). Routledge.

Storrie, K., Ahern, K., & Tuckett, A. (2010). A systematic review: Students with mental health problems—a growing problem. *International Journal of Nursing Practice*, *16*(1), 1–6. DOI: 10.1111/j.1440-172X.2009.01813.x

Sudhagar, D. P., & Mary Binu, T. D. (2022). Understanding stakeholders' intention to follow the National Education Policy 2020 using the theory of planned behaviour. *International Journal of Sustainable Society*, *14*(3). Advance online publication. DOI: 10.1504/IJSSOC.2022.125650

Sutar, D. B. (2024). Libraries and the National Education Policy (NEP 2020) of India in higher education. *Library Hi Tech News*, *41*(7). Advance online publication. DOI: 10.1108/LHTN-05-2024-0085

Swiecki, Z., Khosravi, H., Chen, G., Martinez-Maldonado, R., Lodge, J. M., Milligan, S., & Gašević, D. (2022). Assessment in the age of artificial intelligence. *Computers and Education: Artificial Intelligence*, *3*, 100075. DOI: 10.1016/j.caeai.2022.100075

Syafhendry, S., Ganaie, N. A., & Yama, A. (2025). Smart elections or rigged algorithms: The rise of artificial intelligence in electoral governance in Southeast Asia. *Frontiers in Political Science*, *7*, 1672310. DOI: 10.3389/fpos.2025.1672310

Szmelter-Jarosz, A., & Nozari, H. (2025). AI-Driven Decision Intelligence and Human-AI Collaboration in Economic Systems. In *Dynamic and Safe Economy in the Age of Smart Technologies* (pp. 171–190). IGI Global Scientific Publishing.

Tanksley, T. (2023). Employing an Abolitionist, Critical Race Pedagogy in CS: Centering the Voices, Experiences and Technological Innovations of Black Youth. *Journal of Computer Science Integration*, *6*(1), 9. https://digitalcommons.chapman.edu/cgi/viewcontent.cgi?article=1020&context=jcsi

Tan, X., Cheng, G., & Ling, M. H. (2025). Artificial intelligence in teaching and teacher professional development: A systematic review. *Computers and Education: Artificial Intelligence*, *8*, 100355. DOI: 10.1016/j.caeai.2024.100355

Tarricone, P., Mestan, K., & Teo, I. (2021b). Building resilient education systems: A rapid review of the education in emergencies literature.

Tarricone, P., Mestan, K., & Teo, I. (2021a). https://doi.org/DOI: 10.37517/978-1-74286-639-0

Theoharis, G. (2007). Social justice educational leaders and resistance: Toward a theory of social justice-leadership. *Educational Administration Quarterly*, *43*(2), 221–258. DOI: 10.1177/0013161X06293717

Tian, Z., Zou, H., Yang, S., & Hou, Q. (2025). Research on Collaborative Governance of Cross-Domain Digital Innovation Ecosystems Based on Evolutionary Game Theory. *Systems*, *13*(7). Advance online publication. DOI: 10.3390/systems13070558

Tiwari, A. (2022). *National Education Policy 2020: Empowering Teacher Education*. Paripex Indian Journal of Research., DOI: 10.36106/paripex/7008072

Topali, P., Ortega-Arranz, A., Rodríguez-Triana, M. J., Er, E., Khalil, M., & Akçapınar, G. (2024). Designing human-centered learning analytics and artificial intelligence in education solutions: A systematic literature review. *Behaviour & Information Technology*, *44*(5), 1071–1098. DOI: 10.1080/0144929x.2024.2345295

Torraco, R. J. (2005). Writing integrative literature reviews: Guidelines and examples. *Human Resource Development Review*, *4*(3), 356–367.

Torraco, R. J. (2016). Writing integrative literature reviews: Using the past and present to explore the future. *Human Resource Development Review*, *15*(4), 404–428.

Tucker, F. (2021). For-Profit colleges: Neither educationally nor economically equivalent. *Research in Higher Education*, *40*. https://files.eric.ed.gov/fulltext/EJ1296449.pdf

U.S. Department of Education, Office of Educational Technology. (2023). *Artificial intelligence and the future of teaching and learning: Insights and recommendations*. https://eric.ed.gov/?id=ED631201

Uhl-Bien, M., Marion, R., & McKelvey, B. (2007). Complexity leadership theory: Shifting leadership from the industrial age to the knowledge era. *The Leadership Quarterly*, *18*(4), 298–318. DOI: 10.1016/j.leaqua.2007.04.002

Umoke, C. C., & Nwangbo, S. O., & Onwe. (2025). O. A. AI-Driven Educational Policy Design: Enhancing Equity and Access through. *Intelligent Data Analysis*. Advance online publication. DOI: 10.56201/ijcsmt.v11.no3.2025.pg1.19

UNESCO. (2023). *Global Education Monitoring Report 2023: Technology in education — A tool on whose terms?* United Nations Educational, Scientific and Cultural Organization. https://unesdoc.unesco.org/ark:/48223/pf0000385723

UNICEF. (2021). *Policy guidance on AI for children 2.0: Recommendations for governments and businesses to support child-centred AI systems that uphold children's rights*. UNICEF Innocenti. https://www.unicef.org/innocenti/media/1341/file/UNICEF-Global-Insight-policy-guidance-AI-children-2.0-2021.pdf

UNICEF. (2025). *Guidance on AI and children 3.0: Updated guidance for governments and businesses to create AI policies and systems that uphold children's rights*. UNICEF Innocenti. https://www.unicef.org/innocenti/media/11991/file/UNICEF-Innocenti-Guidance-on-AI-and-Children-3-2025.pdf

United Nations Educational, Scientific and Cultural Organization. (2019). Global education monitoring report 2019: Migration, displacement and education—Building bridges, not walls. https://unesdoc.unesco.org/ark:/48223/pf0000265866

United Nations Educational, Scientific and Cultural Organization. (2020). Global education monitoring report 2020: Inclusion and education—All means all. https://unesdoc.unesco.org/ark:/48223/pf0000373718

United Nations Educational, Scientific and Cultural Organization. (2021). Recommendation on the ethics of artificial intelligence. https://unesdoc.unesco.org/ark:/48223/pf0000380455

United Nations International Children's Emergency Fund. (2021). The climate crisis is a child rights crisis: Introducing the Children's Climate Risk Index (CCRI). https://www.unicef.org/media/105376/file/UNICEF-climate-crisis-child-rights-crisis.pdf

Upadhya, A., & Saraf, M. N. (2025). Heralding a New Era for Higher Education Institutes: Moving Towards Implementation of National Education Policy 2020: A Pharmacy Undergraduate Program Perspective. In the *Indian Journal of Pharmaceutical Education and Research* (Vol. 59, Number 1). https://doi.org/DOI: 10.5530/ijper.20250760

Vaccari, V., & Gardinier, M. P. (2019). Toward one world or many? A comparative analysis of OECD and UNESCO global education policy documents. *International Journal of Development Education and Global Learning*, *11*(1). Advance online publication. DOI: 10.18546/ijdegl.11.1.05

van der Vlies, R. (2020). Digital strategies in education across OECD countries: Exploring education policies on digital technologies. *OECD Education Working Papers*, (226), 0_1-45. https://www.proquest.com/openview/e0a555e60c7bd27fbf409c465d41896a/1?pq-origsite=gscholar&cbl=54479

Venkata, R. R., Bhattacharya, P., Lakhtakia, A., & Krishnasamy, S. T. (2025). Recommendations of India's National Education Policy 2020 for higher education. *Proceedings of the Indian National Science Academy*, *91*(1). Advance online publication. DOI: 10.1007/s43538-025-00386-2

Vibhuti, C., & Divyansh, C. (2024). Towards trustworthy AI: An analysis of the relationship between explainability and trust in AI systems. *International Journal of Science and Research Archive*, *11*(1), 2219–2226. DOI: 10.30574/ijsra.2024.11.1.0300

Vigoda-Gadot, E., & Mizrahi, S. (2024). The digital governance puzzle: Towards an integrative theory of humans, machines, and organisations in public management. *Technology in Society*, *77*. Advance online publication. DOI: 10.1016/j.techsoc.2024.102530

Villegas, A. M., & Lucas, T. (2007). The culturally responsive teacher. *Educational Leadership*, *64*(6), 28.

Virella, P. M. (2023). Introducing the pillars of equity-oriented crisis leadership: A conceptual framework. *School Leadership & Management*, *43*(4), 390–410. DOI: 10.1080/13632434.2023.2186848

vom Brocke, J., Simons, A., Riemer, K., Niehaves, B., Plattfaut, R., & Cleven, A. (2009). Reconstructing the giant: On the importance of rigour in documenting the literature search process. In *Proceedings of the 17th European Conference on Information Systems* (pp. 2206–2217).

Vu Nguyen, V. H. (2025). *Finnish Students' Educational Provision Experience Towards Resilience*. Recovery and Renewal of Education Systems.

Vyas, D. P. (2020). National education policy, 2020 and disability rights. *18 ~ International Journal of Research in Special Education, 1*(2).

Walls, T. E. (2017). *Race, resilience, and resistance: A culturally relevant qualitative examination of how black women school leaders advance racial equity and social justice in US schools*. University of Nevada.

Wang, Y., Wu, H., & Wang, Y. (2025). Engagement and willingness to communicate in the L2 classroom: Identifying the latent profiles and their relationships with achievement emotions. *Journal of Multilingual and Multicultural Development*, *46*(8), 2175–2191. DOI: 10.1080/01434632.2024.2379534

Watkins, D. C., Hunt, J. B., & Eisenberg, D. (2011). Increased demand for mental health services on college campuses: Perspectives from administrators. *Qualitative Social Work: Research and Practice*, *11*(3), 319–337. DOI: 10.1177/1473325011401468

Webster, J., & Watson, R. T. (2002). Analyzing the past to prepare for the future: Writing a literature review. MIS Quarterly, 26(2), xiii–xxiii. Whittemore, R., & Knafl, K. (2005). The integrative review: Updated methodology. *Journal of Advanced Nursing*, *52*(5), 546–553. DOI: 10.1111/j.1365-2648.2005.03621.x

Weidlich, J., Gotsch, F., Schudel, K., Marusic-Würscher, C., Mazzarella, J., Bolten, H., & Merki, K. M. (2025). Teacher, peer, or AI? Comparing effects of feedback sources in higher education. *Computers and Education Open*, *100300*. Advance online publication. DOI: 10.1016/j.caeo.2025.100300

Wells, J., Barlow, J., & Stewart-Brown, S. (2003). A systematic review of universal approaches to mental health promotion in schools. *Health Education*, *103*(4), 197–220. DOI: 10.1108/09654280310485546

Whitley, J. (2010). The Role of Educational Leaders in Supporting the Mental Health of All Students. *Exceptionality Education International*, *20*(2). Advance online publication. DOI: 10.5206/eei.v20i2.7663

Wiliam, D. (2013). Assessment: The bridge between teaching and learning. *Voices from the Middle*, *21*(2), 15–20. DOI: 10.58680/vm201324461

Williamson, B. (2017). Big data in education: The digital future of learning, policy and practice. *Sage (Atlanta, Ga.)*.

Williamson, B., & Eynon, R. (2020). Historical threads, missing links, and future directions in AI in education. *Learning, Media and Technology*, *45*(3), 223–235. DOI: 10.1080/17439884.2020.1798995

Williamson, B., Komljenovic, J., & Gulson, K. (Eds.). (2023). *World yearbook of education 2024: digitalisation of education in the era of algorithms, automation and artificial intelligence*. Taylor & Francis. Gianni, R., Lehtinen, S., & Nieminen, M. (2022). Governance of responsible AI: From ethical guidelines to cooperative policies. *Frontiers of Computer Science*, *4*, 873437.

Williams, T., & Liou, Y.-H. (2023). Framing K-12 School Leaders' Roles and Competencies in Times of Crisis. *Journal of School Leadership*, *34*(1), 26–46. DOI: 10.1177/10526846231187576

Wittka, M. (2020). Designed agency in collaborations: Exploring cross-sector collaboration in Finland's artificial intelligence programme AuroraAI.

Woodruff, K., Hutson, J., & Arnone, K. (2023). *Perceptions and barriers to adopting artificial intelligence in K–12 education: A survey of educators in fifty states. Artificial intelligence in education*. IntechOpen., DOI: 10.5772/intechopen.1002741

World Bank. (2019). Ending learning poverty: What will it take? https://documents1.worldbank.org/curated/en/395151571251399043/pdf/Ending-Learning-Poverty-What-Will-It-Take.pdf

World Wide Web Consortium. (2023). Web Content Accessibility Guidelines (WCAG) 2.2 (W3C Recommendation; updated December 12, 2024). https://www.w3.org/TR/WCAG22/

Wu, F., Freeman, G., Wang, S., & Flores, I. (2024). The Future of College Student Mental Health: Student Perspectives. *Journal of College Student Mental Health*, *38*(4), 975–1010. DOI: 10.1080/28367138.2024.2400612

Wyn, J., Cahill, H., Holdsworth, R., Rowling, L., & Carson, S. (2000). MindMatters, a whole-school approach promoting mental health and wellbeing. *The Australian and New Zealand Journal of Psychiatry*, *34*(4), 594–601. DOI: 10.1080/j.1440-1614.2000.00748.x

Xu, Z. (2024). AI in education: Enhancing learning experiences and student outcomes. *Applied and Computational Engineering*, *51*(1), 104–111. DOI: 10.54254/2755-2721/51/20241187

Yanguas, M. L. (2020). Technology and educational choices: Evidence from a one-laptop-per-child program. *Economics of Education Review*, *77*, 101997.

Zarate-Torres, R., Rey-Sarmiento, C. F., Acosta-Prado, J. C., Gomez-Cruz, N. A., Rodriguez Castro, D. Y., & Camargo, J. (2025). Influence of Leadership on Human-Artificial Intelligence Collaboration. *Behavioral Sciences (Basel, Switzerland)*, *15*(7), 873. DOI: 10.3390/bs15070873

About the Contributors

Asma Khaleel Abdallah is an Assistant Professor of Educational Leadership at Sharjah Education Academy, with extensive experience across higher education, school leadership, and educational consultancy in the UAE and Jordan. She previously served as a Visiting Assistant Professor at United Arab Emirates University and Assistant Professor at Abu Dhabi University, alongside her work as a school inspector and professional development consultant with ADEK's Irtiqa program. Her research focuses on teacher licensing, inclusive education, AI in education, and leadership development. She has authored and co-edited several scholarly books with IGI Global, including Building a Unified Teacher Licensing System: Policies, Education Reforms, and Cultural Integration (2025). She has published widely in Scopus- and Web of Science-indexed journals such as Heliyon, BMC Psychology, and Frontiers in Psychology. Dr. Abdallah holds a Ph.D. in Educational Leadership from the University of Jordan. She has been recognized with the Jordanian Independence Medal, First Class, awarded by His Majesty King Abdullah II for her contributions to education. She is an active reviewer for international journals and maintains a strong research profile with a Scopus h-index of 14 and Google Scholar h-index of 17.

Ahmed Akaabi is a researcher specializing in educational leadership and policy innovation, with a strong focus on teacher education and professional development. He holds an ORCID researcher ID: 0000-0001-7220-8087. His work encompasses investigations into licensing systems for educators, curriculum reform, and the intersection of cultural contexts with educational change. Dr. Ahmed publishes regularly in peer-reviewed outlets and collaborates internationally in advancing teacher training and licensing frameworks.

Markus Talvio is an academic researcher with deep interest in educational policy, teacher professional development, and cross-cultural educational leadership. His work focuses on enhancing teacher effectiveness through innovative frameworks and research-based reform. Dr. Markous contributes to international scholarly dialogue through publications, collaborative projects, and advancing practices in teacher licensing and education systems.

***

A.V. Senthil Kumar is working as Principal, Nehru Institute of Information Technology and Management, Coimbatore, India. He has worked as Professor and Director, PG and Research Department of Computer Applications, Hindusthan College of Arts & Science, Coimbatore, Tamilnadu for 15 years and as Senior Grade Lecturer in CMS College of Science and Commerce for 14 years. To his credit he has industrial experience for five years and teaching experience of 29 years. He has also received his Doctor of Science (D.Sc in Computer Science). He has to his credit 86 Book Chapters, 234 papers in International and National Journals, 85 papers in International Conferences in International and National Conferences, and edited 17 books and 3 Text books. He is as Associate Editor of IEEE Access. He is an Editor-in-Chief for many journals and Key Member for India, Machine Intelligence Research Lab (MIR Labs). He is an Editorial Board Member and Reviewer for various International Journals. He is also a Committee member for various International Conferences. He has guided 16 Ph.D scholars and guiding 3 Ph. D scholars now.

Safeya Alkatheeri is a PhD candidate, specializing in Language and Literacy at United Arab Emirates (UAEU). She has a BA in English Education and MA in English Curriculum and Instructions. She was an English language teacher and then was promoted to a leadership position in a common cycle public school. Her research interests include second language teaching and learning, L2 Writing, and culturally responsive education among others.

S Nagakishore Bhavanam having 16 years of Experience in Teaching and Research. In which 11.6 Years of Administrative experience as Registrar, Mangalayatan University, Jabalpur, MP, Assistant Director, IQAC, Acharya Nagarjuna University (ANU), Coordinator, Rankings, ANU, Head of the Department, ECE, University College of Engineering & Technology, ANU and many more positions at Acharya Nagarjuna University, Andhra Pradesh. So far Published 185 research & review articles, 25 Patents are Published and 2 Innovation and 9 Design Patent grants were secured from National & International (UK & Canada) Level. Contributed 11 Text Books, 18 Book chapters in Electronics and Computer Science Engineering field and received 12 awards. Seven (07) doctorate degrees are awarded under my supervision. During my administrative experience more than 60 State level, National, International level Seminars/ Conferences/Workshops are organized. More than 150 ranks received by ANU and 35 ranks received by Mangalayatan University, Jabalpur under my supervision. Delivered more than 65 lectures as resource person/speaker at reputed organizations, Universities and institutions. I am the Potential reviewer for various Elsevier Journals and IEEE Transactions on VLSI Journal.

Nasir Ahmad Ganaie is a scholar of Political Science with a strong academic background and a sustained commitment to rigorous research and scholarly inquiry. He earned his Doctor of Philosophy (PhD) from the University of Hyderabad, one of India's leading centres for advanced research in the social sciences, where his academic training and research focused on issues of conflict, unrest, peace, and stability, supported by systematic empirical analysis. He subsequently received a prestigious post-doctoral fellowship funded by the Indian Council of Social Science Research (ICSSR), which he pursued at the Department of Political Science, University of Kashmir, further deepening his engagement with contemporary challenges of governance, conflict management, and peace-building, particularly within the context of the Indian polity and region-specific political dynamics. His academic work is characterised by methodological rigour, analytical clarity, and a consistent effort to contribute meaningful and policy-relevant insights to the discipline of political science.

Mohammad Ahmad Ismail is a computer engineer with a major in Computer Engineering and a minor in Artificial Intelligence. His expertise lies in system development, IT solutions, and AI-driven technologies, with a strong focus on machine learning applications, automation, and intelligent systems. With a passion for research and innovation, Mohammad has contributed to projects that integrate AI with real-world applications, particularly in education, sustainability, and smart systems. His academic and professional background includes experience in software development, data structures, and algorithm optimization, making him well-versed in tackling complex computational challenges. He is actively involved in scientific research and publishing, contributing to advancements in AI, automation, and emerging technologies. Mohammad's commitment to continuous learning and innovation drives his pursuit of cutting-edge solutions in the field of computer engineering and artificial intelligence.

Irfat Jan is currently pursuing a Bachelor of Education (B.Ed.) at the Department of Education, University of Kashmir. With a strong focus on pedagogy, inclusive education, and the integration of technology in teaching, she is committed to exploring innovative methods that enhance the learning experience. Her broader academic interests extend to the New Education Policy (NEP), where she is particularly passionate about its potential to reform and modernize India's educational system. Irfat is keen to contribute to the implementation of NEP's goals, such as promoting critical thinking, holistic development, and making education more accessible and inclusive for all students. Through her studies and research, she aims to actively participate in shaping educational practices that align with the evolving needs of society.

Eman Y. Mahmoud is a Language and Literacy Education PhD graduate from UAE University. She received her bachelor's degree in English Language and Literature from the University of Jordan and her master's degree in English Curriculum and Instruction from UAEU. Eman has more than 16 years of experience in English Language teaching in basic and tertiary education. She is a researcher and reviewer, and her research interests include L2 teaching and learning, reading, writing, L2 assessment, task-based language assessment, culturally responsive education, learner autonomy, and social emotional learning among others.

Mohammed Borhandden Musah is an Associate Professor at Emirates College for Advanced Education, Data Analytics, Policy, and Leadership Division in Abu Dhabi. BA in Usul Deen from Al Baqa' Applied University, Jordan; M.Ed. & Ph.D. in Educational Administration (Leadership and Management) from International Islamic University Malaysia (IIUM). His teaching experience includes IIUM, UTM, USIM, Abu Dhabi University, and Bahrain Teachers College, University of Bahrain. His research focuses on higher education management, leadership, quality management, followership, PLCs, and teacher leadership. His ISI and Scopus-indexed journal papers were numerous. He authored a Scopus-indexed book and several chapters. He also completed several research projects on education, including Standard Framework of Collegial Supervision for Malaysian Public Secondary Schools, Teacher Licensing and its Effects on Teacher Professionalism: Teachers' Perceptions in Selected Al Ain Schools, etc.. He is a Fellow (FHEA) of the UK Professional Standards Framework, Advance HE, 2022, and has a Certificate in "Visible Thinking: A Project Zero In-Depth Course", Harvard Graduate School of Education, 2022.

K.R.S. Sambasiva Rao, presently as Vice-Chancellor of Mangalayatan University at Jabalpur, Madhya Pradesh, and formerly Vice-Chancellor of Mizoram Central University during 2017-2022 and Rector (Pro-Vice Chancellor) and Vice-Chancellor (i/c) of Acharya Nagarjuna University during 2014-2017. He did D.Sc. in Biotechnology from Berhampur University, in the field of Microbial Biotechnology; Ph.D. in Zoology from Sri Venkateswara University, in the field of Toxicology and Physiology; PhD. in Pharmaceutical Science from Andhra University, on Dosage formulation and Drug delivery systems. Prof.Rao had Post Graduation in M.Sc. Zoology, M.Sc. Psychology, M.Sc. Information Technology, MBA Big Data Analytics and MA Sociology. Prof. Rao earlier worked as a Professor of Zoology and Biotechnology at Acharya Nagarjuna University over 29 years during 1988 to 2017, and worked in the areas of Aquaculture Biotechnology, Microbial Biotechnology and Molecular Biology. Prof. Rao published over 275 research papers in various national and international journals and filed eight patents and edited/authored 20 books.

Index

U

W

www.ingramcontent.com/pod-product-compliance
Lightning Source LLC
LaVergne TN
LVHW081525300926
849161LV00006B/1300